Reading Fiction in Antebellum America

Reading Fiction in Antebellum America

Informed Response and Reception Histories, 1820–1865

JAMES L. MACHOR

The Johns Hopkins University Press

Baltimore

The Johns Hopkins University Press
2715 North Charles Street
Baltimore, Maryland 21218-4363
www.press.jhu.edu

Library of Congress Cataloging-in-Publication Data

Machor, James L.
    Reading fiction in antebellum America : informed response and reception histories,
1820–1865 / James L. Machor
        p.   cm.
    Includes bibliographical references and index.
    ISBN-13: 978-0-8018-9874-7 (hardcover : alk. paper)
    ISBN-10: 0-8018-9874-9 (hardcover : alk. paper)
    1. American fiction—19th century—History and criticism. 2. Reader-response
criticism—United States. 3. Authors and readers—United States—History—19th century.
4. Books and reading—United States—History—19th century. I. Title.
    PS377.M33 2010
    813'.309—dc22   201002227

A catalog record for this book is available from the British Library.

*Special discounts are available for bulk purchases of this book. For more information,
please contact Special Sales at 410-516-6936 or specialsales@press.jhu.edu.*

The Johns Hopkins University Press uses environmentally friendly book materials,
including recycled text paper that is composed of at least 30 percent post-consumer
waste, whenever possible. All of our book papers are acid-free, and our jackets and covers
are printed on paper with recycled content.

for Nancy

CONTENTS

In the first chapter of *Shakespearean Negotiations*, Stephen Greenblatt explains that his motivation for writing the book, as a new historicist, was his desire to speak to the dead. My reason for undertaking this book has been just the opposite. As a reception studies critic, I wanted the dead to speak to us. What I was interested in hearing, moreover, were not narratives of cultural and literary negotiations but the experiences of reading texts and particularly of reading fiction. However, I rediscovered early in the project something I had already known but often placed in the back of my mind: the dead do not speak very openly or extensively about their reading acts. When they do, the traces of their voices are frequently buried in musty, obscure volumes and far-away archives. It is difficult for us to hear and understand those voices not only because they are hard to find but also because the dead do not give up their traces of responses without mediation—in the form of further reading acts. We get at historical readers and their responses to texts, that is, only by doing readings of readings, and such doings can only obliquely be called finding. Reception historians do not so much discover reading acts and responses in the past. Instead, as I have come to realize in the course of doing the analysis of receptions that forms this book, historians of reading do the same thing readers do: we (re)make texts by creating patterns and making sense of them. Reading and interpretation consist of making sense in the double meaning of those words, as an act at once of deciphering and constructing.

In chapter 1, I discuss this issue more theoretically and in more detail, in a way that seeks to explain what it is we do when we study historical receptions and what we can do to advance such work. For reception study itself has had a history, and chapter 1 traces it out briefly—particularly in the form it has taken in literary criticism and in the history of the book—before moving on to the theoretical concerns relevant to reception study as a whole and especially to what I have called historical hermeneutics. The chapter also explains why the reception of American fiction in the antebellum United States is an especially appropriate focus for such historical investigation, while at the same time positioning reception events before the Civil War in the context of several important cultural, economic, and demographic factors. The last part of the chapter specifies the reasons for choosing the four authors whose fiction was the object of the antebellum reception events examined in Part II, as well as for choosing the materials for examining the reception of fiction in the United States from approximately 1820 to 1865. Whenever possible I have drawn on responses from both the private and public spheres, but this study focuses especially upon evidences of reception activities in the latter, manifested most markedly in responses by periodical reviewers. As I explain in chapter 1, there are several good reasons for concentrating on this particular interpretive community, though I want to anticipate one of them here, so as to underscore its relation to one of the book's concerns. Part of my interest in this study is the impact of nineteenth-century readers' responses on fiction writers themselves, particularly on the way they thought about their work and its (and their) relations to their contemporary audiences. While doing this volume I have become absolutely convinced that these writers' conceptions of those relations depended heavily on the public reception of their texts, especially as it played out in the leading periodicals of the time.

Accordingly, chapter 2 turns to a detailed discussion of the various, interrelated components of what I have called "informed" fiction reading in the antebellum United States, which manifested itself most visibly in the public sphere. This chapter charts the various interpretive conventions and reading strategies that formed the basis for the public—and to a certain degree, the private—reception and interpretation of particular novels and short stories by American writers. These strategies at times anticipated twentieth- and twenty-first century interpretive practices but at other times differed markedly from the way people, and especially academic critics, read today. The materials examined in this chapter come from periodicals selected according to three criteria: geographical diversity, circulation, and longevity. Magazines from cities in New England (Boston), the middle-Atlantic states (New York City and Philadelphia), the South (Richmond, Charleston, and New Orleans), and the

trans–Alleghenies West (Cincinnati) were chosen to cover a representative geographical cross section of the antebellum United States. Although magazine circulation figures between 1820 and 1870 vary widely,
sufficient information exists (including data in the U.S. censuses for
1840, 1850, and 1860) to indicate that all of the magazines used in this
chapter reached a circulation of four thousand or above, which was more
than twice the average circulation for periodicals in this period and the
equivalent of the circulations of the *New Republic* and the *Nation* today.
Finally, I selected magazines that lasted at least fifteen to twenty years, a
number that signaled significant success in terms of continued audience
appeal and sustained distribution.

Part II of the book consists of four chapters that offer what I have
called *case studies* of the nineteenth-century receptions of the work of
four different fiction writers. Chapter 3 is devoted to the antebellum reception of Edgar Allan Poe. Discussing at first Poe's conception of his relation to the contemporary fiction-reading public and his connection to
and knowledge of the practices of informed reading, especially through
his editing and reviewing work with several different periodicals, the
chapter then turns to the changing shape of Poe's reception and to his
sometimes elated and at other times dismayed responses to it. In part
my concern is the dynamic movements in the experiences of readers who
would have come to his tales through the strategies of informed reading. The main thrust of the chapter, however, is to map out the striking
change in the conception of Poe's fiction—and of Poe as a fiction writer—
from the mid-1830s through the 1840s.

Chapter 4 focuses on another canonical American author, Herman
Melville, whose antebellum status was quite different from Poe's. While
Melville began as a highly popular author, his fiction quickly fell into
disfavor in the early 1850s. Most modern Melvillians have explained that
descent by depicting Melville as the quintessentially brilliant but misunderstood writer, who grew increasingly alienated from and disdainful of
his contemporary readers because they failed to respond to and appreciate the genius and complexity of his novels. This chapter offers a different perspective on Melville's career and his relation to his antebellum
audience, arguing that the reception of his fiction before 1858 was both
more complex and more nuanced, that the downward trajectory of his
fiction-writing career was not as neatly linear nor as dour as is usually

depicted, and that his repeatedly changing conceptions of—rather than growing disdain for—his audience became a problematic part of that reception history.

Chapter 5 focuses on a writer who was both popular and critically acclaimed in her own day but who fell into obscurity in the second half of the nineteenth century and remained largely unacknowledged and unread through most of the twentieth, until her recovery in the 1980s. The question this chapter asks is "Whatever happened to Catharine Sedgwick?" The answer it offers is multifaceted and involves the interconnections among the highly productive relations Sedgwick enjoyed with publishers, the way those publishers promoted and republished her novels, and the major shift in the public perception of her fiction—and the type of fiction writer she came to be know as—from the 1830s to the 1840s and 1850s. The irony at the center of Sedgwick's reception history before the Civil War is that her very successes turned out to be factors in her neglect for nearly a century and a half afterward.

The final case-study chapter turns its attention to a writer who was not widely read in the nineteenth century and who today is not only outside the canon but virtually unknown: Caroline Chesebro'. Yet the reception history of Chesebro's fiction possesses some intriguing contours. Despite her lack of notoriety, she maintained a successful regimen of novel publishing from the early 1850s until just before her death in the early 1870s, and her novels and story collections were regularly reviewed—and praised—in many of the most prestigious magazines in mid-nineteenth-century America. It was, in other words, not because of neglect by the public sphere before and immediately after the Civil War that Chesebro' fell into such obscurity that even the feminist recovery projects of the 1980s and after have overlooked her fiction. Something else about the ways her novels were read has been at work in the twentieth- and twenty-first century neglect of Chesebro', and the goal of chapter 6 is to offer some answers grounded—like the reception histories of Melville and Sedgwick—in the responses to Chesebro's fiction in nineteenth-century America.

The book's final chapter consists of a combination of extended applications and of returns. The first section examines some of the implications that reception study, and historical hermeneutics in particular, can have for genre and our conceptions of it, as well as for narratives of literary history, especially the conventional literary history of nineteenth-century American fiction. The latter portion of the chapter then returns to several of the theoretical issues discussed in chapter 1 and offers some additional explorations into the problems of and reasons for doing reception histories.

✒

In the course of writing these chapters I have incurred substantial debts to a number of colleagues, friends, and institutions. For offering encouragement and a bracing intellectual collegiality over many years, I want to thank John Carlos Rowe, John Hellmann, Janet Staiger, and Patrocinio Schweickart. A special thanks goes to Phil Goldstein, not only for his friendship but also for working with me on other projects and professional endeavors, which have deepened and reinforced my sense of the value of doing reception study. Several colleagues have read all or parts of this work, and I wish to thank them for their perceptive critiques and valuable suggestions: Steve Mailloux, Gregory Eiselein, Barbara Hochman, and Janice Radway. Several librarians have been most helpful in enabling me to access important research materials: Paul Mercer of the New York State Library at Albany; Adrian Zahnier, Virginia Reynolds, and especially Betty Milum of Ohio State University; Kathy Coleman and Lori Fenton of Kansas State University; Nicholas Graham of the Massachusetts Historical Society; Yvonne Schofer of the University of Wisconsin; and Raynelda Calderon of the New York Public Library.

In its early stages, this project benefited from a summer fellowship from the National Endowment for the Humanities and a quarter of release time from Ohio State University. Kansas State University has been most generous in awarding me two sabbaticals during which I was able to write a large part of the book.

I am grateful to the following institutions for permission to quote from previously unpublished archival materials: the Massachusetts Historical Society for items from the Catharine Maria Sedgwick Papers used in chapter 5; the Department of Special Collections, General Library System, University of Wisconsin-Madison for a brief passage used in chapter 6; and the Manuscripts and Archives Division, The New York Public Library, Astor, Lenox, and Tilden Foundations for materials from the Alfred Williams Anthony collection and the Robert Bonner, William Conant Church, and Duyckinck family papers, also used in chapter 6.

This volume has been, in a sense, a percolating project of long duration, emerging from a series of smaller ventures that saw the light of day as earlier manifestations in other venues. Accordingly, I wish to thank the following journals for the right to include in this study some of my previously published work. A small segment of the first part of chapter 1 originally appeared in "The Object of Interpretation and Interpretive Change" in *MLN* (© 1998 by The Johns Hopkins University Press). Parts of "Fiction and Informed Reading in Nineteenth-Century America," which was published in *Nineteenth-Century Literature* (© 1992 by The University of California Press), are incorporated into chapters 1 and 2. Brief sections of chapter 2 previously appeared in "Poetics as Ideological Hermeneutics," in *Reader: Essays in Reader-Oriented Theory, Criticism, and Pedagogy.* The first section of chapter 3 derives from "Mastering Audiences: Poe, Fiction, and Antebellum Reading," originally published in *ESQ: A Journal of the American Renaissance* and reprinted by permission of the Board of Regents of Washington State University. I also want to thank the Johns Hopkins University Press for permission to reuse in chapters 1, 2, and 7 some material from my essay "Historical Hermeneutics and Antebellum Fiction: Gender, Response Theory, and Interpretive Contexts," originally published in *Readers in History: Nineteenth-Century American Literature and the Contexts of Response,* as well as from my introduction to that book.

As always, among those who have made contributions to my work, none has been more important than my wife, Nancy. Through the years she has continually been nearby, especially when needed most, in ways that make everything possible. To her this book is dedicated with unending love.

PART ONE

Reading Reading Historically

Historical Hermeneutics, Reception Theory, and the Social Conditions of Reading in Antebellum America

R EADING IS NOT ONLY a private act but also an intersubjective, social practice, in part because we are socialized through reading.
We are, moreover, socialized into reading, trained and positioned into
and through social practices for making sense of discourses. By giving
us a way to interpret the world of print and electronic media, reading
in a double sense reads us into society and culture by offering us a set of
moves for deciphering and shaping them.

Although socialized patterns of response have become almost second
nature in the modern world of mass culture and its reception, in the
early nineteenth century Americans for the first time were beginning to
encounter mass reading through the proliferation of books, magazines,
pamphlets, and tracts. At this period, reading took on a new significance
and a new urgency in the formation of individual, communal, and national identity to the point where it became a recurrent topic—directly
or by implication—in the vehicles of an emerging mass culture of public
discourse. This preoccupation with reading and its connection to questions of identity, morality, aesthetics, and power help account for a remark in the *North American Review* in 1844 that warned, "the novelists
who would induce us to take the murderer and pirate to our hearts, show
very plainly where their affections lie."[1] No mere expression of taste that
can be dismissed as sentential posturing or simplistic pontification,
this comment reverberates with implications endemic to the specific
historical conditions and practices of interpretation in the antebellum
public sphere.

This concern with reading certainly did not begin when Americans found themselves suddenly facing the year 1800 nor did it end with the Civil War. But however regnant its role since that conflict, it is no exaggeration to say that attention to reading as an interpretive activity—in the broadest sense, as a process of making sense of signifiers—has achieved a new prominence over the past four decades, particularly in literary criticism and theory. As a number of commentators have noted, the "return of the reader" or a "shift of attention to the reader" has come to constitute an important component of literary and textual studies, marked not only by the development of reader-response and reception criticism but also by a concern with reading, response, and audience within a variety of areas, including semiotics, deconstruction, marxist and feminist criticism, narratology, the New Historicism, cultural studies, cognitive linguistics, and both the history of the book and its more recent "offspring," the history of reading.[2] Arguing that the significance and functions of texts are inextricably connected to the way they are received, reader- and reception-oriented study has helped revise our conceptions of literature by emphasizing that the status, shape, and meaning of texts are functions of reading activities, which, as reception study in particular has emphasized, are communal practices grounded in shared conceptual and interpretive frames.

If literary studies have been altered by this particular turn, it has, moreover, been affected by another reorientation—what has been called the "return to history." That development in turn helped draw attention to a particular question that early reader-response criticism had sidestepped or obfuscated: Who exactly is "the reader" with whom this criticism has been so intently concerned? Although some reader-response critics in the 1970s maintained that "the search for meaning, which at first may appear so natural . . . is in fact considerably influenced by historical norms," this recognition repeatedly gave way in practice to essentialist descriptions that framed reading either as a feature within texts themselves or as an unvarying set of interpretive procedures.[3] In the 1980s, in fact, several critics challenged reader-oriented criticism on precisely this point, charging it with a failure to ground the study of reading in historically specific conditions and procedures. These challenges rightly pointed out that readers of reading repeatedly had conceived the reader as a transhistorical interpreter by implicitly privileging the critic's own response as an experience shared by all competent readers.[4] Such praxis not only fixed reading within a single interpretive formation but also ignored the historical conditions of response that constitute the critic's own activities.[5]

Amid such legitimate critiques, by the 1980s, response and audience studies began to take a turn toward history. This shift was apparent in the first English translations of Hans Robert Jauss's books addressing the theory and practice of reception aesthetics, as well as in the inaugural developments of historically oriented reception study in the United States.[6] Reception-oriented study expanded in the following decades to the point of virtually replacing earlier reader-response criticism and becoming the dominant form of audience-oriented work in literary studies.[7] A problem with this scholarship, however, has been its tendency to share with its 1970s predecessors a lingering formalism that relies on literary texts themselves for information about historical readers, either by treating such readers as thematized elements of the texts or by analyzing the ways texts sought to shape the experiences of broadly hypothetical historical audiences.[8] Although serious about examining the historical contextuality of reading, most practitioners of reception criticism have engaged, on the one hand, in analyzing writers' conceptions of their audiences and authorial theories of response,[9] and, on the other, in exploring authors' responses to previous literary works or charting the changing history of reception by academic critics and professional literati.[10] As a result, much response and reception criticism and its sorties into history remain far from uniting three major objectives of historical reception study: (1) the analysis of activities of actual—as opposed to textualized or hypostatized—historical readers who are not themselves literary authors or academic critics; (2) the exploration of reading as a product of the relationship among particular interpretive strategies, epistemic frames, ideological imperatives, and social orientations of readers as members of historically specific—and historiographically specifiable—interpretive communities; and (3) the analysis of the dynamics of what can be called reception events—that is, the process by which contextual conditions and historically specific reading formations shape the reception of particular texts and authorial oeuvres within the public sphere.[11]

These developments and problems within response and reception criticism do not, however, represent the full range of work in reading and audience studies, since that work has included scholarship within the fairly new, related fields of the history of the book and the history of reading. Although the relationship between these cognate fields and response and reception criticism is a point of debate,[12] it is clear that this new scholarship has produced significant studies of reading as a sociological activity and of the material and cultural conditions affecting the availability of reading materials. Seeking to get at the experiences of what book historians often call "real readers" or "common readers"— usually defined as "any reader who did not read books for a living"[13]— scholars working in book and reading history, and to a lesser extent in reception-oriented literary criticism, have increasingly turned to letters, diaries, memoirs, and surviving marginalia—sometimes combining these materials with reviews—to discover evidence of historical readers and reading. But this work has also had its limitations. At times such studies have taken an excessively narrow scope—for example, looking at the responses to a single work or even of a single reader without considering or adequately addressing the representativeness of such data in relation to broader reception events and reading formations.[14] More broadly, this work has been constrained by its focus on the history of print publication and distribution, literacy, and audience access—that is, who read, what they read, why they read, and under what conditions. Indeed, until quite recently it was accurate to say that while book history revealed much about the way readers in the past viewed and used reading materials, it disclosed little about the processes of response and the dynamics of reception—little, in other words, about how historically specific readers processed texts and how interpretive strategies shaped the way texts worked on their readers.[15]

My caveat about "accuracy" is necessary because over the last five to eight years, a few historians of reading and a few reception-oriented critics have begun to use letters, memoirs, marginalia, and reviews to reveal something about the dynamics of readers' engagement with print and the strategies by which readers in the past made sense of texts.[16] But this work, too, has had its problems, from questions raised by book historians themselves about its underlying assumption that marginalia, letters, and memoirs provide unmediated, representative indices to the experiences of "real," "common," or "typical" readers,[17] to a frequent lack of theoretical grounding, which has caused book historians repeatedly to succumb to the kind of textual essentialism that response and reception theory has called into question.[18] More importantly, this work, still in its embryonic stage, has yet to reveal and explore the connections between the historical response practices of individuals and the broader reading formations and specific interpretive communities of which they are a part—the place, in other words, where historical studies of reading, literary-critical reception study, and response-and-reception theory can and need to come together. As a result, book historians Kevin Sharpe and Steven N. Zwicker's 2003 observation that "the theory of interpretive communities awaits . . . historical specificity" still obtains today.[19]

This is not to say that previous ventures into examining audiences and the history of response have been failures or that this field is incapable of developing a viable historical approach to reception. But if response criticism and reception study—two areas that, as Patrocinio Schweickart has recently pointed out, remain at odds with one another—hope to move beyond their current state, we must reconceive practice to confront the historical dynamics of response and the contours of reception histories.[20] Such a reorientation needs to integrate response theory and criticism, which concentrates on the stages of hermeneutical processing, with the contextual emphasis of reception study and methods from the history of the book to create a historical hermeneutics that identifies specific reading practices and explores the role of interpretive communities in the way texts were read and made sense of in a given era.[21] For an era other than our own, such a turn would necessitate a close analysis of interpretive traces recoverable from the archive. In doing so, however, a historical hermeneutics would go beyond Jonathan Culler's call for a history of reception that merely surveys the legacy of responses to a particular text to describe the codes that produced its various interpretations over time.[22] Instead, a historical hermeneutics needs to reconstruct the shared patterns of interpretation for a specific historical era to define the reading formation of particular interpretive communities. That reconstruction would explore the role a particular interpretive community had—or sought to have—in shaping interpretation, that community's repertoire of interpretive codes, its assumptions about how reading should proceed and about how texts position their audiences during the reading process, and the relation between community-specific interpretive strategies and the cultural contexts in which they were practiced. By attending to audience positioning, I do not mean that historical hermeneutics would return to the assumption of an essential text containing inherent patterns or forms that simply await reader activation. Rather, this approach would operate from the premise that any textual configurations that can be said to do work for or on a reader are always a function of that reader's historically specific interpretive practices. Historical hermeneutics, that is, would provide a framework for examining the way past reading formations, cultural conditions, and readers' engagements with texts intersect as reception events.

Before proceeding as a practice, however, historical hermeneutics needs to address a theoretical issue that has undergirded—and troubled—response and reception study but that has been largely sidestepped since the early 1990s. This issue involves the question, originally raised by early response critics, of where meaning—and the text itself—resides. Do texts have inherent features that contribute to meaning and shape the reading experience (a position that has been termed a realist, positive/positivistic, or essentialist notion of textuality and response), or are readers totally in charge of constructing texts through the act of interpretation (a position characterized as an idealist, negative, or anti-essentialist theory of reading because of its poststructuralist base)?[23] The second position was most forcefully argued by Stanley Fish, in a form that became, according to Michael Bérubé, the central assumption of response and reception theory: the claim, in contradistinction to the principle of Derridean deconstruction, is that "there is nothing inside the text."[24] Though Bérubé does not say so, the problem with this answer was not only that it was never conceptualized into a viable form of practice but also that it entailed a second question that Fish himself raised: If readers construct texts in the act of interpretation, what is the object of interpretation? Or, to put the query more accurately, when we interpret a text, what is it that gets interpreted? What is interesting is that even as Fish was answering this question by asserting that no one can provide an answer, others began declaring that the question of whether the text or the reader—or some combination of the two—produced meaning was an issue that audience-oriented study no longer needed to worry about.[25] However, it would be a mistake to claim that this issue has gone away or to assume, as Bérubé does, that this former theoretical flash point is now somehow passé or irrelevant. On the contrary, this question—or more accurately, implicit answers to it—continues to be at work in the underlying, often unspoken, premises of current scholarship in reading history and reception study. For such work shares with other forms of critical practice a set of moves that rely on making claims about textual properties, whether those properties are the operation of a political unconscious, a subtextual ideology, a structure of narrative forms, a generic profile, or even the indeterminacy and infinite regress of signification. In other words, most critical practice—including contemporary forms of audience, reading, and reception study—implicitly address the question of what gets interpreted by making tacit assumptions about the object of interpretation.

Unavoidable as a critical inquiry, the issue is whether that question can be addressed without invoking a problematic textual essentialism or succumbing to a Fishian exasperation that says there is no explanation. I want to argue in the next section that an answer to the question of what gets interpreted can be theorized, as a form of historically embedded practice, without recourse to textual essentialism and that historical hermeneutics can help provide that answer.

When engaged in practice, critics and scholars of reading and interpretation have tended to shy away from positing a totally empowered interpreter and to assume instead that texts possess some inherent characteristics that exist before reading begins. Most commonly, this assumption subscribes to an interactive or transactional model of reading, which either maintains that the text possesses inherent meaning (or conceives the text as containing an inexhaustible plenitude of meaning), or attributes to the text intrinsic features—for example, generic markers, image patterns, plot structures, narrative conventions, implied reading roles, or semiotic gaps—from which readers take directions to build (or deconstruct) meaning.[26] Whether they assume that texts embody meaning or argue that readers create meaning from the "signals" provided by a text's formal elements, both approaches quickly run into trouble once the question arises over how such meanings or signals are known. Any assertion of intrinsic meaning has difficulty explaining how these are manifested without positing the reader as a mere blank slate or passive recipient of imparted textual messages. Because even the most tendentious arguments for intrinsic meaning draw back from this assumption, however, and agree that readers help shape meaning, they cannot cogently answer the question of how intrinsic meaning is to be distinguished from the reader's constructions—that is, how anyone could know which is which—without going outside the text itself by invoking interpretive principles that determine what counts and what does not count as evidence. A version of the same problem destabilizes realist/essentialist claims for the presence of formal properties, signals, and directions in texts. As Steven Mailloux has persuasively argued, the attempt to answer the question of how "textually embedded conventions determine [or contribute to] interpretation . . . leads . . . toward some kind of correspondence model: interpreters recognize conventions in a text because they have . . . an internalized set of interpretive conventions."[27] Essentialists thus ground their defense by invoking, as a metacritical principle, the reader's interpretive work as a form of literary competence that is always and everywhere the same. Both strategies thereby succeed only in undermining their premise of textual immanence by admitting to the primacy of interpretive conventions while denying historical variety in interpretation except as a form of incompetence or error.

Still, those who maintain that texts do contribute to meaning have on occasion invoked a different argument based on what might be called a principle of textual restriction. This position is exemplified in Umberto Eco's claim for the "limits of interpretation," particularly through his discussion of a scenario in which someone finds in a bottle a note that reads, "Dear Friend, In the Basket brought by my Slave there are 30 Figs I send you as a present. Looking forward. . . . " Eco points out that such a message could be interpreted several ways. The message could be read as a code in which "*basket* stands for 'army,' *fig* for '1,000 soldiers,' and *present* for 'help,'" whereby the meaning of the note refers to a military operation. Or *Figs* could be taken in "a rhetorical sense (as in such expressions as *to be in good fig, . . . to be in poor fig*), and the message could support a different interpretation." Or the reader, being a medieval scholar, might interpret the note as "an allegory of 'Divine Grace,' and so on and so forth." But while the note could be variously interpreted, Eco asserts that "there are some senses that would be preposterous to suggest"—for example, "that it means that Napoleon died in May 1821." Hence, Eco concludes, "there is at least something which the message cannot positively say."[28]

Although it is not difficult to imagine a reader who could invoke a different code to read this note as meaning "Napoleon died in May 1821," I doubt Eco would be troubled by this additional way of reading the message in the bottle. Rather, his point is that, while words may have a plenitude of meanings, a word, by its particularity *as* a word, limits those meanings to a particular range. *Roof* may mean "the covering of a structure" or "upper palate" or "the sky" (as in "heavenly roof"), but it does not mean "basement" or "car" or "my dead aunt Agnes." *Light suit* may signify "lacking sufficient weight" or "of the wrong color or material for winter" or ironically signify "too heavy" or "too dark," but it cannot mean "oversized," "poorly cut," or "explosive." A single text, in other words, cannot mean just anything.

How credible is such a claim? To consider it, let us imagine a situation involving two people driving a car through the backcountry of Italy, when they are forced to stop for a group of school children crossing the road. While waiting, the passenger turns to the driver and says "go." In this scenario, the meaning of *go* becomes ambiguous in that the driver must conclude that the passenger is either insane or homicidal or that he is being ironic. But according to proponents of textual restriction, there is a limit to the meaning *go* can have. It cannot mean *eat, read,* or *smoke your pipe,* nor can it nonironically mean *stop.* But consider this scenario further. Suppose the driver had earlier informed the passenger that he was hungry and wanted to eat a sandwich they had packed but had been unable to do so because they were on a serpentine road that required repeated gear shifting. As they stop for the children, the passenger says "go," which the driver, not unreasonably, takes as a suggestion that he now have his sandwich. *Go* suddenly is interpreted to mean "eat." Or we could imagine that the driver had expressed the need to use a restroom and had said to the passenger, "If we don't find one soon, I may have to pull over and use nature." In this case, the passenger's "go" could be taken to signify a quite different meaning from "proceed forward." In other words, it is possible to describe situations in which *go* may mean anything from "eat" or "run over behind those trees and take care of you bodily needs" to "check the oil." Should someone object that these situations involve unusual or even abnormal circumstances, we can only reply "abnormal or unusual in relation to what?" Normal circumstances are always context specific, and they always consist of the shared interpretive conventions that determine what meaning(s) apply in a particular interpretive situation.[29]

Where, then, does this leave us regarding the question with which we began: In interpretation, what gets interpreted? If one were to remark that the previous discussion shows that different situations are interpreted differently, my reply would be that that is precisely the point— or more accurately the first point to be made in recognizing what gets interpreted. For the object of interpretation is not some historical context existing "out there" independent of interpretative codes. As Derrida persuasively argued, because context is "an essential nontotalization," its specification must be formulated and marked; hence, context must be constituted in a "performative operation."[30] What counts as context—the shape it takes, the features that are noticed—is itself the product of interpretation. Not only does any speech act or written text become meaningful through an act of interpretation within the active relationship of epistemic frames, ideologies, and interpretive codes constituting the reading formation of a historically specific interpretive community. Any interpretive move also operates within a formation that itself is shaping the context that will not only produce meaning but determine what moves are necessary for its creation.

Consequently, what interpretation interprets is itself: the network or interpretive *field* of reciprocal relations and codes of which the text has become a part by virtue of the linguistic status it is accorded within that field. When a novel, poem, newspaper article, or any text, as sign, enters the field, it becomes part of the site for interpretation. What gets interpreted is not the text but the portion of the interpretive field or reading formation in operation during the particular sense-making act. Interpretation is a self-deciphering activity because the reading strategies, beliefs, and so on that make up the field do not occupy the same plane but operate in a hierarchical arrangement in which decisions about more particular or higher-level interpretive moves are made by lower-level or more "foundational" ones, some of which are shared by more than one interpretive community (e.g., that different genres of writing exist, that an interpretation needs to be as inclusive as possible, that story is an inherent feature of narrative).[31]

But, one might ask, if interpretation interprets itself as an interpretive field, wouldn't interpretation be an infinitely regressive act consisting of an endless chain of decisions about other decisions? In one sense, yes. Interpretation is endless because we are always intersubjectively deciphering signs and shaping contexts, but no particular interpretive act ever operates this way because of what could be called the rule of closure: whenever a reader interprets a sign or a particular collection of signs, he or she moves on to the next collection because the interpretation performed satisfies, to some degree, that reader. Precisely why such satisfaction occurs or what it consists of cannot be theorized as a formal principle since it is always particular to a historically specific reading formulation. But such closure is necessary because without it a reader would find it impossible to function in a world in which new signs need to be dealt with. And it is possible precisely because of the hierarchical arrangement of interpretive codes and beliefs, in that higher-order decisions will yield a satisfactory interpretation because they themselves have been decided upon—that is, interpreted as appropriate—by more foundational principles so deeply embedded in the formation that they function as facts or truths in no need of further decisions.

This explanation, however, leads to another question. If an interpretation is always historically specific in the sense that what gets interpreted is always a portion of a contextually specific interpretive field, why include the text as part of the field? Since a text can mean anything a particular field decides it to mean, such an explanation seems to do away with the text by turning it into a Rorschach blot or an empty set that cannot be differentiated from any other text. I would argue, however, that this is not the case because the materiality of the signifier cannot be ignored. It *does* matter that a particular set of graphemes or phonemes in a particular order is read or heard just as it matters that in listening to music one hears a particular set of sounds in a specific temporal order. How does such a claim, however, square with the fact that a reader can interpret "Sally threw the ball" and "The ball was thrown by Sally" to mean the same thing? If "It's bright in here" can mean "It's too light in here," "It's cheerful in here," "Turn down that spotlight," or "My eyes hurt," it would seem that neither the particularity of the words nor their order matters.

Addressing this issue requires recognizing that when a reading formation interprets itself it does so through a process of decisions and judgments about what interpretive strategies to invoke and what way they are combined, tested, discarded, and reformulated. The fact that the material text consists of signs in a particular order matters because the meaning a reader might create for those signs will result from a particular combination of interpretive moves that differs from other combinations producing different meanings from that material cluster. While "It's bright in here" may mean "The lighting is too intense" or "It's colorful in here" or "Close the drapes," these meanings will be the product of the different shapes each reading formulation takes, just as the shape will vary among formulations in which the same meaning is produced from different clusters. Those differences in shape eventuate, in part, because each formulation makes meaning—and in the process makes the text—in relation to what can be called a particular *pre-text* that becomes, not an anchor for interpretation, but only part of the interpretive field by virtue of the interpretive act itself. The pre-text is not a stable entity, a collection of formal features that is the same for all readers, nor is it the object of interpretation. Rather, the pre-text is the *occasion* for an interpretation, but its status as occasion is itself the product of the reading formation that has determined that the self-deciphering act of interpretation should begin.[32]

Besides providing a viable answer to the question of what gets interpreted in a way that takes into account the historically specific conditions of response, the premises just given as the theoretical basis of historical hermeneutics allow for a reformulation of the relation among interpretation, communication, textual production, and the role of authors and intentions. If interpretive formations are always interpreting a part of themselves, it would seem at first glance that these last three elements drop out of the equation, either as irrelevant or nonexistent within historical hermeneutics. Such an assumption, however, need not—in fact, cannot—be the case, since ignoring those components would lead to the counterintuitive position that we never understand each other. For one thing, production and communication remain within the equation but, in one sense, shift registers once it is recognized that a reading formulation is a construct that produces the text. In this sense, reception is an activity that changes the site of production from the author to the reader or interpretive community. Communication remains an essential part of this process because as the reading formation produces the text by interpreting itself, the formation also attributes to the pre-text, as a collection of signs, the capacity to produce ideas in the minds of readers. Communication thus takes the form of the interpretive community creating a communication with itself, conveying by its act of textual production not only what the text means but how that particular part of the interpretive field, which has produced that meaning, functions.

What needs to be stressed, however, is that as readers we do not experience communication this way, in terms of what we assume happens as we read. Rather, most readers approach texts as acts of communication, designed by someone—usually taken to be the author—who intends to convey some type of meaning (whether as ideas, information, or feelings) to them. This is not to imply that readers are deluded in what they do; on the contrary, the assumption of authorship and authorial intention is necessary within the communication model most readers hold, which treats texts as containers and conveyors of meaning.[33] To recognize this is not to assume that meaning is inherently authorial meaning or that there is no such thing as intentionless meaning. Rather, the point is that when readers, in the act of responding to a linguistic text, read to obtain communicated meaning—the situation, to varying degrees, of most readers today as well as in earlier historical periods—they formulate a concept of the author's intended meaning as the sense they seek. An audience's constructed conception of intentions and authors (what Michel Foucault called the author-function) as producers of texts and as realities independent of and prior to interpretation is an integral part of the history of response.[34] Historical hermeneutics, therefore, cannot sever production from reception but needs to treat the two as processes intertwined and co-extensive in particular ways within historically constituted reading practices.

Consideration of production, however, cannot be limited to the readers' function as producing agents because production in another form is already at work before reading itself begins. Here the materiality of the pre-text comes into play in that the physical form of the text, including the way it is delivered, can affect the shape of response. Such factors are perhaps most obvious in dramatic productions where lighting, the arrangement of props, and other staging practices can have an impact on audience conceptualization. But conditions of material production also play a role in dealing with print. As Diana Goodrich has pointed out, "the book a reader will take up is inscribed in a complex, highly mediated circuit that includes . . . the far-reaching distribution of the text as object . . . and the participation of publishers, editors, and even distributors in a network of financial relationships."[35] A publisher's decision to reprint a work in an unexpurgated or "restored" version or in a deluxe edition can likewise become a factor in the way texts are made sense of. That these production factors result from decisions that are themselves interpretations goes without saying, but that principle itself underscores in one more way the interconnections between production and response in any reading situation.[36]

Those interconnections, moreover, include authors, not only as projections of audiences but as projecting readers. The significance of this factor involves more than the shopworn saw that authors are readers too. Even if communication consists of an interpretive community communicating with itself, the interpretive field inevitably includes as part of its formation a pre-text that itself must be physically constructed as a sequence of signs. That pre-text, furthermore, is the product of interpretation in that its construction as a sequence transpires in a context that includes both the author's previous reading (as interpretive work) and the interpretation that accompanies composing and revision. And what do writers interpret? The answer is "the same thing as other readers": a segment of the interpretive field in which they are positioned. This includes a working sense of the reading conventions that constitute the audience they assume they are addressing and the codes of interpretation they share with other members of one or more interpretive communities. Since those codes inevitably include assumptions about the way reading might or should proceed, any interpretive formation a writer inhabits will involve some working conception of the audience he or she seeks to address. Indeed, as Peter Rabinowitz and others have maintained, "an author . . . cannot begin to fill up a blank page without making assumptions about the readers' beliefs, knowledge, and familiarity with [interpretive] conventions."[37] As social, intersubjective practices, authorial assumptions about audience are always formed within a historically specific reading field that an author shares to some degree with his or her contemporary readers. The importance of that relation cannot be overstated, because, when production and reception are operating within a shared historical grid marking the activities of both author and reader, the interrelations between response and production are most at work. It is precisely at such moments that a historical approach to response, taking into account the nexus of author and audience, is especially valuable and necessary.

Since any historical discussion of authorial intentions, conceptions of reading, and assumptions about the author-reader nexus is itself a product of critical interpretation, we seem to have come full circle. That same circularity would appear to mark any attempt to disclose the shape of response within a given historical context. To put the matter another way, because any description of interpretive codes and reading processes proceeds from the critic's own act of reading—and thus is inherently an interpretive act—would not a historical analysis of response constitute just one more critical construction no more valid nor valuable than ahistorical examinations? Would it not yield just one more reading of reading? In the remainder of this section I offer a partial answer to this question, but because a fuller response ultimately depends upon the way historical hermeneutics is pursued as a practice, I will return to this issue in the last chapter.

If we agree that the critic is always a reader first, it follows that any attempt to reconstruct a set of historical conventions and integrate them with an analysis of reception events will itself be mediated by the critic's own interpretive strategies. Hence the critic's role as interpreter, which itself is historically constituted, cannot be eliminated. Yet that mediation is not only inevitable but necessary, since the relation between historical conventions and the reader's practices and role cannot be pursued solely through the interpretive conventions of a pre-text's original audience. To modify one of Jauss's insights, because an audience's encounter with a pre-text, when it first appears, can involve both fulfillment and reorientation of that readership's interpretive horizons, the critic "must bring his own experience into play, since the past horizon of old and new . . . problems and solutions, is only recognizable in its further mediation, within the [critic's] present horizon."[38]

The inevitability of the critic's role in the reading experience does not mean, however, that a historical hermeneutics must succumb to a temporal solipsism that covertly naturalizes—by tacitly ignoring the conditions of—the critic's own historically constituted response. A historical hermeneutics would militate against this tendency by recognizing that the representation of historicized response consists of an intertextual relation between the experience at the work's origin and the reconstitution of that experience by posterity's interpretive practices, both of which are always (pre)structured by the reader's own position in an interpretive community. While a historical hermeneutics, therefore, cannot eliminate such prestructuring by posterity, what it can do is mitigate it by fashioning an intersubjectivity that counterpoises two different horizons of expectation playing off one another: the set of conventions (re)constructed as the basis of textual response within the historical context formulated, and the horizon governing the critic's created account of reading within and against those original strategies. The purpose of such an approach would not be to proscribe other interpretations of reading as unacceptable or to try to provide a purportedly "objective" description of historical reception events, but, in explicitly confronting the historical nature of reading, to open out and historicize accounts of reading practices. A historical hermeneutics would thereby offer a "fusion of horizons" that is always partial, provisional, and thus open to the flux characterizing interpretation as an intersubjective historical activity.

The decades in the United States from 1820 to 1865 offer an especially appropriate period for examining reception events through the lens of historical hermeneutics. Called by some historians an era of "reading revolutions," the antebellum years witnessed an upsurge in the production and dissemination of reading materials and an unprecedented growth in population—and especially in urban population—that dramatically increased the audience for print.[39] An important byproduct of urbanization was its concentration of resources necessary for the publication of books, periodicals, and printed matter on a scale to match this population. By 1850, according to estimates by some historians of book publishing, the number of publishing and printing houses in the United States totaled over seven hundred. With the founding of such major firms as Wiley, Little Brown, Scribner's, and Putnam, publishing had grown from a small-town cottage industry to a big business; by the 1850s Harper and Brothers had become the largest publishing house in the world.[40]

As large as it was, Harper's output comprised only a fraction of the marked growth in the production of books and other printed matter in the United States. At a time of relatively stable prices, the value of books produced rose from $2.5 million in 1820 to over $16 million in 1865. Between 1820 and 1852, the number of book titles alone averaged eight hundred a year; from 1855 to 1858 that number more than tripled. In all, the total number of imprints mushroomed from 2,500 in 1800 to almost seven thousand in 1844 and continued to climb at a comparable pace right up to the Civil War.[41] What was true of book production in general was true of fiction in particular. Of the 1,400 titles of American fiction published between 1720 and 1850, more than half appeared from 1840 to 1849. By 1855, when the total number of works of fiction published in the United States reached four hundred, that genre comprised almost 30 percent of all titles for that year.[42]

This concurrent growth in population, urbanization, and the availability of printed matter in the first half of the nineteenth century was, to be sure, not unique to the United States. Not only were all three factors regnant through most of the Euro-Atlantic world; the yearly production of book titles in England and France equaled or outstripped that of the United States in the 1850s. However, the ratio of volume production to population was higher on the western side of the Atlantic. In the late 1830s, total volumes printed in the United States and England were about equal at a time when the British population was nearly 50 percent greater.[43] After 1850, the difference became more pronounced, and sales figures for individual titles corroborated the trend. Richard Altick has put the upper limit of sales for any British work at this time at two hundred thousand, a figure achieved by W. H. Russell's account of the Crimean War in 1855–56. By contrast, *Uncle Tom's Cabin* sold one hundred thousand copies in the first five months after its appearance in book form in 1852 and over three hundred thousand copies by 1853. In fiction, the differences in book sales and print runs were most pronounced. Two years before Dickens's *Bleak House* (one of his most popular novels) sold forty thousand copies during its first year of publication in 1853, the American novelist Susan Warner had sold over one hundred thousand copies of *The Wide, Wide World*. Nor was this an isolated contrast. In Victorian England, "ordinary circulating-novels," writes Altick, "seldom had an edition of more than a thousand or 1,250 copies"; by contrast, according to Cathy Davidson, as early as the 1820s in the United States it was possible for the first printing of a new novel to have a run of ten thousand copies. Aided by the availability of inexpensive pirated editions of British novels in the absence of an international copyright law, by the 1850s America had far surpassed England in the sales of fiction.[44]

The growth in print matter in antebellum America was most noticeable, however, in newspaper and periodical publication. Whereas in 1790 there were approximately ninety newspapers in the United States, by 1827 that figure had ballooned to just under one thousand—nearly a third of all newspapers published in the world. When that total grew to 1,600 in 1840, the United States had more than twice the number of newspapers in England and France, the next leading producers of that medium.[45] A similar ascendancy marked U.S. periodical production. Although there were fewer than one hundred magazines in the United States in 1825, that number expanded to nearly seven hundred by 1850; twenty years later the total in Britain had not yet reached five hundred. At a time when France's population still exceeded that of the United States and the number of American periodicals was approaching seven hundred, the total of all periodicals *and* newspapers in France was under six hundred.[46]

Several factors contributed to the greater production of print matter in the United States vis-à-vis Europe. Although technological advances in the methods of book production—including innovations in typesetting, the advent of machine-made paper, and the introduction of the Napier-Hoe cylinder press in the 1840s—contributed greatly to the general outpouring of printed material in the Western world, these developments were especially pronounced in the United States, where stereotyping and electrotyping were more extensively used and where the vast majority of cylinder presses were in operation.[47] Equally important were changes in the organizational and investment practices of American publishers. In this period the activities of printing, binding, and selling became segmented, with the resulting specialization contributing to greater efficiency and to greater capital outlay for new technologies. As they increased their investments in equipment and buildings, publishers sought to expand their markets from local to regional, and eventually to national, audiences for books and magazines. One result was the development in the 1840s and 1850s of nationally distributed periodicals such as *DeBow's Review, Graham's Magazine, Harper's New Monthly Magazine,* and *Godey's Lady's Book.*[48]

Technological advances in transportation further facilitated the expanding regionalization and nationalization of publishing. By the 1820s and 1830s, the Erie Canal and extensive use of steamboats along the Mississippi and Ohio valleys enabled print matter to be shipped to areas it had never reached before. Even more important was the development and growth of the railroad. In 1840, when railroad mileage in all of Europe totaled 1,800, the United States had three thousand miles of track covering an area less than half the size. By the early 1860s, U.S. rail miles would surpass thirty thousand—more than three times the total in Great Britain and more than the total for all of continental Europe.[49]

Such changes and the concomitant growth in the volume of printed matter do not by themselves, however, prove that the antebellum era was marked by a substantial increase in reading that was most pronounced in America. Any claim for such an increase must take into account not only production but also consumption. Although the dramatic growth in newspapers and periodicals and the unprecedented sales figures for some novels indicate that more printed matter was being consumed than ever before, such data may indicate not that more people were reading but that the same number of Americans simply were reading more.[50]

Several factors nonetheless suggest that the increased consumption of print in antebellum America did result from more people reading. Besides growing dramatically in size, the American population was becoming more literate. White adult literacy rates in the first decade of the nineteenth century stood at 75 percent in the North and 50 to 60 percent in the South, but a continual increase above and below the Mason Dixon line caused the literacy rate to reach 90 percent by 1840 for white adults nationwide. Literacy especially grew among women, to the point where rates for men and women had become roughly equal by the 1840s. In 1850, when the adult literacy rate was under 70 percent in England and Wales and not yet at 60 percent in France, literacy among white American adults had become the highest in history at approximately 95 percent.[51] Still, as James Allen has pointed out, "a distinction must be made between simple literacy and the sophisticated ability to participate actively in the world of print."[52] Reading is a function of such factors as access to print materials, education, and the presence of social and cultural conditions that encourage or require reading proficiency and provide situations in which reading can occur. It was precisely the presence and interrelated growth of such factors that characterized antebellum America.

Besides the expansion of the publishing industry and transportation advances that extended distribution and lowered the costs of shipping books, a proliferation in the number of bookstores and the expansion of libraries increased access to printed matter.[53] Between 1790 and 1815, more than five hundred new subscription libraries were established in New England alone, and that number doubled by 1850. In the same period nationwide, subscription libraries increased fourfold. The number of commercial libraries, which circulated books through rental, similarly increased. Although public libraries as we know them (that is, free circulating libraries supported by public taxes) were virtually nonexistent before 1850, 259 were established in the United States before the end of the Civil War. Between 1825 and 1850, the number of subscription, commercial, free public, and school libraries in American had tripled to fifteen thousand, or one for every six hundred free adults; by 1860 that total nearly doubled again to over 27,000.[54] Besides expanding access to print, the growth of libraries in America encouraged reading by offering more opportunities and space for that activity.

The library movement acted in consort with an educational expansion, which saw the number of schools in the U.S. grow to 150,000 by 1860, more than twice the number in more populous France. That rise was accompanied by a substantial increase in school enrollments, length of the school day, and total number of school days attended.[55] The most significant development in this area came in public schooling. Although most elementary schooling was church affiliated or otherwise private through the first decade of the nineteenth century, by the early 1830s funding for public common schools was established in virtually very state along the eastern seaboard from Massachusetts to South Carolina. By the 1850s, a national public school movement, with a goal of "universal access" to education, was at work in the United States, extending to western states such as Ohio, Indiana, and Illinois.[56] This commitment to state-supported schools came much earlier and proceeded at a faster pace than in Europe. Part of the reason, according to Ira Katznelson's and Margaret Weir's study of the history of public education, was that "the principle of free public schooling that proved so contentious for ruling groups in other countries," who saw it as dangerous, "was accepted as a given by virtually all the social classes and groups in the United States" by the time of the Civil War.[57] Another factor was the rapid acceleration of capitalist modes of production in the United States. The increasing number of workers involved in merchandising and commercial activity, which required skills in deciphering written orders and reading delivery schedules, needed the literacy public school education could provide.[58] In the wake of these developments, the number of public schools and total public school enrollment grew enormously from 1840 to 1860, thereby increasing access to reading instruction and to opportunities for reading.

Besides the growth in bookstores, libraries, and education, other factors contributed to the improved opportunities for people to read more and for more people to read. Advances in illumination—first through kerosene lamps and then through gas lighting in the 1840s—extended the hours available for reading, while improvements in eyeglasses, which began to be produced on a large scale in the 1830s, opened reading to children—and prolonged it for adults—whose visual impairments would otherwise have prevented them from exercising that skill.[59] Further opportunities for reading outside schools and libraries resulted from changes in American homes and in leisure time. Homes increasingly were built to provide family members with individual bedrooms, which offered privacy and quiet space for reading. This change in domestic architecture was driven in part by a general expansion and reorganization of leisure time in this period. The growing separation of work and home space under industrial capitalism enabled more workers to circumscribe the time spent in the workplace, which enlarged and concentrated leisure hours that could be devoted to reading. As the activities of economic production moved outside the home, thereby redefining domestic activity primarily as nurture and consumption, women and young adults still living at home had more time to exercise their reading skills.[60]

Proving as important to the promotion and spread of reading as these material developments was a signal cultural formation of the antebellum years: what Lee Soltow and Edward Stevens have called an "ideology of literacy," which linked literacy, citizenship, and socialization. Combining a growth in nationalism following the War of 1812 with what John Higham has termed a "pan-Protestant ideology that claimed to be civic and universal," antebellum ideology identified the advance of Christianity with the development of the American republic through the twin agencies of education and literacy—a linkage that not only spawned the American Tract Society (an institution that would distribute more than 200 million tracts, periodicals, and books between 1826 and 1855) but helped fuel the expansion of libraries and public schools.[61] The result was a symbiotic relationship between the ideology of literacy and the expansion of institutions whose growth further promoted the idea that the country's social, moral, and political health depended on a well-read citizenry. Indeed, it would be accurate to say that this way of thinking constituted not so much an ideology of literacy as an ideology of reading, for what was valorized was not simply attainment of basic literacy skills but greater access to print and increased, regular engagement with reading materials.

This ideology of reading was further fueled by an emphasis on female literacy, which had begun to build in the late eighteenth century under the assumption that the republic could best succeed if its mothers raised their children to become good citizens. Encouraging women to become better educated through reading, this incipient ideology expanded in the antebellum period under what historians have come to call the "cult of domesticity" that developed within the capitalist separation of work and home. Along with the redefinition of home as a place of nurture, womanhood was redefined, with women conceived as uniquely endowed with the ability to teach children because, by their nature or God's will, they were more moral, patient, and nurturing. Mothers were encouraged to read to their children (and become better readers themselves) to promote learning, Christian values, and respect for the social order and to provide the young with the means that would facilitate future economic success.[62]

The growth in reading that resulted from the increase in print matter and the expansion of cultural formations promoting print consumption did not, however, spread uniformly or penetrate equally into all segments of antebellum society. Though the number of public and total elementary schools grew in all regions, much of the increase was concentrated in towns and cities. Even when schools were available, attendance was more irregular in rural areas, where the separation between work and home was less pronounced owing to the nature of farm labor. Spending more time in production than their urban counterparts, rural children had less time—and fewer undisturbed blocks of time—to attend school, a problem exacerbated by the seasonal organization of farming. In 1840s and 1850s Massachusetts, for example, where literacy was among the highest in the nation, both the length of the school session and the average number of school days attended per child were 40 percent greater in towns of ten thousand or more inhabitants than in less populous areas. Nationwide, available data indicates that literacy rates for counties of one hundred inhabitants or fewer were fifteen percentage points lower than in counties of ten thousand or more. The lower literacy skills required in farming occupations also curbed the influence of the ideology of literacy, while the continued blend of work and home spaces caused the cult of domesticity and its attendant impact on the ideology of reading to be much less pronounced in rural areas.[63]

Access to reading materials was also more limited in those areas, since most publishing firms, bookstores, and libraries were concentrated in urban areas. Although one of the main sources of book distribution before 1830, the itinerant book peddler, has come down to us in the image of a print-sowing Johnny Appleseed trudging along lonely roads to isolated farms and villages, most book peddlers concentrated their efforts on towns to maximize profits.[64] Ironically, the coming of the railroad only intensified that trend. In the South, most rail lines linked major cities, while in the North and West, railroad expansion was closely tied to industrialization and thus concentrated in and around urban areas. Consequently, book distribution by rail was marked by a predominantly urban geography.[65]

If the growth in reading was predominantly an urban development, it was, however, no more equally spread among city and town dwellers than it was among the national population. Rather, economic and cultural factors caused the growth in reading and the numbers of readers to be concentrated in the urban middle class. Over the last thirty years, historians have begun to delineate the nature of this segment of the antebellum population. While questions remain about whether the term *middle class* is historically accurate and about what exactly marked middle-class status, most who have grappled with this issue agree that the forty years before the Civil War witnessed the emergence and expansion of an American middle class marked less by specific income categories than by a cluster of social, economic, and cultural features. These included an especially strong concentration of the ideology of reading, of access to print, and of opportunities for reading. As one American commentator in 1855 remarked, the "ability to read and the consequent love of reading have developed in this nation especially [among] an immense middle class of ordinary readers."[66]

One reason for such class differentiation was that access to education and to the reading skills that went beyond functional literacy was not equally distributed in urban America. Children from working-class families attended school less frequently and for shorter periods than their middle-class counterparts, primarily because working-class families needed the income from children laboring in the workplace. By contrast, for middle-class children the school rather than the workplace was the site of social development, with the result that literacy rates were substantially higher among middle-class youths.[67]

Disparities in access to reading materials and to locations conducive to reading further restrained reading among the working class and facilitated it for middle-class city dwellers. Most working-class families did not benefit from the restructuring of domestic architecture in this period, since homes offering the private space provided by individual bedrooms were beyond the reach of the laboring class.[68] While public libraries began to appear in this era, the vast majority of libraries continued to be subscription or commercial institutions, with the former charging annual dues from $4 to $25. Such costs were simply outside the means of day laborers and factory workers, whose wages averaged $5 to $6 per week.[69] Although the price of books in general—and novels in particular—declined in the 1830s and 1840s, hardcover books continued to cost between seventy-five cents and $1.25 throughout the antebellum period, while the price of a novel in the standard two-volume format had risen back to about $1.50 by 1850. The equivalent of a day's wages for working-class men and a half-week's wages for working-class women, the price of a single book was too high for most urban laborers. Although cheap pirated editions of British novels and the introduction of paperbound volumes helped reduce costs somewhat, the era of widely available cheap paperbacks did not occur until the 1860s with the advent of Beadle's dime novels. As a result, in the 1850s the average cost of a novel in a New York City bookstore was about $1, and the average book sold for a little over fifty cents, a figure still beyond the means of most unskilled laborers. While newspapers and periodicals represented an alternative source of print matter, most periodicals had to be purchased through a yearly subscription, which ran anywhere from $2 (e.g., for the *Home Journal*) to $6 (e.g., for *Littell's Living Age*), the equivalent of two days' to a week's wages.[70]

Although cost and availability limited working-class access to print and to literacy training, these factors were part of a larger set of conditions that disproportionately concentrated reading activity within the urban middle class. The increasing prosperity of that class, combined with the labor surplus provided by the first large influx of immigrants from Germany and Ireland, enabled many middle-class families to hire servants and to purchase commodities that had formerly been produced by labor in the home. Both developments helped produce an increase in that class's leisure time.[71] Moreover, owing to the need for most working-class children and women to participate in the labor force, the separation between work and home developed primarily as a bourgeois social formation, in which middle-class women were "free to attend to the concerns of direction, . . . propriety, culture, and sentiment"—concerns that they learned to cultivate through reading and that included reading as an activity marking cultivation.[72] Localizing the cult of domesticity primarily within the middle class, the resulting reconceptualization of motherhood produced a structured bourgeois leisure that shifted domestic time into caring for the health, comfort, and education of children as an identifying mark of the successful middle-class home.[73]

This emphasis constituted part of an especially strong concentration of the ideology of reading within the middle class. The conditions that coded the home as a domestic space of feminine instruction also elevated reading to a defining bourgeois activity for men and women. Education and learning, along with other social signifiers such as dress, housing, and decor, served as markers of one's character and of one's social class. As a result, according to R. Laurence Moore, "the habit of frequent reading" and of systematic, informed reading "became in antebellum America a sign of middle-class behavior," a form of what Pierre Bourdieu has called cultural capital. The goal was not so much social advancement as it was fashioning and maintaining the individual's and the family's bourgeois and urbane status.[74] In conjunction with the economics of access to print and to leisure for reading, such class-conscious inflection of the ideology of reading made the consumption of print, and its growth in antebellum America, a predominantly urban, middle-class phenomenon.

What did all this mean for what was often cited at the time as the most popular form of reading matter: novels and periodical fiction? Traditionally, literary and social historians have echoed the antebellum claim that fiction grew into the most widely consumed form of print, but one historian, Ronald Zboray, has challenged this assumption, arguing that "fiction little benefited from [the] large potential readership" of the time. As an index, Zboray enlists the sales figures of the most popular novel before the Civil War, *Uncle Tom's Cabin*. While Harriet Beecher Stowe's novel reached the unprecedented figure of three hundred thousand copies sold, that number represented only a little over 1 percent of the population in 1852. As further evidence, Zboray cites the holdings of the New York Society Library, in which novels represented only 3.3 percent of its 11,700 volumes.[75]

Two problems, however, inhere in this revisionist challenge. Although the number of copies Stowe's novel sold constituted a small percentage when measured against total population, the same was true of any single volume of the time, with the possible exception of the Bible. By such a measure, no genre could be said to have benefited—a dubious conclusion in the face of the massive increase in the production of books, periodicals, and newspapers in antebellum America. Nor do the *holdings* of the New York Society Library provide an adequate gauge, even if we grant their representativeness. A very different picture emerges, in fact, from the charge records Zboray provides for that subscription library for 1847–49 and 1854–56. Of the 5,688 books checked out in those years, novels accounted for 34 percent of the charges, which was two and a half times the rate for the second most popular genre, travel books. While novels accounted for 21 percent of charges in 1847–49 (highest of all categories), that percentage more than doubled to 45 percent in 1854–56, which was four times the checkout rate of the next category.[76] Such records, in consort with the unprecedented sales figures of novels such as *Uncle Tom's Cabin*, Warner's *The Wide, Wide World,* and Maria Cummins's *The Lamplighter,* and the massive increase in novel titles published, suggest that fiction did benefit from the upsurge in literacy and reading in the forty years before the Civil War. However, the growth in fiction reading was no more systemically national than the growth in reading. Instead, the expanding middle-class urban audience provided the bulk and accounted for much of the growth in the readership for fiction.

Although the audience for fiction was more restricted than literary historians have usually assumed, in another sense it was broader than conceived by some antebellum commentators and subsequent historians. The assumption here involves gender, as reflected in the remark of the magazine writer cited earlier who, after identifying ordinary readers as "middle class," contended, "this great middle class is composed four-fifths of women, inasmuch as the hard-working men of the day have little leisure and taste for any thing beyond the sphere of counting-houses." Although literary historians have echoed this assumption, there is no strong evidence to support the claim that the audience for fiction consisted mostly of women.[77] On the contrary, subscription lists for periodicals such as the *Southern Literary Messenger,* which contained substantial offerings of serialized novels and short fiction, included more male than female subscribers. Similarly, leading women's magazines such as *Godey's Lady's Book,* which regularly included fiction in their pages, enjoyed a substantial male readership. The charge records of the New York Society Library cited above provide further evidence of gender parity in the fiction-reading audience. Of all charges for men, 33 percent were for novels, while the figure for women was only slightly greater at 36 percent. Moreover, while the percentage of novels charged by women went from 23 percent in 1847–49 to 44 percent in 1854–56, the increase for men over the same period was even greater: 20 to 46 percent.[78]

Resulting in part from the factors that had led to a concentrated increase in reading in general among the urban middle class, the growth in fiction reading among that population also stemmed from a change in bourgeois attitudes toward fiction. The older distrust of novels, which had characterized fiction as lies or simply as a waste of time, gave way in the antebellum era to a public recognition—manifested and conducted most volubly in the periodical press—that Americans were devoting increasing amounts of leisure time to fiction reading. "The mass of American reading consists of newspapers and novels," remarked the *Home Journal.* Numerous periodicals made similar statements, including the *Ladies' Repository,* which announced, "One of the characteristics of the literature of the present time is the prominent position occupied by prose fiction."[79] The vast majority of magazine journalists realized that this phenomenon could not be addressed, as it had in the past, simply by censuring such reading. "The day has passed," wrote the *Southern Literary Messenger*, "when works of fiction would be dismissed with a contemptuous sneer" (May 1842: 342), while another review in the *Home Journal* added, "It is futile to attempt to prevent the young, and the many not young, from the perusal of prose fiction" (Mar. 24, 1855: [3] no pag.). Echoed frequently in the pages of *DeBow's Review, Graham's Magazine, Godey's*, the *North American Review,* and other literary and popular periodicals, such remarks emanated from more than a sense of resignation. In the face of growing demand, editors of periodicals recognized that offering fiction was an effective way to increase subscriptions and boost profits. Redefining fiction as economically advantageous, magazines also reconceived it as a form of cultural capital. Framed within the bourgeois ideology of reading, fiction reading was touted as a vehicle of public advancement and personal education. Hence, while *DeBow's Review* was claiming that "fiction has become the chosen vehicle of information and instruction for the present generation of readers" (Dec. 1860: 745), the editor of *Godey's* maintained that "novels are now the great vehicle of public sentiment, where . . . all new ideas . . . are promulgated" (Apr. 1850: 290). In a virtual about face from earlier censure, a writer in the *Southern Literary Messenger* even claimed that the "influence of these fictitious histories . . . has been . . . on the whole, advantageous to general literature, and of the most humanizing effect upon society" (May 1835: 479). Interestingly enough, the same claims were being made about periodicals.

This connection between fiction and magazines was important, but not simply because periodicals became a major venue for the publication of fiction. Magazines also became important vehicles for thinking about and responding to fiction. In the new mass media that the periodical press was creating, reviews and literary essays served as the primary means of disseminating and assimilating ideas about the relation between fiction and reading practices.

This role carries important implications both for the reception of fiction in antebellum America and for the enterprise of historical hermeneutics. Although fictional texts are made meaningful within a field of reading practices, intersecting ideologies, epistemic frames, and material conditions, an historical study of reception must be grounded in analyses of the particular interpretive strategies preserved in the historical archive. Of the two main types of archival material available—responses contained in letters, diaries, memoirs, and marginalia, and reading patterns informing public reception events—the second provides a more extensive and viable basis for several reasons. As John Frow, John Fiske, Eugene Kintgen, and other scholars and theorists in literary criticism, cultural studies, and book history have maintained, we need to study not just readers but reading, as manifested in interpretive practices and what Frow has called reading "systems." That is, fashioning a historicized sociology of reception grounded in affective practices of shared interpretive codes requires, in Jonathan Culler's words, a focus foremost on "public interpretive practices."[80] Reviews in periodicals provide such a basis for fiction reading in antebellum America. Often appearing in magazines with relatively large circulations or in periodicals with a national reputation, reviews enjoyed a publicly sanctioned authority buttressed by the institutional imprimatur of the publishing industry itself. That status does not preclude letters, diaries, and annotations from having some value for an exploration of antebellum reception events. Indeed, this study makes use of comments in letters and other marks of interpretive activity, when available, in chapters 3 through 6, in part to reveal parallels between private and public responses. But because antebellum reviews were not merely individual responses but expressions whose content was corporate and communal, reviewers formed an interpretive community that played an important role in the collective reception of fiction in the early nineteenth century.[81]

To say this is not to imply that the reading practices of reviewers determined or precisely mirrored the responses of the mass audience. But it is impossible to discount the influence of reviewers, in part because the gap between them and "common" readers was not as large as it is today, owing to what James Wallace has called "the peculiar circumstances of intellectual life in early nineteenth-century America." Most reviewers in the United States were not professional critics but "moral and intellectual leaders of the community" who shared a common "social standing, education, and opinion" with the fiction-reading public.[82] Residing primarily in cities and towns, that public consisted largely of the same middle-class audience that bought and read periodicals. Nor should we forget that to be a member of that class meant defining oneself through the values, habits, and practices of bourgeois culture, including its reading practices. Since a main source of learning about those practices, particularly in terms of responding to fiction, were the magazines written for and consumed by the middle class, the desire for group membership through class identity was a powerful impetus for employing the codes of cultured, bourgeois reading exemplified in periodicals.[83] The result was the creation and extension of a public sphere of interpretation that paralleled and helped form middle-class reading formations for the reception of fiction.[84]

This intersection of periodical reviews, public interpretation, and middle-class reading constituted an important context not only for the reading of fiction but also for its production. At a time when producing literature was becoming a profession, fiction writers were facing a new type of relation with their audience, who had become consumers in the new mass market for fiction. Under such conditions, explains William Charvat, antebellum "writers recognized the new reading class as a force and attempted to adjust themselves to it" by producing novels and tales "written with reference to buyers' tastes and reading habits."[85] In the urban mass market, however, that audience and its reading practices were no longer directly knowable. Confronting a faceless audience, writers nonetheless had a potential index to the reading practices of the day in the reviews and literary essays that composed the public forum of response. This was less a matter of exact equation and more a case of writers locating a discursive space for conceiving their relationship to a readership and anticipating audience response. Many writers were cognizant of the reading practices of magazine journalists and were keenly aware of the potential impact of the periodical press on the response patterns of the mass audience. Poe, for example, maintained that "the popular 'opinion' of the merits of contemporary authors . . . is adopted from the journals of the day."[86] Whether writing popular fictions or advocacy novels or pitching their stories to what Melville would call the "eagle-eyed reader," authors as diverse as Melville, Poe, and Catharine Sedgwick could not ignore this community. An analysis of its interpretive strategies, therefore, is important not only to understanding the reception of fiction in early nineteenth-century America but also for examining the way fiction writers sought to engage the contemporary audience.

Such a bi-directional approach to antebellum reading opens an avenue into the historically constituted interplay of literary reception, interpretive practices, discourse production, and the dynamics of response to the fiction of that time.

It is important to stress that production within that relation involved writers' particular conceptions, embedded within a matrix of ideas about fiction reading, audience engagement, and the function of fiction within the larger culture. Indeed, a writer such as Poe was actually a member of the community of "magazinists," as periodical reviewers and editors were called at the time. For much of the twentieth century, however, literary critics and historians have assumed that major authors such as Melville, Hawthorne, and Poe wrote as oppositional writers by producing novels and tales that disrupted or otherwise challenged the values of the dominant culture. Such writers were thereby conceived to be the opposite of popular authors such as Stowe and Sedgwick, whose texts were said merely to duplicate or accommodate the cultural mainstream. Over the last three decades, however, this dichotomy has been increasingly inverted as revisionist critics have argued that the texts of canonical writers were often accommodationist, while popular women writers produced works that subtly or overtly challenged standard social and ideological formations. Neither of these characterizations is adequate. No text can fully challenge its audience and still remain readable—that is, recognizable in some way within the reading formation into which it is inserted. Similarly, no text can be totally accommodating and still be considered new, offering its readers something they have never quite experienced before. Although all fictions affect their audience through both accommodation and disruption, what needs to be stressed is that such effects are a function of the work readers do on the texts and the interpretive formation(s) in which a novel or tale is always embedded. One purpose of a historical approach to the reception of antebellum fiction is to explore the varied forms that work took or may have taken as a product of the public strategies of interpretation at the time.

The chapters in part 2 of this study seek to provide such analysis by focusing on four writers who have occupied different places within the changing history of readers' assumptions about how their texts function and how they are to be valued. I have chosen authors whose positions have varied in terms of the popular or critical recognition they have enjoyed—or the neglect or marginalization their works have experienced—in their own day in comparison to ours. That is, the writers discussed in these case-study chapters represent each of four positions in a matrix: being popularly and/or critically acclaimed in their own day and in ours, having mixed success in their own day but canonized in ours, being popular and acclaimed in their own day but marginalized today, and experiencing mixed success in their own day and neglect in ours. Although the focus of these chapters is on the relation between these texts and the interpretive conventions of antebellum readers and not on our own contemporary reading codes, the two, as previously noted, are inextricably entwined. Indeed, one of the interesting dimensions of exploring the reception of antebellum fiction is the parallels and contrasts between our own reading formulations and those of the antebellum era.

For the category of dual recognition, several canonical authors could have been chosen, but I have selected Poe, in part because of his own work as a reviewer but also because the dynamics of accommodation and disruption that antebellum readers experienced through Poe's stories could assume such intriguing shapes. By contrast, Melville is a writer whose canonical status today is quite different from his position among antebellum readers; while Melville enjoyed brief popularity from 1845 to 1850, the popular and critical disfavor and neglect that befell his fiction shortly thereafter makes him the only canonical writer to occupy this position. For the other two categories, many choices could be appropriate, but I have selected the novels of Catharine Sedgwick for one of these categories because, while her novels achieved both public acclaim and popular success in the antebellum United States, she has been consigned, despite recent critical interest in her, largely to the margins of the canon over the last one hundred years. For the last category, a chapter is devoted to Caroline Chesebro', who, like many other antebellum fiction writers, received only modest attention in her own day and remains in virtual obscurity today. But because the antebellum reception of her novels reveal significant differences both in itself and in comparison to reactions to her fiction after the Civil War, the reception of her work offers an interesting opportunity to examine divergences and shifts in nineteenth-century interpretive and axiological practices. In conjunction with the reception histories of Poe, Melville, and Sedgwick, those shifting patterns of response provide an additional perspective on the relation between past reading formulations and our modern perceptions of nineteenth-century texts and authors.

Preparing the way for those particular reception histories requires turning first to the specific shape of the interpretive assumptions comprising the public forum of response in the forty years before the Civil War. Doing so constitutes in its own right an important component of the work of historical hermeneutics: addressing the question of what shapes fiction reading, as an interpretive activity, took in early nineteenth-century America. But just as importantly, the shapes that reading took provide a basis for enhancing our understanding of the relation among writers such as Poe, Melville, Sedgwick, and Chesebro', their contemporary receptions, and antebellum interpretive practices.

CHAPTER 2

Interpretive Strategies and Informed Reading in the Antebellum Public Sphere

ALTHOUGH ACCEPTANCE OF FICTION as a popular form of reading and as an object for public discussion and interpretation in the periodical press rose in the forty years before the Civil War, neither developed without reservations. Reviewers, editors, and other magazine contributors remained somewhat chary about fiction reading as a danger to individual and social well being, in part because they assumed that writers could wield tremendous power over readers. As a reviewer for *Godey's Lady's Book* explained, the "thrilling stories" of many novels create a "fascination . . . that carries the reader along a willing slave" (July 1848: 59). In more general terms, reviewers repeatedly spoke of novel readers being "under the spell of a great master" (*North American Review* July 1836: 136) and of popular novelists such as Walter Scott being "enchanter[s] whose spell has entranced thousands" (*Ladies' Repository* Sept. 1848: 265). What concerned magazinists was that this "controlling power of authors," according to the *Southern Literary Messenger,* "is perhaps no where more evident [than] in our country, where the people are emphatically a reading people" (Apr. 1840: 289). Unfortunately, warned reviewers, novelists too often abused this power as a kind of black magic under which "the novel reader," as the *Ladies' Repository* lamented, "behaves little better than a lunatic, and passes his hours in dreams of rapture and anguish" (Sept. 1844: 248).

Although such remarks sought in part to encourage better fiction, reviewers did not believe that the problem or its solution rested solely on the shoulders of fiction writers. Whatever authors may do, "the purity of literature," noted *Graham's Magazine,* "depends on the decency of its readers" (Mar. 1851: 159). Believing, as the *Southern Literary Messenger* announced, that "every step taken by the mass of readers in defiance or disregard of any of the forms of excellence, becomes a stride in the downward pathway that leads to vandalism and ignorance" (Mar. 1845: 172), reviewers held that the failure to read fiction carefully, thoughtfully, and responsibly posed the true threat. As another reviewer in the *Messenger* put it, "It is the *abuse* and not the *use* of novel-reading which we reprobate. . . . [W]henever we abuse this privilege, then it is that works of fiction become productive of many grievous evils" (June 1839: 421). In this conceptualization, reviewers shared a concern with many educational reformers in this period, in that both groups, despite promoting literacy, believed that in the absence of public control, the freedom that reading offered could run rampant, threatening educational advancement and social stability.[1]

Into such a potentially inflammatory scenario, reviewers and editors thrust themselves, not to oppose fiction or even primarily to change it, but to mediate its relation to middle-class readers. Acting as surrogates and guides, reviewers and editors directed that audience not only to read certain types of fiction but to read fiction in particular ways.[2] As one writer for the *North American Review* explained, "Reviewers are supposed to know more than most people about new publications. . . . We are proxies for the public, who now . . . trust to newspapers, magazines and reviews" for their ideas about fiction (Apr. 1847: 403). Reviewers who addressed this issue repeatedly identified a similar objective. While "it has been our constant duty to guide our readers aright in their choice of literary amusement," announced *Godey's Lady's Book*, it is also the concern of periodicals to let readers see "that this 'delight' or amusement should be guided by sound principles" (Mar. 1863: 304). A review in the *Southern Literary Messenger* similarly asserted that "a Review now" is far more than "what it used to be in the old days": "[F]rom being a mere guide and director of the reading public, in the choice of books, . . . it has risen to a higher position, and considers it to be now its duty to form and correct the taste, by pointing out beauties and defects, and by analyzing the one and the other till the origin and nature of both are made apparent. More frequently, too, leaving behind it the paths of pure aesthetic criticism, it brings into more prominent notice new and important views or exposes rash and improper deductions" (July 1852: 177). In this role, reviewers thought of themselves as partners with the middle-class periodical- and fiction-reading audience, which they inferred as one that desired such a tutelary relation. As the *New York Review* explained, "We address ourselves . . . to the genial reader. . . . We suppose him . . . to ask of us some hints, at least, of the criticism which he requires; to furnish him with a guide, who shall be qualified to lead him" (Jan. 1838: 56). The motor driving such remarks about reading and guidance was the idea that magazines, and particularly their reviews, were to act as avatars of response by directing and refining the fiction-reading practices of a middle class that sought such guidance, so as to bring those practices in line with the strategies of reading epitomized in the reviewers themselves.[3]

In this sense reviewers conceived of their roles as conservative and even, to an extent, regulatory. But to designate reviewers, editors, and other magazinists as "watchdogs," as several literary historians have, is to overstate and oversimplify the relation among this interpretive community, antebellum culture, and the fiction-reading audience.[4] Although operating through varying degrees of (sometimes unacknowledged) ideological conservatism, magazinists by and large subscribed to and championed the notion that reading was becoming democratized and believed that no one could or should dictatorially proscribe practices for "the people." As the *North American Review* proclaimed, "the great problem of the age is not how to repair the old barrier against the power of the people,—this would be impossible and preposterous, even it if were not an unrighteous, attempt—but to make the power of the people more salutary . . . by enlightening the great mass" (Oct. 1837: 484). Reviewers conceived their role as part of a democratic process because they assumed they were part of the "people," acting as its informed agents. This assumption entailed, on the one hand, practicing methods of response consonant with what the "people"—that is, the urban, middle-class audience of periodicals and fiction—already subscribed to and, on the other, modeling strategies as a form of guidance, reinforcement, and refinement of those methods. Sharing with educational reformers a commitment to managed democratic education, reviewers envisioned their role less as watchdogs and more as tutelary agents empowering the reading public. This idea is precisely what the *New-York Mirror* articulated in 1835 when it explained that the task of reviewers was to "enlighten the public mind, . . . that each may become the judge of what he reads."[5] Implicit in such a view was the assumption that reviewers and editors were to act as cultural stewards of the public, its reading, and its welfare—to act as social and, as they sometimes referred to themselves, "literary philanthropists." And as *Godey's* made clear, the duty of the "literary philanthropist" was "to strengthen the bands of society by instruction" (Sept. 1857: 275).

How far the middle-class audience accepted this role is, of course, difficult to say. Most magazinists believed such acceptance was widespread, in part because reviewers assumed that they and the middle-class audience were virtually of one mind. In the words of the *Southern Literary Messenger*, "the benefits and glories of the press are familiar to every mind. . . . Being a universal mental aliment, it moulds, and fashions, and directs the thoughts and feelings of the man. Thousands and thousands of minds are developed by its effects" (Jan. 1835: 222). *DeBow's Review* likewise asserted that "the tone of the public mind is at this era of the world's history almost entirely directed by the periodical press" (Dec. 1860: 793), while one novel reviewer in *Saroni's Musical Times* even claimed, "The only difference between critics and other readers is that the former *print* their opinions. Oral and published criticism generally agree" (Sept. 29, 1846: 6). Nonetheless, it is evident that the influence of reviewer responses and their affinity with middle-class reading practices were never total, since reviewers sometimes complained that readers were reading the wrong kinds of fiction or were reading it improperly. Nor did magazinists naively believe that they exercised complete sway over the middle class or that their responses were in exact harmony with those of the fiction-reading audience as a whole. This recognition, however, was hardly a stumbling block for most reviewers, since their goal was not to achieve the impossible task of exact conformity between their response to a particular work and those of the broader fiction-reading audience but to guide that audience's reading experiences by inculcating particular and general reading strategies. Some readers accepted and desired such guidance, as evidenced by an anonymous letter from a subscriber to the *Home Journal*. According to this reader, the public wanted "the sturdy stalwart and responsible critic [to] step forward . . . and be to those of us who need it an intellectual guard and guide—a literary conscience so to speak—in whom we can put our trust" (Aug. 16, 1856: 2 [no pag.]).

In fulfilling this capacity as guides and exemplars, reviewers discussed fiction by reading it through an array of interpretive strategies that conceptualized fiction as a semantic and formal discourse. Included in this activity was the articulation of a poetics of fiction that emphasized such structural elements as plot, character, and narrative, which were conventional categories that reviewers had inherited from the classical tradition and from their eighteenth-century British predecessors.[6] However, that poetics itself was integrated into a reading formation that included strategies for determining how and when particular principles applied and for conceptualizing the elements of fiction as operative features in the first place. Poetics thus slid into hermeneutics in mutually constitutive ways. Such connections obtained because reviewers assumed that both the form and content of a work and the audience itself played a role in the experience of fiction. Subscribing to an interactive model of the relation between a work of fiction, its author, and its audience, reviewers not only spent substantial effort attending to that relation but specifically advocated the need to do so. "In literature, indeed, where the author and the public reciprocally act and react without intermission among each other," explained the *Southern Literary Messenger,* "it becomes of especial importance that we should examine the peculiarities of the reader, with the same care with which we determine the characteristics of the writer" (Nov. 1844: 673).

This emphasis upon readers' interaction with and role in fiction emanated from a virtually universal belief among reviewers that fiction reading and writing possessed inherent social implications. An important element of this assumption was the conception that fiction was inherently instructional, either for good or bad. As a reviewer in *Graham's Magazine* asseverated, "a novel should be more than a mere piece of intellectual mechanism, because if not, it is injurious. . . . A fiction which does not do good does harm" (May 1848: 298). While providing entertainment through a good story was generally taken to be the essential feature of all fiction,[7] its instructional capacity, as the *Graham's* remark indicates, was both inseparable and important. Hence, while "the didactic purpose of the novel . . . should be only incidental," explained the *Ladies' Repository,* it should "not, therefore, [be] subordinate or secondary" (Feb. 1860: 125). One characteristic of this assumption was that it functioned simultaneously as a descriptive, a constitutive, and a regulatory convention.[8] In describing fiction as an inherently didactic discourse, reviewers both constituted the reading experience as essentially instructional and prescribed the need for it to be salutary. Since all novels and tales were deemed educational in some way, this tutelary relation meant that for reviewers the reader of fiction was inherently susceptible to and in need of instruction from novels and tales.

While this relation was assumed to exist in many types of discourse exchanges, reviewers tended to ascribe to the audience for fiction a lower reading competency than that possessed by readers of history or philosophy. As a reviewer for the *Christian Examiner* maintained in a kind of Bunyanesque allegory, "It is easier to read a novel than to study political economy or theology, and while there are few who are willing to travel along the hard and difficult path to truth, there are thousands ready to lounge along the broad highway" (Nov. 1855: 355). Epitomizing this idea, the *Ladies' Repository* proclaimed that "we live in a fiction-reading age," in which the "masses must have easy reading, or they will not read at all" (Apr. 1865: 202–4). But if fiction readers as a whole possessed shortcomings, especially problematic were "the large class of readers who crave and seek to stimulate their palled [*sic*] appetites with something highly spiced" (*American Review* Mar. 1846: 244–45). Characterizing this group through a type, which we might call the "indiscriminate reader," reviewers frequently lamented this audience as one that "cannot understand or appreciate . . . refined or elevated sentiment, original and profound thought," and for whom "the commonplace, the superficial, the sensual, the gross, and the gaudy, are alone adapted to their torpid intellectual tastes" (*DeBow's Review* Nov. 1859: 516). Such readers were guilty of consuming fiction indiscriminately without regard for its moral probity and capacity for truth. Instead, they "fall, with a wolf-like appetite, on husks, which, if the lower animals were readers, would appear intended for creatures much lower than mankind" (*North American Review* Apr. 1846: 102). "Ravenous" for the kind of sensationalist fiction that "deprave[s] the taste, and too often the morals" (*Graham's Magazine* Feb. 1846: 95), these indiscriminate readers, according to reviewers, devour fiction with an indulgence that "is [the] diseased . . . consequence of fever and delirium" (*Southern Literary Messenger* Sept. 1844: 540).

Taken as a group, these remarks about indiscriminate readers and fiction readers as a whole seem both curious and problematic when considered vis-à-vis the periodical-reading audience that reviewers were addressing. If the audience for periodicals was largely the same as the

audience for fiction, would not such unflattering characterizations of fiction readers offend and alienate the very readership on which periodicals
depended? Would not such remarks consequently be counterproductive
and even in conflict with magazinists' conceptions of their self-appointed
mission?

Several answers seem possible. One is that American reviewers were
simply imitating a practice of British periodicals, which also characterized the mass of fiction readers in this way.[9] Incorporating the same principle into their own conceptions of the audience for fiction, American
magazinists may have been unaware of its implications for their rhetorical (and socioeconomic) relation to their own reading constituency as
well as the incompatibility of such a conception with their support for
the value of the supposed democratization of reading within the United
States.

However, when we consider the reviewers' conception of their role
as guides within the larger context of middle-class cultural formation
and the bourgeois ideology of reading that had developed at this time, it
seems more likely that this unflattering picture functioned as a means of
catering to and reshaping the bourgeois fiction- and periodical-reading
audience. For one thing, reviewers recognized that not all fiction readers were middle class, that some short fiction and serialized novels were
being consumed by the working class through penny-issue story papers
such as the *Flag of Our Union* and the *New York Ledger*.[10] Such readers
may well have been the group reviewers had in mind when talking about
the "mass" of fiction readers; that is, "mass" referred less to numbers than
to what reviewers conceived as the untutored hoi polloi—the "uncultured, every-day people" the *Ladies' Repository* described when referring
to "the masses [who] must have easy reading." If such a conception were
at work—and reviews such as the one in the *Repository* suggest that it
was—then such remarks and their invocation of the mass, indiscriminate
reader served as vehicles for inscribing and reinforcing a differentiation
and hierarchy among readers that would appeal to bourgeois class status. It was, moreover, a differentiation that could suit bourgeois reading
practices in that the mass reader or indiscriminate reader could function
as a cautionary model of what not to do.

The indiscriminate reader, however, was only a part of a larger con-
figuration of reader types that reviewers used to conceptualize another

public strategy for reading, one that involved reader roles. If reviewers conceived the relation between text and audience as interactive, it was also for them reciprocal. Some novel readers might lack intellectual rigor, seek the easy read, or savor sensationalism and frenzy while reading, but novels and tales provided what such readers wanted and were pitched to such expectations. Since "the *masses now* read," explained one reviewer in *DeBow's,* "[e]verybody tries to write *down* to them, to indulge in 'ad captandum'; to clothe vulgar, sensual ideas in slipshod, careless, gaudy style; to shun what is true, and seek what will 'take'" (Jan. 1860: 82). Although disagreeing over whether the fault lay with readers, who encouraged such kinds of fiction, or with texts that produced such reading practices, reviewers did conceive novels and tales as addressing particular types of readers through form and content. Assuming that all fictions assigned a role to their readership by what they did and said, reviewers' frequently discussed the nature and appropriateness of the reader's role that a particular text was supposedly implying.

For reviewers, this implied reader was sometimes an overt feature of texts, manifested in direct address to the audience in the narrative or in a preface.[11] For example, a review of James Kirk Paulding's *The Puritan and His Daughter* in *Graham's Magazine* noted that "the work is dedicated . . . to 'the most high and mighty sovereign of sovereigns, King People,' and scattered through the novel are abundant pleasant impertinences, sufficiently marked by individual whim and crochet, that stimulate th[at] reader" (Dec. 1849: 380). Their remarks also indicate that reviewers conceived the implied reader as an intrinsic but at times covert element of any work. Because this strategy of reading was a product of the supposed inherent didactic relation between fiction and its audience and the moral implications ascribed to instruction, reviewers frequently couched their observations about implied reader roles within judgments about a work's probity and propriety in addressing an audience.

Lauding texts of salubrious morality and deriding those with dangerous moral tendencies, reviewers determined any particular tendency by linking it to the type of reader they inferred the text to be addressing. A properly ethical novel implied an audience for whom the experience of reading fiction would be morally uplifting. A review of Henry Wadsworth Longfellow's *Kavanagh* in *Graham's Magazine,* for instance, approvingly noted that "the effect of the whole is not to thrill or exalt the reader, not to inspire terror or awaken thoughts 'beyond the reaches of his soul,' but to fill him with the highest possible degree of intellectual and moral comfort" (July 1849: 71). More explicitly, *Godey's* said of *The Castle Builder* that "the high moral and religious tone of this work will be its surest passport to the hearts of all pious and reflective readers" (June 1855: 564). Conversely, a work that encouraged sympathy with rogues, cutthroats, and reprobates, or in other ways inculcated dubious ethics, was assumed to address a reprobate readership or to encourage the mass of readers to become so. Such logic lay behind a review in *Graham's* that characterized *Wuthering Heights* as "a compound of vulgar depravity and unnatural horrors" written "for the education of blackguards" (July 1848: 60) and another in the *North American Review* that complained *The Lady Alice; or the New Una* "seems adapted to minister to the lowest possible passions, and to justify the lowest style of manners and opinions" (Jan. 1850: 235). At work here is not simply an objection to the moral tenor of particular fictions. The operating principle is an interpretive notion of textual strategy: because such works offer an unsavory role to their audiences, their fault lies in their orientation to the wrong kind of implied reader.

An additional factor in this attention to implied readers was the supposed lack of intelligence of many novel readers. Although the assumption that fiction should be instructive caused reviewers to admire texts of intellectual substance, they were skeptical of subtlety because such a quality posited an audience that did not match the reality of some novel readers as conceived by reviewers. Caution especially arose when the text's moral relation to its audience was at issue, as it was in a review of George Sand's novels in *Harper's New Monthly Magazine.* Addressing an ongoing debate regarding the morality of Sand's fiction, *Harper's* intoned, "It has been frequently urged, in defense of her novels, that they do not assail the institution of marriage, but the wrongs that are perpetuated in its name. Give her the full benefit of her intention, and the result is still the same. . . . Her eloquent expositions . . . have the final effect of justifying the violations of duty. . . . The bulk of her readers—of all readers—take such social philosophy in the gross; they can not pick out its nice distinctions, and sift its mystical refinements. It is less a matter of reasoning than of feeling" (June 1850: 95). One interesting feature of this response, which was reprinted in the *Home Journal* (June 22, 1850:

1 [no pag.]), is its interpretation of the relation among author, text, and the implicit address of the audience. Although reviewers generally ascribed the creation of an implied audience to authorial intention, they also assumed that the former need not depend on the latter: implied audience was a feature of the free-standing text, a function or result of its discourse, its characterization, or its "exposition," and took its particular shape regardless of—and sometimes contrary to—what an author may have intended. Thus, despite the good intentions of Sand's "eloquent expositions," her novels' implied audience failed to square with the limited capacities of the mass audience as reviewers conceived them. This separation of text and author, however, was not total because reviewers assumed that authors were responsible for creating this distinction in the first place. As the *Harper's* reviewers explained, "a writer who really meant to vindicate an institution [in this case, marriage] against its abuses, would adopt a widely different course; and it is only begging George Sand out of the hands of the jury to assert that the *intention* of her writings is opposed to their *effect.*" Failing to unite intention with effect, Sand could only imperil individual readers and—in a telling though not unexpected turn of response—society as a whole because she had created a text that defined the reader's role in a way that would encourage "violation of duty" while "sap[ping] the foundations upon which the fabric of domestic life reposes."

Reviewers' connections between interpretations of implied readers and assumptions about actual audiences extended to reading formulations that did not entail questions of morality. In commenting on Washington Allston's *Monaldi*, the *North American Review* objected that the novelist would "have done better to draw out the varied passions of the story at greater length . . . and then to explain and justify the overwhelming catastrophe" rather than relying on "many hints and intimations," which only "the observing reader notices in a second perusal" (Apr. 1842: 400). In this case, the inference of the novel's projected reader comes into play for a purely formal dimension—the development and unraveling of the plot. Because of the way it is structured, *Monaldi* fails with "the great mass of readers, who never take up a book but once" and thus "will remain discontented with the manner in which the destinies . . . are wrought out." According to this reviewer, Allston had written for an implied reader who looks for subtle connections and "intimations," but such a strategy was misguided. Instead, the novel should have addressed an audience that needs the plot connections developed more fully—the audience reviewers assumed most readers comprised.

In one sense, these remarks about Allston's and Sand's novels are somewhat curious when considered in relation to the way reviewers characterized the mass audience for fiction. When reviewers conceptualized that readership as lower in intellect and desultory in its reading habits, they were not only supposedly describing it but lamenting these traits as needing correction through education in more attentive and subtle reading practices. A writer in the *North American Review,* for example, who referred to the "multitudes" who devour fictions indiscriminately and superficially, contrasted such readers to "intelligent persons" and praised the "mature" novels pitched to them (Apr. 1846: 102). According to such a strategy, Sand and Allston should have been praised for refusing to pander to the mass or indiscriminate reader rather than censured. Yet censure is precisely what marked reviewers' responses. Sand or Allston— or any writer for that matter—seems to have been put in a double bind: Write for the mass audience and be damned for addressing the wrong readership or write for the discriminating and be criticized for making their novels problematic for improperly educated readers. What were Allston and Sand to do, assuming they were listening? And what did reviewers expect writers to do in dealing with this problem?

Magazinists seldom if ever offered answers, at least in specific terms, and their silence, as well as the internal contradictions in their responses, would seem to promise only confusion and frustrations as guides to writing—that is, as a poetics of audience engagement. But when we recall that reviewers were as much, if not more, interested in the reader's role in the transaction between text and audience, their remarks take on a different coloration. Since reviewers were engaging in hermeneutical practices that modeled and implicitly encouraged particular strategies of fiction reading for their middle-class audience, whatever problems such interpretive practices might cause for a writer was, in a sense, beside the point for reviewers. Good writers supposedly would find a way to deal with and overcome these problems. The main goal of reviewers was to provide readers with strategies for making sense of a text's status vis-à-vis audience(s) and thereby empower readers as properly educated partners in the transaction with the text.

In treating response and the relation between readers and fiction, reviewers thus engaged in a reading of reading that encompassed but was not limited to the responses of the "mass reader" or the "indiscriminate reader" and constituted a kind of "informed" reader capable of exerting control over the textual experience. Moreover, whether they spoke about readers or not, reviewers were giving to their audience the implicit message that the reviewers' own strategies could serve as a master code for informed response by middle-class readers.

❧

As a reading formation, the antebellum informed code of response consisted partly of the global strategies reviewers practiced for the relation between author/text and audience. The informed reader would be expected to pay attention to that relation, to decipher a reader's implied role in a work, and to distinguish whether that role was appropriate and acceptable. Such global practices depended, however, on more specific responses to a text's form and content that included attention to generic distinctions, formulations of character and action as meaningful units, notions of authorial authority, and conceptions of novels and short stories as tutelary narratives. It included as well many of the elements of reviewer poetics that John Pritchard, Nina Baym, and others have documented, since these poetic principles often emanated from hermeneutical strategies.[12] For example, the frequently invoked principle that character and action were to be judged by their naturalness was based on the strategy of reading character experientially by reference to an observable reality; the idea that plots were to be unified drew on a probabalistic code of meaningful recurrence, sequential linkage, and causal relations; and the assumption that narrative voice should be consistently under control depended on reading according to codes of unity, coherence, and candidness. The capacity to exercise judgment in these areas and in the relation between text and reader suggests that an informed reader was to be more than a passive recipient of fictional discourse. In the implicit dicta of public reading formations, an informed reader participated in the reading experience by exercising choices, including the choice to accept or reject a particular role that a text "implied" for its audience.

At the more general or foundational level of reading principles, reviewers advocated thoughtful, intelligent, and even dedicated engagement with fiction—a willingness to stay with a text, to move through it carefully, to contemplate its shape and implications, and to read it more than once if necessary. A review in *Harper's* of George Curtis's *Trumps, A Novel* virtually defined such attentive reading as a desideratum by contrasting it to its inadequate opposite: "In spite of its popular form and brilliant entourage, 'Trumps' is one of the novels which challenge a deliberate and faithful perusal for its full appreciation. It abounds with beauties which do not reveal their whole power without study; many of its fine successes are in the form of evanescent suggestions, which appeal only to the sense of the sympathetic reader; and its frequent passages of combined wisdom and pathos are lost upon impatient and superficial seekers of mere literary entertainment" (May 1861: 844). Significantly, the sympathetic reader is not delineated as one in emotional tune with the text but is conceived in terms of an intellectual kinship that this novel requires from its addressed audience. In this instance, the sympathetic reader is envisioned as a version of the informed reader. But if all serious fiction required such responses, one had to know which novels or stories were serious and mature in the first place. By implication, therefore, all fiction required some careful thought and analysis as part of the reading dynamic. The editor of *Godey's* made this point explicitly: "In reading any work, it greatly conduces to the development of the judgment, to make frequent pauses, and trace out the inference, and the particular bearing and tendency of detached portions of it; and upon its completion, to consider the general scope, its moral tone, the correctness of the sentiments advanced, and the character of the style" (Apr. 1838: 191).

Such thoughtful, careful reading required an educated audience that had learned to exercise analytical and critical-thinking skills and to apply them to fiction. But the informed reader was also expected to come to a text with a broad knowledge of previous fiction and literature. Sometimes reviewers simply assumed that knowledge of a particular author or text actually was widespread, as did a commentator in the *Home Journal* who referred to "that large class of readers who never tire of Defoe" (Oct. 6 1840: 2 [no pag.]). Similarly, *Godey's* claimed that "there are few readers who are not, more or less, acquainted with the Fairy Queen [*sic*]" (July 1840: 31). Often this competence was demarcated through repeated references in reviews to textual elements used by previous authors. A review of Robert Bird's *Calavar* in the *North American Review*, for example, praised the novel's "power of seizing on the prominent features of a scene, and of thus giving a picture of the whole" by paralleling this quality to descriptions in works by Shakespeare and Scott with which readers would have an expected familiarity. "Those who recollect the words of King Duncan as he enters the castle of MacBeth" or who know *Rob Roy*, explained the reviewer, "will require no explanation of our meaning" (Jan. 1835: 258). Somewhat more indirect in connecting informed reading to literary knowledge was a review in the *Home Journal*. After briefly discussing the disquisitions on clothing in *The Lady Alice; or the New Una*, the reviewer asserted, "We need not point out to the informed reader in how far this 'majestic principle of drapery' may have sprung from that great modern thinker, who found all philosophy concealed under the philosophy of clothes" (June 7, 1848: 3 [no pag.]). Such allusions indicate that this literary competence as intertextual knowledge among fiction readers was to encompass a variety of genres and areas.

Among the more specific codes that constituted higher levels of reading competency, strategies for dealing with plot were frequently exemplified by reviewers. To confront plot in the first place meant, of course, that informed readers would share with mass readers an elementary recognition of plot as a structural feature—that is, they would read a work of fiction to look for connections between events that formed some kind of linear, developmental pattern. Reviewers in fact seemed to have assumed this capacity as an inherent part of any reader's experience with fiction, in part because plot was conceived as the distinguishing structural feature of narrative fiction.[13] One went to fiction to experience first a good story that aroused uncertainty and suspense. As *Graham's Magazine* put it in a review of *Mercedes of Castile*, "we want, indeed, all that exciting suspense, without which a novel is worthless" (Jan. 1842: 48). Yet reading to take in, or be taken in by, plot was only the initial step in dealing with this element of fiction. Informed readers also needed to possess a working conception of what plot was as a formal feature. Hence readers were instructed that "plot . . . properly defined, is *that in which no part can be displaced without ruin to the whole,* . . . in which none of the *leading* incidents can be *removed* without *detriment* to the mass" (*Graham's Magazine* Apr. 1841: 197–98). Similarly, as the *Southern Literary Messenger* reminded readers, "It is a rule of art . . . that a work of fiction should be so joined together, that every passage and incident should bring about an inevitable though unexpected catastrophe" (Oct. 1852: 631).

Such an understanding was necessary to enable readers to make informed judgments about the success or effectiveness of a particular work's story; plot was to be an object for examination and analysis. Response here involved several interpretive strategies. The first was a principle of unity and coherence. Informed readers would pay attention to the difference between plot and a mere sequence of incidents, even if the latter were individually thrilling. Reviewers inculcated this idea by repeatedly pointing out "ill-jointed" plots, as the *North American Review* remarked about James Fenimore Cooper's novels (July 1850: 71), or deriding novels in which incidents failed to cohere into plot, as *Graham's* did in describing *Henry Esmond* as a "story [that] has . . . no development of plot, no unity of purpose" (Jan. 1853: 103).

Even a coherent plot was not necessarily to be viewed uncritically since informed response to plotting entailed assumptions about verisimilitude. In responding to plot, readers needed to decide if individual events or the overall shape seemed far fetched or natural, in the sense of being either true to life or probable within the sequence of occurrences in the story line. As *Godey's* put it as one of "our simple rules" for reading, "plot and incident[s] should be probable, at least possible, and arranged with a thought to the ordinary sequence of events" (Feb. 1852: 147). Thus, an informed reader would recognize that a novel such as Alessandro Manzoni's *The Betrothed* succeeded because "the whole story . . . is so well woven together, that one part seems to follow the other like real life" (*North American Review* Oct. 1840: 358). Reviewers implied that recognition, analysis, and judgment of pivotal developments were especially important. Models in this area were provided by reviewers such as the one in the *Southern Literary Messenger* who castigated Edward Bulwer-Lytton's reliance on "the introduction of some extraordinary agent who suddenly appears, just in the nick of time, like Jack out of the box, or *Deus ex machina*" to solve in a jerry-built, unrealistic manner the complications of his plots (Feb. 1859: 155). This privileging of verisimilitude explains how reviewers could sanction tight plotting and still censure such a practice for its own sake—a principle articulated, for example, in the *North American Review*'s comment that "so far as the novel is intended to be a reflection of life," a "plot, too regularly contrived, may be the ruin of even an able author" (Oct. 1842: 292). If loose plotting displayed an inability to handle the tools of art, excessively refined plotting, it was assumed, constituted a failure to match artistic form to the purpose of fiction: to reflect real life so as to instruct the reader.

One way to judge a plot's probability—and unity and coherence—was through a code of causality. As the *North American Review* explained, "The successful novel of the present day . . . must be able to prove its conclusions follow fairly from its premises, to show that its effects proceed from sufficient causes. Too many liberties with probability are inadmissible for the purpose of bringing about the catastrophe" (Oct. 1856: 342). Another method was through recognition of previous plot patterns or conventions—a strategy that again connected reading plot with the assumption that informed response was, in effect, intertextual. If a novel or tale used a standard plot pattern, the expectation was that it would follow and fulfill that pattern through the course of the story. The most common pattern to which readers were alerted was the love story and marriage plot, which, once begun, needed to be carried to its logical conclusion. Hence, a reader should recognize that a novel such as John Cooke's *Ellie* was a failure, since "if ever there was a young female that deserved a husband . . . it was Ellie. Yet the last we see of this tender Genvieve she is looking out of the carriage window . . . with never a love to bear her company." Continued this reviewer, "we submit that Ellie has been badly treated and the reader defrauded of a pleasurable excitement that by every rule of fictitious composition he was entitled to expect" (*Southern Literary Messenger* Aug. 1855: 519). Recognition and judgment about the love-and-marriage plot was important because, according to reviewers, it was such a staple of fiction.

The recognition of regularity, however, carried further implications for responding to fiction. A novel or tale that consistently handled a plot pattern could still be judged inadequate if it was formulaic. Informed readers needed to be able to recognize plot patterns as a way to orient themselves to a work by grouping it in a familiar type and as a step for judging a work's unity, but they also needed to take into account originality. By "beginning with a family at home, and ending with wedding-time," the *Elder Sister*, as the *Home Journal* reminded its readers, was simply one of "the orthodox sort of novels" (Oct. 20, 1855: 3 [no pag.]). Readers ought to recognize that "the plot is a hackneyed one" when it simply is "depicting the various fortunes of a heroine, from the days of school-girl propriety, through numerous reversals and trials, to a happy denouement" (*Harper's* Nov. 1854: 859). By contrast, an informed response to novels such as Augusta Evans's *Beulah* would give "double praise" according to *Godey's* because, while the "heroine of the story is taken as a child from the depths of poverty, and brought, through a variety of moral and mental struggles, to an elevated womanhood," Evans "succeeded in investing an old and almost wornout [*sic*] subject with fresh interest" (Dec. 1859: 560). Such remarks were not just judgments about particular works or plot patterns. They were strategies of informed response designed to provide readers with ways for thinking not only about how fictions handled plot but also about how texts engaged their audience through plot. Within informed reading, audience was conceived as an agency of plot.

The reason for this conception was that in the interpretive practices of reviewers effective plotting was as much an affective as an aesthetic issue. Original plots were valued as a tool for engaging audience interest, and creating interest, as the *North American Review* noted, depended on the way the "mysteries of the story are developed" (July 1834: 192–93). The creation of mysteries, in the general sense of "uncertainties" and their resolution, constituted the essence of determining effective plotting to the degree that such structures induced suspense for readers. In this area, informed response took shape as a version of what Roland Barthes called the "hermeneutic code," which consists of "the various (formal) terms by which an enigma can be distinguished, suggested, formulated, held in suspense, and finally disclosed," so as to "structure the enigma according to the expectation and desire for its fulfillment."[14] This code was to be a functioning component of informed response from the moment the reading experience commenced. For example, in recounting the plot of *The Betrothed* and its effects upon the reader, a reviewer in the *North American* explained how the "first scene [which] is the meeting of Don Abbondio with the bravoes" stimulated the reader to pose a series of questions. "From this moment you are interested for Lucia and her lover. Who are they? What is the meaning of this tyranny? What is there in a simple country girl, that a noble of the land should resort to such high handed measures in order to prevent her marriage?" (Oct. 1840: 358). As they invoked this code, informed readers needed to determine if the plot of a novel or tale effectively elicited such engagement. When fictions "throw a . . . mystery over the issue of every event," explained a writer in the *Southern Literary Messenger,* readers should decide "if the disclosure be made artfully" so as to engage the audience's "own superior discernment" (Nov. 1838: 729).

Pacing, as an interpretive assumption, also was an important issue to consider. As we might expect, a laborious plot was considered defective, but informed readers would realize that a loss of interest could also result if the plot were too fast paced or contained excessive uncertainties. One fault of "excessive rapidity of movement," as the *North American Review* explained in commenting on Y. B. Saintine's *Chrisna,* was that "the reader has no repose" (July 1859: 262). Readers needed to feel an occasional loosening of the emotional squeeze of suspense or run the risk of the emotional overindulgence so often disparaged as a mode of indiscriminate reading. Moreover, excessive suspense through rapid pacing threatened to close off analysis and thoughtful consideration, as a review in *Godey's* suggested when explaining that "the incidents" in *The Second Marriage* "are introduced so rapidly as to leave little time to the ... reader for profitable reflection" (July 1856: 83). By contrast, prolonged uncertainty could create its own tedium, a point made in an article on Bulwer-Lytton in the *North American Review*: "Mr. Bulwer makes a plot, but ... has one artifice, which, we think, has an effect contrary to his intention. He apparently pleases himself with mystifying the reader, by way of working up his interest, instead of which he fairly runs down his curiosity. He is kept in the dark so long that he becomes indifferent to it" (Apr. 1837: 433). Another strategy linked assumptions about pacing with the hermeneutic code of mystery/solution. Exemplifying this move, a review of the *Marble Faun* in *Littell's Living Age* read Hawthorne's novel as one that "tantalizes us ... but ... defeats our expectations by sketching out a plot that comes absolutely to nothing." The review explained further: "A mystery is set before us to unriddle, and at the end the author turns round and asks us what is the good of solving it. Mr. Hawthorne really trades upon the honesty of other writers. We feel a sort of interest in the story ... because our experience of other novels leads us to assume that, when an author pretends to have a plot, he has one. A story-teller who ends up asking why he should clear any thing up is not dealing quite fairly with us" (May 1860: 323). An interesting feature of this response is the way it combines strategies for reading plot with interpretive assumptions about literary competence, textual familiarity, and a writer's obligations in dealing with audience. This version of informed response sees Hawthorne as less than honest by unfairly denying closure to the reading experience, which readers rightly expect from their knowledge of previous fictional plots.

Paying attention to issues of plotting, meant, of course, that readers needed to be able to decide upon the key elements of any fictional narrative to build a sense of plot. This capacity was part of a larger set of codes of recognition, and one component of this category of response consisted of codes of privileged position. To decipher a text correctly, readers were to pay special attention to certain components, especially the ending, the beginning, and the title, which were seen as keys to a text's unfolding pattern. "One is apt to form some opinion of a work from its title page," explained the *North American Review* (July 1825: 84), adding a few years later that "the title of a book, like a lamp at the street-door, is expected to throw some light on what we enter" (Jan. 1847: 237). Such a response could be linked to the hermeneutic code, as the *Southern Literary Messenger* demonstrated in reviewing Bulwer-Lytton's *What Will He Do with It?*: "the reader very naturally asks, what will *who* do with it? Who is the hero?" And what is the *it*? (Sept. 1859: 213). Beginnings were interpretively privileged because, as *Graham's* explained, in the opening of a novel, "the author works busily for a chapter or two with a view of bringing matters in train for a certain end" (Nov. 1841: 248), while conclusions were important because they were regarded as a key to a work's artistic merit in achieving reader engagement and satisfaction through proper closure.

Close attention to conclusions could, moreover, work with other interpretive strategies, particularly those concerned with a novel's moral tendency and tutelary obligation. A good novel concluded by properly distributing rewards and just punishments. Linking this interpretive principle with assumptions about verisimilitude, the *North American Review* explained that "so far as the novel is intended to be the reflection of real life, its aim is . . . the carrying [of] its characters to a certain point, where the ends of poetical justice having been accomplished, they are to be left forever" (Oct. 1842: 292). That reviewers practiced this combination—and promoted it as a strategy of informed reading—is evident, for instance, in reviews of *The Scarlet Letter*, which, despite objecting to the dangers Hawthorne's story posed in invoking sympathy for the morally problematic Hester, praised the novel because of its acceptable moral closure.[15] This strategy, which can be termed the code of "final authority," also came into play in determining whether that authority was properly handled in relation to the rest of the work. Generally, the kind of thing the *North American Review* found acceptable in Hawthorne's novel was decried within the logic of informed reading. As a review in *Godey's* asserted, "where we are made to feel interest in a guilty character, and to pardon easily his transgressions, there is a moral fault in the book, no matter how it ends" (Apr. 1860: 368). Similarly, a reviewer in *Graham's* explained, "Neither do we like the convenient morality of an author in writing a book directly injurious, and then hoping to atone for it all by a page of morality at the finale" (Sept. 1840: 144).

On a lower or more general level, rules of notice could help readers decipher or position a fiction according to its type. Distinctions among genres at this time, as several modern critics have demonstrated, were often idiosyncratic, inconsistent, and frequently in flux.[16] Nonetheless, among the generally agreed upon categories were domestic fiction, historical fiction / historical romance, and advocacy fiction,[17] each identifiable through certain features in form and/or content decipherable through rules of notice—for example, the presence of historical events and actual historical agents or, for domestic fiction, a plot pattern "beginning with a family at home, and ending with marriage." Reviewers were especially adamant about the need to distinguish between what they considered fictional and nonfictional forms and to admonish stories that mixed the two. Speaking of G. H. Lewes's *The Three Sisters*, a reviewer for *Graham's* wrote, "Fine as the novel undoubtedly is, the author has not given it the requisite artistic finish to produce a harmonious impression. Speculations on matters connected with literature, art and politics, essays on passion and the will, appear in their naked character amid romantic incidents and imaginative representations" (Dec. 1848: 368). For reviewers, the problem with such fictions was that their authors, by creating a generic cacophony, were botching their relation to audience. Hence, a reviewer for the *North American* faulted Cooper's later fictions as "not novels, or romantic fictions, in the proper sense of the term, but tedious arguments, or querulous pleas addressed to the community's sense of justice" (July 1850: 123). By mixing "imaginative incidents" with polemical essays, political treatises, and philosophical disquisitions, novelists such as Cooper, according to this logic, were creating roles for readers that would lose the mass audience or be aesthetically crude to keener sensibilities.

Advocacy fiction posed somewhat different problems for reading. Since novels and tales designated by that term were using made-up incidents and characters to advocate a particular and often controversial real-world belief, practice, or reform, such fictions were at best inherently incapable of proving their truths or at worst culpable for tendentiously misleading readers. The *Southern Quarterly Review* articulated precisely this response in warning its readership about the sophistry of advocacy fiction: "To make truth depend upon a fiction or to argue a truth by means of fiction, or to endeavor to inculcate a body of moral opinion through the agency of a tale which requires the invention of facts, is a very doubtful, if not dangerous practice. Art will sway . . . and the truth will become as clay in the hands of the potter" (Jan. 1853: 266). Besides involving a misguided attempt to solicit readers' acquiescence, advocacy novels were the most striking instance of generic hybrids that readers were urged to regard as distortions of the very nature of fiction. Hence, the *Southern Literary Messenger* reminded its audience in the strongest terms that when a novel begins "mingling in the fumes and gross odours [*sic*] of political or polemical dissension," that "novel . . . has . . . assumed to itself a more vulgar mission, incompatible with its essence and alien to its original designs" (Dec. 1852: 721).

Reviewers did not denounce all social criticism or reform as inappropriate for fiction, but such advocacy was to be judged through an awareness of what constituted legitimate targets. Subjects such as dueling, intemperance, child labor, and the plight of the working poor were acceptable. *Graham's Magazine* could recommend T. S. Fay's *The Countess Ida* for "teaching morality and not polished villainy" by imparting the "maxim that dueling is unnecessary" (July 1847: 47), while *Godey's* lauded Charles Burdett's *The Elliott Family; or, the Trials of New York Seamstresses* for being "well calculated to awaken the deepest sympathy in behalf of our oppressed and suffering class of females, hundreds and thousands of whom may be found in our cities" (July 1850: 60). Controversial issues or those too close to home, however, were viewed as anathema because they threatened dissent and social disharmony. Consequently, reviewers denounced Cooper's diatribes against the American legal system, while Dickens's attacks on the British judiciary, safely across the Atlantic, deserved praise from readers. *Godey's* made a general point that combined this criterion with the assumption of the caustic nature of such fiction by objecting that "the form of the controversial novel, where circumstance, characters, and arguments are purely the creation of the author and yet profess to imitate a state of things actually existing, is peculiarly adapted to misrepresenting an opponent's opinions, and for venting all the bitterness of sectarian animosities" (Mar. 1857: 274).

These interpretive paths had an additional twist, however, in that controversial subjects could be included in fiction provided they were handled in a way that, according to reviewers, was uncontroversial. Even slavery was acceptable if the novel or tale avoided advocating a particular position. This was the governing principle in a *Home Journal* review of the *Master's House,* which praised the novel for presenting "the incidents of Southern life . . . as they most naturally arise, developing the various social relations, enlightenments and clearances, belonging to a story of mixed interest. We cannot discover that the writer inclines to either side" (July 15, 1854: 2 [no pag.]). Similarly, *Godey's* approved of the *Planter's Daughter* because "the author has taken care not to introduce any of those modern devices . . . which have rendered so many works, north and south, . . . destructive to those fraternal feelings which should knit together all sections of our common country" (Jan. 1858: 85). Even religious fictions deserved censure when they fomented controversy by advocating one set of tenets over another. For according to another review in *Godey's,* "satirical representation" of competing creeds or denominations exacerbated "the bitterness of sectarian animosities" among readers (Mar. 1857: 274–75).[18]

This last remark from *Godey's* points to another strategy of informed response: reading for satirical elements in fiction. This strategy sometimes connected a work to comparable texts that were supposedly more familiar to the audience. *Harper's* recommended *Peter Schlemihl in America* as a novel in which "the satire is equal to that of Don Quixote. . . . The hits at society in this country are admirable and well pointed" (July 1848: 57). Reviewers did not stop, however, at simply invoking the term or referring to previous examples; recognizing that the fiction-reading audience might not know what satire was, reviewers sought to provide a workable conception. According to the *Home Journal,* satire entailed "bringing our sham-festivities, and our fashionable follies, into contempt" (May 20, 1854:2 [no pag.]). More specific was a *Harper's* reviewer, who instructed readers that satire, as exemplified in Thackeray, "does not mainly consist in the creation of oddities of manner, habit, or feeling; but in so representing actual men and women as to excite a sense of incongruity in the reader's mind—a feeling that the follies and vices described are deviations from an ideal of humanity always present to the writer" (Feb. 1853: 207). Playing a role here was a working conception of irony, since satire, according to this reviewer, operated through an implicit comic "antithesis of actual and ideal" that "suggests a standard higher than itself, *not* by any direct assertion of such a standard, but by an unmistakable irony." That such irony would be "unmistakable" assumes, of course, a fiction- and periodical-reading audience that already shared a common set of ideal standards.

Informed readers, however, needed to do more than have a working sense of satire and irony and be alert to their presence in fiction. Like other strategies of response, reading for satire was both a descriptive and proscriptive convention that would enable readers to decide when a work's satire, sometimes called comic "hits" or "sarcasms," was appropriately handled. Determining the difference between legitimate satire and invective or personal attacks was one strategy, as exemplified in a review of the *School for Politics* in *DeBow's Review*. "This is an admirable hit at the tergiversations and somersets of the politicians of the day," explained the review, because the "author . . . disclaims all intention to be personal in his delineation of the characters." While "the characters are, in truth, so well-delineated [*sic*] that every reader will fancy that the author had some particular individual in his eye," the informed reader will recognize that this novel is truly satiric because "the individual is but a type of this kind; and a description sufficiently correct to lead us to a knowledge of the genus cannot but be recognized as a faithful portrait of every individual of the family" (Nov. 1854: 543). Even "legitimate" satire, which ridiculed types and foibles rather than individuals, could be interpreted as a failure if it seemed misdirected or too dominant. A reviewer in the *Southern Quarterly Review* exemplified this move in responding to *Bleak House*: "The error of Mr. Dickens is in allowing his *satire* to get the better of his *fiction*. The joke, which concludes two such monstrous volumes, should have been a more pregnant one. We see that there is a terrible satire in a finale to a case which has had so many victims; but we feel how pointless and ineffective it is, when addressed to the ear of a Lord Chancellor, whose big whig must effectually keep it out" (Jan. 1854: 228). Two criteria are at work in this judgment. One is the inherited idea that satire is ridicule designed to correct by holding up the type as a mirror. According to this reviewer, Dickens's satire fails because it holds the comic mirror up to those who will refuse to look and thus is directed at the wrong audience. The second criterion relates to the code of generic uniformity. While satire may be an acceptable part of fiction, *Bleak House* had gone too far. By "allowing his *satire* to get the better of his *fiction*," Dickens had turned his novel into a satire, thereby positioning it in a genre that it could not occupy and still remain fully true to its status as fiction.

One thing that these conceptions of and responses to satire, advocacy fiction, and genres as a whole make clear is that informed reading required attention to both form and idea. The two were, in fact, inextricably intertwined because, in responding to plot patterns and irony as formal elements, reviewers had to create meaning and sense from these elements. In this regard, it is necessary to revise substantially Nina Baym's assertion that "never—not in a single instance—did [reviewers] talk about the act of reading novels as one of producing meanings, interpretations, or readings."[19] Whatever reviewers may or may not have said, they clearly *practiced* interpretation. Their repeated emphasis on unity of plot, on attention to beginnings and endings, and on the need to examine the role texts created for the audience depended on interpretive strategies of decoding, selection, and amalgamation. More importantly, it is evident that most reviewers assumed that fiction did possess a meaning that informed readers would ferret out.

Whether dealing with plot, character, or the text as a whole, thematic interpretation was deemed essential to deciphering a work's purpose. Though seldom invoking the words *meaning* or *theme*, reviewers often spoke about the "ideas," "philosophies," "doctrines," "reasonings," or "theories" in a novel or tale, as did one reviewer for the *North American Review*, who wrote of the novel *Margaret*, "One of the doctrines intimated in this work is the sufficiency of every mind to itself, thus implying that every human spirit can solve for itself the problem of existence" (Jan. 1847: 104). A concern with thematics punctuated a *Home Journal* review of Bulwer-Lytton's *Zanoni*, which explained that "the doctrine of the book [is] that the highest scientific attainment, or amplest culture of the understanding . . . involves and requires the negation of human passion and affections" (Sept. 13, 1856: 2). Other examples abound. A *Graham's* reviewer pointed out that "to the thoughtful reader," Hawthorne's stories "are not merely tales, but contributions to the philosophy of the human mind" (Apr. 1842: 443); *Godey's* commented on the "sagacious reasonings upon many evidently important questions of philosophy and social life" in John Sterling's *The Onyx Ring*, noting in particular its "great truth that every one should be contented with his own mental and physical qualifications" (May 1856: 472); and a reviewer in the *Southern Literary Messenger* offered a brief reading of Herman Melville's *Pierre* as a cautionary tale, explaining that "the purpose of the Ambiguities . . . we should take to be the illustration of this fact—that it is quite possible for a young and fiery soul, acting strictly from a sense of duty, and being therefore in the right, to erect itself in direct hostility to all the universally-received rules of moral and social order" (Sept. 1852: 574). At times reviewers even invoked the terms *meaning* and *theme*. *Godey's* noted that Caroline Glover's *Vernon Grove* made "love its principal theme—not love the guilty passion but that love . . . of duties fulfilled" (July 1859: 85), while a review in *Harper's* commented about the *Marble Faun* that "its theme is properly the elevation of a being, not quite human, through suffering" (June 1860: 128). Asserting the practice of thematic interpretation as a general principle, *Graham's Magazine* intoned that fiction reading "unravels the web of an author's mystery to interpret his meaning" (Jan. 1842: 69).[20]

To be sure, the extensive thematic analysis that characterized much twentieth-century academic criticism rarely marked antebellum reviews, but to juxtapose the two is to draw a false comparison. Antebellum reviewers responded to thematics in a manner more analogous to that of modern reviewers in national or regional magazines oriented to a general, educated audience. Like their twentieth- and twenty-first century counterparts, these earlier reviewers did not privilege exegesis; they did, however, make attention to theme a significant part of their interpretive strategies. Moreover, they encouraged readers, in the words of *Godey's*, to "take pleasure in solving the philosophy of fictions" (Apr. 1855: 370). Where antebellum reviewers differed from their modern counterparts was in the tendency to equate theme, as a principal of fictional form, with a story's message—a practice consistent with the nineteenth-century assumption that the aesthetic and the didactic were interconnected in the reading process.

Despite this difference, the conviction of antebellum reviewers that themes, ideas, or doctrines emanated from the form of a novel or tale indicates that they shared an assumption with many modern critics regarding the relation between theme and action or plot. According to Wolfgang Iser, "plot is not an end in itself—it always serves a meaning, for stories are not told for their own sake but for the demonstration of something that extends beyond them."[21] Whether Iser's comment identifies a truth about this relationship is not the issue. The point is that his remark instantiates an interpretive assumption common to modern critics *and* to antebellum reviewers. For example, a reviewer in *Godey's*, in commenting on Sarah Wentz's *Smiles and Frowns,* noted that "there is, besides, a leading *idea*, not set forth in so many words, but interwoven with each separate history [of the events in the characters' lives], that love and marriage are not to be looked upon simply as an addition or completion of earthly happiness, but as part of the discipline which is to prepare us for the truest joy" (July 1856: 94). Similarly, the *Home Journal,* after discussing the philosophy of clothing contained in *The Lady Alice; or the New Una,* added, "We dwell upon the philosophic peculiarities of this curious book because . . . the heroine is a 'new Una'—a very new one. She, like the Elizabethan heroine, is meant to typify faith in distress, and the glorification of loving and sorrowful purity; and she personifies it by refusing to marry her lover because he is a Catholic" (June 2, 1849: 3). Another review in *Godey's* maintained that the plot of Cornelius Matthews's *Big Abel and Little Manhattan,* with its "minute account of the nooks and corners of the city . . . [is] merely an . . . undercurrent to the main thesis," which articulates "the true value of the savage and civilized states" (Nov. 1845: 218). As these remarks indicate, plot and action were not to be read merely for suspense or unity. Because "idea, plot and character" are "mutually dependent," as an article in *Littell's Living Age* explained, the interaction of characters and the unfolding of plot constituted elements in which readers were to discover themes, ideas, and doctrines (June 1860: 718).

Readers needed to be aware, additionally, that the interrelations among action, character, and meaning could require a particular type of reading: allegorical interpretation. A reviewer in the *Southern Literary Messenger*, for instance, pointed out that F. W. Shelton's *Crystalline: or, the Heiress of Fall Down Castle* should be understood as a "sustained allegory" in which "the author aims . . . to recreate a sort of fairy tale, with an undercurrent of much deeper meaning than anywhere appears upon the surface" (June 1850: 382), while a review in *Godey's* asserted that Bulwer-Lytton's *A Strange Story* "is, in fact, an allegorical work," since it employs the "chief characters of the work" for "illustration of the grand moral which he has striven to inculcate" (May 1862: 510). Often reviewers seemed to believe that drawing attention to the presence of allegory was enough and that readers would be able to decipher allegorical meaning on their own. Occasionally, however, a reviewer would explicitly draw out the allegorical implications, as a review in *Godey's* did in designating *Salander and the Dragon* "a very interesting little allegory . . . illustrating the danger of uttering, or of lending a willing ear to, unkind words and insinuations against the reputations of neighbors and acquaintances" (May 1851: 333). The comment in the *Messenger* about *Crystalline* as a "sustained allegory" indicates, moreover, that allegory was not necessarily conceived as a device that could be easily decoded by reading action and character as transparent vehicles for meaning. Since the significance of an allegory could consist of a "much deeper meaning," allegorical reading required close analysis and attentive penetration in the process of response.

Such an assumption obtained in part because the model of reading as an interaction between text and reader did not assume that the search for meaning, including allegorical significance, was necessarily governed by authorial intention. Reviewers assumed that a reader could legitimately infer a particular allegorical significance in a work of fiction even if the author was not fully aware of its presence. After explicating the "allegory of the crystal mountains" in Hawthorne's "The Great Carbuncle" as "a *damper* to all imagination that would with the lofty sanction the low," a writer in *Littell's Living Age* pointed out, "No such intention may the allegorist have had; but at least he might have guarded against so justifiable a gloss by using a more intelligible cipher" (July 1853: 156). A similar strategy was at work in a review of Bulwer-Lytton's *Lucretia* in the *Southern Literary Messenger*, which read the plot relations between characters as a parallel to the relation between readers and the text. Noting that the character of Dalibrand trains Lucretia in metaphysical speculation without regard to morals, the reviewer warned that the novel tries to do the same thing to its audience: "While the mind of the reader or spectator is assiduously engaged in the recognition of the metaphysical phenomena, the strictness and the intensity of the abstractions which such contemplation requires must keep out of vision the accessory, but more important considerations, which address themselves to moral feelings. . . . For it was exactly by this process, as represented in the novel itself, that Dalibrand was enabled to infiltrate his corrupting venom into the mind of Lucretia" (July 1848: 397). One interesting feature of this response is the way it marks the presence in informed reading of a particular kind of allegorical interpretation—that is, reading a novel or tale as an allegory of reading. In this instance, the allegory of reading in *Lucretia* not only exists as a feature of the text that perforce is deciphered, it also needs to be judged within the frame of proper reader-writer relations, which identifies the allegory as a moral danger to readers. More tellingly, after speculating about how much Bulwer-Lytton was "aware" of this dangerous allegory, the review asserts that the novelist should have noticed it, since "there is no excuse for even a momentary failure to take note of it." In light of the reviewer's example, the same applies to the informed novel reader, who has no excuse for failing to decipher this insidious allegory, resist it, and censure Bulwer-Lytton and his novel in the process.

While allegorical interpretation could take several forms, a related strategy of reading that did not appear to be part of informed response was reading a work symbolically—at least in the modern sense of reading images, characters, actions, or scenes as both significant in themselves and resonant with multiple, even contradictory, meanings inseparable from the symbol. While several reviewers did employ the designation "symbolic" or "symbolical" in discussing texts, their comments indicate that they conceived symbolism as an allegorical device. In speaking of the method of "allegorists," *Littell's Living Age* explained that when "the places of the human actors are perhaps occupied by appropriate symbols of some predominant sentiment or characteristic which each of the group subsequently embodies," then "the tale seems allegorical" (Jan.–Mar. 1861: 220). In other cases, reading symbolically meant reading emblematically, in the sense of interpreting an element of a text as typifying a single, abstract (often larger) idea, condition, or value—much as flower books deciphered particular flora as emblematic of peace, hope, or innocence.[22] Such a strategy is instantiated in a *Harper's* comment on *Little Dorrit*, which explained that "the stupid confession of the important young official, who lives in precedents and an agonized and reverend chaos, when he drops his eye glasses . . . is symbolical of the entire humbug of the system of which he is a cipher" (May 1856: 848). In a like manner, an article in *Littell's* explained that Hawthorne's Pearl is a character "who, by a suggestive symbolism, is made to typify in her nature the mixture of conflicting influences which her parents seem to have bestowed" (June 1860: 716). In these kinds of interpretive moves, Pearl and Dickens's young official are treated as emblematic of a particular abstract value possessed by other elements in their respective novels.

Although reading for theme, idea, or meaning was deemed essential to any informed response, reviewers recognized that some fiction made ideas a central concern of their narratives and that in some cases those ideas were complex. Most reviewers, however, treated such learned fiction as problematic. For one thing, learned fiction looked too much like an essay or a philosophical treatise and thus violated the code of generic uniformity. Another problem entailed assumptions about the limitations of the mass audience: since philosophical issues and complex ideas had to be treated with subtlety to do them justice, reviewers assumed most readers would simply by baffled—or bored—by them. Even Dickens, otherwise praised for his accessibility, came under rebuke in this area. According to *Godey's*, the *Haunted Man*, though "admirably written," will have "not so much honest interest to the great mass of readers." Having "more philosophy in it" than Dickens's other Christmas tales, "it will be a mystery to those who do not read it carefully"; hence, concluded the magazinist, "we do not like this story so well" (Mar. 1849: 222). Another problem was that learned fiction, whether through its ideas or through other marks of erudition, could become pedantic. Such was the conclusion of the *Southern Literary Messenger*, which complained that the *Caxtons* "is charmingly cursed with one of Bulwer-Lytton's greatest faults, his pedantry. Proud of his extensive and varied reading, . . . he is forever thrusting fragments from out of the way authors under your nose, and with juvenile conceit, looking up in your face, as it were, saying 'Haven't

I read a quantity?'" (Jan. 1862: 13). Taught to view intellectualized and erudite fiction as a roadblock to effective engagement of the audience, antebellum informed readers were encouraged to be on guard for its various problems and to be skeptical of its merit.

Like other interpretive conventions, reading for ideas or themes—whether emblematic, learned, or neither—was not advocated for mere intellectual or aesthetic purposes, however. Because of the didactic and social implications attributed to fiction and its relationship with readers, reviewers advocated thematic awareness as a means for determining the ethical orientation and value of a novel or a tale. If fiction reading were to serve its instructional purpose in an uplifting and legitimate way, readers had to understand the leading ideas of texts to allow them to perform their appropriate cultural work, particularly by maintaining and reinforcing traditional values and institutions and curtailing dangerous new ideas. Such logic is evident in the review in the *Southern Literary Messenger* that read *Pierre* as a tale cautioning against the pitfalls of a commitment to a personal sense of duty which contravened "universally-received rules of moral and social order," as well as in a review in *DeBow's Review,* which punctuated its remarks on Alice Haven's *The Coopers* by explaining that "the moral of the tale is to be found in the practical workings of married life, the experiences of which are truthfully delineated" in the actions and characters (Oct. 1858: 490). Such readings not only identified certain fictions as appropriate but served as models for how to interpret the sociothematic worth of such texts. Accordingly, by this logic *Godey's* could recommend *The Blithedale Romance* as a worthwhile fiction for its audience because "in [its] serious lessons on the mental follies . . . of the times," it "may, in some manner, be relied upon for its influence in checking the exuberance of 'new ideas,' and in bringing back bewildered, but well-meaning people to the usages and requirements of common sense" (Oct. 1852: 311). Thematic reading was thus a means of defusing potentially subversive texts by turning them into advocates of "common sense"—the very "foundation," according to Barthes, "of the bourgeois statement of fact."[23] In this way, reading for meaning could aid readers in resisting texts that might be construed as challenging middle-class ideology. At the same time, such thematic reading offers one of the clearest examples within antebellum informed reading of the way an interpretive formation functions by interpreting itself. In this instance, self-interpretation entailed privileging foundational values of middle-class culture and applying them through an interpretive move that constructed *Blithedale* as a textual embodiment of those values.

Such formulations rested, of course, on the assumption about the instructional and moral obligations of fictional texts and fiction readers and the determination of a fit between the two. A central conviction was that fiction must be evaluated by how well it balanced instruction and formal control and whether that balance created a proper role for its audience. Narrative technique was a factor in this area in that reviewers, as Pritchard and Baym have demonstrated, distinguished between fictions that engaged in appropriate instruction through the dramatic situation and those that merely layered such instruction on the narrative proper.[24] Though maintaining that an uplifting, tutelary relation was intrinsic and necessary to fiction, reviewers directed readers to look for and sanction the relation that was subtle and consistent rather than overt, intrusive, or intermittent. We should recall here the objection of the *Graham's* reviewer cited earlier who complained, "Neither do we like the convenient morality of an author in writing a book directly injurious, and then, hoping to atone for it all by a page of morality at the finale" (Sept. 1840: 144). One reason for such objections was that intermittent preaching, particularly at the close of a novel, was inadequate for achieving a proper moral relation with readers whose interest depended on plot and characters—in other words, the weak-minded mass readers.

At work as well in strictures against intrusive narration was a concatenation of more general interpretive assumptions about authorial authority, implied readership, and proper narrative technique as features of effective communication. Moralistic intrusions marked only one instance of the ineffectiveness that resulted when a narrative was seen as attempting to overdetermine the reader's response. That problem could also proceed from excessive exposition. As a writer in the *Southern Literary Messenger* pointed out in condemning the way G. P. R. James's *The Smuggler* handled its description of the hero's military prowess, "If we are told of his profound and skillful 'combinations' once, we are told of them fifty times." In the grip of such expositional redundancy, "the reader can have no possible escape; he is held by the button until he yields a ghastly admiration" (Sept. 1847: 535). Since reviewers repeatedly emphasized that good fiction united subtle artistry with exemplary instruction, a novelist who relied on heavy-handed intrusions or excessive dramatization inadvertently exposed the machinery by which the novel was expected to do its work. According to this interpretive logic, such techniques prohibited an author from retaining his or her rightful authority with readers, whether they were the "mass" fiction readers, who would be put off because they lacked the patience for dealing with overt instruction and dramatic redundancy, or more informed readers, who would interpret these elements as technical blunders.

The underlying assumption of authorial authority in the handling of narration carried with it other strategies for treating this dimension of fiction. Throughout the antebellum period reviewers assumed that novels were narrated by the author, a conviction that identified narrative voice and point of view as an authority readers could—and would—trust.[25] This assumption, however, included a recognition of variation. Although never using the term *point of view,* reviewers reminded readers that fiction could be delivered through different narrative agents. Amid the general belief that authors were their narrators, reviewers recognized that some fictions used first-person narrators, which they called "autobiographical" fictions, a term that seems to have marked the source of information in a work and maintained in an indirect way the continuity between narrator and author.[26] But what, then, of the possibility for an unreliable narrator? Because of the author-narrator affinity and the principle of trust reviewers ascribed to that link, the idea of an unreliable narrator seems not to have been part of their analytical lexicon.[27]

Yet in regard to this protocol, several qualifications need to be made. Despite the general assumption of reliability, reviewers occasionally questioned whether a particular type of first-person narrator was a legitimate choice. For example, a reviewer in the *American Whig Review* found Hawthorne's Miles Coverdale "a most repulsive being . . . who forsakes the rough, healthy life of Blithedale because he pines for Turkey carpets and a sea-coal fire." But instead of seeing these traits as a conscious artistic strategy by which to undermine the reliability of Coverdale's narration, this reviewer disdainfully concluded, "Such is the man upon whose dictum Mr. Hawthorne would endeavor covertly to show the futility of the enterprise in whose favor he once enlisted" (Nov. 1852: 419). In effect, this reviewer judged Hawthorne in error for mishandling the "proper" relation between reader and text by choosing a narrator who could not effect the authoritative voice required for fiction. By implication, informed readers would conclude the same.

Other reviewers' comments, however, reveal a turn in the 1850s in treating autobiographical narration, as some reviewers sought to instruct readers in a more subtle and complex response to this type of fiction. Commenting on Thackeray's method in *The Luck of Barry Lyndon*, a reviewer in *Graham's* pointed out that "as the story is told in an auto-biographical form, the author has an excellent opportunity to exhibit ... the whole psychology of villainy." The reviewer added that Thackeray's method of choosing a narrator whose ethics and entire view of life are questionable enabled him to produce "a masterly satire [that] holds up cruelty, selfishness, hardheartedness and impudence to mingled execration and derision, by ironically stating their claims to respect and admiration" (Mar. 1853: 363). Similarly, another review of *The Blithedale Romance* (this one in the *Southern Literary Messenger*) asserted that the "interest" of the narrative "is mainly kept up by the fact that the story is told by one who had been only a looker on, and not an actor, and the results are thus invested with an extraordinary effect ... on account of the supposed ignorance of the narrator" (Aug. 1852: 512). By the 1850s reviewers were beginning to define narration as a technique in which deliberate unreliability was a legitimate aesthetic strategy and to alert their readers to use that interpretive paradigm for making sense of potentially problematic and disruptive texts.

This attention to narrative reliability incorporated more than aesthetic and cognitive principles. Believing that the relation between fiction and its audience always entailed ethical issues, magazinists extended that principle to the relation between readers and narrators. To understand what a novel or story presented required understanding its point of view and making informed judgments about the morality, immorality, or amorality in the narrative perspective of the work. Here the strategy of informed reading gave audiences a choice. The reader could censure a novel for its improper point of view, either because it was immoral or because the point of view failed to match the work's instructional aim. In the 1850s, however, formulation of the concept of unreliable/ironic narration gave informed readers the option to "rescue" a text by turning its ostensibly dangerous message into a covertly palatable one. What united these two options was the imperative to control texts that otherwise would be subversive and dangerous. As a product of the reviewers' cautionary attitude toward fiction reading and their belief that it should enhance traditional values and social stability, the concept of unreliable narration developed as an interpretive strategy by which readers could construct a text and its relation to the audience in conformity with the ideology undergirding informed reading.

Because of the underlying equation of narrators and authors, responding to the relation between readers and narrators inevitably led to conceptions of the audience's relation to the author. Readers were expected to take from a work of fiction some sense of who the author was—above all as an artist but also, if possible, as a person.[28] Affirmative judgments about the unity of plot, proper handling of the reader's role, choice of narrators, and other elements would be interpreted as indices that the writer was a successful artist. The moral tone of a novel or tale and the ethical relation it established with its readers were to be taken as indices to an author's moral character. As the *North American Review* explained, "novelists who would induce us to take the murderer and pirate to our hearts, show very plainly where their affections lie" (Oct. 1844: 435). Fiction that was too learned or cabalistic in its erudition could hint to readers that the writer was egotistical or pompous. What was true of ethics and erudition, moreover, was applicable to any ideas a writer embodied in a novel or tale whenever those ideas had some impact. According to *Harper's*, "Every author, indeed, who really influences the mind, who plants in it thoughts and sentiments which take root and grow, communicates his character" (July 1857: 279). Accordingly, "to a discerning reader," noted the *Southern Quarterly Review*, "the work will serve an important purpose,—that of revealing the character of the writer's mind" (Apr. 1846: 509).

While this knowledge frequently was advocated as a means for readers to make proper judgments, in the 1840s some magazinists began arguing that one needed to know the author for full enjoyment and understanding of a fictional work. Called by its proponents "reproductive criticism" or "aesthetic criticism"—and by its detractors the "transcendental-Boswell" or "Sub-Goethian" method—this strategy of response involved abjuring or at least bracketing judgment in favor of entering through the text into the mind of the author to experience the work in a manner similar to the way it was written.[29] Anything less, according to its advocates, left the reader deprived, as *Godey's* argued: "When a critic cannot get out of himself to . . . read another's work in the very atmosphere it was written, he will not show us the truth" (Jan. 1847: 52).

Although some magazinists continued to champion this strategy into the 1850s, it is fairly clear that the reproductive response obtained among only a small minority of reviewers and thus served as a minor strategy of informed reading. Part of the problem, according to its opponents, was that the reproductive method was inadequate for dealing with the relation among author, text, and reader and represented an abandonment of the reader's responsibility to make informed "objective" judgments. Another difficulty was that readers could not be sure they had gotten at the true experience of an author and his or her purpose, since works of fiction—or at least some of them—were hardly transparent windows to the author's mind. "When we know exactly what an author aims at, we have a specific standard . . . of the excellence of the performance," admitted the *North American Review*, "but when his purpose is so obscurely shadowed forth, as to leave the most painstaking reader in doubt whether he has any definite object, the book can be judged only by the general impression it produces, its obvious moral tendency, and the skill it shows in its construction as a work of art" (Apr. 1856: 368). The injunction for informed reading here seems to be something like this: employ a reproductive response if the work is clear, but, if its purpose is more "shadowed," use external standards, which in turn will enable you to decide if the shadowing is a mark of subtlety or of turbidity. What drives the logic in this case is the reviewer's implicit adherence to the idea that intention does not govern significance and performance. Hence, while admitting that "we may thus misjudge the author's intention" by abjuring the reproductive strategy, the reviewer in the *North American* remarked that we "shall perhaps arrive at a truer valuation of his work, because, not being in his secret, we shall not incur the risk of being misled by any fancied connections between the mark and the precision of the shot."

Although in theory any feature of a novel or tale could serve readers as an index to the author's ability, temperament, mind, or moral character, one of the primary vehicles to which readers could attend was the work's characters. The type of characters presented, the way in which they were developed, and the sympathy (or lack) with which they were treated could be read—and were read by reviewers—as revealing signs of an author's own character. The facility with which this move was made is evident in an article on the novels of Fredrika Bremer in the *Southern Quarterly Review,* which noted that "the mind which could originate such a character [as Elsie Frank, whom the reviewer styles "the good mother"] must be full of beauty" (Oct. 1843: 504). Not that reviewers equated fiction writers with their characters. For the most part they did not, no more than reviewers or academic critics do today. But just as some novel readers today conflate the opinions or ideas of characters (or the values they embody) with those of the author, so apparently did a segment of the antebellum audience. Or at least, some reviewers believed readers did so and encouraged them to recognize that the "ideas a particular character expresses should not be taken as universal truths" espoused by the author. Rather, "[e]ach character . . . speaks for itself" (*Littell's Living Age* Nov. 1844: 182).[30] Informed readers needed to understand that the presence of a reprehensible character did not inherently indict an author as a person of questionable repute or as a poor artist. What mattered was how the author treated that character. Attending to that treatment would give readers not only a window for determining and judging an author's moral probity but also an index to a writer's artistic success or failure in creating an appropriate role for readers vis-à-vis such characters.

Reading through character to get to the author was, however, only one strategy for conceptualizing and dealing with this element of fiction. That conceptualization consisted most basically of treating characters as amalgams of traits that readers could assemble into identifiable representations. As such, it was grounded in the same assumption that guided responses to plot: the idea that fiction was a mimetic medium referring to an empirical reality outside the text. One dealt with a character by getting to know him or her in the same way one got to know a person: attending to traits and qualities as indices for deciphering the character of a character.

Because they assumed that any action, speech, or thought performed by a character or any narrative comment about him or her could disclose a trait, reviewers did not articulate a precise typology of such indices. Their practices nonetheless drew attention to some strategies. Attention to characters' names, for one thing, could be important. Read through a rule of notice, "names," as a reviewer in *Graham's Magazine* pointed out, can "be indicative of peculiarities of person or character"

(Nov. 1841: 252). Names might be taken as emblematic, as a review in *Godey's Lady's Book* explained by noting that in *Lorimer Littlegood* "the name of the principal character foreshadows the nature of his exploits" (Dec. 1856: 563). Or names might simply be suggestive, as the *Southern Quarterly Review* illustrated in discussing the method of Dickens in *Bleak House,* where the characters' "hideous attributes," whether of "decay, bad passions," or other "personal deformities," are "sufficiently indicated . . . in his names of persons" (Jan. 1854: 226). Another strategy consisted of reading character through principles of accumulation and juxtaposition. A series of actions that accorded with one another could collectively indicate a particular trait in a character. According to *Harper's,* for instance, in finding a character who "is ready to give up her fortune to the poor little sister" and "will cheerfully die for the lover to whom she hasn't a kind word to say," readers could rightfully conclude that that character "is as generous as the sunshine" (Oct. 1857: 661). An incongruity between what a character does and says or between what she thinks and says also could be telling. Such was the case, according to a review in the *Southern Literary Messenger,* in *Adam Bede,* in which "the contrariety between thought and speech" in some of the characters reveals a gap between "the heart within and the mask without, which we call a face" (Sept. 1859: 232).

While we might be tempted to call such responses a "natural" way of reading character, they were also practices emanating from shared cultural codes common to the interpretive community of antebellum reviewers. The logic for such conceptualizations of character inhered in the need to justify fiction reading as a worthwhile activity that would inform the reader about real life. This principle was as much a prescriptive as a constitutive strategy within informed reading, as reviewers made clear by repeatedly gauging characters according to their perceived verisimilitude. Readers were told that Cooper's "personages are mere wooden images, with no semblance to life" (*North American Review* Oct. 1838: 489), but that in Thackeray's *The Newcomes* "the great charm of its portraitures is their perfect naturalness" (*Home Journal* Oct. 6, 1855: 2 [no pag.]). Woodenness or unnaturalness could be detected in a number of ways, but the most commonly invoked method was to ask if a character was idealized or stereotyped. A character lacking "shadowing," as it was called, by being all good or all bad was unacceptable. Thus, readers needed to understand that in *Who Shall Be Hers?* "the characters of Rosiland and Vivian are almost too perfect, as is that of Cottrell too bad" (*Godey's* Mar. 1841: 144). Driving such a response and the criterion of verisimilitude in characterization was the assumption that short stories and novels, as the *North American Review* expressed it, "are patterns of life and that characters presented in them must have that diversity and even contrariety of feeling, motive, and conduct . . . which are daily written among our friends, or we do not acknowledge the fidelity of the imitation" (Jan. 1838: 21).[31]

Besides invoking fidelity as a mark of verisimilitude, reviewers instructed readers to look for consistency as an index to true-to-life characterization. Using this strategy, the *Home Journal* objected to the "inconsistency and indelicacy of the portrait" of Laura in *Pendennis* because, though "possessing every generous feeling, every good gift," Thackeray makes her "faithless to that first affection for Pendennis (July 14, 1855: 1 [no pag.]). At times within informed reading, such a flaw could mark only a single characteristic, but more frequently the strategy of consistency was invoked in relation to the full assemblage of traits constituting character. Periodical readers learned, however, that looking for consistency was a tricky strategy. Was a reverend rake such as Arthur Dimmesdale or the taciturn yet garrulous Natty Bumpo to be viewed as an inconsistent and thus implausible character or were such diversities of feelings and conduct faithful to life? And what of a character who seemed consistently inconsistent? According to some reviewers, such a character could still be natural. At least that is what a review of *Jane Eyre* in *Littell's Living Age* explained to its audience. Jane may be "zealous and fanciful, yet cool and prudent, impulsive yet deliberate, foreseeing yet not calculating" and thus "molded from a heap of opposites, but her composition being once admitted, she is consistent in every act and thought" and thus is true to nature (Feb. 1848: 324). Reading for consistency was clearly a slippery procedure that informed readers could not expect to employ without some second-guessing and uncertainty.

Somewhat less problematic was the strategy of looking for change in character. Change was not required for verisimilitude, but it also was not objectionable as incompatible with consistency. Although reviewers often conceptualized change in terms of the process by which an increasing number of a character's traits became known to the reader, reviewers also noted that some characters undergo alterations in their established character because of turns in the plot. Such change might take the form of a reversal, either "upward" (for example, an inebriate is reformed or a coquette becomes a dutiful wife) or "downward" (for instance, a believer loses faith). But reviewers also reminded readers that change could be lifelike through the growth of some embryonic laudable trait or the festering and deepening of some flaw. According to the *Southern Literary Messenger,* such characterization was precisely the strength of Maria Edgeworth, for "it is in tracing the gradual evolution of some original fault or vice of character by the action of circumstances, that she displays the most consummate ability. . . . With the most minute observation she follows the progress of some pernicious propensity . . . [and] depicts its natural development [*sic*] in the ordinary course of events" (Sept. 1849: 582). What readers needed to watch for in determining verisimilitude was whether change was effected in a plausible manner—that is, in the "ordinary course of events," and gradually rather than abruptly. Thus a review in *Godey's* alerted readers to be chary of the "astonishing" and "sudden alterations of characters" in some novels (Feb. 1850: 151).

Any change, according to reviewers, had to be properly motivated as well, but this principle was a particular form of a more general criterion of motivation as a gauge of effective characterization. A character was expected to act in a way that was appropriate to the circumstances of the plot and setting and that resulted from sufficient cause. Readers, that is, were to attend to the way an author develops "his personages by unveiling the process of their thoughts, taking up the train with events that suggest it, and following it down to the act that results from it" (*North American Review* July 1853: 206). The idea that proper motivation would combine causal relations and a delineation of characters' thoughts and feelings meant that readers needed to read with an eye for the inner dimensions of character.

In drawing attention to inner characterization, however, reviewers modeled several different and ostensibly conflicting codes for informed readers. On the one hand, inner development was viewed as superior to other forms of characterization. In part this was a function of a link within informed reading between character development and types of fiction, and the valuation of some types over others. As *Littell's Living Age* explained, "a sensation novel, as a matter of course, abounds in incident" but lacks "[d]eep knowledge of human nature, graphic delineations of individual character, vivid representation of . . . the workings of the human soul—all the higher features of the creative art" (June 1863: 437). Another factor in the valorization of inward characterization was the belief that it was more true to life, constituting a method, as the *Southern Literary Messenger* explained in speaking of Balzac's fiction, by which "readers [can] participate in the essential life and not merely behold the outward experience of his characters" (Feb. 1859: 84). What is curious is that amid such approval, reviewers also berated inward characterization, thereby suggesting that readers were to find something amiss in this method. Dismay with authorial expression and exploration of a character's inner traits formed the core of a comparison between Fielding and Thackeray in the *North American Review*, which proclaimed that Fielding "exercises over his characters an absolute right of property. He establishes himself in the inmost recesses of their minds, and displays the secret thoughts which no conjecture founded on action will reveal." In contrast, "Thackeray takes no such unfair advantage of the offsprings of his imagination" but positions his readers in a more lifelike relation to his characters. "We open one of his books, as we enter a company of strangers. What we first notice is their . . . features and dress, their occupations and their peculiarities of action; and on these observations we found our conjectures as to their characters" (July 1853: 207–8). Such devaluation of inner characterization was repeated by a review in *Littell's Living Age*, which informed its readership that if an author is to achieve effective characterization, "it will be by a close study of human nature from its objective side, and by checking the propensity to dive into psychological problems and the complex mechanism of motives and feelings" (Jan. 1862: 316).

What appear as incompatible strategies in these responses, however, may have been part of a more subtle set of distinctions within informed reading. The objections to inner characterization seem directed not against reader access to that dimension of character but against the methods some writers used to achieve it. Developing a character's inner traits through narrative comments constituted a failure because it was an instance of intrusive narration that sacrificed mimesis to diegesis. Hence, the objections in the *North American Review*, cited above, to Fielding's methods. According to the logic of informed response, readers should rightfully expect more subtle techniques of revealing inner traits through outward means, such as a character's actions or speech. Suggestiveness was one key here, as indicated in the *North American Review*'s praise of Thackeray's ability to present characters in such a way that readers could productively speculate about and thereby gain insight into characters' inner beings.

This is not to say that reviewers did not struggle with reading characters through the code of verisimilitude. Especially troubling was the matter of deciphering the status of allegorical or emblematic characters. Reviewers held that allegory was a particular type of fiction that had certain principles or necessities for characterization built into the nature of its form. Readers, accordingly, needed to give a certain allowance to allegories by regarding their characters, despite their thinness or lack of shading, as legitimate if they contributed to the instructional goal of the allegory or were interesting. This was the case with Hawthorne's works, according to the *North American Review*. The "figures" in the *Twice-Told Tales* "are not persons, they are passions, emotions, spiritual speculations"; nonetheless, they "hold the mind with a Lamia-like fascination" (Oct. 1864: 545). Even so, reviewers conveyed the idea that because such characters lacked verisimilitude, they could never be fully satisfying or adequate when considered within the overarching principles of naturalness and individuality. This was a typical problem, according to *Graham's Magazine*, with Bulwer-Lytton's characters, which lack "personal identity—they are only embodiments of certain passions or peculiarities. His actors are like the knights of Spencer [*sic*], mere stalking horses for particular vices or virtues" (June 1842: 355). These various remarks constituted part of a two-tiered strategy for responding to such characters. An article on "Fiction" in the *Ladies' Repository* explained the basis for this strategy in these terms: "characters in second-rate fictions are ideas; those in novels of a more artistic grade are real people, used as lay figures, to exhibit metaphysical fabrics upon" (Apr. 1865: 205). Informed readers were to grant leeway to characters presented primarily as vehicles for ideas when such characterization was either necessary to the form or functional for a work's thematic purpose; however, readers were at the same time to view such characters as inferior within a hierarchical scale of representation.

Besides responding to characterization within codes of representation and aesthetic competency, informed readers needed to decipher their own relation to characters of a novel or tale. Most basic was determining whether characters, especially the protagonists, were interesting. This quality could take any number of forms, from characters being "natural" and thus like actual people, to having an aura of mystery about them, to being striking in a way that made them different from other fictional characters. Hence, *Harper's* explained that Currer Bell "is so direct, life-like, and human . . . and withal keeps you in such provoking, yet delightful uncertainty, with regard to the real characters of her heroes and heroines—that her writings exercise a relentless fascination" (Apr. 1853: 714). The interest readers can take in the title character of Marian Harland's *Miriam* results because "[s]he is altogether different from the namby-pamby class of girls which novelists too frequently consider as being especially qualified for heroines. Miriam is characterized by energy, strength of purpose, dignity, and rare intellectual gifts" (*Godey's* Jan. 1863: 97). At times, as such remarks indicate, interest was linked to admiration. But a character could also be interesting when, according to reviewers, he or she merited censure. Perhaps the most noticeable examples of this principle were reviewers' fascinated responses to Hawthorne's Arthur Dimmesdale and Thackeray's Becky Sharp, but characters by Bulwer-Lytton, Dickens, Edgeworth, and a number of other writers also received similar reactions. The *North American Review*, for example, pointed out that in Bulwer-Lytton's *Last Days of Pompeii*, "Abraces, the Egyptian, . . . is the most striking personage" precisely because "as a man skilled in all learning of the day, and deeply read . . . even in demonology," he is "a cool and calculating impostor. . . . Subtle and unprincipled, he is checked by no scruples; and . . . withheld by no fear of retribution" (Apr. 1835: 451–52).

Readers were to consider a character's capacity to be interesting through another criterion—whether he or she evoked sympathy or empathy in the audience. According to the *Southern Quarterly Review*, readers must ask of any novel or tale, "Do we sympathize with the actors? Do we enter into their feelings, link ourselves with their destiny, and anticipate . . . the result?" (Jan. 1854: 19). Invoking the same principle was a review in the *Southern Literary Messenger*, which reminded readers, "We must have something in common with the *dramatis personae* or we will care nothing about them" (Oct. 1853: 647). Sympathy depended first of all on recognizing traits shared alike by characters and the audience and thus was a function of reading for verisimilitude. But beyond that link were the ethical tones decipherable in characters and the implications those tones had for reader sympathy. Readers were encouraged to attend to such indices as a character's actions or speech or to a narrator's comments to determine whether a character was laudable or not and consequently deserving or not deserving of sympathy. Though assuming that in many cases this would be an easy task for readers, reviewers also recognized that deciphering a novel's or tale's moral inflection of its characters could require attentive, close reading. Such was the strategy needed for reading *Martin Chuzzlewit,* according to the *Southern Quarterly Review.* Urging readers to "look at" the text's "words in consecutive order" as they describe Pecksniff and his daughters, the reviewer pointed out that "there is not one word of this to be taken in its true and literal meaning." Paying attention to Dickens's "delicate vein of irony" would reveal to readers that the text "gives the leer to the hypocritical gravity of his portrait[s]" for a purpose quite opposite to "preserv[ing] the respect of the reader for them" (Oct. 1843: 296).

Readers were to recognize, however, that such markers of sympathy or repulsion, empathy or derision, had to be read in consort with other codes. Texts, in other words, could not be granted sole or final authority by which readers should determine their alignment with characters; readers had to decide whether a text's attempt to create sympathy or identification was appropriate or not, especially when a character's ethics were at issue. If a text promoted sympathy with a disreputable character, that sympathy was to be resisted as a violation of fiction's ethical obligation to its audience. Relevant to this area were codes involving character change, final authority, and implied audience. A reprehensible character, for example, still might legitimately warrant reader interest and sympathy if in the course of the work he or she reformed, but readers needed to be aware of how the shift in reader response was evoked. If a novelist encouraged both admiration and disgust before the change—and especially if what inspired admiration also prompted the disgust—readers were to see this as a moral problem in characterization and reader engagement, and draw back. This point was the gist of a review in the *Southern Literary Messenger* that inveighed against the "much graver error" of *Guy Livingston* "in drawing the picture of a dashing, devil-may-care young gentleman in colors so attractive that we cannot but admire while we condemn him, and after leading him through the world of fashionable vice and debauchery, presenting him to us as extremely repentant and purified" (Oct. 1857: 319).

Reviewers recognized, in other words, that determining one's emotional relation to characters—especially when ethical issues were involved—required a certain amount of sophistication and thoughtful weighing and balancing of several different factors. And once again, verisimilitude came into play. If characters were to be truly natural, even admirable individuals would have faults; conversely, even reprehensible ones might possess traits that readers should be rightfully drawn toward. Such was the point of a comment in the *North American Review* about Walter Scott's Highlander in the Waverly novels. Though emphasizing that, as a matter of principle, "we would say nothing in defense of any doubtful character" in fiction, the reviewer pointed out that readers had to approach the Highlander by recognizing that "Scott has recommended him to our compassionate respect and not as an example." Extrapolating from this instance, the reviewer added the following as a general principle "with respect to characters": "as long as we have to do with mixed characters"—that is, characters that are natural and life-like by being morally shaded—"we must regard them with mixed feelings" (Apr. 1843: 414). The key was in recognizing what one's response should be to the various shades of a character to avoid blurring distinctions and/ or to recognize and censure fictions that problematized the reader's ability to do so. That possibility was one about which readers needed to be chary in responding, for example, to *Vanity Fair*, according to a reviewer in *Littell's Living Age*. Thackeray's novel was one of a class of "distressing books" in this area because, ironically enough, the "personages are too like our everyday selves and neighbors to draw any distinct moral from. . . . Palliatives of the bad and disappointments in the good are perpetually obstructing our judgments" as readers, explained the reviewer. Consequently, "We cannot see our way clearly" (Mar. 1849: 448). In informed response, reading for and sanctioning verisimilitude in characterization was appropriate, but readers were to understand that when it left the audience morally adrift, verisimilitude had gone awry.

Amid this careful rounding up of variations, this repeated effort to cover the contingencies of potentially disruptive relations between characters and readers so as to keep both in conformity with the bourgeois ideology of reading, reviewers nonetheless believed that it was appropriate for a novel or tale to use characterization to challenge readers in some ways. Creating uneasiness in readers could be appropriate work for fiction because experiencing that uneasiness could help readers learn more about themselves and their relation to others. According to a review in the *Southern Literary Messenger,* our experiences in life cause us "chiefly to consider the differences between ourselves and other men, often utterly forgetting the grand fact of an underlying unity," but "good novelists" unsettle this way of thinking. When we read such texts we "hear the author exclaiming, 'You see all those people that appear to be different; I tell you they are alike. You despise that wretch; thou art the man. See what a monster I have painted; I am that monster'" (Sept. 1859: 230). Such disruptions of the reading self, however, were not conceived as challenges to the reader's beliefs so as to cashier or deform the core of middle-class values and the dominant ideology of antebellum America. Instead, challenge was conceived in such encounters as a way for readers to reestablish their connection to traditional, "universal" truths, as the *Messenger* reviewer made clear by adding that the reminder that we too are wretches and monsters "is but a secular rendering of the deepest sentiments of Christianity . . . which teaches us . . . that we all have got an evil corner in our hearts." What readers were supposed to learn from such fiction was the underlying veracity of established truths somehow forgotten or their own failure to live by those truths.

Reviewers did not assume, however, that in responding to character or to plot, theme, methods of audience engagement, or other elements of a novel or tale, informed reading should proceed in exactly the same form for men and women. Subscribing to a representational poetics in which fictional value was determined by its fidelity to an empirical reality built on sexual difference, the informed code of reading posited that responses to fiction should at times take a distinct shape for women. Although all readers were to derive instruction from fiction and to judge it by how well it reflected life, its utility for women depended on their ability to extract practical information relevant to their social roles. Thus a reviewer in the *Southern Literary Messenger* recommended *The Image of the Father* because "our lady friends will find in the character of Mrs. Farquhar . . . a bright example of an obedient and *useful wife*" (Nov.

1848: 704). Although such criteria were to guide women's responses to domestic fiction especially, the informed woman reader was expected to glean practical benefits from novels and stories that did not overtly provide them. Historical fiction was especially touted for this advantage; as another reviewer in the *Messenger* asserted, "One of the most beneficial and interesting modes in which fiction can be employed, is that of illustrating historical events" (Sept. 1839: 632). For readers of fiction, and especially women, explained another writer in the same issue, "the advantages of correct knowledge of history must be obvious," primarily because such knowledge can "invigorate the sentiments to virtue." For this reviewer, history in the guise of fiction was important for a woman as a means to cultivate those virtues necessary to her state—a state in which "her vocations are domestic and her duties solitary" (598–99).

The gendered inflection in informed reading appeared most noticeably, however, in reviewers' conceptions of emotional response and didacticism. The concern with readers' sympathy toward characters indicates that emotional response was held to be an important part of the fiction-reading experience for all. But reviewers assumed that women readers were more naturally inclined to respond emotionally to fiction. The "genius" of woman, explained *Godey's Lady's Book*, lies in the way "she could enter into and appreciate as a man could not, the struggles of the spirit"; thus, a novel such as *Silverwood*, with its "vein of religious feelings," would be especially appreciated by women, "who sympathize with affliction" (Apr. 1848: 247; June 1857: 564). Nonetheless, when discussing emotional response, reviewers sometimes criticized it as femininely inferior. One writer for the *Southern Literary Messenger* looked forward to the day when the novel-reading public would no longer be deluged "by tears which have fallen from the eyes of every grade of society, from the countess who sobbed herself to sleep . . . over the Children of the Abbey, up to the seamstress in her garret, or down to the scullery maid . . . who wiped her eyes on the duster, at the sorrows of Malvina" (Jan. 1862: 11). Another reviewer similarly complained about the "sentimental propriety which claims . . . the female mind" when reading (*Christian Examiner* Jan. 1860: 120). Such contradictory remarks about emotional responses were paralleled in reviewer's comments about reading didactically. Though generally critical of overtly didactic fiction as unpalatable to the truly informed reader, reviewers' comments indicate that such didacticism was another matter when the gender of the reader was a factor. One reviewer for *Graham's*, though complaining of "a consistent intrusion of ethical reflection" in Bulwer-Lytton's *Harold, the Last of the Saxon Kings*, nevertheless affirmed that such passages "will doubtless much edify all young ladies" (Sept. 1848: 179). Gendered assumptions about sympathy and didacticism as principles of informed reading underlay an essay in the *Southern Literary Messenger* that offered an ironic bit of advice about how to cope with and avoid heavy-handed passages. Speaking of such moments in the novels of G. P. R. James, the essayist quipped, "We were once greatly assisted in avoiding them by reading one of his books after a lady, who had drawn pencil lines about every such passage as an expression of her sympathy and admiration" (Sept. 1847: 534–35). What is telling about this flippancy is that it comes at the expense of the very role reviewers identified as appropriate for the female audience. As such, it signals the presence of contradictory scripts that were provided ostensibly to educate women but seemed designed, simultaneously, to immobilize their response.

An adequate understanding of antebellum informed reading, however, needs to recognize that it did not develop along a fault line of gender. The vast majority of the interpretive strategies within this reading formation were promoted as a means to empower both men and women of the middle class as active, informed participants in the culture of fiction.[32] In practicing and disseminating a rather uniform version of informed reading for character, plot, meaning, and other elements of fiction, reviewers did not, however, promulgate a rigid pattern of codified response; many recognized that diverse types of fiction existed and that audiences needed to adapt. In one sense, this principle of adaptation was implicit in the various categories reviewers used to classify fiction. Because correct response depended on knowing the type of fiction being read, poetics in this area dovetailed with hermeneutics. But the criterion of adaptability extended to other areas, since one assumption of informed reading was that if a work of fiction failed to display control or merit in one area, it nonetheless could compensate by satisfying other interpretive expectations. As a reviewer for *Godey's* explained in evaluating Ann Stephens's *The Heiress of Greenhurst*, "although many of the incidents of this volume are scarcely within the bounds of probability, there is yet a lively interest created and sustained by the animated descriptions of scenery and character" (Aug. 1857: 181). Reviewers assumed that truly informed readers needed to recognize and give credit to a writer who violated reader expectations, provided that the work offered something in return. Cognizant that the novel was a protean form, informed readers were expected to approach fiction with an horizon of expectations flexible enough to account for and appreciate noteworthy variations in a work that might otherwise trouble standard response strategies.

This flexibility, moreover, was not to be applied only when responding to texts of unusual merit that seemed to disrupt some interpretive criteria. The need to adjust reading codes was also imperative for other dimensions of response, including reading fiction for its moral tendency. This strategy is typified in the objections, cited earlier in the *Graham's* and *Godey's* reviews, to the immorality of novels that nonetheless ended morally—objections that privileged one reading code by bracketing another. In lieu of employing the code of final authority, the reviewer in *Graham's* implicitly told his audience what the reviewer in *Godey's* made explicit: that "the morality of a narrative" has "little to do with . . . how it ends," and that readers instead needed to be aware that "it is the prevailing impression, not the catastrophe, that is important" (Apr. 1860: 368). For responding to certain works, particularly where the question of ethics obtained, the strategy of final authority may need to give way to a code of "prevailing impressions" for determining the role such texts implied for their readers. Flexibility was thus a convention with multiple strains within informed reading.

By practicing these interpretive conventions as a means to encourage readers to activate such codes in their response patterns, reviewers espoused a conception of literary engagement that both reflected the continuing impact of Enlightenment defenses against the potential antisocial threat of fiction and anticipated what Daniel Schwarz has called the "humanistic formalism" that dominated Anglo-American criticism through most of the twentieth century.[33] For the modern and Enlightenment traditions enclosed the antebellum period within a set of assumptions which maintained that fiction has a social function because human behavior is the central concern of its representational mode. Yet reviewers hardly saw their interpretive strategies as a historically constituted set of procedures. According to reviewers, the conventions they proffered supposedly constituted a natural, timeless way of responding to fiction that readers should follow as an informed audience.

Given the way reviewers conceived of themselves as caretakers of culture, such an approach was almost inevitable. Dedicated to preservation, not creation, to replication, not rupture, reviewers did not define fiction reading as an experience that produces self-revelation and startling insights. Nor did reviewers envision it as a means to create new strategies for interpreting texts that might productively challenge old assumptions. Instead, fiction reading was to be a form of self-validation and confirmation of the already known. Through a strategy of informed reading that was essentially conservationist, reviewers sought to multiply their practices as incarnations of bourgeois culture, which middle-class readers could employ as a means of socializing the discourse of novels and tales while valorizing order and control in the production and consumption of fiction.

The interpretive conventions of antebellum reviewers thereby formed a potentially powerful vehicle for configuring fiction and its reception. However, neither readers nor writers before 1865 monolithically followed the model. Reviewers and middle-class readers who employed the codes of informed reading inevitably differed among themselves in the way they combined and privileged specific interpretive strategies. For such strategies and the experience of reading fiction intersected with political allegiances, ideologies, and varying social formations that made informed reading a patchwork of overlapping—and at times divergent—interpretive experiences rather than a seamless whole. At the same time, while fiction writers had to be aware of these strategies and to accommodate them in order to be read, the very demand for novelty and originality in fiction encouraged writers to try to find fresh, viable ways to engage the expectations and assumptions of this bourgeois reading formation. In the context of these interpretive strategies, therefore, the relation between antebellum fiction and its audience transpired as a process of reconciliation and transgression that took shape most visibly in the public sphere. In that process, the formulations of informed reading constituted both challenges and pathways to the forms fiction and its reception could take in early and mid nineteenth-century America.

PART TWO

Contextual Receptions, Reading Experiences, and Patterns of Response

Four Case Studies

CHAPTER 3

"These Days of Double Dealing"

*Informed Response, Reader Appropriation,
and the Tales of Poe*

AMONG NINETEENTH-CENTURY American writers, perhaps no one
had a more acute sense of audience than Edgar Allan Poe. Conceiving the form, unity, and originality of literature as a function of its effect
upon readers, Poe defined fiction and poetry as discourses intrinsically
involved with reception. This recognition of the need to engage readers
within the developing literary marketplace of the 1830s and 1840s repeatedly surfaces in Poe's critical commentary and accounts for his treatment of literature in "The Philosophy of Composition" as an instrument
for securing the public's attention during a single sitting. Long before
that essay, however, Poe had made his concern with reception a component of his fiction in the design for his Folio Club Tales, a planned
collection of stories written by members of a literary club and linked by
the members' responses to their colleagues' tales. Yet if Poe's attention to
readers took various forms throughout his career, his greatest interest lay
in the magazine audience for fiction.

Poe's involvement with magazines, begun in his youthful reading of
British periodicals, extended throughout his life. His stints as editor of
the *Southern Literary Messenger* (1835–37), *Burton's Gentleman's Magazine* (1839–1840), *Graham's Magazine* (1841–1842), and the *Broadway
Journal* (1845–46) immersed him in the world of magazines and magazine fiction and helped convince him, as he asserted on more than one occasion, that the "whole tendency of the age is Magazine-ward." Believing
of "the Magazine literature of America" that "there can be no question as
to its extent or its influence," Poe was certain that authorial achievement
depended on skillful navigation through this growing medium.[1] Since
magazines spoke to and for "the tastes of the day," the successful writer
would write for those tastes, and "not . . . merely for the taste of the taste-

less, the uneducated, but for that also, of the few."[2] What was true for writers in general was especially the case for writers of the increasingly popular mode of prose fiction. The "writer of fiction who looks most sagaciously to his own *interest*," claimed Poe, will "combine . . . his loftier efforts" with "such amount of less ethereal matter as will give general currency to his composition" (*ER* 312).

Despite his enthusiasm for magazines as the ascendant vehicle of fiction and audience engagement, Poe nonetheless recognized danger in writing the popular. Although he generally believed that a work's popularity did not automatically signal artistic flaccidity, he also maintained that "a book may be exceedingly popular without *any* legitimate literary merit." By the early 1840s, Poe even began expressing doubts that popularity was something a true artist would want. In a review of Charles Lever's widely read novel *Charles O'Malley* in 1842, Poe claimed that seeking popularity in fiction represents a "stooping to conquer" and then sounded almost a proto-modernist warning that "the popularity of a book is *prima facia* evidence . . . of the book's *demerit*" (*ER* 311–12).[3] Not that Poe would ever renounce public approbation, since he continued to relish the popular success of "The Gold Bug" and his Dupin stories. But like Robert Browning's duke, Poe preferred never to stoop. Popular and critical success, he believed, needed to come on his own terms.

Poe's double strain in thinking about fiction and the popular audience found a parallel in his interactions with reviewers and the informed pattern of response they disseminated to the middle-class magazine audience. In fact, Poe's binary connection to informed reading holds double significance because of its relevance both to the shape of his career as a writer and to the reception of his fiction in antebellum America. Yet Poe's dialogic relation to the public codes of reading in his own day was largely overlooked by most twentieth-century critics, who underscored his departure and independence from antebellum critical assumptions.[4] To be sure, Poe took on the reviewing establishment of New York and Boston, objecting in particular to the "cliques," glad-handed corruption, truckling toadyism, and "disingenuousness" among reviewers whose praise or critique of a work too often depended on regional biases or under-the-table dealings between editors.[5] Despite his objections to what he called the "mere dogmas and doctrines, literary, aesthetical, or what not" that formed the "ruling cant of the day," Poe nevertheless was deeply embedded in their practices (*ER* 290). Only recently, in fact, have we come to understand, as one Poe critic has noted, that "in most instances, his critical opinions agree with those of his contemporaries" in *Graham's, Godey's*, the *Southern Literary Messenger*, the *North American Review*, and other leading periodicals.[6] Behind those opinions and Poe's commentaries as a whole lay a set of interpretive practices that linked Poe inextricably with the codes of antebellum informed reading.

If modern students of Poe often missed the connection, part of the reason is that Poe tended to exaggerate his differences from other reviewers, sometimes by creating readerly straw men. A case in point occurs in his second review of Charles Dickens's *Barnaby Rudge* when Poe claims that reviewers as a group are wrong in their consensus that a work of fiction has to "disregard" or "contravene" established principles of art to be a popular success (*ER* 226). What Poe fails to mention is that his counterargument that a work could be both popularly and artistically successful paralleled the principle of most reviewers, who maintained that popular and critical success were not necessarily at odds and that the best fiction could achieve both.[7] Such an assumption, in fact, caused reviewers repeatedly to single out Dickens, Walter Scott, and the James Fenimore Cooper of the Leather-Stocking Tales as writers whose works deserved praise as models of that dual accomplishment.

Poe shared a number of other assumptions with informed reading, beginning with the belief that reviewers and magazinists exercised substantial influence as guides for the fiction-reading public. The "general opinion" about an author, Poe maintained, "is never self-formed" but is decided "by reference to the reception of the author's immediately previous publication," a process that makes the actual responses of the audience "a species of critical shadow" (*ER* 372). Even more explicit was his assertion in one of his "Literati" sketches that "the popular 'opinion' of the merits of contemporary authors . . . is adopted from the journals of the day" (*ER* 1118). Besides acceding to the prevailing belief that magazinists were shaping the audience for fiction, Poe exercised many of the specific practices of informed reading. In addition to reading for conventions of characterization that included identifying such fictional types as the "hen-pecked husband," the "intermeddling old maid," the "beautiful governess," and the "high-spirited officer," Poe subscribed to codes of verisimilitude and uniformity in characterization, as reflected in his comment that in Robert Bird's *Hawks of Hawk-Hollow* too often a character "proves inconsistent with himself" or lacks a "fidelity to nature."[8] With other reviewers, Poe believed that characters could be read as indices to their authors, as evidenced by his remark that Seba Smith's eponymous Major Jack Downing "is not *all* a creation; at least one half of his character actually exists in the bosom of his originator."[9] Poe also attended to plot conventions and how they were deployed. He could praise a work for handling plot to produce "poetical justice" and take to task a novel such as Edward Bulwer-Lytton's *Night and Morning* for its "absurd sacrifices of verisimilitude" in the "main events" (*ER* 214, 154). In treating genre, Poe embraced the code of uniformity, which caused him to upbraid novels such as Cooper's *Mercedes of Castile* for being "neither fish, flesh, fowl, nor good red herring."[10] Regarding narrative technique, while Poe felt that authorial commentary had a place in fiction and that "the *commenting* force can never be safely disregarded" by the "successful novelist," he also shared with other magazinists the belief that "it is possible to have too much of this comment" and that intrusive narration resulted when writers relied on a "superabundance" of "authorial comment" (*ER* 328, 104).

What is interesting is the way Poe's own practices directly contravene some of his objections to the way reviewers read fiction. Despite his oft-cited fulminations against what he called "the heresy of *The Didactic*" and his claim that any fiction must be "[v]iewed as a work of art, and without reference to any supposed moral or immoral tendencies," Poe's responses to novels are littered with remarks on the instructional and moral probity of fiction (*ER* 75, 103). As much as any reviewer, Poe could object to the unseemly, the immoral, and the vulgar in novels as an affront to informed readers, inveighing, for example, against *Charles O'Malley* for the "disgusting vulgarism of thought which pervades and contaminates this whole production" and from which the "lofty mind will shrink as from a pestilence" (*ER* 320). Conversely, he could praise J. P. Kennedy's *Horse-Shoe Robinson* for the way a "high tone of morality, healthy and masculine, breathes throughout the book" (*ER* 653).[11] While seldom expatiating on the tutelary merits of particular works, Poe did engage in the negative principle of didactic critique in informed reading by lambasting novels that imparted immoral lessons. Such was the gist, for instance, of his response to a novel entitled *Mephistopheles in*

England, which struck him as having "no just object or end" except "to cherish and foster the malice, the heart-burnings, and evil propensities of our nature. The work must, therefore, as a whole be condemned."[12]

Even Poe's idea of effect connected to the interpretive practices that dominated public responses to fiction. This linkage involved more than the obvious point that effect requires someone to be affected and thus necessitates thinking about fiction's relation to its audience. Undergirding Poe's concept of effect and his privileging of it as "indispensable" to the brief tale was the assumption in informed response that the successful author would be a virtual enchanter who controlled the audience with his or her spellbinding artistic performance. Like other reviewers, Poe believed that the successful work of fiction resulted from and testified to the ability of the author to wield the "wand of the enchanter," whose "vigorous, and glorious *imagination* . . . induces the reader . . . to muse in uncontrollable delight over thoughts" (*ER* 216). As he explained most pointedly in one of his reviews of Hawthorne's stories, when "in the brief tale . . . the author is enabled to carry out the fulness [*sic*] of his intention" and achieve the effect he desires, then "[d]uring the hour of perusal the soul of the reader is at the writer's control" (*ER* 572).[13]

Such connections and parallels should come as no surprise given the extent of Poe's immersion in the world of antebellum periodicals. Because Poe was steeped in the public discussion of fiction, the interpretive practices through which it proceeded played a formative role in his conception of his relation to his audience and the impact he wanted his fiction to have on readers. He understood that to work, a story had to address its audience's horizon of expectations. This engagement was not, for Poe, a matter of pandering to the popular, since the optimal goal was to produce a text and an effect that "should suit at once the popular and the critical taste" (*ER* 15). It also was never a matter of pure accommodation to that horizon since Poe understood, again in accordance with informed reading, that a work of fiction had to be different, had to depart from or even disrupt expectations to be seen as original and achieve its effect. In defining originality as "novelty of effect," Poe believed that such "originality . . . demands in its attainment less of invention than negation," an undercutting of audience expectations so as to destabilize or at least reorient the reading experience (*ER* 580, 20–21).

The interrelation of accommodation and disruption in Poe's conception of authorial engagement of the audience emerges most clearly in his three reviews of Nathaniel Hawthorne's *Twice-Told Tales,* where Poe also expressly addressed the nature of effect. Although he sometimes spoke of "effect" as any impact a work had on the reader, his comments on Hawthorne reveal a more specialized conceptualization. In explicitly linking the status of the "skillful literary artist" with the ability to achieve "a certain unique or single *effect*," so that "the soul of the reader is at the writer's control," Poe observed that in such Hawthorne tales as "Sights from a Steeple," "Little Annie's Ramble," and "The Haunted Mind," a thoughtful reader would "note their leading and predominant feature, and style it *repose*. There is no attempt at effect. All is quiet, thoughtful, subdued" (*ER* 570–72). Such a comment indicates that, for Poe, effect achieved by the "skillful artist" does not inhere in just any impression or impact. Hawthorne may produce repose, but he does not produce effect because effect cannot consist of calmness, satisfaction, or ease but emerges only when the reader is made to feel emotional and mental disruption. Because Poe believed that "[a]ny strong mental emotion stimulates all the mental faculties," he held that only the strong stimulation of mental faculties produces true effect (*ER* 1354). And herein lay the problem with feelings such as repose and comfort. Lacking strength, they could not produce effect, since they could not compel the reader's mind and soul to fall under the fiction writer's irresistible control. Effect resulted instead from the writer's ability to produce in the reader the opposite of repose, to disrupt the reader's ease by instilling disquietude and even disorientation so as to maintain authorial mastery over the reading experience.

Poe's ideas about effect and reading signal that his departure from the assumptions of informed reading did not consist of rejecting its interpretive codes but emerged instead from elevating some of those principles to paramount importance in defining his own relation to the fiction-reading audience. For Poe, more was at stake than a particular tale's success or failure to achieve its effect. What mattered was the exercise of power and control as the sine qua non of his artistic identity. Indeed, it would not be amiss to assert, as Stephen Railton has tellingly observed, that "control is . . . the central, informing preoccupation of Poe's uneasy career as an American writer"—a career in which he was driven by the idea that "no word can be permitted to escape the writer's control, and no reader."[14] What bothered Poe was not only the potential of the unruly text to elude authorial authority once it passed from the writer's hands. Greater problems lay in the control reviewers had (or Poe believed they had) over the fiction-reading public and the attendant power of that public, especially within the reading formation of informed response, to determine a work's meaning, impact, and status.[15]

Poe, to be sure, recognized that readers had a necessary role in fiction and were not simply passive receivers of an impact. In the second Hawthorne review, Poe explained that a tale, when composed with "care and skill" to produce a "single *effect*," "leaves in the mind of him who contemplates it with a kindred art, a sense of the fullest satisfaction" (*ER* 572). To be truly appreciated, a work of fiction requires a reader who not only contemplates its form and meaning but does so in harmony with the author's purpose by bringing to the text a shared aesthetic sense or "kindred art." Poe, however, never felt comfortable with this dependence on the reader, despite his enthusiastic support for the popular world of magazine fiction and its mushrooming audience. If popularity could necessitate an unacceptable "stooping to conquer" by the author, the activities of the audience posed the danger of reader usurpation of control over the text and, thereby, an appropriation of power from the author. Since Poe equated success in fiction writing with mastery of the reader's soul, such usurpation could only signal authorial failure.

The potential for readerly appropriation existed most dangerously in particular ways of reading, especially those that Poe believed were tendentious. Hence, he objected to didactic and moral readings of fiction even though he practiced both forms of interpretation. He also developed a marked uneasiness with the assumption that one can read from a text to the writer, particularly by identifying a narrator with an author. For Poe, such an interpretive strategy gave readers the power to erase the magic of a writer's mercurial genius by reducing the fictional text to a reflection of authorial personality and temperament.

In Poe's way of seeing things, however, any reading that invested ultimate authority in the audience's interpretations and judgment, which was precisely a central tenet of antebellum informed reading, posed a threat that made him anxious. Poe was hardly alone among his contemporary fiction writers in feeling an anxiety over his relationship with readers.[16] What distinguished him, however, was the way he approached that relation as a virtual battle for authority, waged as both frontal assault and guerrilla warfare.[17] Properly pursued, a covert struggle would be especially valuable to Poe for undermining the audience's ability to fix his identity through his fiction. As a counter to the problematic agon with readers over authorial mastery of the text, Poe accordingly sought to make himself into the writer as shape shifter, whose artistic magic and sleight of hand would be so forceful yet subtle that it would disempower readers while leaving them in bewildered awe.

Yet a question arises in this context: Which readers were the target of Poe's disorienting strategies? This issue merits consideration because the most frequent critical anatomy of Poe's relation with readers has defined his approach as one characterized by a bifurcated notion of audience. Modern critics repeatedly have claimed that Poe wrote partly for the masses and partly for an astute minority of readers. According to one version of this argument, Poe segmented his stories by readership, creating his tales of horror for the mass audience and his literary hoaxes for the attentive minority. Terence Whalen, Benjamin Fisher, and others have countered that Poe did not align particular tales with different audience groups since such a strategy, in Whalen's words, "would have either limited his best works to the smallest circulation, or . . . condemned them to oblivion. Instead, he viewed his texts as split or divided objects." In this characterization, each tale contains elements pitched to thoughtful readers as well as something designed to work on the masses.[18]

Such arguments hold a certain degree of credibility, given Poe's repeated assertion that the fiction writer needs to engage both popular and discriminating readers; on one occasion he even claimed that the "judicious artist" would include in a work of fiction "qualities which are interesting to all, as a passport for those of a more intellectual character" (*ER* 312–13). Such a division, however, was never paradigmatic for Poe because as a defining principle it could not fit his notion of artistic mastery and the imperative to control all readers. Thus, it would be a distortion to view his tales of crime and horror or his fictional hoaxes as stories in which the majority of the audience was to become immersed in or duped by events and characters while other readers would step back from that experience in a more thoughtful and analytical way so as to understand and admire the art of the effect. Though Poe could happily talk of leading "the nose of a mob" by "its imagination," he also increasingly believed as his career progressed that imagination and analytical intellect, as "the two divisions of mental power[,] are never to be found, in perfection, apart" (*ER* 1455, 549).[19] Consequently, the accomplished artist, who seeks perfection in both the text and its engagement with readers, would strive to tap both analysis and imagination in all audience members.

Even as Poe sought a response that merged imaginative credulity with analytical insight and appreciation, he also conceived the informed audience and the mass readership as a common ground for staging effect as a means of asserting authorial power. For if effect entailed disruption, then all readers had to be disrupted, disoriented, or to some degree duped, even the reader of "the kindred art." After all, a reader who understood too much about a text's artistry could not remain in the writer's control, or, as Poe put it on two occasions in his Marginalia pieces, a work in which a reader can see the method cannot produce the effect it seeks precisely because "the wires are . . . not concealed" or "the trap is not properly baited or set" (*ER* 1404, 1365). The trick was to create a degree of understanding while still keeping the reader in the dark by producing an illusion of perception achieved or insight shared. In his third review of Hawthorne, while discussing originality in fiction, Poe suggested how this strategy could take in even the most kindred-spirited reader: "true originality—true in respect of its purposes—is that which, in bringing out the half-formed, the reluctant, or the unexpressed fancies of mankind, . . . combines with the pleasurable effect of apparent novelty, a real egotistic delight. The reader . . . feels and intensely enjoys the seeming novelty of the thought, enjoys it as really novel, as absolutely original with the writer—*and* himself. They two, he fancies, have, alone of all men, thought thus. They two have, together, created this thing. Henceforward there is a bond of sympathy between them, a sympathy which irradiates every subsequent page of the book" (*ER* 581). Interestingly, Poe defines this intimate bond with the reader by taking away as much as he gives. In the truly resourceful engagement, the reader is induced to feel a bond, to "fancy" achievement as a kindred art, that remains in part an illusion, staged by the writer who has kept his true accomplishment—the wires controlling the scene—hidden behind the curtain of his craft.

Every member of the audience, including the reader of a kindred art, was for Poe a potentially double addressee to be simultaneously engaged and kept at a distance, enlightened and mystified, even amused and ridiculed. Thus, if Poe's relation to the fiction-reading audience was ambivalent, it was not because, as Michael Williams has claimed, Poe conceived his readers as "potential victims or lurking villains."[20] His ambivalence toward his audience consisted of conceptualizing them as a necessary part of artistic effect even as he chafed under that necessity because it threatened loss of mastery. For Poe, that is, all readers were legitimate victims *because* they were potential villains. Informed readers, both as reviewers and as the middle-class magazine audience, were nemeses and desiderata of the powerful author, who would turn them into unwitting co-conspirators of their own capitulation.

The undercurrent of uneasiness that marks this conception meant that as much as he sought power over his readership, Poe did not conceive himself as a mere puppet master. His goal involved maintaining a balance between eliciting admiration while dominating the fiction-reading audience, but it was a balance always in danger of tipping toward self-cancellation, since a writer's true genius could never be fully appreciated, in Poe's logic, unless it was fully understood. Yet full understanding paradoxically would break the spell that marked authorial mastery. In the form Poe conceived it, the struggle with the audience for artistic control always threatened to do in the writer no matter how much he or she succeeded.

A battle with readers constituted one of several important elements in the reception of Poe's tales and the public conception of him as a fiction writer in the 1830s and 1840s. A combination of fascination, dismay, and pleasure marked the audience's encounter with his short stories; however, it was not the same pleasure that most twentieth-century readers have identified with Poe's fiction: the *frisson* of horror. Instead, from 1833 until the late 1830s, Poe was viewed—and achieved some popular success—as a writer of comic tales. Certainly, the public discussion treated stories such as "Hans Pfaall," "Ms. Found in a Bottle," and "Lionizing" that way, and there is little if any evidence to suggest that the middle-class audience who read these and other Poe stories in the *Southern Literary Messenger,* the *Saturday Courier, Godey's,* and *Graham's* received them any differently. The issue of the *Messenger* containing "Lionizing" called it "an inimitable piece of wit and satire," while the *Baltimore Republican* dubbed "Hans Pfaall" a "capital burlesque upon ballooning," a response echoed by the *Baltimore Gazette*.[21] Six months later the *Messenger* was calling Poe a writer whose stories as a whole were marked by a "uniquely original vein of imagination, and of humorous, delicate satire" (Dec. 1835: 1). The *New York Corsair*, still later, referred to the "sparkling dash of fancy, sentiment, and wit intermingled" in Poe's tales.[22] Interesting is the preponderance of these comic readings even though tales such as "Pfaall," "The Duc de L'Omelette," "Metzengerstein," "King Pest," "The Assignation," "Berenice,"—in fact, virtually every one of the eighteen tales Poe published before 1839—can be read as narratives peppered with what critics today call conventions of gothic fiction but which, in the terminology of antebellum informed reading, marked out the sensational German tale or the story of "Germanic mysticism" and horror.[23]

Certainly Poe's contemporary audience could have perceived in those tales features that they would have identified as marks of "Germanism"— a term loosely connected with mystical philosophy, antiquated (often Old World) settings, ruined habitations, necromancy, and an aura of desolation. The settings in dark European castles or palaces in "Metzenger-stein," "The Bargain Lost," and "The Assignation" would have been salient, as would the encounters with the demonic in "Duc" and "Bargain," the mysticism of "Metzengerstein," and the plague-ridden atmosphere of "King Pest." Informed readers could also have pointed to the live burial of "Loss of Breath," the mutilation in "Berenice," and the corrupt aristocratic characters of "Duc," "Metzengerstein," "The Assignation," "King Pest," and "Von Jung" as indications that these were stories of Germanic mysticism. Besides the conventions connecting these tales to that genre, the magazine audience could have used rules of notice to do the same thing. For attentive readers, the epigraphs from Schiller and Goethe heading the first published version of "The Assignation" and the subtitle of "Loss of Breath" as "A Tale a la Blackwood" (the British periodical well known to American readers for stories of Germanic horror) could have been telling signs of these tales' modes. In light of the fit between reader horizon and the interpretive occasion provided by these tales, it is not surprising that a few readers did view some of these as stories of Germanic mysticism and, following the principles of informed reading, denounced them as sensationalistic. According to the *Augusta Chronicle*, "Berenice" and "Morella" were stories "belonging almost peculiarly to . . . the German school" in their "gloomy exhibition of passion" (June 11, 1835, *PL* 156); likewise, the *Southern Literary Messenger* objected that in "Berenice" there is "too much horror in his subject" (Mar. 1835: 387). Even more strongly, the *Richmond Compiler* said that "The Duc de L'Omelette" "is calculated to produce effects permanently injurious to sound morals" and urged "Mr. Poe" to "disenthral himself from the spells of German enchantment and supernatural imagery."[24]

Such responses, however, were the exception rather than the rule in the reception of Poe's fiction before 1839. The question is, why? How was it that a writer known throughout the twentieth century as perhaps the quintessential gothic writer in American literature was read primarily as an author of fictional satires and burlesques for the first third of his career?

In some ways it is not difficult to see why reviewers and magazine readers took these tales as risible, particularly if we consider them in light of antebellum interpretive assumptions about informed reading. Readers could have found support for comedic interpretations by invoking a rule of notice: attending to character names as an index to a story's meaning. Readers would hardly have found it difficult to locate a humorous drift in such characters as the Prince de Foie-Gras, Abel-Shittim, Mr. Windenough, Mrs. Lackobreath, the Duchess of Bless-my-Soul, Don Stiletto, and Her Serene Highness the Arch Duchess Ana-Pest.[25] Moreover, since informed readers were to be, at least in theory, well read, certainly some would have seen many of these tales as marked by allusions to or imitations of other fictional works generally held to be in the Germanic or sensational mode. The prophecy about the destruction of a castle and the portrait of an animal that comes alive in "Metzengerstein" would recall parallel developments in Horace Walpole's Germanic "classic" *The Castle of Otranto*, while readers would recognize the entire drinking scene in "King Pest" as a virtual duplicate of the grotesque Palace of the Wines episode in Benjamin Disraeli's popular novel *Vivian Grey*. Anyone familiar with Theodore Fay's widely read *Norman Leslie* could not help but see echoes of it in "Von Jung," and "Morella" would have looked remarkably like another version of Henry Bell's "The Dead Daughter" or the classical story of the child-eating Lamia.[26] Such allusions and parallels, which are now virtually inoperative for most readers of these tales, would have been part of the reading formation—and thus the experience of these stories—for many antebellum readers. The combinations of such connections with the jocular names may well have caused Poe's contemporaries to see these stories as part of a tradition they would have known: the popular subgenres of literary parody or Germanic satire.[27]

Such reading practices and expectations, however, would not necessarily have led all readers to a comic response, particularly those coming to any single tale without a working sense of the type of writer Poe was. Though informed readers supposedly would not have encountered Poe's tales in such an ignorant state, even the best-prepared reader would have read his first published tale, "Metzengerstein," in that condition. A question worth asking, therefore, is what would the experience of "Metzengerstein" have been for those first-time readers of Poe's first story.

Informed readers certainly would have been struck by the story's opening paragraph, beginning with its reference to "horror" and "fatality" and its announcement that the tale is set in Hungary during a period when "a settled although hidden belief in the doctrines of the Metempsychosis" flourished.[28] Such announcements would have looked like the standard trappings of Germanic mysticism. Yet readers also would likely have paused at the mention of metempsychosis, since it was not only a subject of mystical philosophy; it was also known to readers as a pseudo-phenomenon, a form of contemporary quackery employed by sharpers and spirit-rappers to deceive a credulous public. Then, too, the narrator's comment at the end of the opening paragraph must have added to the audience's sense that some rethinking about this tale and its subject might be necessary. For after commenting that, "[o]f the doctrines themselves—that is, of their falsity, or their probability—I say nothing," the narrator adds that "much of our incredulity . . . *'vient de ne pouvoir être seuls.'*" Readers had to wonder whether "incredulity" referred to a lack of belief in metempsychosis or a lack of conviction about its falsity, but if the former were the case, the phrase "comes from not wanting to be alone" (a reasonable English translation of the French) hardly would seem an apt cause for doubting metempsychosis.

With the second paragraph, more oddities might have struck antebellum readers. Not only does the narrator call metempsychosis a "superstition" that, even at the time of the story, was "fast verging to absurdity," but the quotation rendering the belief of the Hungarians as they "said" it is given in the French of "an acute and intelligent Parisian" (1: 19). Taken together, such additions would seem either to give an absurdly contorted view of the belief or to deny it altogether.

Of course, to reach such conclusions, readers would have had to be able to translate the French in both paragraphs, and that ability would not necessarily have been widespread in the middle-class audience. Yet even those who could not make the translation could have reached two conclusions shared with those who could: first, that "Metzengerstein" looked like a typical Germanic tale in several ways, including the reliance on sprinklings of foreign phrasing that typified that genre; and second, that it also looked atypical because instead of using that foreign phrasing to create mystery, "Metzengerstein" seemed to be employing it to produce obscurity. That sense of obscurity would have been reinforced, furthermore, when the magazine audience reached the story's fourth paragraph, in which the narrator, after invoking the prophecy that "the mortality of Metzengerstein shall triumph over the immortality of Berlifitzing," discloses that "the words themselves had little or no meaning" (1: 19).

To reconstruct the experience of reading the tale in this way would seem to indicate that, for antebellum readers encountering it through codes of informed reading, "Metzengerstein" would have started to look like an absurdly comic version of the Germanic tale of horror or a parody of such Germanic novels as Walpole's *Castle of Otranto*. However, I do not necessarily want to claim that the initial readers of the tale in 1832 would have reached such a conclusion, particularly if we consider antebellum codes of reading as distinct from modern ones. From a modern perspective, that is, such involutions and abrupt contradictions designate comedy precisely because, as G. R. Thompson has argued, they disclose a narrator who does not understand the very story he tells and thereby becomes, as obtuse gothic yarn-spinner, an object of satire.[29] For antebellum readers, however, such a reading would have been virtually impossible since it depends on a code that was not among the interpretive strategies of the 1830s: the assumption of an unreliable narrator. Instead, the involuted comments and the narrative's lack of help in making sense of them more likely would have led Poe's magazine audience to conclude that the story was a technical, aesthetic blunder by Poe himself. From such a perspective, antebellum readers could have regarded "Metzengerstein" as a botched tale of Germanic horror, a bad imitation of a *Blackwood's* tale or of *Castle of Otranto*.

The point here is not that this was the conclusion that the antebellum audience reached about "Metzengerstein" but that for informed readers in 1832 an interpretation of the story either as a turbid parody of the Germanic tale or as a flawed but seriously intended version of that mode would have been possible. Coming upon this initial Poe tale in the *Philadelphia Courier*, the audience of that periodical would thus have probably been perplexed by the story and by their difficulty in deciding exactly what it was. For such readers, it was a matter of having to choose between a bad Germanic horror tale or a poorly performed Germanic burlesque that was, in either case, connected to an inherently flawed and dangerous genre. For those readers, the story's inability to identify its status would have been a further sign of its weakness.

By 1836, however, when Poe republished a slightly revised version of "Metzengerstein" in the *Southern Literary Messenger*, the tale would have looked quite different. Readers could take it unequivocally as a witty parody "in imitation of the German" (the story's subtitle), but the reason was not the changes Poe had made. Nor was it a matter of readers finally coming to their senses and interpreting the tale correctly. The controversy marking twentieth-century commentary on "Metzengerstein" belies any claim that a comic or a serious reading of the story is the "correct" one.[30] Rather, readers in 1836 could create a comic "Metzengerstein" instead of a tale that they may have originally found confusing because the conditions for reading Poe's tale had changed. By 1836 Poe's reputation as a comedic author of such tales as "Loss of Breath," "Bon Bon," "The Assignation," "Lionizing," and "King Pest" (all of which had preceded the reprinting of "Metzengerstein" in the *Messenger*) had been established in the reception events that had collected around Poe's fiction. Public responses to his stories by that time were regularly identifying them as burlesques, satiric "hits," or comedic "quizzes" aimed at the faults, foibles, and pretenses of the day. In that vein, the *New York Courier and Enquirer* styled "Loss of Breath" a "capital burlesque of the wild, extravagant, disjointed rigmarole" in *Blackwood's*;[31] the *Augusta Chronicle* explained that "Lionizing" "has all the humor, animation, and satire of Sterne's man from the promontory of Noses" (Aug. 7, 1835, *PL* 164); and the *Richmond Compiler* identified "Hans Pfaall" as "a burlesque upon the mania for ballooning" (Nov. 26, 1835, *PL* 181). Moreover, if a comment by James Kirk Paulding has any truth to it, the response to

Poe as a comic writer was not limited to reviewers. In an 1836 letter to Thomas White, proprietor of the *Messenger,* Paulding claimed that Poe's "quiz on [N. P.] Willis" in "Lionizing" and his "Burlesque of 'Blackwood'" in "Loss of Breath" "were not only capital, but what is more, were understood by all."[32]

Especially significant for establishing this version of Poe's fiction were the publication and reception of "Ms. Found in a Bottle" (1833, reprinted in the *Messenger* in 1835) and of "Hans Pfaall" (1835). Both tales originally were taken as nonfictional reports. A letter in the *Baltimore Patriot,* for instance, announced that "Hans Pfaall" is "no less than a true and authentic narrative of a voyage made by Mynheer Phaal [*sic*], from the city of Rotterdam to the Moon" (Aug. 7, 1835, *PL* 164). Part of the reason for such credulity was that these stories looked to their readers much like the true-to-life but breathtaking narratives of voyages and exploring expeditions that formed a staple of newspaper and magazine offerings, particularly at a time when experiments in ballooning were gaining public attention. Then, too, as several commentators pointed out at the time, the verisimilitude of these two tales in their detailed descriptions—especially of balloon construction, atmospheric measurements, and topography in "Pfaall"—struck readers as earmarks of the real thing. The *Messenger* commented, for instance, that "Hans Pfaall" renders its events "with a minuteness so much like truth, that they seem quite probable,"[33] while the *Charlottesville Jeffersonian* remarked that the actions of the story "are pictured . . . with all the detail of circumstances, which truth and the fearful reality might be supposed to present" (Jan. 1, 1835, *PL* 186).

The phrasing in some of the public commentary nonetheless indicates that not all readers were taken in completely by "Hans Pfaall" regarding its status as fiction or nonfiction—and some were not fooled at all. Only a day after the story's publication, the *Baltimore Athenaeum* called "Pfaall" a "well imagined" story that "displays much ingenuity" (July 11, 1835, *PL* 162), and a month later the *Richmond Whig* pointed out that "[t]here is a great deal of nonsense [and] trifling" in the tale (Aug. 7, 1835, *PL* 163). Those readers familiar with Poe's stories previous to "Pfaall" had, in fact, good reason to be skeptical, since they would have known that only a year and a half earlier, "Ms. Found in a Bottle" had created a modest stir as a successful hoax that had induced a good laugh among the reading public. Even at the time of its publication in 1833, moreover, some readers had been able to see through the public misconception that "Ms. Found in a Bottle" was a work of nonfiction, apparently by seizing on several factors. Attentive readers noticed that it was being published in the *Baltimore Saturday Visitor* as the declared winner of what had been announced over the previous months as a competition for the best imaginative tale submitted to that paper. Consequently, taking "Ms. Found in a Bottle" as a hoax did not depend on readers interpreting it though the concept of unreliable narration but involved reading for genre by determining its status as a work of fiction disguised as nonfiction. Such a move entailed, for some, linking Poe's tale to a precedent. As the *Charleston Courier* reminded its audience upon the republication of the story in 1835, "Ms. Found in a Bottle," in working on "the credulous," had drawn on the writings of Captain John Symmes (October 17, 1835, *PL* 175). Informed readers in 1833 who made that interpretive connection and recalled that Symmes's 1820 *Symzonia: A Voyage of Discovery* had itself been exposed as a hoax would have had a further warrant for taking Poe's tale as a fictional fabrication playfully designed to mislead readers about its genre profile.

By 1836, the interpretive horizon of informed readers had been well prepared through a series of reception events, reviewer comments, and previous reading experiences to expect a certain type of fiction from Poe. In place was a contextual horizon of expectations for taking any new or republished tale by him—including "Metzengerstein"—as a satire, burlesque, or potential hoax.

It would be inaccurate, however, to assume that all of Poe's contemporary readers were configuring his tales as comedic or that those who did so were doing it in a uniform manner. Besides the occasional reviewer remarks already noted about dangerous German horror, one of Poe's readers, J. P. Kennedy, conveyed in a letter to Poe some dismay at the reception of Poe's tales as humorous performances. In case Poe did not realize it, Kennedy explained, "Some of your *bizarerries* have been mistaken for satire—and admired too in that character. They deserved it, but *you* did not, for you did not intend them so."[34] Another reader privately complained of "Lionizing" that "it has neither wit nor humor; or, that if it has any, it lies too deep for the common understandings to fathom it." No doubt there was an element of truth to the latter part of this remark, contrary to Paulding's claim that Poe's burlesques "were understood by all."

Early in 1836, Harper Brothers turned down Poe's proposal to publish a collected edition of his tales on the grounds that the satire of the stories was too fine and required a familiarity and knowledge that many readers simply did not possess.[35] Whatever degree of accuracy the Harpers' conclusion may have reflected in describing the reading audience, there is no doubt that many readers nonetheless were being schooled to view Poe's stories as ludic and to read them, despite the occasional public objection, as moral tales that combined humor with tutelage. The *Baltimore Republican*, for instance, in commenting on "Lionizing" as "an admirable piece of burlesque," noted that Poe's tales possessed "an ability to afford amusement or instruction" (June 13, 1835, *PL* 157). More emphatic was the *Richmond Compiler*. Reading "King Pest" as a satiric temperance tale, in which "the evils and maladies attendant upon intemperance are all portrayed in the allegorical personages," the reviewer added that "few of Mr. P's tales are without aim or moral" (Nov. 26, 1835, *PL* 181).

The general drift in the public reception of his fiction in the mid-1830s must have pleased Poe quite a bit, in part because the comic response that dominated the discussion seems to have been what he was striving for in at least some of these tales. As he explained in reply to Kennedy's letter about the public "misreading" of several stories, "You are nearly, but not altogether right in relation to the satire of some of my Tales. Most of them were *intended* for half banter, half satire. . . . 'Lionizing' and 'Loss of Breath' were satires properly speaking." Seven months later, in a letter to Harrison Hill, Poe likewise identified the "series of Tales, by myself—in all seventeen," which he had been publishing (and republishing) in the *Southern Literary Messenger* during the previous eighteen months—as marked by a "bizarre and generally whimsical character."[36] Besides according with his professed goal, the comic readings of the tales had to please Poe as evidence of his authorial success at controlling reader response and thus validated his developing theory about effect. Indeed, the success of the hoaxes and the accompanying audience credulity would have strongly confirmed—and served as a satisfying index to—his ability to disorient and dominate his audience by leading them by the nose of their imagination.

Poe, in fact, was so delighted by the triumph of "Hans Pfaall" and "Ms. Found in a Bottle" that he was willing to claim more for them than he apparently had sought in the first place. Although taking credit in 1835 for the successful deception he had achieved with "Pfaall," Poe admitted ten years later, in an unusual public disclosure, that fairly early in the composition of that tale "I gave up the idea of imparting very close verisimilitude to what I should write—that is to say, so close as really to deceive." He even admitted that it was only in the three weeks following the story's publication, when "the first of the 'Moon-hoax' editorials made its appearance in 'The Sun,'" that "I understood the jest" (*ER* 1215–16).

Poe's remark here suggests that he was encountering some troubling implications in the reception his tales were getting in the mid-1830s. It was as if readers had taken some of them in directions other than what he had wanted, and Poe was finding it necessary to redefine them as comically efficacious so as to reclaim them under his mantle of authorial control. Poe surely must have been bothered by some of the other responses, particularly those that read his tales as didactic or cautionary stories for imparting moral lessons or that objected to them as degenerate Germanic stories designed to harm the fiction-reading public. His frustration with the latter as early as 1835 is evidenced in his letter to Thomas White, who apparently had objected to "Berenice" as a story marred by sensationalism and bad taste. Wrote Poe in reply: "The history of all Magazines shows plainly that those which have attained celebrity were indebted for it to articles *similar in nature*—to Berenice. . . . You may say all this is in bad taste. I have my doubts about it. . . . But whether the articles of which I speak are, or are not in bad taste is little to the purpose. To be appreciated you must be *read*, and these things are invariably sought after with avidity."[37] It is difficult not to sense Poe's defensiveness in such remarks, as though he felt the need to take back control of his stories by claiming for them a calculated popularity based, as he explained to White, on "the ludicrous heightened into the grotesque: the fearful colored into the horrible: the witty exaggerated into the burlesque." Although modern critics have wrestled with these passages, seeking to decipher exactly what Poe meant by "the grotesque" and "the ludicrous," what is most striking in the context of Poe's reception is the evasiveness of his comments. Is "Berenice" "ludicrous" or "horrible"? Grotesque or burlesque? Witty or fearful? Granting the story's horror, Poe denies it by asserting the tale's humor, even as he qualifies its comedic status by aligning it with fear. At work here is the same kind of shape shifting Poe practiced in his letter to Kennedy when discussing the supposed satire of his tales. After his remark about intending them as "half banter, half satire," Poe added in the same sentence, "although I might not have fully acknowledged this to be their aim even to myself." In effect, Poe tells Kennedy that his tales were intended as humorous, though he might not have sought to make them funny, and that he designed the humor to be both inconsequential "banter" and serious "satire." Under the oppressive potential of even ludic readings of his works, which threatened to fix him as comic writer, Poe shifts his profile before Kennedy's eyes in an effort to avoid Kennedy's ability—and the ability of the rest of the audience Kennedy had mentioned—to pin him down.

What is ironic is that Poe was able to get his wish about not being typecast as a comic writer. Despite how the interpretive horizon for the magazine audience had become contoured by the conception of his fictions as burlesques, satires, and hoaxes, a curious shift started to emerge in the reception of his stories from 1839 to 1840. Responses increasingly began to characterize his tales as only a few commentators had done previously by stressing the horror, crime, outré philosophy, and unnaturalness in their pages and by treating them as serious (and for some, dangerous) Germanic tales. The *Southern Literary Messenger* complained that "The Fall of the House of Usher" "leaves on the mind a painful and horrible impression" and accused Poe of being "too much attached to the gloomy German mysticism" (October 1839, *PL* 272). The *Saturday Evening Post,* while commenting on "Usher," "William Wilson," and the earlier "Morella," noted more appreciatively that Poe "is deeply imbued with the spirit of German literature, and as one of that class of writers has few equals" (Nov. 2, 1839, *PL* 275). *Alexander's Weekly Messenger* disclosed that "William Wilson" "reminds us of Godwin and Brockden Brown" (October 16, 1839, *PL* 274), while the *New York Evening Star* called "Usher" a "*chef d-oeuvre*" one would usually find "in the pages of Blackwood" (Sept. 7, 1839, *PL* 269). As part of this reorientation in the response to Poe, the *Boston Evening Gazette* offered this characterization of his fiction, with a special emphasis on "Morella," "Ligeia," and "Usher": "The wilder and more impassioned tales of Mr. Poe, are of a dark, mystic, German character, the most ideal, shadowy and strange, like the phantasmagoric dream of an opium-eater."[38]

By the close of 1839, following the publication of Poe's *Tales of the Grotesque and Arabesque,* reviewers were uniformly emphasizing the sober and Germanic elements of his tales despite the fact that, of the twenty-five stories in the collection, two-thirds had been previously read and publicly discussed as burlesques, satires, and hoaxes. The *Philadelphia Saturday Courier* reported that readers would find these tales "generally wildly imaginative in plot; fanciful in description, often times to the full boundaries of the grotesque" (Dec. 14, 1839: *PL* 281). The *Saturday Evening Post,* after noting that the *Tales* is comprised largely of Poe's republished pieces, emphasized that "[t]hey are strongly infused with the German spirit, [possessing] a metaphysical style to which the writer is ardently attached" (Dec. 7, 1839, *PL* 280). Although admitting that there is an element of "the quaint and the droll" in the volume, a reviewer in the *Philadelphia Pennsylvanian* underscored the way the tales are "marked with all the deep and painful interest of the German school" (Dec. 6, 1839, *PL* 279). Less flexible and more captious was a response in the *North American Review,* which announced, "These tales betoken ability on the part of the author to do better. Let him give up his imitation of German mysticism, throw away his extravagance, . . . and leave all touches of profanity to the bar room" (Dec. 10, 1839, *PL* 280).

Undoubtedly, Poe was aware of these responses and was likely pleased by the praise several accorded the tales as well as by the turn in his reception, insofar as it signaled a departure from the assumption that had fixed him as a writer of comic fiction. Yet it is also clear that he was chagrined by the shift even before it hardened into a new paradigm via the reception of *Tales of the Grotesque and Arabesque.* In a November 1839 letter to Joseph Snodgrass, Poe expressed hope for a "complete triumph over those little critics who would endeavor to put me down by raising the hue & cry of *exaggeration* in style, of *Germanism* & such twaddle."[39] By the time that *Tales of the Grotesque and Arabesque* was being readied for publication, the conception of his fiction as Germanic had reached enough of a pitch that Poe found it necessary to try in his preface to the collection to counter that conception.

At stake was not just the way Germanism was being leveled against the tales as a moral indictment of the harm they posed to their audience. More perfidious, for Poe, was that such an epithet ascribed to his stories a derivative status by implying that they were mere imitations of a foreign model—and a questionable one at that. Hence, in his preface, Poe carefully asserted that any terror in these tales was legitimate and original because it was not of foreign import: "If in many of my productions terror has been the thesis, I maintain that terror is not of Germany, but of the soul,—that I have deduced this terror only from its legitimate sources, and urged it only to its legitimate results."[40] Even more dangerous was the manner in which the "German" bent of the responses threatened to overwhelm Poe's authorial power by enabling the audience to pigeonhole his stories in a neat, pejorative category.

The bulk of Poe's preface can be seen as seeking to blunt this interpretive turn through an evasive "clarification" of what these tales are. After explaining that the "epithets "Grotesque' and 'Arabesque' . . . indicate with sufficient precision the prevalent tenor of the tales here published," Poe counters this characterization by asserting that "it cannot be fairly inferred," based on the stories in this collection, "that I have, for this species of writing, any inordinate, or indeed any peculiar taste or prepossession." Having severed his artistic identity from the fixed category that he has just identified as applicable to the tales, he then turns to the direct charge of Germanism by agreeing with it: "Let us admit, for the moment, that the 'phantasie pieces' now given *are* Germanic, or what not. . . . These many pieces are yet one book. My friends would be quite as wise in taxing an astronomer with too much astronomy, or an ethical author with treating too largely of morals." In other words, Poe implicitly asks, how can the stories be charged with doing what they do since that is what they do? They cannot do anything else any more than a moralist can avoid addressing morality. But having virtually defended Germanism as the tales' inviolable essence, Poe then tells his audience that "the truth is that, with a single exception," which he does not identify, "there is no one of these stories in which the scholar should recognize the distinctive features of that species of pseudo-horror which we are taught to call Germanic." Poe's strategy here works by sleight of hand: Now you see the Germanism, now you don't. Of a piece with such attempted disorientation of the reader to protect Poe's own authority as author is his brief second paragraph of this two-paragraph preface. There he notes that "[t]here are one or two of the articles [i.e., magazine stories] here, (conceived and executed in the purest spirit of extravaganza), to which I expect no serious attention, and of which I shall speak no farther." Drawing attention to at least a couple of the tales that had been received as comedic and simultaneously disclaiming their importance, Poe can assert the diversity—and, hence, the intractability—of his creative powers while aloofly dismissing the assertion as a mere afterthought hardly meriting his attention.

It was an intriguing tactic, even a brilliant one—if it had worked. Of course, it did not, as illustrated by the responses to the *Tales of the Grotesque and Arabesque* cited above. Yet the sticking point in all this is not the ineffectiveness—or even the shape—of Poe's response to his audience's responses. The question is why this shift in the public perception and interpretation of Poe's fiction occurred in the first place.

It is tempting to claim that the answer is the tales themselves. One version of this explanation might build on Meredith McGill's point that the "publishing histories" of some of Poe's stories in "altered states" created for his contemporaries "all kinds of confusions about authorial identity"[41]—including confusions or shifts in readers' conceptions of Poe as a comic or Germanic writer. By this logic the altered material forms of Poe's tales, resulting in part because of the revisions Poe made whenever he reprinted them, caused readers to take as Germanic what they formerly had read as comic.

Both the changes themselves and reviewer comments, however, indicate that material changes did not play a role in this rereading of Poe's previous fictions. For one thing, between their original appearance in periodicals and the reprinting in *Tales of the Grotesque and Arabesque,* only three of the twenty-five stories in the collection had undergone any extensive revision. One of those, "The Signora Zenobia," Poe divided into two separate stories for the *Tales.*[42] Nor did the physical form of the collection seem to have any effect. Lea and Blanchard, which published the volume, issued it in a standard format with no special features (e.g., black letter typeface or suggestive illustrations) that might have led readers to see the text as a compilation of Germanic pieces. Nor was it a matter of gathered impact. No reviewer identified—or even hinted at—a connection between reading the stories as a group and their genre profiles, so that stories that had looked ludic when read individually now as a group were interpreted as Germanic.

The other textualist explanation involves claiming that the shift in the response to Poe, which began treating him as the author of serious tales of German horror, resulted from a shift in the type of stories Poe began writing in 1839 and after—a change evident in the stories' formal and thematic properties. Such an explanation certainly meshes with what has served among twentieth-century Poe scholars as the standard narrative of his career. According to this paradigm, Poe began as a writer of hoaxes and satires, which he conceived as a group that he had hoped to publish as the Folio Club Tales, and then only in the late 1830s, with "Ligeia," "The Fall of the House of Usher," and "William Wilson" (or, according to some versions of the story, "Berenice" and "Morella") did Poe turn to the serious gothic fiction that would characterize the rest of his career.[43]

Such a formalistic explanation unfortunately runs into several problems, not the least of which is the way response and reception theories call into question its essentialist premise that there are formal and thematic elements in a text that exist prior to and independent of the way it is read. The history of how Poe's fiction has been interpreted also problematizes any claim for the texts themselves as the cause. Recall that the responses to the *Tales of the Grotesque and Arabesque* tendentiously emphasized their Germanic sobriety despite the fact that eighteen of the twenty-five stories in the collection had previously been occasions for viewing Poe as a writer of comic fiction. Moreover, despite the standard modern story of the "shift" in Poe's fiction writing, twentieth-century critics and scholars hardly have agreed about which Poe stories are comic and which are serious gothic narratives. A number of the early stories, including "Hans Pfaall" and such Folio Club Tales as "The Assignation," "Metzengerstein," and "Ms. Found in a Bottle" have been read by some as comic *and* by others as serious fictions.[44] The same has obtained in critical discussion of the supposedly clear-cut hoaxes and satires published after 1840, such as "Mesmeric Revelation," "The Facts in the Case of M. Valdemar," and "The System of Doctor Tarr and Professor Fether"—fictions whose "clear-cut" comedy itself problematizes the standard narrative of the shift in Poe's writing style. Daniel Hoffman has even claimed that all of Poe's hoaxes "have a serious interest."[45]

Conversely, the tales often thought of as Poe's most chilling and pensive gothic stories, including "Ligeia," "Usher," and "William Wilson," have been turned on their heads and "exposed" as playful comedies or mordant satires.[46] More tellingly, some twentieth-century critics have argued that all of Poe's tales, even his most serious narratives of the dark side, are to some degree comic, whether as prickly satires, as burlesques of other forms, or as self-parodies.[47] Perhaps unsurprisingly in the face of such shifting interpretive winds, several critics have agreed to a gentlemanly throwing up of hands and announced that "it is impossible to tell when Poe is playing games with us and when he is being serious" in his fiction.[48]

Indeed, we cannot tell, if by "telling" we expect to determine on the formal level of the "tale itself" which ones belong to which category. Such indeterminacy, of course, accords quite nicely with Poe's goal as the shape-shifting fiction writer; however, before we get too heady about ascribing a tidy fit between intention and effect and crown Poe with artistic laurels for a feat well done, it is worth pointing out that even Poe recognized, to a degree, that the explanation for the response to his tales did not lie in the fiction itself but in the way it was read. Significantly, Poe used that recognition as part of his strategy in his preface to the *Tales of the Grotesque and Arabesque* when countering the charge of Germanism. Just after "admit[ting], for the moment, that the 'phantasy-pieces' now given *are* Germanic," Poe added that the reason is that "Germanism is 'the vein' for the time being. To morrow I may be anything but German, as yesterday I was everything else." Although ostensibly a description of his past, present, and future proclivities as a fiction writer, the contexts for this comment—both the shift in the antebellum response to his tales and his own assertion a few lines later that his stories are *not* Germanic— provide an alternative explanation: that Poe is describing the supposed Germanism of his tales as a product of the altered way they were being read in 1839.

Poe's explanation clearly begs the question as to why Germanism was the vein of the day, but it also opens an avenue for examining the reasons for the interpretive shift. It resulted not because more writers were producing Germanic mystical fiction to the point where anything that even faintly looked the part got the label. Evidence suggests, in fact, that just the opposite may have been the case by the late 1830s.[49] Rather, Poe's stories became Germanic because "the German," as an interpretive marker, had undergone change as a cultural and literary category for signifying and judging fictional forms. Understanding the transformation in the responses to Poe's fiction thus requires attending to that shift as a product, in part, of altering cultural conditions and their impact on the interpretive practices of informed reading.

In his study of nineteenth-century attitudes toward death, Greg Laderman has disclosed how conceptions of death began to change in antebellum America, as the traditional Christian response of resignation was giving way to extreme feelings of loss and an expansion of rituals of mourning, particularly among the middle class. Americans were not facing any sustained increase in the incidence of death, but there were periods of significant fluctuation in mortality rates, particularly when what Laderman calls "changes in living and work patterns" resulted from market expansion in the capitalist economy.[50] Those expansions bought with them periods of economic upheaval, with one of the most significant being the Panic of 1837 and the depression that followed. By 1839 and 1840, the privations, increases in urban crimes, and fatalities that marked the depression—coupled with the attendant change in attitudes toward death—made it increasingly difficult for the middle-class audience to read stories of disease, crime, and human demise as in any way humorous.[51]

Contributing to this change in the conditions of reception was the growing uneasiness with certain developments abroad that signaled a threat to American society and to the Republic. Americans began to express fear over what were seen as potential perils accompanying an influx of certain types of immigrants. For this era witnessed a rampant suspicion about Roman Catholics, not just through Irish immigration but through German as well. If association with "the Germanic" came under increasing suspicion, it was not, moreover, only because anti-Catholicism was on the rise. Political radicals with protosocialist ideas began to arrive in the United States from Germany, and those ideas and their proponents were seen, particularly by the American middle class, as an Old World threat to the young republic.[52] In the wake of such cultural paranoia, "the Germanic" and anything associated with it, including fictional forms, took on increasingly ominous implications. The medieval settings and Old World trappings associated with the Germanic tale no doubt further served to connect Catholicism and German mysticism in a way that enhanced the perceived danger of the latter as a literary form.[53] By 1839–40, it consequently became almost impossible for readers to respond to Germanic elements in tales as minor components subservient to other ends—especially the comedic. Nor was it necessary for Poe's audience at this time to think of him as a writer who had gone from comedy to Germanic tales. If reviewers and the magazine audience could take the collected *Tales of the Grotesque and Arabesque* as Germanic, it was because what formerly had been comic in his fiction now looked Germanic.

The dynamic of the audience's encounter with Poe's stories is important to consider here because these changing cultural contexts were not a hegemonic force working outside the experience of the fiction. That experience and the trajectory marking the reception of his stories—as well as other Poe writings—also were central to the reconstruction of Poe as a writer of serious fiction—for good or ill.

Part of that encounter involved the reception of Poe's only novel, *The Narrative of Arthur Gordon Pym*, in late 1838. Although a few readers wondered about its factuality, most reviewers responded to *Pym* by situating it as a type of fiction reminiscent of Daniel Defoe's *Robinson Crusoe* or Jonathan Swift's *Gulliver's Travels*—an adventure/travel narrative of striking verisimilitude and/or social commentary. *Alexander's Weekly Messenger* called *Pym* a novel written "after the manner of Defoe," while the *New York Review* said it had "that air of reality which constitutes the charm of *Robinson Crusoe*." The *Knickerbocker* spoke of *Pym*'s "Robinson Crusoe-ish sort of simplicity," and the *New York Albion* exclaimed that "the author is a second Capt. Lemuel Gulliver."[54] But having made some sense of *Pym* through a code of genre identification, readers were at a loss to decipher what Poe was doing in that mode. A reviewer in the *Albion* pointed out that *Pym* "does not deal in political or moral satire" in the vein of Swift and Defoe (Aug. 18, 1838, *PL* 254) and, in fact, had no higher purpose, according to the *Gentleman's Magazine*, other than to "require his insulted readers to believe his ipse dixit" (Sept. 1838, *PL* 254). Several reviewers began to suggest that *Pym* was a lark for its own sake and pointed to the improbabilities, the discrepancies, and the preternatural events as reminiscent of Sinbad the Sailor, Baron Munchausen, and Jack the Giant Killer.[55] Perhaps, some reviewers suggested, the novel was a hoax, in the mold of Richard Adams Locke's well-known "Moon-Hoax" of 1835—or Poe's own "Hans Pfaall." If so, however, it was a bit much, marked by heavy-handedness and sanguinary excesses, according to the *Knickerbocker*, and what the *New York Review* termed "too many atrocities, too many strange horrors." The *Monthly Review* objected that

"some of the most elaborate scenes" in the novel "are disgustingly horrible," while the *Naval and Military Gazette* warned that *Pym* was fit
fare "[f]or those who possess a genuine love of the horrible" (October 20,
1838, *PL* 257).[56] The problem was not simply a matter of too much horror
going on for too long. The sticking point for informed readers was that,
in light of Poe's comic reputation, the horrifying elements had not been
countered sufficiently by the comic—whether as satire or hoax—with the
result that readers interpreted *Pym* as a failed "Hans Pfaall" or as an
egregiously uncontrolled collection of atrocities—or as both. The question readers asked, in effect, was what Poe was doing with this novel. Was
it truly an authorial gaff, a sign of decline, or was Poe up to something
that was not quite clear?

Readers had to be suspicious because by 1838 it was difficult simply to
dismiss Poe as a hack novelist, not only because of his proven successes
as a fiction writer but also because of the reputation he had gained via
his editorship of the *Southern Literary Messenger.* His nonfiction may
indeed have played a role in the reconceptualization of Poe that would
come in 1839 and 1840. Although Poe had begun as an outsider to the
magazine literary scene, by the late 1830s he had become recognized as a
voice to be reckoned with. In the logic of informed reading, such a writer
could not have been using his stories simply to lampoon other genres or
to create fictional bagatelles. Poe had to be a writer of serious literature
that was above the faults he leveled at other writers. Then, too, the content of some of his editorial pieces may have served readers as a clue to
Poe's "true" nature as a fiction writer. For example, his review of Henry
Chorley's *Conti the Discarded* in the February 1836 *Messenger* heaped
praise on the "very powerful influence" of the "*Kunstroman,*" which, he
explained, instills "admiration and study of the beautiful, by a tissue of
bizarre fiction, partly allegorical, and partly metaphysical." From "Germany alone," he added, could so "profound" a form have come.[57] Readers
who saw in such comments enthusiastic support of the Germanic as a
potent porridge of the bizarre, the allegorical, and the mystical could
have found in Poe's words an index for deciphering his own fiction as
forms in which the mystical and bizarre serve as vehicles for metaphysical allegory in the Germanic mode.

When magazine readers turned to "Ligeia," "The Fall of the House of
Usher," and "William Wilson" in 1839, they did so with a different horizon

of expectations than what had been in place for Poe's reception only two years before—a horizon that caused them to ask different questions and reconceptualize the gaps in Poe's tales. In speaking of antebellum readers confronting gaps in Poe's tales, I do not mean that this was a novel experience for Poe's audience in 1839. Like all works of fiction (and all texts) Poe's stories always "had" gaps, but they were constituted, as gaps, in particular ways through the audience's specific reading formations. As we have seen, for antebellum readers the gaps "in" "Metzengerstein" were not intrinsic to the text but were a function of particular strategies of reading, which also determined the way readers could fill the gaps with comic significance by the mid-1830s. With the failure of *Pym* and Poe's altered public status, however, readers were constituting different gaps in "Ligeia," "Usher," and "William Wilson."

An index to that difference comes from a remark on "Usher" by John Heath in his letter to Poe shortly after that story's publication. Heath complimented the tale but expressed his lack of pleasure at finding himself "reading tales of horror and mystery." A parallel response characterized Washington Irving's comment on "William Wilson" in a letter to Poe two months later, in which Irving explained that the story induced a "singular and Mysterious" interest.[58] Significantly, both responses employ a term that had not previously been applied to Poe's short stories: *mystery*. It is as if these two readers were finding gaps in the respective tales that they were having trouble filling—a problem analogous to the one reviewers of Pym had encountered. Exponentially more puzzled by the "mystery" of Poe's new tales was Philip Cooke, who remarked in a letter to Poe, "Of 'William Wilson' I am not sure that I perceive the true clew. From the 'whispering voice' I would apprehend that you meant the second William Wilson as an embodying of the *conscience* of the first; but I am inclined to the notion that your intention was to convey the wilder idea that every mortal of us is attended with a shadow of himself—a duplicate of his own peculiar organization—differing from himself only in a certain angelic taint of the compound. . . ; I cannot make myself understood, as I am not used to the expression of a wild *half thought*. But although I do not clearly comprehend, I certainly admire the story."[59] This remark is telling in several ways. Faced with uncertainty, antebellum readers such as Cooke employed an interpretive strategy that enabled them to position the tale in a particular way—as a "wild" tale of the supernatural and the mystical in the German mode. Just as importantly, Cooke's response indicates that one of the uncertainties is what a story such as "William Wilson" was about in terms of its philosophy or theme. If not satire, burlesque, or parody, what were "Wilson," "Usher," and "Ligeia" saying? For this reader, the solution to the mystery was to read "William Wilson" first through the didactic code as a moral allegory about conscience and then on a "deeper," perhaps emblematic, level as a vehicle for exploring a metaphysical theory. But also clear from his professed uncertainty about perceiving "clews" is that this reader felt less than comfortable with his allegorical or emblematic reading as a solution to the mystery of Poe's tale.

Interestingly enough, readers seem to have done the same kind of thing in responding to "Ligeia," following a rule of notice to identify its epigraph from Glanville as a clue to deciphering the story. At least that is what a reader for the *Southern Literary Messenger* did. Interpreting "Ligeia" in light of the Glanville epigraph as a "wonderful story, written to show the triumph of the human will even over *death*," the *Messenger* commentator treated the tale as an allegory or emblematic vehicle for presenting a philosophy about human volition (Jan. 1848: 36).

To get from the epigraph to this thematic response, any antebellum reader would naturally have had to go through a number of interpretive turns that, in all likelihood, would have begun with the title. Exercising the hermeneutic code of mystery/solution in conjunction with a rule of privileged position, informed readers would most likely have asked what the title refers to. That is, what or who is Ligeia? Although perhaps a bit unsettled by the narrator's initial inability to provide information about family name or origin of acquaintance, readers nonetheless could discover by the story's second paragraph that Ligeia was a woman—and the narrator's wife and friend. Certainly, Ligeia would have struck the audience as an unusual woman and consequently as a female character who could not be viewed as a comic or parodic stereotype. While readers might have taken her as belonging to the convention of the pale, slender beauty of many stories, that reaction probably was followed by a sense of Ligeia as a character who was also a mysterious stranger and a learned tutor. Her proficiency in classical languages—a rare accomplishment for women by antebellum standards—would only have enhanced the audience's sense that they were dealing with an unusual character of exceptional parts. Despite the husband-narrator's praise of Ligeia, however,

Poe's contemporaries must have wondered how to take her. For readers would have discovered by the story's sixth paragraph that Ligeia was also the purveyor of esoteric knowledge that led the narrator, as he admits, toward "the goal of a wisdom too divinely precious not to be forbidden" (1: 316). It is difficult to think that antebellum readers would not have seen in this phrase allusions to such stories of transgressive knowledge as the Faust legend and, more poignantly for middle-class Christians, the temptation and sin of Eve. Combined with her abnormal erudition, Ligeia had to strike middle-class readers— male and female—as a woman who had gone dangerously beyond the bounds of true womanhood. The ideology of the antebellum cult of domesticity would have provided the logic for such a response, which would have had even greater support through a development in Jacksonian American to which Charles Sellers has pointed: the growing bourgeois fear of a connection between strong women and male indulgence in illicit behavior.[60] Such a connection, along with Ligeia's excesses, could only have been strengthened in the minds of Poe's contemporary readers by the disclosure of "Ligeia's more than womanly abandonment to a love" (1: 317).

Among readers for whom such dark implications would have accumulated midway through the story, a gap would have opened about the narrator himself: How is one to take his fascination with and continued adulation of this woman? That question could only have intensified by the end of the tale when antebellum readers confronted what must have struck them as a monstrous Ligeia responsible for Rowena's death and the supernatural violation of her body.

Yet even while experiencing such problems in the story, informed readers may already have been fashioning an answer by seizing on the narrator's comment that Ligeia's attractions had the "radiance of an opium dream" and his later admission that he had become "a bounden slave in the trammels of opium" (1: 311, 320). Pointedly enough, when "Ligeia" was republished in 1845, a comment accompanying it in the *New World* emphasized that element of the story, drawing attention to the "ruined and specter-haunted mind of the narrator" as "suggest[ing] a *possible explanation* of the marvels of the story, without in the least weakening its vigor as an exposition of the mystical *thesis* which the tale is designed to illustrate and enforce" (Feb. 15, 1845, *PL* 502–3). This was not, it should be stressed, a reading of the story as the fantastic in prescient anticipation of Tzvetan Todorov's modern theory. The commentator in the *New World* did not identify a psychological or naturalistic explanation as an uncanny counterpoint existing in tension with the marvelous elements in the story. Instead, in interpreting the mind of the narrator as "ruined" by opium, this reader saw such an implication as in no way diminishing the story's mystical thesis about the supernatural power of the human will. Such a reading, moreover, would have gained additional credence for some readers from the fact that, at Ligeia's death, the narrator repeats in his own mind Glanville's words about the power of the human will.[61] For if the narrator, by such an action, makes this belief his own, antebellum readers could justifiably have concluded that the narrator's transgressive fascination with Ligeia is part of his guilt in that he too is responsible for the subsequent death of Rowena and the commandeering of her body by Ligeia's dark spirit.

If this is a reasonable reconstruction of the experience of "Ligeia" by antebellum informed readers, it would nonetheless seem to raise a problem. Would not such an experience entail, and even depend on, readers identifying the tale's narrator as unreliable—precisely the kind of thing that many modern critics have done?[62] In other words, would not this reconstruction depend on ascribing to readers an interpretive move that would have been impossible for them to make in 1839–40? I do not believe so. While an antebellum reader experiencing the tale as I have described would find something specious, it would not be the narrator but the tale itself. For the informed audience, the story was an "autobiographical" tale and thus, according to the interpretive convention for processing that technique, was told by a narrator who, as an imagined mind of the author, surely shared the author's mentality. Any problem with the narrator, therefore, could be interpreted as a flaw in Poe's handling of the story as a vehicle for conveying its "thesis" on the power—and perhaps the danger—of the human will.

A version of this kind of reading formulation appears, in fact, to have been the motor behind a comment by Poe's sedulous correspondent, Philip Cooke. Shortly after reading "Ligeia," Cooke had written Poe to let him know that

I of course "took" your "idea" throughout. The whole piece is but
a sermon from the text of "Joseph Glanvil" [*sic*] which you cap it

with—and your intent is to tell a tale of the "mighty will" contending with & finally vanquishing Death. The struggle is vigorously described . . . until the Lady Ligeia takes possession of the deserted *quarters* . . . of the Lady Rowena. There I was shocked by the violation of the ghostly properties—so to speak—and wondered how the Lady Ligeia—a wandering essence—could, in quickening *the body of the Lady Rowena* . . . become suddenly the visible, bodily, Ligeia. If Rowena's bodily form had been retained as a shell or case for the disembodied Lady Ligeia, and you had only become aware *gradually* that . . . a soul of more glowing fires occupied the quickened body and gave an old familiar expression to its motion—if you had brooded and meditated upon the change . . . and then . . . broken into the exclamation which ends the story—the *effect* would not have been lessened, and the "ghostly properties" would, I think, have been better observed.[63]

Explaining how he comprehended the story's idea, Cooke nonetheless objects to the way it is presented. What bothers him in particular is the way the theme is actualized through what the narrator says and observes about the transformation of the resurrected Rowena into Ligeia. In his reading, this problem in the handling of the narrative, while not disrupting the theme, interferes with the story's "ghostly properties" and thus with his ability, as a reader, to decipher his position vis-à-vis the characters. To be sure, Cooke seems more concerned with the shape of Ligeia's metempsychosis and the probability of the plot (as deciphered by the code of causality) than with the narrator's authority, but as a good informed reader Cooke would not have seen these issues as separate, since narratorial authority always was, in informed reading, a matter of authorial authority and competence in telling and plotting a tale. Significantly, Cooke's response embodies precisely that connection in the way he refers to the narrator of "Ligeia" as "you," as if Poe himself (or at least an autobiographical projection of Poe) "became aware" of Rowena's transformation and blurted out the story's last words.

To some degree, Poe must have been amused by such remarks, but he also must have found responses such as Cooke's disturbing, even as he had to take some satisfaction both from them and from reviewer comments about "Usher" and "William Wilson." The disquietude and disorientation of those comments accorded with the kind of disruptive effect that Poe equated with excellent fiction.[64] Yet even if the match were that neat, Poe had to have been concerned because, to work in the fullest sense, it would require an understanding of the artistry behind the disruptions of these tales and thus the establishment of an aesthetic distance in which the reader perceives the controlling wires and lays bare the traps. To succeed, in other words, Poe's tales depended on the audience's triumphant understanding. Compounding the problem was that Poe could not even know for certain whether such cognizant appropriation of the text's power was going on. Instead, in light of comments such as Cooke's tempered chiding, Poe confronted responses against which he had to defend himself. By late 1839, faced with the need to recapture his own sense of authority as a fiction writer, Poe began pursuing a two-pronged strategy.

One tactic involved directly addressing readers, both publicly and privately, via counter readings of his tales that were coupled with a playful evasiveness through which Poe could become the author as chameleon. Hence, the deft dodgings and arch acrobatics of his preface to *Tales of the Grotesque and Arabesque*. Likewise, in his response to Cooke, Poe chose elusiveness as part of his strategy. Despite telling Cooke that "[t]ouching 'Ligeia' you are right—all right—throughout" and that a "*gradual* perception" that Ligeia lives again would produce "a far loftier and more thrilling idea than the one I have embodied," Poe never changed the conclusion of the text, despite making other (and in some cases substantive) revisions each of the three times he republished it.[65] This is not to imply that Poe revised "Ligeia" as he did simply to confound Cooke. The lack of change to the ending suggests that Poe probably did not see it as flawed and that his "admission" to Cooke may have been a hoax of the moment. In other words, from Poe's perspective, if the tale had not served as an irresistible force of authorial power in working on Cooke and readers of his ilk, the problem was not with the tale itself but with a dense, officious, and uncooperative readership.

By 1839 Poe seemed, in fact, to be growing increasingly perturbed with the fiction-reading audience. After expressing his satisfaction that "Ligeia" was at least "intelligible" to Cooke, Poe announced, "[a]s for the mob—let them talk. I should be grieved if I thought they comprehended me here." A similar disdain marked the advice Poe offered to his friend

Frederick Thomas a year later in response to Thomas's inquiry about how to succeed as an author. "If you would send the public opinion to the devil," advised Poe, "forgetting that a public existed, and writing from the natural promptings of your own spirit[,] you would do wonders."[66]

As the other prong of his strategy, Poe sought in the early 1840s to construct his tales in a way that would counter the problematic element in the reception of the stories in the *Tales of the Grotesque and Arabesque* by keeping the audience off balance and eliciting awe while simultaneously achieving understanding from readers who would nonetheless not quite comprehend what happened to them. It is as if Poe could not relinquish his desire, despite his growing uneasiness with the popular magazine readership, to somehow affect an audience who would be both overpowered and appreciative.

In composing his tales, accordingly, Poe combined several tactics. To avoid being fixed by his audience, Poe sought generic diversity by returning to the successes of his past through stories that could elicit a comic response. Poe had begun to employ this strategy even before the reception of his collected tales as he became aware of the shift to the Germanic emphasis in responses to his fiction. Publishing "The Psyche Zenobia" ("How to Write a Blackwood Article") in 1838, he followed it in 1839 with "The Devil in the Belfry"—a melange of fabricated authorities and identifiably humorous names that Poe simply called an "extravaganza"—and "The Man That Was Used Up," a tale that Daniel Hoffman has asserted would have been recognizable to Poe's contemporaries as a political satire probably aimed at Winfield Scott.[67] To these Poe added two new hoaxes, the serialized "Journal of Julius Rodman" (1840) and "A Descent into the Maelstrom" (1841), as well as "Never Bet the Devil Your Head" (1841), "Diddling" (1843), "The Spectacles" (1844), and "The Literary Life of Thingum Bob, Esq." (1844).[68] In several of these, Poe went after targets that the contemporary magazine audience could readily have identified as "hits," from con games and human vanity to the puffery of literary journals. Other stories, however, could be read several ways—or at least Poe wanted the comic swath to cut broadly. When one reader wrote to him about "Never Bet the Devil Your Head" as a satire on New England transcendentalism, Poe demurred by retorting with a counter reading: "You are mistaken about 'The Dial.' I have no quarrel in the world with that illustrious journal. . . . My slaps at it were only in 'a general way.' The tale in question is a mere Extravaganza levelled at no one in particular, but hitting right & left at things in general," from homeopathy and child-rearing practices to antigambling tracts.[69]

To enhance his reputation for diversity, Poe also turned to a fictional mode he called "something in a new key": his tales of ratiocination and detection beginning with "The Murders in the Rue Morgue" (1841) and "The Mystery of Maria Rogét" (1842).[70] Achieving significant popularity, these tales enabled Poe to tap the magazine audience's interest in such topical events as the widely reported, mysterious death of the "beauti-ful cigar girl," Mary Rogers, in New York City and more generally in the crime reporting that was a staple of mass-circulation newspapers. Such stories also provided him with what he hoped would be a vehicle for mys-tifying and dazzling the audience without being tarred with the brush of "Germanic horror," and his plan apparently worked, at least for some readers. The *Pennsylvania Inquirer* marveled at "Rue Morgue" for the way "[a]t every step it whets the curiosity of the reader, until the interest is heightened to the point from which the mind shrinks with something like incredul[i]ty; when with an inventive power and skill, of which we know no parallel, he reconciles every difficulty" (July 1843, *PL* 430). The *Literary Gazette* said of the same tale simply that its "marvelous chain of analytical reasoning" causes readers to feel that "the horror of the in-cident is overborne by the acuteness of the arguments" (Jan. 31, 1846, *PL* 621).

One interesting dimension of Poe's experimentation with this "new" mode is that, at a time when his dissatisfaction with the fiction-reading public and its demands was growing, readers found these tales accom-modating by discovering in them something informative, useful, and reassuring. According to the *Saturday Museum*, "Murders in the Rue Morgue" provided "the man of legal lore an opportunity of acquiring an insight into his profession, more thorough than his long days and studi-ous nights could ever glean from all the records of criminal practices" (July 22, 1843, *PL* 429). Making a broader claim for the value of the Dupin tales as a group, the *American Review* informed readers that these stories, while designed "to surprise the mind into activity," also "relieve the curiosity of the reader from the tangled mesh of mystery, in which it is caught and confined" in a manner that "makes him aware of the practi-cal value of such mental acuteness in the ascertainment of truth."[71]

It would, nonetheless, be a mistake to push any claim of accommodation too far in drawing out Poe's relation to fiction readers in the 1840s. Poe wanted the upper hand, and playing the part of the accommodating writer was one more role he could take on as a means to display his abilities as a writer of multifarious modes and masterly diversity. Poe's concern with diversity as a principle of his reception is perhaps most evident in his reaction to the Wiley and Putnam 1845 publication of their collection of twelve of his stories, which Evert Duyckinck had selected from the roughly sixty-five tales Poe had published. Despite the pleasure Poe took at the success of the Dupin stories and other ratiocinative tales such as "The Gold Bug," he complained afterward that Duyckinck "made up the book mostly of analytic stories. But this is not representing my mind in its various phases—it is not giving me fair play. In writing these Tales one by one . . . one of my chief aims has been the widest diversity of subject, thought, & especially *tone* & manner of handling." Cloaking his consternation by wrapping self-aggrandizement in a mantle of objectivity, Poe went on to claim, "Were all my tales now before me in a large volume and as the composition of another—the merit which would principally arrest my attention would be the wide *diversity and* variety."[72]

Yet the impression such diversity would ostensibly create of him as a writer was hardly enough, since such an impression meant only that readers had not been able to channelize him. It fell short as an index to the kind of control over the audience and the fiction-reading experience that Poe regarded as a hallmark of great authorship. For such an effect, more was needed, and to achieve it Poe turned to the more aggressive and potentially dangerous part of his strategy: to subtly entrap his audience in stories that would, like "Ligeia" and "William Wilson," affect readers by destabilizing the reading experience and eliciting awe, while preventing them from mastering the tale.

I am referring here to the strategy Poe pursued through the stories many twentieth-century readers view as his quintessential tales of mystery and horror: "The Tell-Tale Heart" and "The Black Cat," both published in 1843. Antebellum readers were certainly prepared to receive both tales as anything but comedic, despite the fact that "Descent into the Maelstrom" and "Julius Rodman" had gone the rounds as successful hoaxes only two years before. Not only had Poe's reputation as a serious Germanic writer been implanted in the magazine readership by 1839 and 1840; the intervening publication and reception of "Maria Rogét," "The Oval Portrait," "The Masque of the Red Death," and "The Pit and the Pendulum" further entrenched that interpretive assumption. Just as formatively, middle-class readers came to "The Black Cat" and "The Tell-Tale Heart" at a time of growing public interest in urban crime—and in the psychological and moral condition of criminals and the criminally insane.

For centuries insanity had been viewed as a possible cause for crime and for murder in particular, with the condition of the insane criminal conceptualized as a form of total and permanent mania, measured by the criterion of the "wild beast." But by the mid-1830s, doctors, jurists, and legal thinkers began to argue that criminal insanity need not be total nor constitutional. Instead, such insanity could manifest itself intermittently so that, if eventuating prior to and as the impetus for an act of homicide, such insanity precluded moral culpability on the part of the killer. The logic here was that the criminal, as a victim of an "irresistible impulse," was unable to prevent his or her own temporarily heinous behavior. Termed "moral insanity," the concept became the basis of debates about criminality and guilt as part of a new form of insanity defense. By the early 1840s, according to Norman Dain, the issue of moral insanity, the status and treatment of the criminally insane, and the insanity defense "became an important and controversial subject in America."[73] Through published trial accounts and articles in newspapers and magazines, these ideas and the developing controversy were disseminated to the same middle-class audience that was reading "Tell-Tale Heart" and "Black Cat." The controversy even seems to have reached something of a peak in 1843, the year both tales appeared, in the murder trial of a man named Singleton Mercer, whose trial and insanity defense were treated extensively in several New York papers.[74]

There seems little doubt that the antebellum audience would have interpreted both stories as criminal narratives. When the narrator in "Tell-Tale Heart" says in the second paragraph that "I made up my mind to take the life of the old man," readers would have had more than a clue (2: 792). In "Black Cat" the warrant for such an interpretation comes even earlier, if more subtly, when in the opening paragraph the narrator blurts out "to-morrow I die, and to-day I would unburthen my soul" (2: 849). The combination of impending death and confession of wrongdo-

ing would have enabled readers to infer, if not impending capital punishment, at least a transgression so bad as to signal criminality. In both
stories, informed readers would have quickly seized on elements of the
pre-texts to identify them as part of the mushrooming genre of crime
fiction.[75]

As a reviewer in *Graham's* pointed out, however, "Tell-Tale Heart" was
more. Attuned to the autobiographical form of fiction in "Heart" and
"Black Cat," the reviewer concluded that "Mr. Poe probes a terror to its
depths, and spreads it out to the reader" by "leading the mind through
the whole framework of crime and perversity, and enabling the intellect
to comprehend their laws and relations." As an "anatomist" of the well-
springs of wickedness, explained the reviewer, Poe provided the audience
of his two stories with an insight into the criminal mind.[76] Thus, when
each tale's narrator mentions madness, readers could readily have made
a link between dementia and criminality.

In moving through "Tell-Tale Heart," antebellum readers would have
become involved in the issue of the narrator's madness by his early ac-
cusation that "You fancy me mad" (2: 792). At issue, given the contemporary controversy over the insanity defense, was a question of the relation
between insanity and crime in this narrator and the story he tells, but
more was at stake for antebellum readers than a question about whether
the narrator is insane or not. In light of assumptions about the moral obligation of fiction, informed readers had to ask how they should be relating to this narrator and his tale and what Poe's purpose was in providing
this "anatomy" of the criminal mind.

Here, too, context was a factor in that, as David Reynolds has pointed
out, by the early 1840s crime pamphlets and crime fictions increasingly
were representing the criminal sympathetically.[77] Even if the middle-
class audience were not necessarily reading such fiction, they knew of it
as part of the sensational tales that reviewers and editorialists regularly
castigated. A question for this audience was whether "Tell-Tale Heart"
represented such a sympathetic treatment by casting the narrator's
crime in the category of "moral insanity" and the narrator as a victim of
an abnormal mental failing that had tormented him into a heinous act
beyond his control. Then, too, what was Poe suggesting by such sympathetic treatment (if sympathetic it was)? Was the tale making a case for
the new insanity defense?

These were more than questions prompted by interpretive curiosity. They raised unsettling moral issues, and one of the reasons they did so was the story's narrative voice. Informed readers would have come to "Tell-Tale Heart" expecting a tale's narrative voice to serve as a guide to a character's actions and speech, especially if questions arose as to whether they should be construed as acceptable or deserving of sympathy. Even Poe, as we have seen, subscribed to the interpretive convention of reading for such a controlling voice and modeled that practice as a reviewer. But in this story readers would have been hard pressed to find such a guiding perspective. If that were not enough, the encounter with the tale's conclusion would have produced further disorientation. Though the narrator's admission of his crime to the police would probably strike antebellum readers as a resolution that restores order, his shriek and his comment that the dead man's heart continued to beat beneath the floor hardly would have seemed an ending that drains the tension from the narrator's frenzy and the reader's close—and possibly sympathetic—involvement with it. In other words, attentive readers would have noticed that the conclusion only highlights their own investment in emotional excitement and that the experience of the tale has encouraged them to indulge in a self-implicating violation of the morality of informed reading.

The combination of audience expectations and the way the pre-text of "Tell-Tale Heart" could serve as an occasion for grappling with interpretive and readerly identity had the capacity to create an uneasiness that fit Poe's goal: a disorientation in the reading experience that would thwart readers' ability to draw back with charges of Germanic mysticism or through other judgmental moves. Moreover, any sympathy readers found themselves feeling for the narrator may have stymied a retreat to analytical safety, since by such sympathy readers, in effect, admitted to being co-conspirators who shared the criminal guilt of a story that they had tried to master.

It would be naive, however, to assume that all of Poe's audience gave him what he sought or that the story itself, as one modern critic has claimed, defies rational analysis.[78] However troubling the experience of the tale may have been, a commentator in the *New York Tribune* confidently and even contumaciously declared "The Tell-Tale Heart" to be a story about an insane murderer—and a disgusting one at that. As the

Tribune put it, Poe's tale was "overstrained and repulsive" in its "analysis of the feelings and promptings of an insane homicide" (Jan. 13, 1845, *PL* 395). The problem was not only the gruesome details of the iniquity, which looked like something out of the sensational criminal reports of the penny press, but the way the experience of the tale, by encouraging a psychological intimacy with the criminal that could induce sympathy, jeopardized the audience's moral equilibrium. In its own way, "The Tell-Tale Heart" looked from such a perspective to be another version of the suspect sensational tale, which posited the wrong role for its audience. Even for antebellum readers who were not sure that the narrator was insane or was to be viewed sympathetically, the question of what Poe was doing by linking criminality and insanity in the same tale would provide a pathway for seizing analytical control of the story. For whether Poe was supporting or calling into question that link, the status of the story as a proponent of one of these positions meant that it was a form of advocacy fiction and thus belonged to an inherently suspect and inferior genre.

It is necessary, however, to raise a complication in this anatomy of antebellum experiences of "Tell-Tale Heart." Any reading that assumes the narrator is or might be insane would be an interpretation that casts doubt on the reasonableness and accuracy of the narrator's reports and judgments. Consequently, what returns here is the issue that arose in reconstructing an informed reading of "Ligeia": Does not the assumption of insanity depend on the conception of an unreliable narrator, which was not part of the interpretive lexicon of informed reading in the 1840s?

The question is unavoidable because it arises as well for "The Black Cat," a story Poe's contemporaries recognized, as the *Aristidean* noted, as "a reproduction of the 'Tell-Tale Heart,'" though with "an amplification of one of its phases" (October 1845: 317). That recognition is not surprising, for we have already noted the way the experience of the opening of "Black Cat" likely would have paralleled that of "Tell-Tale Heart" within antebellum informed reading. Readers of "Black Cat," however, would have grappled with other elements in deciphering the story's philosophy and purpose, both in itself and in relation to the audience. One would have occurred, I believe, at some point after realizing that the narrator is a murderer who, as he explains in the opening, will die on the morrow. Antebellum readers could have concluded that the narrator is "unburthen[ing] my soul" by telling his tale from a prison cell, which means he has likely unburdened himself with a confession before he begins his tale. That conclusion, in turn, could have led to the question of why the narrator is confessing for a second time. In raising this question, however, I do not believe antebellum readers would have decided, as one modern critic has, that such a situation means that the narrator's story lacks value as an unburdening confession and seems merely "arbitrary and compulsive" in its motivation.[79] For antebellum readers, the re-confession that the tale stages could have been interpreted as a form of penitence born either of the need to humble oneself in sin or from an inborn desire to do the right thing by offering a cautionary tale. If the first depended on Christian principles, readers could configure the second explanation from what had become a growing conviction in the nineteenth century that human beings, by their nature, were drawn to the good and the right.

Even more significant would be a third possible interpretation, which readers could have located in the narrator's admission that he had been subject to "the Fiend Intemperance" and that his "more than fiendish malevolence" was "gin-nurtured" (2: 851). Many antebellum readers would have been familiar with the fact that in nonfictional accounts of murder at the time, intemperance often was cited as a motivating factor.[80] For those readers, the narrator's disclosure of his drinking problem would have provided a rationale for his homicidal behavior and his story as confession. The confession he is now making for the first time is the secret tale of his life: the etiology of his self-destruction under the horrors of demon drink. To answer the question of why the narrator tells his tale, readers could have interpreted his story as a temperance tale in the mold of T. S. Arthur's popular *Ten Nights in a Bar-room,* which had appeared only a year earlier.

More importantly, such an interpretation would have enabled antebellum readers to see the narrator as a victim of insanity without having to interpret him as unreliable. The logic would have run as follows. Owing to his intemperance, the narrator suffered from moral insanity during the time he committed the two killings and afterward while walling up his wife's body and the second cat. At the time of the telling of the tale, however, the narrator is not insane—a conclusion conforming to the theory of moral insanity—and consequently is quite trustworthy, not only in his version of the events but in his claim that currently "mad am I not"

(2: 849). Such a conclusion about the narrator would have fallen neatly in line with the linkage of alcohol, insanity, and illness among middle-class reformers who used that sutured triad to define the alcoholic as psychologically wayward yet reclaimable through the social technologies of disciplinary health care.[81] Consonant with middle-class values, such a view could readily provide magazine readers with an ideological base for deciphering "Black Cat" as a reassuring temperance tale.

This response to the tale nonetheless could hardly have come without its own difficulties. Because this era witnessed a growing tendency to view the alcoholic with sympathy, readers could well have found themselves in the same problematic situation that accompanied any feelings of sympathy for the narrator as a victim of insanity in "Tell-Tale Heart."[82] Both responses brought readers into a dangerous emotional bond with the deviant. More disturbing to readers of "Black Cat" would have been the narrator's comment, shortly after his disclosure about his alcoholism, that the "final and irrevocable" impetus to his actions was the "longing of [his] soul to *vex itself*—to offer violation to its own nature—to do wrong for the wrong's sake only" (2: 852). The problem informed readers would have endured with such a disclosure lay not only in its serving as an explanation for the narrator's actions but also in the murderer's claim that this "spirit of PERVERSENESS . . . is one of the primitive impulses of the human heart . . . which give direction to the character of Man" (852)—a claim at odds with prevailing antebellum ideas about human nature as inherently inclined toward the good. In addition, readers would have had to wonder about the black cat itself, since the interpretive rule of privileged position would probably have led to the question of what exactly *is* the nature and significance of the titular feline. The problem of answering that question was no doubt compounded by the narrator's intimation that something supernatural is at work in the second cat, which leads to the discovery of the murdered corpse.

This last turn is especially problematic because it would seem to raise again the issue of unreliability, in that readers who assumed this narrator to be sane at the time of the telling would have to account for his continued adherence to a supernatural explanation for the tale's pivotal events. Of course, one move to make would have been to treat this as a tale of the supernatural and thereby dismiss it as far-fetched, which is precisely what a reviewer in the *Literary Annual Register* did. According to that reader, "the 'Black Cat' is a striking but improbable story of a murderer haunted by a cat with the mark of a gallows on her breast, and finally by her agency brought to justice."[83] But for readers who had invested in the interpretation of the story as a temperance tale and/or a narrative about criminality and moral insanity, such a conclusion would have been less than satisfying. Instead, such readers would apparently have been confronted at the close with the question of whether the narrator was confused, haunted, or perhaps still mentally unbalanced.

Rather than reaching an interpretation involving narrative unreliability, however, some antebellum readers addressed the question of what was going on in "Black Cat" by allegorizing its problematic elements as figurative or emblematic vehicles. According to a reviewer in *Littell's Living Age*, while the second cat of the tale would appear to "have been a proper inmate for the 'Castle of Otronto' . . . it may be argued that the Black Cat is a figurative personification for the dark-brooding thoughts of a murderer, murder being the climax of the story" (Nov. 1845: 343). What is most noticeable in the public discussion of the story at the time is the way readers interpreted the "Black Cat" as a tale in which everything is a vehicle, not just of the narrator's murderous mind but more specifically for his explanation of events as products of his spirit of perverseness. Or as some readers of the time viewed it, the tale was a vehicle for *Poe's* theory of perverseness as the etiology of the story's events. As the *American Whig Review* explained, "'The Black Cat' is a story, exceedingly well told, illustrative of a theory, which the author has advanced . . . respecting perverseness, or the impulse to perform actions simply for the reason that they ought not to be performed." Despite noting, moreover, that "[t]he theory is ingeniously represented in the case of an imaginary character," this reviewer attributed the character's comments to Poe himself: "For this devilish spirit, Mr. Poe claims the honor of being 'one of the primitive impulses of the human heart—one of the indivisible primary faculties, or sentiments, which give direction to the character of man'" (Sept. 1845: 309). Here was an informed response situated squarely within the interpretive code for autobiographical fiction: though the autobiographical narrator is a created fictional character, he still speaks the author's mind in the way that any narrator must do. Interestingly enough, *Blackwood's* magazine in Britain reached the same conclusion about "Black Cat." Although noting that Poe "appears at first to aim at rivalling the fantastic horrors of Hoffmann," readers "soon observe that the wild and horrible invention in which he deals, is strictly in the service of an abstract idea which it is there to illustrate. His analytical observation has led him, he thinks, to detect in men's minds an absolute spirit of 'perversity,' prompting them to the very opposite of what reason and mankind pronounce to be right."[84]

For such readers, if something was amiss in the explanation of the tale's events, the problem was not the narrator's; it was Poe's. Hence, the *American Review* added that the "Black Cat" "is not much to our taste" because "[t]he perverseness, to which the author refers, seems to us to be rightly classed, not among the original impulses of human nature, but among the phenomena of insanity. . . . It is a moral disease, not a primitive impulse." The logic behind this decision to clear up the tale by reading it as a story of "moral insanity" over which Poe had lost control is understandable, and the reason is hinted at in the *Blackwood's* comment about what "reason and mankind pronounce to be right." If the story, as an illustration of Poe's theory of perversity, dismayed readers, the reason was that such a theory was an heretical affront to rationality, to the view of human nature as inherently good, and to antebellum Christian values. As a result, readers could interpret the tale as itself perverse and distorted, presenting its theory, as *Blackwood's* complained, in "a turn of circumstances as hideous, incongruous, and absurd as the sentiment itself." In this response, the disruptions and incongruities of the "Black Cat" were akin to those of Germanic sensationalism, this time bodied forth in an absurdly plotted and abhorrently confused allegory.

It is not difficult to imagine the dismay Poe must have felt in reading such responses, since in one form or another they echoed the old taunt of imitative Germanism now coupled with a charge of flaccid thinking. By treating the narrator's ideas in "The Black Cat" as if they were Poe's, such readings implicitly labeled Poe as the one with the deviant mind. Nor could Poe have been much happier as he looked elsewhere at his public reception and found the interpretations of his Dupin tales as tutelary narratives for lawyers and right-thinking gentlemen. More, of course, was at issue than these responses to specific tales, which represented for Poe the worst aspect of the didactic propensity in informed reading—at least when applied to his own fictions. Especially troubling was the cumulative result of such readings in implying a loss of mastery through an inability to control his texts' effects on his readership. Poe was reaching the point where even responses that lauded elements of his stories were becoming galling, as if such responses signaled readers' presumptions about their ability to comprehend his artistry. Thus, even as he relished the praise he received for the ingenuity of his ratiocinative tales, he dismissed such reactions as a sign of the audience's misunderstanding. As for those tales, Poe explained in another letter to Cooke, "people think them more ingenious than they are—on account of their method and *air* of method. In the 'Murders in the Rue Morgue,' for instance, where is the ingenuity of unravelling a web which you yourself (the author) have woven for the express purpose of unravelling? The reader is made to confound the ingenuity of the supposititious Dupin with that of the writer of the story."[85] By such dismissal of the reader's awe, Poe could claim that the true brilliance of those stories' method lay in their artistic sleight of hand. Seeking to define himself as once again a step ahead of his readership led Poe to identify his Dupin stories as virtual aesthetic hoaxes.

Indeed, the power Poe associated with the fictional hoax as a tool of control over his audience grew in the mid-to-late 1840s, when he wrote such deliberately designed impostures as "The Balloon Hoax" (1845) and "Von Kempelen and His Discovery" (1849). Regarding the latter, Poe explained in a letter to Duyckinck accompanying the manuscript that "I mean it as a kind of 'exercise,' or experiment in the plausible or verisimilar style. Of course, there is *not* one word of truth in it from beginning to end." Convinced that "such a style, applied to the gold-excitement [in California], could not fail of effect," Poe added, "[m]y sincere opinion is that nine persons out of ten will (even among the best-informed) *believe* the quiz."[86] His conviction that the fictional hoax provided an answer in his battle with the informed audience is suggested further by his response to the public reception of such tales as "Mesmeric Revelation" (1844) and "The Facts in the Case of M. Valdemar" (1845). On several occasions Poe quietly admitted that in "my 'Valdemar Case' . . . I had not the slightest idea that any person should credit it" and that he "never dreamed" of "Mesmeric Revelation" as being anything but a story without "veracity" concerning the events recounted. Instead, he explained, "Mesmeric Revelation" was written to "introduce . . . to the world" his "philosophy . . . in a manner that should insure [*sic*] for it attention. I thought that by representing my speculations in a garb of vraisemblance . . . I would secure for them a hearing. In the case of Valdemar, I was actuated by similar motives."[87] A curious thing happened, however; both stories were received as factual accounts of incidents in which mesmerism had been used either to prolong human life or to verify "scientifically" existence beyond the grave. Newspapers and magazines reprinted "Mesmeric Revelation" and "Valdemar" with introductory remarks calling each story a "statement of facts" or suggesting that it may well be authentic, while several of Poe's friends, including George Eveleth and Sarah Helen Whitman, wrote letters to inquire whether the stories were true.[88] Only after such responses did Poe begin declaring that "'Hoax' *is* precisely the word suited to M. Valdemar's case" and start chortling in print over the joke he had played on the credulous press and much of its public.[89] Yet Poe was playing a dangerous, self-incriminating game here that ironically removed from him as much power as it garnered. For among those "hoaxed" by his retrospective claim for "Valdemar" and "Mesmeric Revelation" as impostures, as one modern critic has suggested, was Poe himself, in that "he was forced by public clamor to acknowledge, ultimately, that which he never intended."[90]

That public clamor was not one-sided, however, since a substantial segment of the magazine audience had its doubts about the authenticity of the two tales. A good deal of the public discussion, in fact, was devoted to clarifying that each story, as the *New York Tribune* put it, "is of course a romance" and to interpreting "Valdemar" and "Mesmeric Revelation" in the same way reviewers had treated "The Black Cat": as fictional conveyances for Poe's own philosophy.[91] The *Aristidean* called "Mesmeric Revelation" "nothing more than a vehicle of the author's views concerning the DEITY, immateriality, spirit, &c." (October 1845, *PL* 587), while the *Literary Gazette* took it as a tale in which Poe "daringly attempts a solution to that deepest of riddles, the nature of the Deity" (Jan. 31, 1846, *PL* 621). Such responses, of course, were precisely the ones at which Poe claimed to have aimed, yet the credit he took for both tales as successful hoaxes had strategic relevance even for the interpretations that matched his intentions. Such a claim provided Poe with one more opportunity to assert authority over those who had ostensibly read the tales "correctly," in that the status of these stories as successful hoaxes implied that they were more elusive and powerful than even readers of a kindred art had realized.

No more than his other tales, however, did Poe's claimed hoaxes free him from the problem of depending upon the audience's expectations, beliefs, and interpretive strategies for the success of his fiction. To work as hoaxes, after all, stories such as "Valdemar," "Mesmeric Revelation," and "Von Kempelen" depended on the capacities of the audience, first to be taken in by and then to see through the hoax as a jest. A hoax unrecognized cannot achieve its goal of being understood and admired as a successful imposture. In like manner, readers who cannot see that they were taken in cannot know the extent of their delusive attempts at textual mastery; their incrimination remains invisible. What does the mischief is that such understanding by the audience *makes* the story work and thus constitutes a masterful response by the reader. The problem was that such mastery invested readers with final power in what Poe continued to view as the struggle between audience and writer over control of a text and its effects.

Not that Poe's readers always felt in control, particularly when it came to believing that his stories represented the kind of fiction they wanted. Much of the public response to Poe in the late 1840s expressed just the opposite sentiment. Despite Poe's efforts at diversity, despite the way several of his tales were received as clever comedies or intriguing mysteries, and despite his goal of countering the charges of Germanism, the overall response to his tales from 1843 until his death in 1849 consisted of viewing them as stories of Germanic sensationalism or mystical humbuggery—and often chiding them for being so. *Graham's* called him "an anatomist of the horrible and the ghastly," whose "pertinacity" at "prob[ing] a terror to its depths . . . is a peculiarity of his tales" (Sept. 1845: 143). The *New Haven Courier* found that his stories continued to be "full of more than German mysticism, grotesque, strange, improbable," while the *Southern Patriot* emphasized that Poe "is fond of mystifying in his stories."[92] More direct in their dismay were reviews of the 1845 *Tales* in *Littell's Living Age* and the *Knickerbocker*. While the latter termed the collection part of "the force-feeble and the shallow-profound school," the former announced, "We object, for the most part, to the tales . . . because they uncurtain horrors and cruelties" that "form no part of the glories of literature" (Nov. 1845: 343).[93] Several reviewers even suggested a link between the diseased sensationalism of the fiction and Poe himself. According to the *Harbinger*, "Mr. Poe's tales are . . . clumsily contrived, unnatural, and every way in bad taste. There is still a kind of power in them; it is the power of disease; there is no health about them, they are alike in the vagaries of an opium eater." A similar innuendo marked a notice in the *Richmond Compiler*. Although admitting that Poe's stories "manifest unusual talent, and indeed genius," the reviewer added that it is "of a morbid, unpoised character; they resemble the strange outpourings of an opium eater, while under the influence of that stimulating drug."[94]

Such comments reflected the fact that by the mid-to-late 1840s, other factors had come into play in the reception of Poe's fiction. The battles he had waged over the years, particularly with the literati and magazinists in Boston and New York, had made him such enemies that the public response strongly swayed to the critical and even damning in the periodicals of those cities. The acrimony reached the point where several of Poe's enemies, including Louis Gaylord Clark at the *Knickerbocker*, were spreading rumors and libelous stories in 1846 about Poe's personal habits and moral health—accusations accompanied by innuendoes that Poe was succumbing to mental instability. Those stories were picked up and reprinted in newspapers in New York, Baltimore, and St. Louis.[95]

Exacerbating the situation was the cumulative effect of years of responses to Poe's tales within antebellum assumptions of autobiographical narration that identified Poe with the moral and psychological conditions depicted in his stories. The interpreted connection between Poe and his narrators (or characters) received an additional boost through the public commentary that accompanied the publication and immense popularity of "The Raven." Often while ladling praise, reviewers spoke of the poem as a "conversation carried on between Mr. POE and 'The Raven'" (*Knickerbocker* Apr. 1845, *PL* 523) or claimed that in the poem, as the *Aristidean* announced, the reader hears "the poet tell his own story" (Nov. 1845: 400). Struck by the poem's haunted narrator, the *Southern Quarterly Review* observed, in an eerie echo of responses to the 1845 *Tales*, that "[i]t seems as if the author wrote under the influence of opium, or attempted to describe the fantastic terrors which afflict a sufferer from *delirium tremens*" (July 1848, *PL* 739). Apparently the tone and point of view of "The Raven" and his "Germanic" tales could be so taken as a reflection of Poe's own state that even his friend George Eveleth told Poe in a letter that he "was afraid, from the wild imaginations manifested in your writings, that you were an opium-eater."[96]

Such equations, it should be remembered, were an important component of the broader assumption of informed response that one could read from (or through) the fictional text to the author himself, and by 1848 that assumption had become a recurrent element in Poe's reception. By the time of his death in late 1849, the idea that Poe's tales, though interesting and often brilliant, displayed a deviancy that reflected a problem in the man himself was well on its way to becoming established in the public sphere. There is little doubt, moreover, that Rufus Wilmot Griswold's infamous biography of Poe in his libelous "Ludwig" article did much to extend and disseminate this equation of Poe and his tales.[97] But in depicting Poe as having a moral and mental character only slightly above such creations as Roderick Usher, William Wilson, or the criminal narrators of "The Black Cat" and "Tell-Tale Heart," Griswold was following, not inventing, the interpretive assumption that the points of view and characters of Poe's tales were an extension of the man.

Nor was Griswold the last of Poe's readers before the Civil War to interpret Poe and his fiction in this way. Just after Poe's death, an article in the *Model American Courier* explained how Poe "passed his hours in studies which were only pursued in chambers litten [*sic*] with sepulchral lamps, of various colored chemical fires, which he afterward described in the spirit-haunted apartment of the Lady Rowena" in "Ligeia."[98] Extrapolating to a higher level of generalization, a trio of reviews in the *Southern Literary Messenger* in March 1850 told its readership that "nearly all of Poe's tales are biographical," being marked by a "despair, [a] hopelessness[,] and the echoes of a melancholy extremely touching to those who read with remembrance of his broken life" (174, 180). Less than a year later, the *Democratic Review* employed almost the same phrasing to claim of Poe, "Nearly all that he wrote in the last two or three years . . . was in some way biographical" (Jan. 1851: 162). So close were man and tale, so aligned were writer and created character in this formulation that an 1853 article in the *National Magazine* presented Poe as a warning against intemperance by claiming that his tales, "unhealthy" in their adherence to "the dyspeptic school," are colored by "the shadow of mania a potu" that shaded the writer's own life.[99]

The final irony in the antebellum reception of Poe's fiction is that even some of those who came to his defense and to the defense of his tales against the charges of Griswold, Clark, and others contributed to the reading of Poe as a version of his criminal and haunted narrators and to the assumption that his tales' characters were dark reflections of the man himself. In the *American Whig Review* in 1850, George Peck defended Poe against his attackers by praising his genius and arguing that for thoughtful readers, "Poe's stories must be healthy diet." In the course of his defense, however, Peck concluded that "in several passages in his tales Poe has unintentionally personated himself" (Mar. 1850: 305). More poignant was the brief book-length work on Poe published by his friend and admirer Sarah Helen Whitman in 1860. Part recollection, part impassioned defense of Poe and his writings against the calumnies of Griswold and company, Whitman's version of Poe duplicated the interpretive logic of the very readers she hoped to counter. In seeking to explain the complexity of the man and his work, she pointed out that in "Ligeia" "we look into the haunted chambers of the poet's own mind and see, as through a veil, the strange experiences of his inner life." In her reading, tales such as "Morella," "Elenora," and "Ligeia" are narratives in which "the author's mind seems struggling desperately and vainly with the awful mystery of Death." Indeed, claimed Whitman, all of Poe's "graver narratives" are "attributable, not so much to a delicate artistic purpose, as to that power of vivid and intense conception that made his dreams realities, and his life a dream."[100] As the troubled and misunderstood romantic genius, Whitman's Poe is the spontaneous maker whose mind and temperament are reflected in the character of his prose and the nightmares of his characters.

The image of Poe as the tortured soul whose own psyche resides in the narrators, characters, and atmospherics of his tales hardly ended with these defenses or even with the nineteenth century. Interpretations of his stories as indices to the man, rendered by narrators who in some way serve as Poe's psychological doubles, continued throughout the twentieth century, even among some Poe scholars.[101] Yet to stress this point is not to imply that such responses have "misread" Poe's tales and thereby provided an inaccurate version of his fiction—and of Poe himself. From the perspective of historical hermeneutics, the significance of such responses and of their continued currency, both in and outside the academy, lies in their being the legacy of reception events that first took shape as interpretations of Poe's fictions constructed by the codes of antebellum informed reading.

CHAPTER 4

Multiple Audiences and Melville's Fiction

Receptions, Recoveries, and Regressions

I**F EDGAR ALLAN POE** had one of the keenest senses of audience among antebellum fiction writers, Herman Melville was not far behind. Though never as obsessive as Poe in conceptualizing his readership, Melville came to fiction writing through experiences that helped make him aware of, and at times deeply sensitive to, audience responses to his tales.[1] Those encounters were initially oral and face-to-face, first aboard the whale ships and the man-of-war he sailed on from 1840 to 1844 and then at home in Lansingburgh, New York, where he found opportunities and encouragement to hone his story-telling abilities by relating to family and friends narratives of his nautical exploits.[2] Ultimately, however, the same public discussion in which Poe was involved became Melville's main index to ideas about his relation to readers. While never an inveterate reader of periodicals or deeply involved in the world of reviewing, Melville was—or would become with the publication of his first novel, *Typee*—habitually drawn to reviews of his own fiction. He developed from them not only a sense of informed reading but also a rough working conception of the audience he would need to engage with his narratives.[3] Melville, in fact, is a striking case of a writer whose career in the antebellum literary marketplace—involving the reception of his fictions and his conceptions of his craft—was shaped by the way his fiction was read and discussed in the public sphere. For those conceptions underwent significant changes amid the shifting seas of his public reception during his fiction-writing career in the 1840s and 1850s.

Scholars and critics over the past seventy-five years have largely agreed about the pattern of that career. Melville began in 1845 as a writer seeking popular success, but during the growth of his literary ambitions while composing *Moby-Dick* (or, as some maintain, as early as *Mardi*) he reconceived the role of the fiction writer as a kind of double agent (or aesthetic confidence man) who composed for two audiences, which he defined in his 1850 essay "Hawthorne and His Mosses" as the "superficial skimmer of pages" and the "eagle-eyed reader."[4] However, in the wake of disappointing sales and responses, first to *Mardi* and then two to three years later to *Moby-Dick*, Melville grew increasingly antagonistic toward his contemporary readership to the point where he virtually turned his back on his audience before abandoning his career as a professional fiction writer.[5]

As a critical consensus, this master narrative of Melville's career has a hefty weight of credibility. Melville clearly was dismayed on a number of occasions with the responses to his books, referring to some reviewers at one point as "so many numskulls" and announcing in an 1849 letter to his friend Evert Duyckinck that "an author can never—under no conceivable circumstance—be at all frank with his readers." In tones almost of despair, he lamented to Hawthorne two years later that "not one man in five cycles, who is wise, will expect appreciative recognition from his fellows, or any one of them. . . . [W]e pigmies must be content to have our paper allegories but ill comprehended."[6] Moreover, his frustration and ambivalence toward the antebellum reading public waxed as Melville's career wore on in the 1850s.

Nevertheless, this version of Melville's relationship with his audience is both jaundiced and oversimplified. The two-tiered audience theory Melville articulated overtly in "Hawthorne and his Mosses" was not the product of a sudden inspiration charged by his galvanic encounter with Hawthorne's stories in 1850. Melville had been thinking about multiple audiences since *Typee*. More importantly, he never acrimoniously abandoned the reading public during his fiction-writing career, nor did he even become exclusively—or even primarily—antagonistic toward his contemporary readers. Instead, amid a mixture of successes, disappointments, celebrations, and frustrations, Melville repeatedly sought to redefine for himself the nature and shape of the multiple audiences he projected, and he struggled to adjust his fictions to them. In this regard, Lawrence Buell has suggested that "our view of Melville may become more usefully complicated if we impute to him a multiple and shifting notion of the implied reader."[7] What needs attention is not only the shape of that transforming projection but the angst and hopefulness that characterized Melville's attempts to wrestle with it in the face of the reception his works received.

In this facet of authorship some affinities between Melville and Poe certainly existed. Like Poe, Melville believed, at least in part, that authorship was "an exercise in freedom," as Wai-chee Dimock has put it;[8] however, for Melville it was not a freedom from readerly control or a freedom by the writer to control the reader. It was a freedom to tell the truth to the audience—and if need be, at times, in spite of the audience. More than Poe, Melville also came to understand that authorial freedom vis-à-vis the fiction-reading public was more a matter of desire than a fully achievable end. He did not seek the kind of authorial domination over readers that Poe so ardently craved. To be sure, Melville had his egotisms, which included an attraction to the romanticized idea of imperial authorship.[9] He also shared the conception within informed reading that the great writer was both a genius and a mesmerizer, and, like Poe, he could occasionally express contempt for popular appeal as "mere mob renown," as he disparagingly termed it in "Hawthorne and His Mosses."[10] Melville, however, expressed in that essay his strong attraction to an idea of authorship as a practice that could "breathe the unshackled democratic spirit" (249), and he subscribed to the conception within informed reading that the great writer could speak to a broad and diverse audience, educating and entertaining readers of various stamps. For Melville, the majestic writer needed to be a democratic leader of learning and insight, who could guide the populace as a man of the people.[11]

To say this is not to characterize Melville as a naive optimist about the fiction-reading public, the literary marketplace, or even his own abilities. Besides repeatedly struggling, as Elizabeth Renker has demonstrated, with the physical act of writing itself, Melville believed that "a certain tragic phase" marked the labors of any serious writer. However, his commitment to democratic authorship, enhanced by his attraction to the politics of liberal romanticism, fueled in him a belief that the truly democratic author would redefine the relationship between authorship and audience, the individual and the mass, the learned and the popular.[12]

To achieve that end Melville concluded that form would be a factor in any such engagement. As Ann Douglas has pointed out, Melville "increasingly grasped that the author meets his reader's expectations or doesn't, earns his reader's trust or fails to, punishes or rewards his reader through form," since form offers "the negotiating ground for writer and reader."[13] In this light, Sheila Post-Lauria has argued that Melville's novels themselves, especially in the way they combine genres and interlard forms, testify to Melville's desire to engage multiple audiences by supplying different elements to different types of readers.[14] There is, of course, a problematic circularity in going to the novels themselves for evidence about implied audiences and strategies for engaging readers, since the evidence supposedly "in" those texts is itself a product of a reader's interpretive acts. Yet other indicators do exist to support the claim that Melville repeatedly engaged his readers in a variety of ways via shifting strategies—most notably his discursive remarks in letters to his publishers and literary confidantes, but also the very responses that constituted the core of his literary reception. In this regard a suggestive and representative index—if not to intention, at least to impact—comes in a comment in an 1857 review of the *Confidence-Man*. In looking over Melville's career as a fiction writer, this contributor to the British *Westminster and Foreign Quarterly Review* explained that the novel's titular character is "like Mr. Melville in his earlier works," because in those previous fictions Melville "asks confidence of everybody under different masks of mendicancy, and is, on the whole, pretty successful."[15] Whatever Melville's specific intentions were, his continual struggle to engage an audience led him to produce pre-texts that his contemporary readers repeatedly found to be composed of diverse forms that bespoke Melville's effort—often for ill as for good effect, according to the codes of informed reading—to redefine "under different masks" his relations with readers.

Melville's antebellum reception, therefore, is significant not only for what it tells us about what it meant to read his fiction before the Civil War or what such reading suggested to Melville about himself and his art. That reception also bears examination for what it indicates about the widespread twentieth-century critical interpretation of Melville as a writer increasingly alienated from his contemporary readership. For if that view is an oversimplification of the complexity of Melville's conception of audience, it is an interpretation that stems from the responses of antebellum readers and reviewers who, by the mid-1850s, were reading Melville as a writer increasingly prone to turn his back on his audience. Like their modern counterparts, a part of Melville's contemporary audience subscribed to such an interpretation of his fiction as a method for making sense of his career. The difference between the two resides in the fact that for twentieth-century scholars and students the alienated Melville they have constructed represents the tragically heroic Melville, misunderstood by his contemporaries and increasingly defiant of their simplistic responses, which trivialized his most ambitious work, from *Mardi* and *Moby-Dick* to *Pierre* and *The Confidence-Man.* For antebellum readers, however, the disdainful Melville was an interpretive formulation developed to comprehend his later novels as a falling away from the early achievements of *Typee* and *Omoo*—a decline that resulted because a successful and promising writer had given up on his obligations to his craft and to his audience.

😀

Antebellum readers certainly agreed with the twentieth-century view that Melville's first novel was composed for broad accessibility. A review in the *Charleston Southern Patriot* explained that *Typee* "reminds us of those delightful volumes of our boyhood, the voyages of Cook, Carteret, Byron and Anson, over the plates and pages of which we so loved to linger (Apr. 25, 1846, *CR* 47), while the *New York Morning News* said that it "has the sufficiency . . . to be one of the most agreeable, readable books of the day" (Mar. 18, 1846, *CR* 17–18). Such remarks were repeatedly echoed in the approximately 150 reviews of *Typee* that appeared in American magazines and newspapers from Maine to New Orleans—a number that made *Typee* Melville's most talked about novel. That public notoriety was matched by a popularity among the book-buying audience. The first American edition of two thousand copies rapidly sold out following its March 1846 appearance, and by January 1849 Wiley and Putnam, Melville's American publisher, had sold 6,380 copies of the 6,500 they had printed. Though not a bestseller when compared to such novels as *Uncle Tom's Cabin, The Wide, Wide World,* or *Ruth Hall, Typee* clearly was a popular success among middle-class readers and reviewers.[16]

If we ask what made *Typee* so popular, no single answer will do, but one factor certainly was the politics of American expansionism that gave the book a ringing topicality. U.S. involvement in the Pacific had been in the news since 1842 when the French sent a squadron of ships to annex the Marquesan Islands and Tahiti under protest from the United States, which had had interests in those archipelagoes ever since one of its agents had unofficially claimed them for the United States nearly thirty years before. Only a year after the French action, an even larger controversy developed over the Hawaiian (a.k.a. Sandwich) Islands, when the British under Lord George Paulet provisionally claimed that group before "formally relinquishing" them to the United States later that year. Making such events especially newsworthy was President John Tyler's declaration of U.S. policy in December 1842, which, for all intents and purposes, extended the Monroe Doctrine to the Pacific to include the Sandwich Islands. That look westward was part of an imperial design that included in this period the northwest section of Mexico and the Oregon Territory. Not insignificantly, the same issue of *Hunt's Merchants' Magazine* that carried a brief review of *Typee* (May 4, 1846) also had a lengthy article on "The Value of Oregon," helping to link Melville's book with popular interest in America's "Manifest Destiny."[17]

Other reviewers were even more explicit in suturing Melville's book to the logic of empire and the popular interest in the westward "destiny" of the United States. Referring to Polynesia as a "region [that] is destined to a rapid rise in Historical and Geographical importance" and where "[r]ecent events . . . have attracted much attention," a review in the *Southern Literary Messenger* alerted readers to "the work of Mr. Melville" by focusing on the passages of *Typee* that recount the "motives of the French occupation of Tahiti, and the provisional cessation of the Sandwich Islands to Lord Paulet" (Apr. 1846: 256). Similar connections appeared in a review of *Typee* in the *United States Magazine and Democratic Review* and the *Anglo American Magazine*.[18] What such remarks indicate is that one attraction to *Typee* lay in the way readers found in it what they were looking for. Coming to the book with an interpretive expectation that any good narrative should have a didactic purpose, readers discovered in Melville's volume information about far-flung places about which their interest already had been aroused.

Not that *Typee* was absolutely novel as a travel narrative offering a "peep" at its exotic locale. As the *Literary World* remarked a few years later, what readers found in Melville's narrative was "pretty much the identical things" that had been available "in the pages of Bougainville, Onga, Ellis, and Earle."[19] Indeed, only a month before *Typee* was published in the United States, *Littell's Living Age* ran a two-page review of John Coulter's *Adventures in the Pacific*, which it described as a book expressly meeting the expectations of "readers [who] feel a strange kind of interest in nautical adventure removed from the routine of civilization" (Jan. 1846: 71). From the early 1830s, following the publication of Charles Stewart's *A Visit to the South Seas* (1831), the audience for an "informative treatment of the South Seas," according to Leon Howard, was growing, and to meet that readership "travel literature dealing with the region had been increasing in quantity for more than a decade."[20] This lack of novelty in *Typee*, however, actually contributed to reader interest because readers could find in Melville's book more of what they already had been exposed to and had thoroughly enjoyed. That pleasurable redundancy involved the information they discovered in *Typee* as well as fulfillment of expectations about genre, since the public reception of *Typee* linked it to *Robinson Crusoe*, the foremost travel narrative of adventurous encounters with the exotic, which was a favorite with antebellum readers. From the *New York Weekly Tribune* and *Daily and Weekly Mirror* to the *Richmond Enquirer, Cincinnati Morning Herald,* and *Washington National Intelligencer,* reviewers repeatedly remarked on the similarity between *Typee* and Daniel Defoe's narrative in both subject matter and treatment.[21]

Not to be ignored as a factor of popularity was another link readers made, only this one involved a different precedent available via periodical reviews. That factor consisted of the reviews of *Typee* in British magazines, which on the whole were quite positive. Melville was one of the few American authors at the time to circumvent the lack of international copyright laws by arranging for simultaneous publication of his novels in England and America. For his first six books—including *Typee*—that arrangement actually entailed having the British edition of each in print roughly a month before its American twin. Consequently, the first British reviews of any one novel had already made their way across the Atlantic and were available to both the novel-reading public and reviewers in America just as the American edition was coming off the presses. It was not uncommon, therefore, for the early American reviews of Melville's first six books to refer (often approvingly) to what had been said about them in the *London Spectator, Athenaeum,* and *John Bull.* For *Typee* that meant that the laudatory British responses were already available as a precedent facilitating American enthusiasm about the narrative.[22]

Placing *Typee* in relation to previous works enabled readers to see it as, among other things, an adventure narrative, a travelogue, and a nautical reminiscence, and for some reviewers this diversity was a central part of the book's charm. As the *New York Morning News* explained, "Typee, in fact, is a happy hit whichever way you look at it, whether as travel, romance, poetry, or humor" (Mar. 18, 1846, *CR* 17). For others, however, such a diversity marked a problem because it raised uncertainty about exactly what genre *Typee* belonged to. One troubling dimension of this concern involved a question first raised by several British reviews. Although John Murray, Melville's British publisher, had put out the book as part of his Home and Colonial Library, which consisted entirely of works of nonfiction, several British reviewers wondered if *Typee* was an authentic autobiographical work.[23] By April, similar doubts were being raised in the *New York Evangelist* and the *Morning Courier.* Even the *Albany Argus,* which defended the book's authenticity, pointed out that some American readers were taking *Typee* as "a beautiful fiction" that was "too strange to be true" (Apr. 21, 1846, *CR* 47).

For some, the smoking musket lay in their encounter with the early part of the book, particularly the account of Melville/Tommo (the two had to be one if this were nonfiction) and Toby's jungle rovings and descent into the Typee valley. The reviewer in the *National Intelligencer* thought that "[t]here is a great poetic exaggeration in the height of cliffs and waterfalls and the depth of chasms, across which our fugitives make their way to the vale of Typee" that did not square with what the reviewer had found in previous accounts, such as David Potter's 1815 *Journal of a Cruise Made to the Pacific Ocean.* The *Intelligencer* also remarked that "the tumbling over the sides of precipices, so judiciously practiced by Herman and Toby . . . is a thing which has no possibility out of romance. A more enormous sailor's *yarn* has seldom been heard" (May 27, 1847, *CR* 74). Nor was such doubt expressed only in public. In a letter, George Duyckinck reported reading the same section of the novel with a skepticism that prevented him from "taking it for sober verity." Duyckinck found that Melville's "exploits in descending the waterfalls beat Sam Patch," the legendary folk figure.[24]

For others the problem was not any one part of the book; instead, it was the prevailing impression that the narrative read very much like a romance, a term that the *Southern Patriot,* the *Argus,* and the *Boston Universalist Review,* among others, applied to *Typee.* Here the interpretive link to *Robinson Crusoe* proved as much of a problem as a boon, for if *Typee* were like Defoe's novel, then by generic affiliation it had to be fiction. Indeed, for some, the resemblance between *Typee* and other fictional travel narratives was clear. For a reviewer in the *Boston Post,* that meant placing *Typee* "with Robinson Crusoe and Gulliver" (May 5, 1847, *CR* 101). The *Morning Courier and New York Enquirer* went further, declaring overtly that *Typee* "is a *fiction* . . . from beginning to end" (Apr. 17, 1846, *CR* 46).

More was involved in this issue of the genre of *Typee* than mere taxonomy. Within the codes of informed reading, it was a question of how to interpret and value the book, including the implied role Melville was asking his readers to assume. Deciphering genre affected interpretations of what readers construed as the two key thematic or philosophical issues the book raised: the contrast between primitivism and civilization and the role of Christian missions in the Pacific islands. What was Melville saying about the civilized-primitive dichotomy and about the missionaries? Most readers agreed that some kind of criticism was going on in the treatment of both of these ideas in *Typee* but disagreed over what it was and what it portended.

A few reviewers interpreted *Typee* as an unconscionable attack on missionary work in the Pacific and by extension an unacceptable attack on Christianity itself. As several Melville scholars have pointed out, these responses appeared primarily in a smattering of religious periodicals in New York and Boston.[25] Yet such responses no doubt reflected more than the reactions of a few cantankerous evangelical reviewers, since such magazines prided themselves on representing the sentiments and beliefs of members of the denominations with which they were aligned. Moreover, the same critical reactions occurred in several secular magazines such as the *American Whig Review,* which called the book's criticism of the Pacific missions "prejudiced and unfounded" (Apr. 1846, *CR* 35). Part of the problem for such readers was the genre issue, for if *Typee* were a novel making an argument about religious matters, it was, in effect, an advocacy novel—and a religious one at that—and, thus, doubly suspect according to the logic of informed reading.

The objections to Melville's critiques of missionaries, though not limited to the religious press, were, nonetheless, a minor note in the responses to *Typee.* In a way, this is surprising, yet the context for the public response to what were perceived as attacks involved more than shared Christian sensibilities in the American audience. Some readers did not find Melville's treatment of the missionaries troubling because such missionary work was itself suspect for some Christians. In this period, an anti-missionary movement existed among some conservative denominations in the United States, driven by the conviction that conversion resulted from divine influence and could not be effected by human intervention. Suspicion of American Protestant missionary work in the Pacific was especially strong among Roman Catholics; thus, it is not surprising that a four-page discussion of *Typee* in an article on "Protestant Missions in the Society Islands" in the *United States Catholic Magazine* praised Melville's criticism as a welcome exposé of Protestant failures. Nor were some reviewers the only ones sympathetic to what were seen as *Typee*'s excoriation of the missions. Elizabeth Elkins Sanders, a trenchant critic of South Sea missions, defended Melville's animadversions against the "scandalous and wicked transactions . . . of the missionaries in the Sandwich Islands" in her 1848 *Remarks on the "Tour Around Hawaii,"* adding that "the degradation and suffering of the natives from intercourse with civilized men, and particularly since the introduction of christian [*sic*] missionaries, cannot be denied."[26]

Even those supportive of Pacific missionaries in some form were not necessarily troubled, since what the book actually questioned was one of the interpretive issues. Some readers took *Typee* not as a wholesale condemnation of evangelical Christianity or even of the Polynesian missions but as a legitimate corrective aimed at specific missionary errors. In the view of the *New York Morning News* (in a review reprinted a week later in the *Weekly News*), *Typee* "represents the missionary rule in the Sandwich Islands as for the most part a vulgar and miserable mismanagement. We have no respect whatsoever for a vulgar missionary . . . and we say, Show him Up by all means" (Mar. 21, 1846, *CR* 21). Similar responses appeared in the *New York Evening Mirror* and the *Newark Advertiser,* with the latter giving its "grip of approval" to Melville's "account of the character" of the natives "under the two-fold influence of sailors and missionaries" (May 10, 1847, *CR* 106). More explicitly, the *Mirror,* apparently thinking especially of chapter 26 in *Typee,* praised the way Melville candidly "treats of clerical despotism and evangelical tyranny" in the South Seas missions, particularly how "the prostitution of the natives is indirectly made a source of revenue to the clerical establishment." Although it "always is a thankless task to expose abuses of this kind," continued the *Mirror* reviewer, "Mr. Melville's remarks on the manner in which the Missionary system is conducted in Tahiti and other islands of the South Seas are deserving of serious consideration" (May 21, 1847, *CR* 110–11).

Such responses would, nonetheless, have been impossible had readers taken *Typee* as a questionable advocacy novel. What made these readings operational was that most people interpreted the book not as fiction but as a factual account tinged with poetry and romance. The *Cincinnati Morning Herald,* for instance, asserted, "The narrative is worthy of the author of Robinson Crusoe in style and in interest, with the additional advantage of being a simple record of facts" (Apr. 3, 1846, *CR* 38), while the *Boston Harbinger* said that "there is no doubt of the facts" in *Typee,* even though Melville had "embellished the facts from his own imagination," since he sought to render "an indefinite amount of romance mingled with the reality of his narrative" (Apr. 4, 1846: 264). According to *Debow's Review, Typee* has "all the attraction of elevated romance" even as "it gives truthful views of life in the far distant isles of the sea" (Nov. 1849: 465). Privately, Sophia Hawthorne expressed the same idea in a letter to her mother, in which she called *Typee* "a *true history,* yet how poetically told—the divine beauty of the scene, the lovely faces and forms."[27] Indeed, the quality of being romanticized nonfiction, according to many readers, constituted a salient part of the charm of *Typee,* and their responses provide a further index to the book's popularity. The *Southern Literary Messenger* called it "a new chapter in book-making. Nothing like its poetic reality had ever before issued from traveled brains" (Apr. 1851: 256). Likewise, the *Springfield Republican* claimed, "It is no small merit in the author, to have written a book so consistent in its details, and so plausible" while also having the "*coleur de rose* . . . thrown round the incidents related [which] seems to reside in the author's mind" (July 7, 1846, *CR* 80).

Taking *Typee* as nonfiction with an aura of romance did not preclude interpretive debate about what was seen as its other—and, for some, more troubling—major thematic concern: the relative merits of civilization and primitivism. Some reviewers interpreted *Typee* as an indictment tout court of civilization (which they equated to Western civilization) and an unabashed panegyric to primitivism—a view that caused them to object to the book as a naive or misguided idealization. The *New York Morning News* offered a tempered version of this response, terming Typee a "rose colored account of a tropical race" that idealizes the islanders as if they were "performers in some rich ballet rather than as actual inhabitants of this labor stricken earth" (Mar. 18, 1846, *CR* 17). More vituperative was a review in the *Christian Parlor Magazine*, which objected to the "flagrant outrages against civilization" in *Typee* and its "palpable and absurd contradictions" regarding the supposed beatitudes of native life (July 1846, *CR* 55 and 57). The *New Haven New Englander* asserted that Melville had wandered so long among primitives that he "had forgotten . . . the advantages of civilization" and thus had succumbed to a "moral obtuseness" regarding the relative merits of savagery (July 1846, *CR* 51).

Yet again, these responses were not the only reading formulations of this thematic element in *Typee*, nor were they in the majority. Most reviewers and middle-class readers clearly found intriguing and delightful—and not at all troubling or misguided—Melville's depiction of native life as primitively exotic. Some saw the book as containing its own counterforce to its panegyric by acknowledging the rebarbative side of the primitive. As the *United States Magazine* put it, Melville may offer "pictures . . . of earth's loveliest vallies, rich with green flowers . . . with a warm, mellow light glowing over all," but he also adumbrates "shadows upon the picture," including a "dead man's head, and the fact the author was imprisoned in this lap of luxury" (July 1849, *CR* 238). If this reviewer could make sense of the ideas and events of *Typee* through the *memento mori* of the death's head, a reviewer in the *New York Evening Mirror* simply evoked the most ominous putative feature of the Typees as an index to Melville's balanced and accurate representation. Asking "What are we to think of the little paradise in savagedom?" this reviewer responded, "we see either nothing impossible or improbable in it. Very far, indeed, from being purely etherial . . . [t]he old King [Mehevi] and his retainers are strongly suggested of devouring their neighbors, and the author's lady love . . . eats raw fish" (May 21, 1847, *CR* 108–9). More was operating here than just the "transparency" of textual evidence these readers found or even the activity of filling, in a comprehensible way, the gap they located between the paradisiacal and the horrific in Melville's depiction of the Typees. Behind such responses lay an ethnocentrism that assumed Western civilization was superior to nonwestern existence and that any representations or arguments to the contrary, though engaging to read as fantasies, were undoubtedly exaggerations. Through this interpretive horizon, readers found a way to come to terms with the mixture of romance and reality they attributed to *Typee*. If Melville's work was an authentic piece of nonfiction, then a means to reconcile that status with its panegyric to primitivism in a way that made the text semantically consistent was to ascribe to the text a strategy that combined a pleasant fantasy with a narrative return of the reader to reality via the mark of the cannibal.

The response to Melville's depiction of Typee culture as a charming but clearly demarcated fantasy depended, therefore, on several elements in the audience's interpretive repertoire, and one not to be overlooked, particularly for the second response, was another form of familiarity. For many readers, Melville's idyllic depiction of the primitive was neither unsettling nor problematic because they had often seen it previously in the accounts of others who had visited the Pacific islands and described them as paradises populated by noble primitives. Alluding to such well-known works as David Porter's *Cruise Made to the Pacific Ocean* and Stewart's *Visit to the South Seas,* the *Harbinger* pointed out, in commenting approvingly on Melville's depiction of the Marquesan islanders, "All writers unite in declaring them to be the most perfect specimens of physical beauty, symmetry, and health" (Apr. 4, 1846, *CR* 39). Even Melville's championing of the primitive against the depredations of western civilization, which numerous reviewers pointed to, had been a staple of such works as Stewart's, as well as Frederick W. Beechey's *Narrative of a Voyage to the Pacific and Bering Straits* (1832) and Otto von Kotzebue's *A New Voyage Round the World* (1830), all three of which readers could find cited in *Typee* as corroborating its observations.[28]

Indeed, for many antebellum readers, the corruption and destruction of people of color by white civilization was a well-known phenomenon, as the review of *Typee* in *Graham's Magazine* reminded its audience: "It is the old story of civilization, who, whenever she goes to heathen nations, carries her eternally conflicting implements—ruin and religion" and brings in the process "disease, starvation, and death" to the natives (May 1846, *CR* 49). The *New York Gazette and Times* made a similar observation in discussing *Typee* but added an intriguing link that no doubt struck other middle-class readers: "As with the Indian of our own continent, contact with the white man, has only served to entail upon the primitive, simple and happy people of the South Sea Islands, the worst vices, and to introduce diseases, from the ravages of which the race is becoming gradually but surely extinct. This is a melancholy subject of reflection, but is one nevertheless, which can neither be denied nor extenuated" (May 11, 1847, *CR* 107). Telling here is the ideological connection between Native Americans and indigenous Polynesians as part of one overarching, implacable social pattern. As John Coward has pointed out in his history of coverage of Indian removal in the popular press, from the 1830s onward, newspapers repeatedly represented Native Americans as a people who "in contact with whites quickly lost their native virtue and took up white vices" and attributed that phenomenon to a natural deficiency that marked native incapacity to resist the inevitable inroads of white civilization. In the logic of what has been called the nineteenth-century's cult of the vanishing aborigine, white progress sadly but ineluctably doomed native peoples, including the more "noble savages," to a fated displacement and extinction.[29] By the 1840s, as interest in the South Seas increased, that ideology was being extended to the inhabitants of the Society and Sandwich Islands. For example, an article called "The Sandwich Islands" in the *Home Journal* explained that "the rapidity with which the population of these islands is decreasing is really astonishing," but while shaking its journalistic head over such a regrettable development, the *Home Journal* added that "the grand *reason,* equally applicable to all Polynesians, is, *it is the destiny of the race*" to be supplanted by "a population to be supplied" by "the three great maritime powers" of Britain, France, and the United States (Sept. 15, 1849: 3). In *Typee,* accordingly, the antebellum audience could read Melville's laments about the destruction of native people in the Pacific as one more reassuring instance of the conviction that an unavoidable cost of civilization's destined, progressive advance was the contamination of natives and their inevitable "disappearance."

When taken as a whole, the antebellum reception of *Typee* suggests that Melville had produced a pre-text that had reached various interpretive communities within the larger formation of informed reading and that readers had found it engaging in various ways. That this result accorded with Melville's goals is suggested by what we know about his composition of the book and his responses to the reviews of *Typee.*

After composing the novel in 1846, he eliminated several passages that some readers might have taken as scandalous, such as his account of an erotic dance of the Lory-Lory maidens of Tamaii. Possibly at the suggestion (and perhaps the insistence) of his London publisher, he also added substantial factual material about the islanders, their folkways, and the geography of the Marquesas to contribute to the "intellectual advancement" of his audience.[30] Moreover, while Melville apparently was not much bothered by the few, albeit vituperative, objections to the book's critiques of the missionaries, he agreed to the expurgation of most of the offending passages in the second edition. In a letter to his British publisher, he explained that he was "persuaded" as to the value of the changes, since "the book is certainly calculated for popular reading." Consequently, Melville continued, "All passages which . . . offer violence to the feelings of any large class of readers are certainly objectionable."[31]

Such changes, nonetheless, raise a question. If Melville's desire for audience engagement included a concern about offending a "large class of readers," why did he include the critiques of the missionaries in the first place? One factor may have been his belief that including such claims would enhance sales by fomenting a public debate that would attract middle-class readers to *Typee* out of curiosity. Additionally, Geoffrey Sanborn has speculated that the criticisms of the missionaries and of white civilization may have been "a systematic effort to draw the reader into his own paths of reflection"—particularly the middle-class audience's preconceptions about the process of civilizing and Christianizing the Pacific Islanders.[32] Such a strategy would have been in line with the protocol of informed reading that assumed self-examination was an important potential product of thoughtful reading. Of course, Melville was not naive enough to think that all—or even most—readers would so readily embrace such an opportunity; not even the most sanguine promoters of informed reading assumed such utopian results. Melville instead had to know that only a small segment of his readership might respond in that way. But that assumption itself would have entailed a recognition by Melville of multiple audiences—and multiple reader positions—for *Typee.* For if the exoticism and adventures of *Typee* were pitched to an audience interested in "popular reading," and if the descriptive sections suited informed readers who expected to be enlightened as well as entertained, the critiques could be the stuff of interest for a group within informed reading willing to face some tougher questions about the shape and consequences of the civilizing process.

What is interesting is not only that this segmentation by and large characterized audience responses but also that Melville's desire to include the criticisms and then to delete them indicated that he was trying to adjust his thinking about his audience and to conceptualize different segments or "classes" of his readership. But these shifts in his conceptualization also signal that by the end of 1846 Melville had not developed a clear idea of the various readerships he sensed were part of the public sphere and the middle-class audience. He was casting about in an unsystematic (though surprisingly successful) manner to find ways to write for that audience.

For the most part, Melville was quite pleased by the reception American readers gave *Typee* in terms of sales and the public discussion, as well as the responses to its follow-up, *Omoo,* which appeared in March and April 1847. But shortly after the first wave of reviews of *Omoo* had appeared, Melville commenced writing his third book, *Mardi,* by striking out in a somewhat different—and bolder— direction. Most Melville scholars agree that his artistic ambitions began to grow at this time, largely owing to his exposure to the works of Rabelais, Shakespeare, Dante, Coleridge, and Thomas Browne, which he was voraciously borrowing from the well-stocked library of Evert Duyckinck.[33] The influence of Duyckinck's library—and of Duyckinck himself, who had provided Melville with some preliminary advice on the manuscript of *Omoo*— dovetailed, however, with some of the less flattering reviews of *Omoo* that Melville had seen.

Two especially captious attacks appeared in the *New York Tribune* and the *American Whig Review,* both of which charged *Omoo* with being, as the *Tribune* put it, "positively diseased in moral tone" for what the reviewers saw as its salacious tendencies (June 26, 1847, *CR* 130).[34] Yet more troubling than this outburst, which was quickly countered by other reviewers who defended *Omoo* and its author, was the note first sounded by several British reviews and subsequently echoed in American magazines. What Melville and other middle-class readers had encountered in some of the British responses were comparative evaluations that found *Omoo* inferior to *Typee.* The *London Spectator* said that while *Omoo* was "equal to its predecessor" in some ways, "[t]here are not such elaborate pictures" nor "the same novelty of subject in *Omoo* as there was in *Typee* (Apr. 10, 1847, *CR* 89). Soon after, the *London Home News* called *Typee* "the cream of the author's experience," while "Omoo [*sic*] has more the flavor of skimmed milk" (Apr. 24, 1847, *CR* 94). Finding that "this sequel to the 'Adventures in the Marquesas' is comparatively deficient in romance and incident," the *London Sun* asserted, "'Typee' is pure gold to the lacquer of 'Omoo'" (Apr. 26, 1847, *CR* 95–96). Several American reviewers agreed. A review in the *Washington National Intelligencer* asserted that "to create and sustain the illusion of truth . . . Mr. Melville, in our opinion, has shown himself a great adept, in *Typee*," but "(whether from carelessness or a subject less capable of admitting invention *ad libitum*) only a considerable proficient in *Omoo*" (May 27, 1847, *CR* 73). In a similar vein, the *Knickerbocker* concluded that for attentive readers *Omoo* was an "entertaining work" that would, no doubt, be a success but "[w]ithout being equal in spirit and interest to its popular predecessor" (June 1847, *CR* 125). In the wake of the common assumption among reviewers that an author's corpus should display "progress and development," such remarks implied that Melville had not fulfilled the promise in *Typee* by advancing as a writer.[35]

The conjunction of such implications and of Melville's growing ambition was twofold. On the one hand, Melville sought to turn himself into a writer who could satisfy the expectations of more sophisticated readers— readers epitomized for Melville partly in the reviewers who had called *Omoo* inferior to *Typee* and partly in the well-read Duyckinck himself. On the other hand, Melville's opinion of *Typee* and *Omoo* underwent an alteration in light of his readings and the book he was writing. While squarely in the middle of composing *Mardi*, he told Murray that he had developed "an invincible distaste" for his erstwhile "narrative of facts" and urged Murray "not to put me down on the title page as 'the author of Typee & Omoo.' I wish to separate '*Mardi*' as much as possible from those two books."[36]

Yet in his reconceptualization Melville was neither repudiating those two texts nor renouncing everything they stood for. Nor was he turning his back on what he had sought to do with those books in his quest for a democratic authorship. On the contrary, the responses to *Omoo* and *Typee* as works of mixed genres helped Melville to think of his book-in-progress as a variform text comprehensible to multiple audiences, from the popular readers of adventure tales to the eagle-eyed literati. It is a mistake, therefore, to think of *Mardi* primarily as Melville's "declaration of independence" from contemporary reviewers or as a novel that "leaves his reader behind" as an expression of Melville's hostility to the middle-class audience.[37] With *Mardi* Melville ambitiously sought to engage more, not fewer readers, by addressing an audience both popular and sophisticated.

Part of his strategy consisted of constructing *Mardi* as a work of fiction that could look like fact, as he explained in the book's preface, though this was less a reconceptualization of his craft and more an overt recognition of what some readers saw him doing in *Omoo*. But as Melville told his audience, "[t]his thought was only the germ of others, which have resulted in Mardi."[38] His overt embrace of fiction constituted a strategic move because Melville recognized that the novel was an increasingly popular genre that had an intrinsic capacity, when handled with a reasonable degree of acumen, to entertain and enlighten audiences. Additionally, readers had already seen in his previous two books the earmarks of various types of recognizable and highly regarded fictions, from the verisimilitude of *Robinson Crusoe* to the topicality and humor of *Gulliver's Travels* to the marvelous fantasies of Baron von Munchausen. *Mardi*, in Melville's growing ambition, would have all that and more, thereby satisfying with intrepid brilliance the various expectations of a range of reading groups. As he boasted to Murray, "I doubt not that—if it makes the hit I mean it to—it will be counted a rather bold aim."[39]

Melville was not oblivious to the risks of engaging in his open-ended "voyage tither"; however, we should not attribute too much awareness on his part. He was neither closely attentive to the market nor coolly disengaged from the ambition and the heady intellectual draughts he was taking as he composed his "Romance of Polynesian Adventures." Instead, his self-confident comments to Murray, including his request for a larger-than-normal advance for his new book, suggest that he believed he could overcome the risks of writing as a bold artist because the diversity of his novel would match the variety of interests and expectations he was attributing to readers based on the various responses to *Typee* and *Omoo*. Far from being a text in which Melville was "narrowing" his projected audience, *Mardi* was to be as many things to as many readers as possible, a reading journey through Swiftian satire, Defoesque exoticism, Rabelaisian wit, Carlylesque speculation, Danteian allegory, Brownian flights of rhetoric, and more, all fueled by Melville's imaginative wanderings and capable of transporting readers on their own literary and intellectual voyages.[40]

The boldness in his letters to Murray provides an index to how badly Melville was miscalculating the situation. As a publisher of works of nonfiction, Murray had little interest in a novel, and he quickly rejected the completed manuscript of *Mardi*. Only through the efforts of a friend did Melville succeed in placing the book with the firm of Richard Bentley. Nor did Melville, as Brian Higgins and Hershel Parker point out, "give any indication of understanding how severely he might affront the goodwill of any reader" with *Mardi*.[41] It was not so much, however, a matter of Melville's "misunderstanding" or "miscalculating" as it was of his not calculating much at all. Projecting an audience so vague in its multiplicity yet so simplistic in its dichotomy between adventure-seeking masses and eagle-eyed reviewers, Melville had no clear, viable sense of an implied readership for *Mardi*. As a result, he produced a pre-text virtually guaranteed to puzzle and displease as many readers as it could hope to satisfy.

Responses came first from across the Atlantic, with a few English reviewers leading the way by setting the tone, as they had for *Typee*. Unfortunately for Melville, several set it negatively, including the review in the *London Athenaeum*, which was one of the more influential British periodicals widely available to American readers. According to the *Athenaeum*, *Mardi* did not stack up well to *Typee*, particularly in regard to audience appeal: "Among the hundred people who will take it up, lured by their remembrances of 'Typee,' ninety readers will drop off at the end of the first volume; and the remaining nine will become so weary of the hero . . . that they will throw down his chronicle ere the end of its second third is reached" (Mar. 24, 1849, *CR* 193). Other British reviewers from the *Atlas*, the *Examiner*, the *Spectator*, *Britannia*, *John Bull*, and *Blackwood's* focused on problems in the novel that some American reviewers would also find: puzzling allegories, stylistic extravagances, metaphysical obscurities, and uneven writing, particularly in the second half of the book.[42]

Mardi was not, however, a reception debacle or even the popular and critical "failure" that some modern Melvillians have termed it.[43] The

Harpers, who had become Melville's publishers beginning with *Omoo*, printed over three thousand copies of *Mardi* in its first edition, which was 50 percent more than Wiley had put out in the first American edition of *Typee*. Within six months more than two thousand had sold. In its first three years, *Mardi* sold an average of 215 copies per month, or nearly 70 percent of the average *Typee* had enjoyed in its initial three years.[44] Part of the difference can be attributed to price. A much larger work, *Mardi* sold for $1.75 in its cloth edition and $1.50 in paper—three times the retail price of *Typee* and *Omoo* and high enough to deter purchase by readers in the lower-middle-class income range. Though British sales lagged far behind what *Typee* and *Omoo* had garnered, *Mardi* matched or exceeded the figures for *Redburn* and *White-Jacket*, the two novels most Melville scholars identify as his "comeback" books following *Mardi*.[45]

Moreover, despite the negative grains that peppered British responses, American reviewers' comments on *Mardi* hardly justify the modern critical view that "the reception of *Mardi* is a striking example of the way in which the general readers' latent, deep-rooted hatred of the seriously experimental is flushed to the surface by a work that takes him off base."[46] Such a characterization is another version of the canonical view of Melville as the brilliant, avant-garde artist misunderstood by the narrow and benighted antebellum audience, and it misrepresents the diversity within the public responses and overlooks reviewer attentiveness to the challenging yet engaging variety they found in *Mardi*. Quite in line with Melville's hopes of achieving a multifarious appeal matched to the novel's projected readerships, several periodicals pointed to *Mardi* as a narrative feast offering various types of reading delectables. According to the *New York Albion*, "Parts may be read by the most careless reader, and be enjoyed in the doze of a summer's afternoon—other parts require a wide-awake application or . . . one half the aroma will be lost" (Apr. 21, 1849, *CR* 215). The *Evening Mirror* went further in offering a catalog of both the novel's diversity and the various readers to which its elements would appeal: "Mardi [*sic*], with all its fascinations, its unique style, its beautiful language, its genial humor, its original thought, its graphic descriptions, its poetic flights, its powerful reasonings, its philosophical reflections, . . . stretches before us like a new world, and the mental eye can never weary of gazing upon its strangely beautiful landscape. Here are points of interest for every mind. The scholar can feast upon its classic allusions, the man of erudition can add to his store, . . . the philosopher meet with things startling, the child find entertainment, and genius salute the author as the rising sun" (Apr. 13, 1849, *CR* 207). Even if we take this reviewer's enthusiasm as a hyperbole that may signal a "puff," the idea that *Mardi* marked Melville as a "rising sun" was not a claim unique to the *Evening Mirror*. The *Home Journal* declared, "'Mardi' is in a higher vein than 'Typee' or 'Omoo'" owing to its being "richer in description, fuller of incident, with more humor, wit, character" (Apr. 21, 1849, *CR* 215). The *Literary World* and the *New York Morning Herald* agreed, with the former asserting, "it is evident to us that so far from any flagging from the interest of his previous works, 'Mardi' is, as might have been anticipated, an onward development" (Apr. 7, 1849, *CR* 206).

Besides the multidimensionality and growth these reviewers found, readers discovered in *Mardi* none of the objectionable or problematic elements of *Typee*: the critiques of the missionaries and the question of whether they were reading fiction or nonfiction. Pointing to the book's preface, everyone agreed that *Mardi*, as *Graham's* put it, was "an acknowledged romance" (June 1849, *CR* 235). Readers also could find in it much that looked attractively familiar. The title itself was reminiscent of the exotic-sounding titles that had come to be associated with Melville through *Typee* and *Omoo*. Then too, the plot and events, at least in the first half of the novel, met the audience's horizon of expectations. According to the *Albany Argus*, "the first hundred pages" are in "Mr. Melville's happiest style," recognizable as an autobiographical (i.e., first-person) narrative of "ocean solitudes and the adventures of a whale boat" (May 17, 1849, *CR* 227).

Nor were readers necessarily wearied or stymied by the remainder of the novel, as the Athenaeum had predicted. While the characters of *Mardi* did pose interpretive problems to some readers, others engaged in an allegorical reading to make sense of the book's personages. According to an article in the *Literary World*, Yillah "should represent 'human happiness' sacrificed by the priests," while Queen Hautia is an emblem of "voluptuousness" (Aug. 11, 1849, *CR* 246). Even those who had trouble making such clear interpretive moves made sense of the novel's characterization by reading it through a generic code and the principle of compensation. Though admitting that "Babbalanja philosophizing drowsily, or the luxurious sybaritical King Media . . . are all shrouded dimly in opiate-fumes, and dream-clouds," a review in *Putnam's Monthly* explained that readers can "accept it as a rhapsody." Since *Mardi* was clearly a suggestive allegorical romance, "[w]hatever they say or do; whether they . . . eat silver fruits, or make pies of emeralds and rubies . . . we feel perfectly satisfied that it is all right, because there is no claim made upon our practical belief."[47] Indeed, according to the *Southern Quarterly Review*, the characters of *Mardi* can best be understood emblematically as part of a "fanciful voyage about the world in search of happiness" (Oct. 1849, *CR* 250).

Such allegorical readings represented the most common strategy that antebellum readers invoked for making sense of *Mardi*. Several reviewers pointed in particular to the voyages to Dominora, Vivenza, and Diranda from chapters 138–50 to conclude that "the continents are but isles in Mardi—Mardi is the world," as the *Literary World* explained before going on to interpret "this isle of Dominora and its king Bello, of Vivenza, this Porpheero" as "marvelously like John Bull, America, and Republican France" (Apr. 21, 1849, *CR* 217). In like manner, the *Albion* found in *Mardi* "some delicate satire . . . on men and things in our own and other countries," which were discernible once readers understood that "the United State [is] plainly enough portrayed in *Vivenza*, the British Isles in *Dominora*, *Kaleedoni*, and *Verdanna*, France in *Franco*, and Canada in *Kanneeda*" (Apr. 21, 1849, *CR* 215). A reprint of a foreign essay on Melville in the *Literary World* alerted readers that the allegory went beyond the social. Taji's visit to Alma and Serenia needed to be understood as a spiritual allegory in which "Alma represents the Savior; Serenia his domain" (Aug. 11, 1849, *CR* 248).

These allegories, however, proved a source of consternation for other readers. The *Tribune* felt that the second half of *Mardi* was marred by a "vein of mystic allegory" composed of "transcendental, glittering, soap-bubble speculations" (Dec. 1, 1849, *CR* 288). *Saroni's Musical Times* objected that in the course of the novel "we are taken bodily, and immersed into the fathomless sea of Allegory from which we have just emerged, gasping for breath, with monstrous Types, Myths, Symbols, and such like fantastic weeds" (Sept. 29, 1849, *CR* 249). Nor was this response confined to some reviewers. Melville's wife, Elizabeth, expressed a similar frustration when she commented in a letter to her mother about being "deep in the 'fogs' of 'Mardi.'"[48]

The irony in some of these objections to *Mardi* was that the assumption that Melville was writing (exclusively or primarily) fiction, though helpful in one way, also led readers to apply codes of fiction reading in a way that led to strong criticism. Some readers found that the obscurity of *Mardi* resulted from the excessive erudition of the allegories. This complaint was in part an objection to "learned fiction," based on the belief that such writing wrongly left out or spoke over the heads of too many readers. But it was also a matter of such fiction being ostentatious and affected. For instance, the *American Whig Review* commented that in *Mardi* "[e]very page of the book undoubtedly exhibits a man of genius, . . . but exhibits also pedantry and affectation. . . . We half suspect, however, that Mr. Melville has intended this as a quiz, but at any rate he has overdone it, and made a tedious book" (Sept. 1849, *CR* 248–49). A reviewer in the *Weekly Chronotype* found *Mardi* marred by an "unconscionably pretentious style . . . and a wild license of the fancy which make his book a glittering Mosaic of obscurity and affectation" (June 9, 1849, *CR* 236). According to a review in the *Southern Literary Messenger*, in *Mardi* "there is . . . a continual straining after effect, an effort constantly at fine writing, a sacrifice of natural ease to artificial wittiness" to the point where "every page fairly reeks of 'the smoke of the lamp'" (May 1849, *CR* 223–24). Similar remarks elsewhere pointed to a common conclusion. Overly fond of his own erudition, Melville had engaged in an excessive display of learning that caused him to intrude himself on every page of his narrative in direct violation of what informed reading insisted was a mark of good fiction writing.

Reviewers also responded negatively to elements of the novel's plot or what they felt was a lack thereof. *Holden's* found "no story to interest" but only "a dreamy kind of voluptuousness" (June 1849, *CR* 235), while the *Tribune* complained "[t]he story has not movement, no proportion, no ultimate end . . . winding its unwieldy length along, like some monster of the deep, [with] no significant point" (May 10, 1849, *CR* 226). The reviewer in *Putnam's Monthly* punned, "[w]e would just as soon undertake to give anybody a connected and coherent account of the *Mardi gras* of Paris, on coming out of the *Bal de l'Opéra* at three in the morning" as try to recount the plot of Melville's novel.[49]

Negative responses to the text most frequently targeted what some had seen as the novel's asset: its multifariousness. To a number of reviewers, *Mardi* seemed a farrago of literary forms, which caused it to lack a coherent generic profile. The *Richmond Watchman and Observer* felt that "the form of the book is a . . . sort of a cross between the Pilgrim's Progress, Gulliver's Travels, [and] Sartor Resartus" that causes it to be a "peculiar" amalgam (circa May 12, 1849, *CR* 226–27). The *Tribune* gave a darker tint to its observation along this line, calling *Mardi* "a monstrous compound of Carlyle, Jean-Paul, and Sterne, with now and then a touch of Ossian" (May 10, 1849, *CR* 225). For such readers, it was not only that *Mardi* was a curious compound of various styles, modes, and genres but also that these forms were not integrated. According to *Graham's*, "'Mardi' is of the composite order of mental architecture and the various rich materials are not sufficiently harmonized to produce a unity of effect." Owing to its ill-conceived mingling of "chapters of description, sketches of character, flashes of fanciful exaggeration, and capital audacities of satire, . . . confusion, rather than fusion, characterize the book as a whole" (June 1849, *CR* 236). Several reviewers agreed that in trying to do so many things, Melville had not been very successful at any of them. The *Literary World* quoted a reviewer that had found Melville to be in *Mardi* a "Rabelais without gaiety, a Cervantes without grace, a Voltaire without taste" (Aug. 4, 1849, *CR* 244), while a review in the *New York Eclectic Magazine* reported that if one took *Mardi* "as an allegory, the key of the casket is 'buried in ocean deep'—if as a romance, it fails from tediousness—if as a prose poem, it is chargeable with puerility" (May 1849: 144).

Several reviewers agreed that the problem was that Melville, as the *Tribune* reviewer put it, had "failed by leaving his sphere"—the romance of reality that had characterized *Typee* and *Omoo* (May 10, 1849, *CR* 226). Indeed, asserted the *Boston Post*, Melville would have done "better [to] stick to his 'fact' which is received as 'fiction,' . . . than fly to 'fiction' which is not received at all" and which has made "'Mardi' . . . inferior to 'Typee' and 'Omoo'" (Apr. 10, 1849, *CR* 212). The delightful gumbo that some found in *Mardi* struck others as an ill-concocted stew that left a bad taste in the mouths of readers who had savored the flavors of *Typee* and *Omoo*.

Taken as a whole, therefore, the responses to *Mardi* constituted a mixed reception, but it was a troubling mix for Melville's own sense of where he stood with his audience. If *Typee* and *Omoo* had received praise and some blame, at least Melville could find in the responses what had seemed a clear mandate: He should continue giving the popular audience a good story that at once informed and enlightened, but he ought to reach out to more readers—especially more sophisticated ones—in a way that would demonstrate his growth as an author. Although Melville may have thought that he had achieved those goals with his most ambitious novel to date, readers who found *Mardi* wanting were doing so on the very grounds on which he had staked his art of fiction. The public reception of the novel also appeared to give him contradictory messages: that is, that he had successfully produced a rollicking, multifaceted novel that was also a botched collection of disparate forms, cryptic ideas, and meretricious styles, and that in turning from romances of reality to pure fiction he had engaged a variety of reader interests while improperly forefronting his own authorial presence at the expense of his audience's needs.

Melville's reaction was predictable. In a letter to Duyckinck he said that *Mardi* had been "stabbed at" by reviewers, while to Bentley he described the public discussion of the novel as having "fired quite a broadside into 'Mardi.'" Given the mixed nature of the responses to the book, Hugh Hetherington is right to say that Melville "was exaggerating the hostility of the world's reaction."[50] Yet Melville's response is not surprising in light of the hopes and effort he had poured into his third novel. It is interesting, moreover, to watch Melville in his letter to Bentley attempt to come to terms with the reception of *Mardi*. In trying to decipher what had gone wrong, Melville focuses on the relation between features of the novel and various segments of the audience; he concludes that the problem lay in segmented mismatches between the two. He opines that *Mardi*'s "having been brought out . . . in the ordinary novel format must have led to the disappointment of many readers." Then, too, he explains, "the metaphysical ingredients (for want of a better term) of the book, must of course repel some of those who read simply for amusement." Lest Bentley forget, Melville adds that "the peculiar thoughts and fancies of a Yankee . . . could hardly be presumed to delight" British reviewers.[51] Since Melville, however, had himself engaged in such a presumption and had assumed that he could write in the metaphysical mode without alienating those who read to be amused, his diagnosis is arguably less an exercise in marketplace analysis and more an expression of disguised dismay.

Although Melville was clearly projecting a good portion of his frustration at middle-class readers as much as he was feeling the "stabbings" of reviewers, it is certainly an oversimplification to claim that Melville became hostile to his readers and turned his back on them—or to claim that his frustrations with the popular readership led him to an elitist conception of audience in 1849.[52] For one thing, turning his back on the middle-class audience was not something Melville could afford to do financially. For another, some of his other comments following the reception of *Mardi* suggest that Melville was as much dismayed with the book itself (and himself as its author) as he was with the fiction-reading public. In an April letter to Evert Duyckinck, Melville had confided that his "mood had so changed" toward *Mardi* "that I dread to look into it, & have purposely abstained from doing so since I thank God it was off my hands." Later that year in one of his journal entries, he privately referred to himself as "H.M. author of 'Pedee,' 'Hullabaloo,' & 'Pog-Dog.'"[53] That comic self-deprecation suggests a writer who sees something ridiculously inadequate in his three books with exotic-sounding titles—books that in one way or another had failed at being the multifaceted texts that could reach out to diverse readers with an authoritative and democratic embrace matching their author's ambitions.

Even as the criticism of *Mardi* emerged, moreover, Melville felt that the objections were useful, much as he had assumed that the controversy over the missionaries had contributed to the public interest in *Typee*. He assured his father-in-law, Lemuel Shaw, that "[t]hese attacks [on *Mardi*] are matters of course, and are essential to the building up of my permanent reputation—if such should ever prove to be mine." Even more significant is the next sentence of this letter to Shaw, which explains that while "dunces" may think "there's nothing in it . . . Time, which is the solver of all riddles, will solve 'Mardi.'" This brief assertion signals a striking new wrinkle in Melville's thinking about audience that anticipates what Richard Brodhead has called Melville's idea of "prophetic authorship" in "Hawthorne and His Mosses."[54] The Shaw letter reveals that nearly a year before that essay, Melville was already starting to reconceptualize his audience by adding posterity to his readership and entertaining the idea that the audience of the future might well constitute his truest readers.

Perhaps Melville's most significant response to the reception of *Mardi*, however, was his dive back into fiction writing to produce two novels within six months in 1849: *Redburn*, published in October and November, and *White-Jacket*, published in the following February and March. Although we have little if any evidence of what Melville thought about *Redburn* and its relation to his readership while composing the novel, after its completion—and before the American reviews began appearing—he disparaged the novel privately to family and friends. In a letter to Duyckinck in December, Melville described himself as "a poor devil writer with duns all around him & looking over the back of his chair . . . like the devil about St: Anthony—what can you expect of that poor devil?—What but a beggarly 'Redburn!'" To his father-in-law, he virtually dismissed the novel as having little value to him or to readers: "For Redburn [*sic*] I expect no particular reception of any kind. It may be deemed a book of tolerable entertainment;—& may be accounted dull," but in either case it was a mere "job" from which "no reputation that is gratifying to me" could come.[55] Yet Melville's disparagement was more nuanced than it seems. Although he described writing *Redburn* as little more than hired manual labor, such an equation was not necessarily pejorative for Melville. Two years later he would apply a similar metaphor to writing *Moby-Dick*, referring to "my ditchers work with that book."[56] Moreover, in his letter to his father-in-law he had admitted that, despite having "felt obliged to refrain from writing the kind of book I had wished to," he nonetheless had "not repressed myself much" in producing *Redburn*.

What Melville meant by repressing himself is difficult to say, but certainly middle-class readers and reviewers found *Redburn* to be at once similar to Melville's previous work but also quite different. *Redburn* was, to be sure, a nautical novel, but rather than encountering the exotic South Pacific locales of Melville's first three books, readers found the setting of *Redburn* to be much more like that of the world they knew. That change also involved a shift in reader perceptions of generic affiliations. Instead of seeing Melville's new novel in relation to the adventurous voyages depicted by Defoe, Swift, and Munchausen, reviewers tended to relate *Redburn* to the true-to-life nautical narratives of Richard Henry Dana, James Fenimore Cooper, Tobias Smollett, and Captain Marryat.

The most common response to *Redburn,* in fact, consisted of reading it as a fiction most noteworthy for its verisimilitude. The *Literary World* praised its "fidelity to nature" and the "conviction of reality" in its "fresh natural composition of ocean life" (Nov. 10, 1849, *CR* 275–76), while the *Boston Post* found that "the great charm of the work seems to be its realness. It seems to be *fact* word for word" (Nov. 20, 1849, *CR* 279). Part of that verisimilitude readers found in the novel's characterization and dialogue, as the *New York Literary American* pointed out: "The dialogues are natural: Mr. Melville is a sailor, and he talks, acts, and writes like a sailor" (Nov. 24, 1849, *CR* 284). For others, the verisimilitude inhered in incident and exposition. The *Southern Literary Messenger* asserted, "No one, we undertake to say, can find in this sailor-boy confession any incident that might not have happened—nay that has not the air of strict probability." Not that *Redburn* was fact; rather, the illusion of reality was so strong in the book's "descriptions of life before the mast, of the sailor boardinghouses in Liverpool, of dock service and forecastle usages" that it "sometimes remind[s] us of Smollett" (Dec. 1849, *CR* 286).

However, while virtually all reviewers were struck by the novel's realism, a few raised a more troubling qualifier: the verisimilitude seemed to come at a price. According to the *Springfield Republican,* while *Redburn* had "more of an air of reality" than *Typee* or *Omoo,* "possibly it may be less interesting in consequence."[57] Despite its praise for the book's naturalness, the *Literary American* also found *Redburn* "not as fresh, striking, and imaginative, as his former productions" (284). While several reviewers deemed it an improvement over *Mardi,* others felt *Redburn* represented a dropping off from that work. *Graham's* asserted that *Redburn* "hardly has the intellectual merit of 'Mardi'" and "is less adventurous in style" (Jan. 1850, *CR* 290). According to *Littell's Living Age,* though *Mardi* had been "overwrought with romance and adventure," *Redburn* was absolutely "deficient" in those same areas to the point of being "prosy, bald, and eventless" (Aug. 1853: 483). Indeed, the most frequent response to *Redburn,* after attention to and approval of its verisimilitude, consisted of concluding that it marked a regression from Melville's first three books. In that vein, the *Home Journal* announced that

Redburn "will not perhaps raise the author's literary reputation from the pinnacle where Mardi [*sic*] placed it" (Nov. 24, 1849: 2). More often, it was the standard of *Typee* or *Omoo* of which *Redburn* was assumed to fall short. *Littell's* believed that in its characterization "one misses the breadth and finish of his corresponding description in 'Omoo'" (484), and the *Philadelphia Saturday Evening Post* explained that *Redburn* "is not equal to either 'Typee' or 'Omoo'" because instead of the "glorious islands of the Pacific," Melville has written his fourth book on "the hackneyed subject of a voyage to Liverpool" (Dec. 1, 1849: 2).

There is little record of Melville's reaction to this or any other element of the reception of *Redburn*. Supposedly on one occasion he said he had found the reviews "laughable," but if so, it was a darkly ironic comedy for Melville.[58] If he had "repressed" himself even a tad out of a desire to regrasp a broad, popular audience, the sales of *Redburn* had to be disappointing to him. Though they totaled over 2,300 copies in the United States, they failed to match the success of either *Typee* or *Omoo* and barely outgained *Mardi's* total.[59] Just as importantly, reviewers were telling Melville that he had drawn back too far and thus had come up short of the boldness of *Mardi* and the vigor of *Typee* and *Omoo*. Such results could only confirm Melville's sense that in writing *Redburn* he might as well have been cutting wood or digging ditches.

There was, however, nothing Melville could do to adjust with his next novel, since *White-Jacket* was already completed and about to appear in print as the reviews for *Redburn* were running their course. Given that situation, it is little wonder that he was quick to group *White-Jacket* with *Redburn* as another mere job. Telling himself that he thought so little of the book was a way of deflecting disappointment, since it would allow him to dismiss any negative reactions as exactly what he expected. Melville had little reason, in fact, to expect that the response to *White-Jacket* would be much different from that for *Redburn*; his fifth book was another nautical novel and was even more geared to popular appeal, since its subject—or what antebellum readers identified as its major subject— was more topical: corporal punishment and abuses in the U.S. Navy.

The question of naval discipline had recently come before public attention. During the 1848–49 legislative session, the U.S. House of Representatives witnessed a long debate over a resolution to abolish flogging in the navy, and regular newspaper reports brought the issue before the general reading public. Just as Melville was beginning *White-Jacket,* moreover, a series of articles on naval flogging had begun to appear in the *United States Magazine and Democratic Review.*[60] Upon publication of the novel, reviewers quickly positioned it amid the swirling tides of public discussion and debate. The novel's representation of and comments on flogging were some of the most frequently talked about and quoted passages, as reviewers interpreted Melville's new book as a work devoted first and foremost to the question of naval reform. While *Saroni's Musical Times* simply asserted that "'White-Jacket' discourses most eloquently on . . . the question of flogging in the Navy," which "is now attracting so much attention" (Mar. 30, 1850, *CR* 324), others specified what they saw as Melville's unmistakable position on that practice. The *Boston Evening Transcript* called *White-Jacket* a "graphic and spirited" critique of the "evil effects of the flogging and grogging system in our naval service" (Mar. 25, 1850, *CR* 317); the *Southern Quarterly Review* said that in the book Melville's "role is that of a reformer" in dramatizing "the cruel treatment usually bestowed upon the poor sailor" (July 1850, *CR* 347); and the *Biblical Repository* called the book "an exposé of the wickedness of our 'Articles of War,'" particularly of "the bad tendencies and effects of 'Flogging'" (July 1850, *CR* 347).

Reviewers did not just interpret *White-Jacket* as an exposé of flogging and other naval abuses; with just a few exceptions, they approved it as a welcomed protest. The *New York Albion* announced, "We entirely agree with Mr. Melville in his condemnation of many of the internal regulations of ships of war" (Mar. 30, 1850, *CR* 312), while the *Tribune* praised the way "Mr. Melville has performed an excellent service in revealing the secrets of his prisonhouse, and calling the public attention to the indescribable abominations of naval life, reeking with the rankest corruption of blood and cruelty" (Apr. 5, 1850, *CR* 329). "We are glad," asserted the *Boston Evening Transcript,* "to see that Mr. Melville, in the volume, ably exposes the evil effects of the flogging and *grogging* system in our naval service" (Mar. 25, 1850, *CR* 317).[61]

Such heartfelt and unqualified enthusiasm is somewhat curious. After all, everyone took *White-Jacket* as a novel, since fiction is what readers unanimously assumed Melville had been writing since *Mardi.* But if *White-Jacket* were a novel promoting a specific reform, such an interpretation meant that it belonged to the genre of advocacy fiction; thus, according to the protocols of informed reading, reviewers should have raised doubts about it as a questionable and inferior novel. Yet few did. The question, of course, is why did reviewers so overwhelmingly support and refrain from questioning what ordinarily was a problematic type of fiction?

For a number of reviewers, the book's lifelike reality swept away misgivings. The *Methodist Quarterly Review* pointed out that while "[m]any of our readers simply from the title, will suppose this to be a mere novel," it is also "a most graphic picture of the real life of a man-of-war," which enables it to expose "the evils, abuses, and, in part, crimes of the American Naval Service" (July 1850, *CR* 349). "Unlike the . . . pretending and high wrought romances of Cooper," explained the *Springfield Republican*, *White-Jacket* "deal[s] in pictures so pure and simple" that "the work cannot fail to do much in the reform" of the "baneful effect of the 'cat' and the spirit ration upon the marines in National service" (Mar. 30, 1850, *CR* 325). Indeed, reviewers often spoke about *White-Jacket's* "remarkable air of verisimilitude," its "air of simplicity and truthfulness," its "daguerreotype-like naturalness," and its "matter-of-fact minuteness of detail." One after another they grounded in such traits the book's legitimacy as a work of reform.[62] Through such moves, reviewers read *White-jacket* as a viable reformist text by interpreting it as a real-life romance: a combination of fiction and fact, dominated by the former yet ballasted enough by the latter to not be discredited as something merely "made up."

As much as reviewers took *White-Jacket* as a factual fiction through one interpretive move, the specific objectives that they identified as *White-Jacket's* purpose further enabled them to see it as unsullied by the kind of inappropriate polemics for which advocacy novels ordinarily were decried. Reviewers could accept unproblematically the advocacy profile of *White-Jacket* because they saw in it none of the highly contentious—and thus objectionable—controversy marking advocacy novels. Readers had already been exposed to similar indictments of naval practices in Charles Briggs's *Working a Passage*, Samuel Leech's *Thirty Years from Home*, William McNally's *Evils and Abuses in the Naval Service Exposed*, and, most importantly, Dana's *Two Years Before the Mast*, as well as the series of articles in the *United States Magazine and Democratic Review*.

In the public reports, discussions, and debates, opinion repeatedly came down against flogging and corporal punishment. So strong had public sentiment become that in the same year *White-Jacket* was published, Congress passed a new naval appropriations bill that contained an amendment abolishing flogging on U.S. military and merchant vessels. Consequently, far from initiating or even having much of an impact on naval reform, *White-Jacket* was a latecomer to a public debate already largely won by the reformers.[63] Since Melville's novel was articulating a public consensus, reviewers and middle-class readers were quite willing to accept it as a legitimate work of reform.

It is difficult not to believe that such a response was partly what Melville had hoped would happen or that he had written *White-Jacket,* at least in part, to exploit a topical subject from an acceptable, unthreatening position as a way to regain some of his former popularity. Happily for him, a resuscitation did occur. Not only were the reviews laudatory but of the 4,500 copies of *White-Jacket* printed by the Harpers, nearly 4,000 sold in the first month.[64] Those sales certainly were the highest Melville had experienced since *Omoo,* and the public response that viewed his latest novel as something of a reprise of his first two books (i.e., a hybrid akin to his romances of real life) signaled that most reviewers saw him making an important (re)turn. If features of *Mardi* looked to be signs that Melville was neglecting the needs of his audience, *White-Jacket* struck them as a concerted and welcome effort to come back to the audience he had engaged with his earliest books.

If the responses to *White-Jacket* indicated recovery, such an implication could not have been fully satisfying to Melville. In the prevailing paradigm for considering an author's career, a return to one's writing past, after all, marked regression—or at best stasis—and not growth. Such a conclusion hardly represented what Melville wanted to hear after his ambitious and onerous experience with *Mardi* only a year earlier. Even the relative success of *White-Jacket* had to trouble Melville, as his ideas about his art and its relation to readers continued to change in 1849. As a writer whose aspiration to secure a broader and more diverse readership had grown, a return to the kind of success he had had with *Typee* and *Omoo* was less than satisfying. The problem was compounded by the fact that, as he expressed in his December letter to Duyckinck before the reviews of *White-Jacket* appeared, Melville doubted the viability of such an aspiration if he could not even be "frank" with his audience.

Following the public response to *White-Jacket,* Melville's conception of authorship and audience changed further as his reading, especially in Shakespeare, stimulated his ambitions and expectations. However, his well-documented encounter with Hawthorne and the galvanic bond Melville felt with the slightly older New Englander perhaps made the greatest impact. That friendship would cause Melville to "regard Hawthorne," as he confessed to Duyckinck, "as evincing a quality of genius, immensely loftier & more profound, too, than any other American has shown hither."[65] As the great American genius, Hawthorne became something of model for what has been called Melville's "imperial" notion of authorship.[66]

Yet his other experiences, particularly with *Mardi,* had shown Melville that an author possesses absolute dominion over neither text nor audience. As he began to write *Moby-Dick* in early 1850, he continued to feel the constraints of the literary marketplace, especially the limitations that seemed to accompany writing for a popular audience. Whether that resulted in what Charvat called a "creative tension with [the] reading public" or in bouts of despair and dismissal or in a combination of these effects, after a year of working on *Moby-Dick* Melville had reached the point where he privately but candidly declared his frustration in an early June 1851 letter to Hawthorne. "Dollars damn me," lamented Melville. "What I feel most moved to write, that is banned,—it will not pay. Yet altogether, write the *other* way I cannot. So the product is a final hash, and all my books are botches."[67]

Elements of that frustration as well as of his imperial ambition and his working sense of audience were already evident a year earlier, in part in a letter to Dana and then more fully in "Hawthorne and His Mosses." In the former Melville adds a new link to his coiled chain of ideas about audience. Responding to a letter in which Dana apparently had expressed "congenial feelings" after reading *Redburn* and *White-Jacket,* Melville made the following, almost surprising admission: "did I not write those books of mine almost entirely for 'lucre'—by the job as a woodsawyer saws wood—I almost think, I should hereafter—in the case of a sea book—get my M.S.S. neatly & legibly copied by a scrivener—send you that one copy—& deem such a procedure the best publication."[68] What is striking (even accounting for the playful, flattering hyperbole) is Melville's idea that one sympathetic, understanding reader—particularly if that reader is another author—could fulfill a writer's desire to find an audience. Voicing such an idea for the first time in this May letter, Melville in the summer of 1850 would enhance and project it in the essay in which Hawthorne would become the touchstone of Melville's meditation on author-audience relations.

His "Hawthorne" essay, of course, is where Melville first overtly articulated the two-audience theory that had been part of his working ideas in some form since *Typee*. The essay, however, also provides a lens into his revolving, kaleidoscopic view of audience during the nearly two years devoted to the composition of *Moby-Dick*. Ellen Weinauer has noted how Melville's essay conveys the sense that he sees himself and Hawthorne as part of a "literary fraternity, a 'brotherhood' whose relations are set against the competitive organization of the antebellum marketplace," and it is, indeed, difficult to come away from the piece without feeling that Melville has a good deal of disdain for the mass market for fiction.[69] At one point he refers to the popular audience as a "mere mob" (245) and disparages a whole segment of readers as "superficial skimmer[s] of pages," who, in confronting Hawthorne and other great writers such as Shakespeare, are "egregiously deceived" into overlooking the depth and power of their works (251). Despite such a move, Melville does not simply dismiss such readers as obtusely irrelevant to an author. Though such readers may miss the dark depths of Hawthorne, that failure need not disqualify them as legitimate members of the contemporary audience, as Melville explains: "Nor need you fix upon that blackness in him, if it suit you not. Nor, indeed, will all readers discern it for it is mostly insinuated to those who may best understand it, and account for it; it is not obtruded upon everyone alike" (245). The great writer, in fact, must take into account not only the select few but also the broad multitude, which may well be less discerning, if he hopes to "breathe the unshackled, democratic spirit" (248). Although Melville does differentiate a hierarchy among readers, he creates a convergence that he sees as essential to the work of the true American fiction writer, if he or she is to achieve a democratic patronage "for the nation's sake" (247).

Even as Melville makes his famous two-audience distinction, furthermore, he collapses it. For him, the "superficial skimmer of pages" is not simply one type of respondent distinguishable from the more astute "eagle-eyed reader" he mentions in the next sentence. Rather, these also constitute reading positions between which a reader can move. This is precisely the point Melville makes through his own experience as a reader in explaining that two of Hawthorne's stories (one of which he identifies as "Young Goodman Brown") "did dolefully dupe no less an eagle-eyed reader than myself." Only after carefully reading these tales, admits Melville, did he succeed in going from a superficial misinterpretation to an understanding that "the simple little tale" about Brown "is as deep as Dante" (251). By extension, Melville implies that the same thing happens to others because Hawthorne's text impels readers to such a recognition. "Nor can you finish it," Melville asserts, "without addressing the author in his own words—'It is to penetrate, in my bosom, the deep mystery of sin.'" For Melville, a text such as "Young Goodman Brown" is an allegory of the reader's experience of the tale. But more importantly, it is a trigger for audience discovery that makes eagle-eyed readers from the superficial skimmers the story is designed to engage.

While both differentiating and collapsing these two categories of audience/reading, Melville in the process identifies two other types of readers that Hawthorne and any American fiction writer must deal with. One consists of the "critics of America," and while "several of them are asleep," they still form part of the reading public (247). They may, in fact, be a valuable part because, as Melville explains in an ironic turn, by accusing a writer of failure, such reviewers provide that author and his audience with an index to his genius, since "[f]ailure is the true test of greatness" (248). Since Melville feels, however, that it can take some time for the audience to recognize such backhanded indices and the achievement they signal, he identifies his fourth category of readers, and it is the category he had first invoked in his letter to his father-in-law a year earlier: the audience of the future. A writer such as Hawthorne—and by extension, Melville himself—must also look to "Posterity," since posterity is where an author's hope for understanding and recognition may lie (253).

The "Hawthorne" essay reveals far more than Melville's dismay with the antebellum reading public or a simple dualistic concept of audience. It can be taken as expressing the complex and deep-seated ambivalence of a man torn between, on the one hand, frustration with a contemporary readership of superficial page skimmers and soporific reviewers and, on the other, a tenacious commitment to authorship conceived as a broad engagement capable of reaching a multifarious audience.[70] Its typologies and shifts between distinctions made and then collapsed also reflect Melville's continued and ever-increasing difficulties in trying to determine, amid his quest to chase and capture his literary whale, who his audience was and how he could successfully induce them to ship on his authorial voyage.

Nor did the grueling work on *Moby-Dick* help. On the contrary, that demanding intellectual labor soon caused Melville to question some of his 1850 assumptions about who his readers were or might be. In his June 1851 letter to Hawthorne, Melville expressed little expectation from his audience of the future. "To go down to posterity is bad enough," he wrote, "but to go down as a 'man who lived among cannibals'! When I speak of posterity . . . I have come to regard this matter of Fame as the most transparent of all vanities." His letters from the second half of 1851 also demonstrate that Hawthorne had supplanted Dana as Melville's singular ideal reader, particularly after the former had expressed (in an unpreserved letter) enthusiastic admiration for *Moby-Dick* shortly after its publication. "A sense of unspeakable serenity is in me at this moment, on account of your having understood the book," Melville warmly responded, and in their glow of "fraternal feeling," he added, "your appreciation is my glorious gratuity." Two months later, by contrast, Melville warned Sarah Morewood, a friend of the family, away from his recent novel: "Dont [*sic*] you buy it—dont [*sic*] you read it when it comes out, because it is by no means the sort of book for you. It is not a piece of fine feminine Spitalfields silk. . . . Warn all gentle fastidious people from so much as peeping into the book."[71] In a significant departure from the inclusive vision of his Hawthorne essay of the previous year, Melville was now thinking about who did not belong in the audience for *Moby-Dick*.

However, just as it is an oversimplification to say Melville had turned his back on readers with *Mardi*, so too would it be inaccurate to say that, in his letters to Hawthorne and Morewood, Melville was renouncing the popular audience for fiction. His comment to Morewood about *Moby-Dick*'s not being "fine feminine silk" indicates that the "fastidious people" he thought of as peripheral to the book's readership were women—a conception that paralleled the phallocentric assumption among reviewers that certain novels, though widely read, were outside the proper sphere of the female audience. Melville continued to subscribe to a version of that idea as he turned to his next novel. Although in a letter to Hawthorne, Melville had said that *Pierre* would be a Kraken to his whaling leviathan, he also told Sophia Hawthorne, "I shall not again send you a bowl of salt water. The next chalice I shall commend, will be a rural bowl of milk."[72]

Though we might be tempted to dismiss such a remark as a Melvillian irony, several factors suggest he was being neither evasive nor dismissive with such a comment. Melville appears to have respected Sophia as a reader; in the same letter in which he referred to *Pierre* as a "rural bowl of milk," he also expressed appreciation for her emblematic interpretation of the "Spirit Spout" chapter in *Moby-Dick,* which Hawthorne had conveyed in one of his letters. Additionally, in a letter to Richard Bentley less than three months later, Melville described *Pierre* as "very much more calculated for popularity than anything you have yet published of mine—being a regular romance, with a mysterious plot to it, & stirring passions at work."[73]

These factors suggest that Melville was composing *Pierre* with the idea that it would be another great book—a Kraken—like *Moby-Dick* (and *Mardi*) and, at the same time, a very popular book, and that in thinking about the popular audience he had added the category of gender to his conceptualization. It was an addition, however, that did not clarify his ideas of audience but rather contributed further turbidity by being one more element in an ever-shifting supposition. In writing *Pierre* Melville was not rejecting his contemporary readers so much as operating within a conceptual morass about author-audience relations, which prevented him—to a greater degree than had been the case with *Mardi*—from formulating a viable hypothesis that could guide his drive to write for himself and for his readers.

Those readers would continue to have a say, as Melville learned when the reviews of *Moby-Dick* began to appear while he was working on *Pierre*. Once again British reviewers had the first word chronologically, but it came with a potentially damaging twist. Only two English reviews—in the *Athenaeum* and the *Spectator*—appeared and were accessible in the United States before American periodicals took up *Moby-Dick,* and the pejorative reactions of both those periodicals helped slant the first American reviews toward the negative. Yet the British impact was neither as large nor as deleterious as some Melville scholars have claimed.[74] Nor was the American reception of *Moby-Dick* a barrage of criticisms, as is often assumed.[75] On the contrary, it was an admixture of derogation, admiration, and thoughtful commentary.

While some American reviewers did feel that *Moby-Dick* was an odd fish (or mammal), quite a few found in it much that was fascinating and amenable within their horizon of expectations. For American readers in 1851, whaling and whales were at once an exotic and commonplace subject. Whale products—from the oil used for household illumination to the bone that served as stiffening for umbrellas and clothing—touched the lives of nearly everyone as the whaling industry grew to a $70 million enterprise in the late 1840s. Stories about whaling were in the news, apprising readers of the power, majesty, and ostensible ferocity of whales themselves, including the ones that, according to widely circulated stories, had stove and sunk the *Essex* and the *Ann Alexander*. As the *Tribune* review of *Moby-Dick* pointed out, "Everybody has heard of the tradition which is said to prevail . . . of a ferocious monster of a whale, who is proof against all the arts of harpooning, and who occasionally amuses himself with swallowing down a boat's crew." Melville's new book, continued the reviewer, is "the Epic of that veritable old leviathan" (Nov. 22, 1851, *CR* 383). Reviews in the *Boston Daily Bee* and the *Literary World* made similar connections, thereby directing middle-class readers to expect a stirring fictional representation of real-life events.[76]

For others the familiarity reverberated in different echoes. There were, of course, the characters' names, particularly Ishmael's and Ahab's, with their biblical connections, and attentive readers could recall encountering other Ishmaels in two popular novels from the 1840s: Cornelius Matthew's *Career of Puffer Hopkins* (1842) and William Starbuck Mayo's *Kaloolah* (1849). Two reviewers found older and more prestigious literary affiliations. *Harper's New Monthly Magazine* thought that "some of the leading personages . . . present a no less unearthly appearance than the witches of Macbeth" (Dec. 1851, CR 392), while the *National Intelligencer* found on the whole that the "delineation of character is actually Shakespearean . . . in 'Moby-Dick'" (Dec. 16, 1851, *CR* 400).

More than anything else, what readers noticed in the novel as both familiar and perplexing, delightful and dismaying was the diverse generic concoction they believed Melville had brewed. Reviewers invoked various generic labels to decipher *Moby-Dick,* and in some cases a single review summoned several at once. Both the *Tribune* and the *Intelligencer* were fairly certain it was "a prose Epic on Whaling" (*Intelligencer* 400) or a "Whaliad," as the *Tribune* dubbed it, but the *Tribune* reviewer was less certain that a single descriptor could do, since the novel also contained "occasional touches of the subtle mysticism" that are "relieved by minute descriptions of the most homely process of the whale fishery" (Nov. 22, 1851, *CR* 383). Others could not agree on a particular genre for *Moby-Dick.* The *New York Spirit of the Times* explained, "'Moby-Dick, or the Whale' is a 'many-sided' book" mixing "sermonizing, a good deal of keen satire," the "natural history" of whales, and "romance" (Dec. 6, 1851, *CR* 396). "It becomes quite impossible to submit" such a book, said the *Literary World,* "to distinct classification as fact, fiction, or essay. . . . Moby Dick [sic] may be pronounced a most remarkable sea-dish—an intellectual chowder of romance, philosophy, natural history, [and] fine writing" (Nov. 22, 1851, *CR* 384).

As might be expected, some reviewers objected to this generic gumbo as an affront to the principle that a novel should have a consistent generic footprint. Other reviewers, however, embraced that melange as interesting and highly readable. The *Springfield Republican* announced that "in this, his latest book Mr Melville has woven around this cumbersome bulk of a romance, a large and interesting web of narrative, information, and sketches of character and scenery, in a quaint though interesting style" (Nov. 17, 1851, *CR* 377). The *New Haven Palladium* asserted, "The work possess all the interest of the most exciting fiction, while, at the same time, it conveys much valuable information in regard to things pertaining to natural history, commerce, life on ship board, &c." (Nov. 17, 1851, *CR* 377), while the *Washington Union* called *Moby-Dick* "most readable and intensely interesting" in its union of "numerous exciting incidents," a "variety and completeness of information" about "the natural history and habits of this leviathan of the deep," and its "life-like delineations of character" (Nov. 20, 1851, *CR* 390). Similar comments characterized responses in *Graham's,* the *New York Independent,* and the *American Literary Gazette,* with the last of these calling the novel a work of "great versatility" in being "a fine contribution to natural history and to political economy, united to an original and powerful romance of the sea."[77]

What is surprising is that a good half of the reviewers who responded to *Moby-Dick* through genre codes found so much to approve, since such a mixture ordinarily signaled a flaw according to the tenets of informed reading—as it had been deemed in the responses to *Mardi*. But reviewers seemed more receptive to that admixture in *Moby-Dick*, and several factors may have been influential. For one thing, readers of Melville had come to associate such a congery of forms as an "identifiable" Melvillian trait that became part of their interpretive horizon. Being thus enabled to "place" *Moby-Dick* with a certain degree of comfort, some readers could find Melville's latest book a satisfying generic hybrid. Such a response was exemplified in the *Home Journal*, which saw in the novel's multifaceted modes a conscious authorial strategy designed to meet "the vivid expectation excited in the reading public by his previous books" (Nov. 29, 1851, *CR* 390).

A related factor was the way readers perceived the book's mixture of fact and fiction, romance and realism. Frequently commented upon was its chapters on cetology and whaling life, and the vast majority of American reviewers praised these sections for providing valuable information about an important American industry. Propelled by a nationalistic predisposition toward an American novel that dealt with an American subject, reviewers in the *Literary World, Harper's New Monthly*, and the *Home Journal* combined such leanings with the protocol of informed reading that valued instruction and entertainment in novels to proclaim *Moby-Dick* a fiction that successfully provided both in its combination of modes. Indeed, for some, the "information" chapters on whaling and whales were precisely the needed ballast for the book's romance of adventure and its philosophical forays. Thus, proclaimed the *Tribune*, the book's "intensity of the plot" and "subtle mysticism" are "mixed up with so many tangible and odorous realities that we always safely alight from the excursion through mid-air upon the sober deck of the whaler" (Nov. 22, 1851, *CR* 383). Likewise, the *Troy Budget* concluded that the "great deal of information about the whale, his habits, and the manner of hunting and capturing him . . . hangs on the general thread" of the account of the *Pequod's* quest "as an essential appurtenance, and [is] necessary to the perfection of the picture" (Nov. 14, 1851, *CR* 374). For other readers, the cetology and whaling information chapters were less a complement to the romance plot and more the center of the book; in this interpretation, the romance tale was primarily a glue that held together and gave an engaging shape to the realistic facts. According to the *Newark Daily Advertiser*, while Melville's "object" is "to plainly portray the daily adventure and dangers of the hardy sailor in quest of the great leviathan, . . . [a] semi-marvelous narrative or tale is the link which connects the various chapters and retains the interest of the reader until the very last page" (Dec. 5, 1851, *CR* 393). The code of formal compensation played a role here. If *Moby-Dick* was a generic hybrid that ordinarily would have been problematic, it compensated by using the mixture for legitimate and productive ends. As the *To-Day* put it, while "parts of the book . . . would be of much value if their connexion with other parts of so totally different a character did not cast a shadow of uncertainty over their accuracy," the "form in which it is given, mixed with the events of the story, may perhaps attract more readers than a professed matter-of-fact history" (Jan. 10, 1852, *CR* 413).

Reviewers were less amenable to other dimensions of *Moby-Dick*, though those responses also were mixed. The *Hartford Courant* objected to the "want of unity . . . of a regular beginning and end" in the plot and overall structure, causing it to lack "the form and shape and outline of a well built [*sic*] novel" (Nov. 15, 1851, *CR* 375). While also feeling that *Moby-Dick* lacked a rounded-out and well-proportioned structure, other reviewers nonetheless relished particular sections, with the opening twenty chapters being special favorites. Although "[i]t is some time after opening . . . before we get fairly afloat," the *Literary World* admitted, "the time is very satisfactorily occupied with some strange, romantic, and withal, highly humorous adventures at New Bedford and Nantucket," which "treat the reader to a laugh worthy of Smollet" (Nov. 15, 1851, 376). *Harper's New Monthly* expressed even warmer approval of the scenes at the two whaling ports: "The introductory chapters of the volume . . . are pervaded with a fine vein of humor, and reveal a succession of portraitures, in which the lineaments of nature shine forth. . . . To many readers, these will prove the most interesting portions of the work" (Dec. 1851, *CR* 392).

Characterization received substantial attention, and it too was mixed, both in judgments about quality and in the diversity of opinions about who was the novel's protagonist. The *Literary World* believed that "an infuriated, resolute sperm whale as pursued and destroyed the Ann Alexander is the hero, Moby-Dick, of Mr. Melville's book" (376), an interpretation that the *Utica Daily Gazette* seconded.[78] By contrast, the *To-Day* magazine held that the book's "hero is named Ishmael" (Jan. 10, 1852, *CR* 413), which was completely in line with the common interpretive assumption that an autobiographical novel inherently made its narrator the hero-protagonist, since that narrator was assumed to be a fictive avatar of the author. Such a protocol certainly obtained in reviewer interpretations of Ishmael. The *Tribune,* for example, described the opening events of *Moby-Dick* by explaining that "the writer relates his first introduction to Queequeg, a South Sea cannibal, who was his chum" (Nov. 22, 1851, *CR* 383); the *Albion* explained that "the writer was . . . (or says he was, which is the same thing) but a seaman aboard the vessel whose narrative he relates" (Nov. 22, 1851, *CR* 380); and the New Bedford *Mercury* summarized, "[a]fter some introductory chapters . . . we find our author quitting the good society of old Manhatto, 'for Cape Horn and the Pacific'" (Nov. 18, 1851, *CR* 378). As the *To-Day* reviewer pointed out in articulating the logic behind such an equation, because Ishmael "tells his story in the first person . . . this sort of writing . . . cannot but make the reader feel that his author has experienced what he writes about" (413). Others took a different view by interpreting Ahab as the main character. Despite identifying Ishmael with Melville, the *Tribune* reviewer asserted that "the interest of the work pivots on a certain captain Ahab" (383), while the *Church Review and Ecclesiastical Register* simply declared that the novel "abounds in episodes and marvels, of which Capt. Ahab is the great hero" (Jan. 1852, *CR* 410). A reviewer for the *Spirit of the Times* exemplified the logic behind such an assumption by identifying Ahab's quest as the fulcrum of *Moby-Dick*: "Think of a monomaniacal whaling captain, who, mutilated on a former voyage by a particular whale, well known for its peculiar bulk, shape, and color—seeks, at the risk of his life and the lives of his crew, to capture and slay this terror of the seas! It is on this idea that the romance hinges" (Dec. 6, 1851, *CR* 396).

Ahab himself represented a fascinating and troubling character for readers to decipher, both emotionally and aesthetically; consequently, reviewers evinced a variety of interpretive reactions. Several found him an aesthetically successful, strong, and original character. According to the *New York Churchman,* the "character of the monomaniac Captain Ahab is a novelty, and powerfully drawn" (Dec. 6, 1851, *CR* 395), while the *Albion* concluded that "foremost" among the novel's characters "is the Captain, in the conception of whose parts lies the most original thought of the whole book, stamping it decidedly as the production of a man of genius" (Nov. 22, 1851, *CR* 380). It is not difficult to infer in such comments a fascination that belies the modern critical assumption that "Ahab . . . was thought repulsive by most reviewers of the time."[79] The reviewer in *Harper's New Monthly* articulated the cause for that entrancement: "The character of Captain Ahab also opens upon us with a wonderful power. He exercises a wild bewildering fascination by his dark mysterious nature, which is not at all diminished when we obtain a clearer insight into his strange history" (Dec. 1851, *CR* 392).

Other reviewers, however, responded with some ambivalence. The *Literary World* believed that "the intense Captain Ahab is too long drawn out; some thing more of him might, we think, be left to the readers's imagination. . . . Yet Captain Ahab is a striking conception, firmly planted on the deck of the Pequod.—a dark[,] disturbed soul arraying itself . . . for a conflict at once natural and supernatural" (Nov. 22, 1851, *CR* 385). Similarly, a reviewer in *Littell's Living Age* said, "Captain Ahab is introduced with prodigious efforts at preparation; and there is really no lack of rude power and character about his presentment. . . . His portrait is striking." Yet this reviewer also raised a red flag by describing Ahab's speech as "a lingo borrowed from Rabelais, Carlyle, Emerson, [and] newspapers transcendental and transatlantic" (Aug. 1853: 486).

Indeed, those who objected to Ahab tended to find fault with the speeches Melville gave his monomaniacal captain, and some saw the problem at work in many of the characters in *Moby-Dick*. The *Southern Quarterly Review* found Melville's "Mad Captain . . . a monstrous bore" whose "ravings . . . meant for eloquent declamation, are such as would justify a writ *de lunatico* (Jan. 1852, *CR* 412). Though having pronounced Ahab an "original" character, the *Albion* reviewer likewise objected to "the stuff and nonsense spouted forth by the crazy Captain" and felt that this "[r]arely-imagined character has been spoiled, nay altogether ruined, by a vile overdaubing with a coat of book-learning and mysticism" (Nov. 22, 1851, *CR* 382). Moreover, claimed the *Albion*, the same thing happens whenever "Mr Melville puts words into the mouths" of his characters: "From the Captain to the Cabin-boy, not a soul among them talks pure seaman's lingo" (381). If Melville had designed his novel's "bold and lofty language" to strike a tragic and elevated tone, some reviewers found it an artificial posturing absurdly out of place.

Reviewers also struggled with the themes of *Moby-Dick*. Like Sophia Hawthorne, a reviewer in *Harper's New Monthly* sensed that Melville had written an emblematic novel "not without numerous . . . suggestions on psychology, ethics, and theology" and that "[b]eneath the whole story, the subtle, imaginative reader may perhaps find a pregnant allegory, intended to illustrate the mystery of life" (Dec. 1851, *CR* 391). Though sensing the same thing, other reviewers either had trouble deciphering what the philosophical allegory portended or found it unnecessary or offensive. The *Newark Daily Advertiser* felt that the novel's "metaphysical discussion, half earnest and half banter, might well be omitted" (Dec. 5, 1851, *CR* 391), while the *Argus* objected, "There is an air of irreverence pervading" the book's ideas (Nov. 15, 1851, *CR* 374). The *New York Churchman* also objected to *Moby-Dick*'s "wild rhapsody and bad philosophy," as well as to its "frequent displays of irreligion and profanity" (Dec. 6, 1851, *CR* 394), and similar charges against the novel's "profane" and "irreverent" ideas appeared in the *Boston Evening Traveller*, the *New Haven Palladium*, and *To-Day*. In making these objections, reviewers sometimes spliced together the novel's dramatizations and themes, as the reviewer in *To-Day* did by interpreting Ishmael and Queequeg's shared worship of the latter's idol in chapter 10 as a scene "where sacred things are made light of" (Jan. 1852, *CR* 413).

Reviewers, of course, had made similar objections to Melville's irreverence before, but responses to *Moby-Dick* hardly matched the shrill remonstrances against *Typee* and *Omoo* in this area. Overall, it is fair to say that the responses to *Moby-Dick* were more evenly balanced than *Mardi*'s had been and were divided along a scale similar to what *Redburn* had received. Comparatively, *Moby-Dick* was hardly condemned as a failure by antebellum reviewers.

In one sense, however, the label "failure" is not completely inaccurate; sales for *Moby-Dick* were disappointing. Although Harpers reported selling 1,535 copies in the first thirty days, only 470 more sold in the next three months, and subsequent sales averaged only 120 copies per month—about a third of *Typee*'s sales and only slightly more than half of what *Mardi* had achieved.[80] Cost again seems to have been a factor, as it had been for *Mardi*, but even the hefty retail price of $1.50 for *Moby-*

Dick does not explain the comparatively low sales, given that *Mardi* was slightly more expensive.

An additional factor in the low sales of *Moby-Dick* was the turn in the general perception of Melville's career by early 1852. The middle-class audience could glean from the ongoing public discussion of Melville's books the strong impression that his career had been uneven and that he had never quite lived up to the success and promise of *Typee*. In fact, reviews of *Moby-Dick* in the *United State Magazine and Democratic Review* and in *To-Day* included a retrospective look at Melville's corpus and concluded that his career had taken a downward turn since *Typee*.[81] To be sure, some reviewers had said that *Mardi* was actually superior to *Typee* while *Redburn* had marked a bit a of a falling off. But unlike those who had defined *Mardi* as the pinnacle of his career up to that point, few if any reviewers shared Hawthorne's private opinion that *Moby-Dick* was Melville's best book.[82]

On the contrary, besides seeing it as one more step in the downward spiral from *Typee*, some reviewers were telling the fiction-reading public that *Moby-Dick* evinced a disturbing authorial vanity in its bombastic philosophizing and affected style. The *Boston Post* said that Melville's latest novel was "stuffed with conceits and oddities of all kinds, put in artificially, deliberately and affectedly" (Nov. 20, 1851, *CR* 378), while the *New York Evangelist* informed its readership that "oddity is the governing character" of *Moby-Dick*, through which Melville "has reached the very limbo of eccentricity" (Nov. 20, 1851, *CR* 379). According to the *United States Magazine*, the novel's excesses in "bombast, in caricature, in rhetorical artifice" resulted from Melville's "attempts to display to the utmost extent his powers of 'fine writing'": "The truth is, Mr. Melville has survived his reputation. If he had been content with writing one or two books, he might have been famous, but his vanity has destroyed all chances of immortality, or even a good name with his own generation. For in truth, Mr. Melville's vanity is immeasurable. . . . He will centre all attention upon himself, or he will abandon the field of literature at once" (Jan. 1852, *CR* 410). In his attempts to achieve literary fame, and pumped by his previous successes, Melville had, according to this response, become so full of himself that he was intruding his presence on every page of *Moby-Dick* in violation of an important principle of informed response. Even worse, in his authorial vanity, Melville had over-written *Moby-Dick* as a transparent form of self-promotion.

But whether the problem was a product of solipsism or reckless hubris, such comments implied what some were saying overtly, either in public or private: that Melville was either thoughtlessly alienating or turning his back on readers by writing primarily for himself. In the wake of the responses to *Moby-Dick*, Bentley cautioned Melville that if he "had restrained your imagination somewhat, and written in a style to be understood by the great mass of readers—nay if you had not sometimes offended the feelings of many sensitive readers[—]you would have succeeded" with this latest novel.[83] Publicly, the *United States Magazine* expressed the same idea more acerbically, saying that with *Moby-Dick*, "Mr Melville is evidently trying to ascertain how far the public will consent to be imposed upon" (410). Needless to say, such warnings and the picture they sketched of Melville's corpus could hardly have done much for the sales of *Moby-Dick*, especially given its relatively high price, nor could those responses have induced among middle-class readers much enthusiasm for a writer whose career seemed to be on a downward slope.

The low sales and the damaging insinuations in some of the public discussion, which Melville himself sensed, help explain the dismay and anger with which he reacted to what was, on the whole, an otherwise balanced and at times thoughtful set of interpretations and evaluations of *Moby-Dick*. To Melville, those results seemed only to reinforce his sense that the literary marketplace was trying to force him into more ditch-digger's work and to caricature him as a man whose fame would consist of having lived among cannibals. Especially troubling to Melville, apparently, was the fact that his friend Evert Duyckinck had been responsible for the lukewarm reviews in the *Literary World*, which among other things had called *Moby-Dick* a "conceited" book. In response, Melville wrote a curt note to Duyckinck in February 1852 canceling his subscription to the *World*.[84] Yet Melville's ire was hardly limited to the betrayal he ascribed to Duyckinck. Most Melville scholars hold that he was so annoyed with the reception of *Moby-Dick* that in the midst of writing *Pierre* he changed its tenor by turning the last third into a withering attack on the antebellum literary marketplace, from the publishing industry and magazine reviewers to the fiction-reading public as a whole. What he put before his audience in *Pierre,* writes Ann Douglas, was a "document of despair," in which "Melville punishes his readers in advance for their inevitable failure of comprehension."[85]

Certainly antebellum readers could have found in *Pierre* elements that may well have been, if not punitive, at least dismaying: Pierre's doubts about Christianity, the latently incestuous relationship between Isabel and Pierre, and the section on the literary marketplace beginning with Book 17 and entitled "Young America in Literature." Yet there is no evidence that any readers—including any reviewers—read the last third of *Pierre* as an assault on the fiction-reading public. What that means, among other things, is that the text of *Pierre* itself cannot be taken un-problematically as an index to Melville's view of readers and reviewers in 1853—unless, that is, we make a sweeping assumption that all antebellum readers were simply too obtuse to see what was "really" going on in Melville's seventh novel.

To say this is not to deny the angst Melville was experiencing at this time as a writer in the marketplace for fiction. Ever since *Mardi,* he had been torn between frustration over the need to attract an audience and his desire to engage readers in the broadest and deepest ways possible. Since then, his desire and dismay had grown, increasing the tension between the two until it had reached a pinnacle during the composition of *Pierre.*

The public discussion of the novel indicates that readers felt their own kind of tension in working through their responses to *Pierre,* and one reason was that the American audience had no barometer from abroad. Contrary to what the case had been with virtually all of Melville's previous books, British reviews did not lead the way in the reception of *Pierre*; in fact, they had no impact owing to the manner in which the novel was published. Because Melville and Bentley could not come to terms on editorial emendations to the novel, no British edition of *Pierre* was published; thus, there were no advanced copies distributed to English reviewers. The only British version of the novel, which consisted of bound copies of the remaining sets of sheets from Harper's American printing, came out in November 1852, five months after the American edition.[86] Hence, American reviewers and readers were on their own to puzzle through the text.

And puzzle they did. In the United States, many readers took to *Pierre;*

or, the Ambiguities by taking it apart. Employing rules of notice, several reviewers turned to the novel's subtitle as a guide, but they found it misnamed. Instead of "Ambiguities," said the *American Whig Review*, Melville should have called his book "Absurdities" (Nov. 1852, *CR* 451). The *New York Lantern* had its own candidate for a more apt title: "The book is a mistake, even the name is a blunder—it should be called the *double entendre*" (Oct. 16, 1852, *CR* 441). For a number of reviewers the subtitle was a misnomer because it did not go far enough in reflecting the true nature of the book, since *Pierre*, according to the *Richmond Semi-Weekly Examiner*, was not just ambiguous; rather, "[t]he book is a puzzle" (Aug. 13, 1852, *CR* 425). A reviewer in the *New York Herald* stridently agreed: "Ambiguities, indeed! Once long brain-muddling, soul-bewildering ambiguity . . . without beginning or end—a labyrinth without a clue—an Irish bog without so much as a Jack-o-th'-lantern to guide the wanderer's footsteps" (Sept. 18, 1852, *CR* 437).

Such remarks used the novel's subtitle to define what quickly became the most frequent response to *Pierre*: reviewers' feelings that it was a turbid novel obscured by its own turgidity. The *Literary World* asserted that to read the novel was to enter into a "mystic romance, in which are conjured up unreal nightmare-conceptions, a confused phantasmagoria of distorted fancies and conceits" (Aug. 21, 1852, *CR* 431). Philadelphia's *Church's Bizarre* agreed, finding *Pierre* "wild, wayward, overstrained in thought and sentiments," problems compounded by its style, which was "barbarously outré, unnatural, and clumsy beyond measure" (Aug. 21, 1852, *CR* 432). The problem was not merely the difficulties the novel presented to reader understanding. Such difficulties also prevented readers from doing what one protocol of informed reading said was imperative: deciphering an author's purpose in a way that allowed a novel itself to determine in part a "specific standard" for judging "the excellence of the performance."[87]

Several reviewers sought to address this uncertainty over the novel's purpose by reading *Pierre* as an elaborate joke. The reviewer in *Putnam's Monthly* explained, "When we first read *Pierre*, we felt a strong inclination to believe the whole thing to be a well-got-up hoax."[88] A reviewer in *Godey's* felt that the novel had to have been intended as a satire, but not of reviewers or fiction readers. According to *Godey's*, *Pierre* seeks "to satirize the ridiculous pretensions of some of our modern literati"—

i.e., the extravagances of authors of contemporary novels (Oct. 1852, *CR* 440).[89]

A similar way of thinking may have been at work in other reviewers' attempts to decipher *Pierre* by placing it in relation to other novels and authors. The problem, however, was that for most readers such comparisons did not result in a satiric, parodic, or hoaxing profile for *Pierre* but indicated that Melville's novel was simply a bad imitation of other inept or dangerous fictions. A *Herald* review concluded that Melville "has dressed up and exhibited in Berkshire, where he is living, some of the most repulsive inventions of the George Walker and Anne Radcliffe sort" (July 29, 1852, *CR* 419), while a reviewer in the *Albion* asseverated, "'Pierre' is an objectionable tale, clumsily told" for its "heaping up horrors and trash" in "the spirit of Eugene Sue" (Aug. 21, 1852, *CR* 427–28). The connections between *Pierre* and Radcliffe's novels signaled the way several reviewers saw Melville's novel as a repugnant example of a deleterious mode: Germanic fiction. Both the *Boston Daily Times* and the *American Whig Review* explicitly made that connection, with the latter asserting that "a repulsive, unnatural and indecent plot, a style disfigured by every paltry affectation of the worst German school, and ideas perfectly unparalleled for earnest absurdity" make *Pierre* "deserving of condemnation" by "everybody who has sufficient strength of mind" (Nov. 1852, *CR* 443). Several even saw a resemblance between *Pierre* and Poe's fictions, but not through a logic of guilt by association. Rather, as the reviewer for *Graham's* saw it, Melville "has attempted seemingly to combine in [*Pierre*] the peculiarities of Poe and Hawthorne, and has succeeded in producing nothing but a powerfully unpleasant caricature of morbid thought and passions" (Oct. 1852, *CR* 441).

The *Graham's* reviewer alluded to one of the primary causes behind the antebellum response that identified and condemned *Pierre* as Germanic fiction. Repeatedly, reviewers read *Pierre* as a novel preoccupied with a morbid anatomy of the mind of its titular protagonist. The *Home Journal* called it "psychologically suggestive" yet marked by "eccentricity" and "bewildering intensity" in its probings (Sept. 4, 1852, *CR* 436). Likewise, the *Graham's* reviewer responded, "Pierre, we take it, is crazy, and the merit of the book is in clearly presenting the psychology of his madness; but the details of such a malady . . . are almost as disgusting as those of physical disease itself" (441). The *Washington National Era* agreed even more captiously by asserting that in writing a novel purportedly about "the subtleties of psychological phenomena," Melville produced only "characters [that] are absurdly overdrawn" and grotesque (Aug. 19, 1852, *CR* 426).

For other reviewers the Germanic inhered less in the book's psychological characterization and more in its thematics. The *Troy Budget* found "a sort of gloomy, complaining philosophy pervading" *Pierre* (Aug. 9, 1852, *CR* 424), while the *New York Evening Mirror* warned readers that the novel's "metaphysics are abominable," being both "morbid and unhealthy," and that when—or if—they completed the book, it will be "with something of the feeling . . . we experience on awakening from a horrid fit of the night-mare" (Aug. 22, 1852, *CR* 433–34). The link to the Germanic via the novel's philosophy resulted not only from the morbidity readers found in the book's ideas but also from their obscurity, which several reviewers found reminiscent of the Germanic, transcendental philosophy that U.S. readers associated with Thomas Carlyle. According to the *New York Herald*, "No book was ever such a compendium of Carlyle's faults, with so few of its redeeming qualities, as *Pierre*. We have the same German English—the same transcendental flights of fancy— the . . . same incoherent ravings, and unearthly visions" (Sept. 18, 1852, *CR* 438–39).

Not that all readers found *Pierre* obscure or incoherent. A number of reviewers did attribute specific purposes, themes, or ideas to the novel, though their readings took various forms. The *Baltimore American and Commercial Advertiser* called *Pierre* "a regular romance of love and its dangers and difficulties" (Aug. 6, 1852, *CR* 423), while the *Lansingburg Gazette* read it as a story of "frailty and vice" (Aug. 3, 1852, *CR* 419). *Hunt's Merchants' Magazine* felt that the novel "aims to present the workings of an over-sensitive spirit," exemplified by Pierre himself.[90] Combining elements in the *Hunt's* and the *Gazette* interpretations, a reviewer in the *Southern Literary Messenger* offered a bit more elaborate thematic reading: "The purpose of the Ambiguities . . . we should take to be the illustration of this fact—that it is quite possible for a young and fiery soul, acting strictly from a sense of duty, and being therefore in the right, to erect itself in direct hostility to all the universally received rules of moral and social order" (Sept. 1852: 574). A similar interpretation appeared in the *Literary World*, which explained, "The purpose of

Mr. Melville's story" is "to illustrate the possible antagonisms of a sense of duty . . . to all the recognized laws of social morality; and to exhibit a conflict between the virtues" (Aug. 21, 1852, *CR* 429).

While identifying such purposes, some reviewers, however, felt that these themes were precisely the problem with *Pierre*. As the reviewer of the *Literary World* put it in following up his thematic interpretation, "The most immoral *moral* of the story, if it has any moral at all, seems to be the impracticality of virtue. . . . But ordinary novel readers will never unkennel this loathsome suggestion" (430–31). Yet if the *Literary World* was certain that the fiction-reading audience would never succumb to the impiousness of *Pierre*, other reviewers raised the possibility that the novel could actually corrupt readers. Throughout the novel, according to the *Southern Literary Messenger*, "our sympathies are sought to be enlisted with Pierre," a character whose "follies and crimes . . . overcome every law of religion and morality" (575). By encouraging such empathy, Melville's novel was perverting the reader-text relationship by implying a morally dangerous role for its audience, which informed readers needed to resist. Such a response was precisely what the *Herald* practiced and called for in pointing out that in *Pierre* Melville, in a "fiend nightmare," seeks to curry reader sympathy for a protagonist who is at best a "madman" and even worse, "a murderer in cold blood." Indicting *Pierre* for being, in effect, a sensational novel that induces readers to take murderers to their hearts, the *Herald* declared that with a rogue like Pierre, rightthinking readers will "have no thrill of sympathy, no bowels of compassion" (437).

One interesting feature of these responses, besides being virtual textbook embodiments of principles of informed reading, is the way they integrate thematic reading, interpretation of characters, and consideration of implied reader roles. More than any other Melville novel, *Pierre* was a site not only where thematic interpretation was pronounced but where antebellum responses to characters and ideas were most tightly imbricated. Hence, reviewers who charged *Pierre* with depravity in its themes saw that problem as a product of its reprobate and monstrous characters. If "[t]hought staggers through every page like one poisoned" and if "the moral is bad," claimed a review in *Putnam's Monthly*, the reason is that the book presents a "wretched, cowardly boy for a hero" and a cast of characters in which "[e]verybody is vicious in some way or other.

The mother is vicious with pride. Isabel has a cancer of morbid, vicious, minerva-press-romance, eating into her heart. Lucy Tartan is viciously humble, and licks the dust beneath Pierre's feet."[91]

If Melville had hoped that *Pierre* would be a metaphysical-transcendental-psychological novel that eagle-eyed readers would savor, he soon found from reviewers' comments that he was sadly mistaken. Moreover, if *Pierre* had been calculated for popularity—perhaps as a sensational novel and/or as one that would foment enough controversy to stimulate popular curiosity and generate sales—he had miscalculated badly. Of the 2,300 copies of *Pierre* that Harpers printed, only 283 sold in the first eight months, and while the figure rose to 1,400 copies by the time the novel had been out just over a year, it would take another dozen years to sell an additional 300 copies. Just as troubling, the sharkish reviews of *Pierre* virtually devoured any chance for further sales for *Moby-Dick*.[92]

What hurt Melville as much if not more than the poor sales were the conclusions reviewers and readers were reaching and the implications those presumptions carried. What many reviewers said implicitly, others voiced overtly: that *Pierre* was not only a significant falling off from *Typee* and *Omoo* but also his worst book so far. The *Boston Daily Times* announced that "[n]o man has more singularly abused great original power than the author of this singular work" (Aug. 5, 1852, *CR* 421). Similar sentiments were echoed in the *Boston Post,* the *New York Morning Courier,* and the *Southern Literary Messenger,* with the last of these offering the following summary of Melville's career to date: "from the time that Typee [*sic* for all titles] came from Mr. Melville's portfolio, he seems to have been writing under an unlucky star. The meandering manner of Mardi was but ill atoned for even by the capital sea-pieces of Redburn and White Jacket; Moby Dick proved a very tiresome affair indeed, and as for the Ambiguities, we are compelled to say that . . . one . . . had better leave [it] . . . unbought on the shelves of the bookseller" (Sept. 1852, *CR* 434).

Several reviewers went a step further to conclude that with his latest novel, Melville had clearly abandoned his readers or, worse yet, was deliberately abusing them. The *Morning Courier* concluded that the "wild fantastic irregularities" of *Pierre* "have no other design than to offend all correct judgment and taste" (Aug. 21, 1852, *CR* 432), while the *Literary World* decided that *Pierre* was "meant as a problem of impossible solution, to set critics and readers a wool-gathering. It is alone intelligible as an unintelligibility" (Aug. 21, 1852, *CR* 431). Reviewers in *Graham's,* the *New York Evening Mirror,* and the *Southern Literary Messenger* reached similar verdicts, which in turn caused several to declare—as an *ad hominem* extension of one assumption within informed reading—that Melville, like his protagonist in *Pierre,* was going mad. According to the *New York National Magazine, Pierre* was "an emanation from a lunatic rather than the writing of a sober man."[93] Comparable conclusions emanated from the *New York Commercial Advertiser, Charleston Mercury, Southern Literary Messenger, Southern Quarterly Review,* and *Boston Post.* The last of these, for example, asserted (in a review reprinted in *Littell's Living Age*) that *Pierre* "must be supposed to emanate from a lunatic hospital" (Aug. 4, 1852, *CR* 420). The *New York Day Book* said it all with the scare-headline title of its brief review of the novel: "Herman Melville Crazy" (Sept. 7, 1852, *CR* 436).

Such charges may well have been the responses to which Melville's wife would refer decades later when she wrote that the reception of *Pierre* "was a subject of joke to him." Even if that were true, the other implications of the book's reception were no laughing matter in terms of both his hopes for *Pierre* and his conception of authorship as a progressive path of growth and development.[94] Nor did they bode well for his public reputation or future sales. After all, a work of fiction by a slightly deranged author might have at least some appeal for public curiosity. Witness the response to Poe in the mid-1840s. However, readers would expect very slight rewards—whether as enjoyment, enlightment, or even guilty pleasure—from an author who, some said, cared little if anything for his audience.

↾

Despite the obloquy of the reception events surrounding *Pierre,* Melville was not about to turn his back on his readers, nor were readers necessarily abandoning him. *Putnam's Monthly* in January 1853 once again referred to him by that convivial moniker of "Typee Melville," and in midyear *Littell's Living Age* reprinted a six-page essay that reflected his damaged yet still extant reputation and the public's perplexed fascination with the ambiguous Melville. "Surely," the article concluded, "the man is a Doppelganger—a dual number incarnate (singular though he be in and out of all conscience):—surely he is two single gentlemen rolled into one, but retaining their respective idiosyncrasies—the one sensible, sagacious, observant, . . . and producing admirable matter—the other maundering, driveling, subject to paroxysms, cramps, and . . . penning many pages of unaccountable 'bosh.' So that in tackling every new chapter, one is disposed to question it beforehand" (Aug. 1853: 485). But while readers were still willing to countenance Melville if he would yet smile on them, Melville was in the process of a different form of back-turning—or more accurately, a turning away from the genre of fiction in which he had worked exclusively: the novel in bound format. Instead, his next published works were the short stories that he began to write in spring and summer 1853 and that started appearing in November and December in *Harper's New Monthly Magazine* and the recently founded *Putnam's Monthly*.

The genre of short fiction possessed several attractive possibilities for Melville. Writing tales would tax him far less than writing novels, which was no small relief given that vision problems were now making the physical act of writing and revising a strain for him. Additionally, the medium itself offered potential benefits. *Putnam's*, one of the new "paying" magazines, offered him $5 per page irrespective of sales, and Melville convinced the Harpers to compensate him at the same rate for contributions to their magazine. Consequently, he could count on specific royalties upon acceptance of a story rather than worry, as he had with his last five novels, whether sales would even cover his advances. The anonymous publication format of the two periodicals also offered him opportunities to engage readers outside the usual horizon of expectations they had for fiction from the pen of "Typee Melville" and to continue testing ways of reaching audiences without the risk of further damage to his reputation if readers found the stories wanting.[95]

The turn to that medium seems to have worked for Melville, at least to some degree. Although his anonymity was not preserved, as word of his authorship for most of his stories eventually leaked out, he did make over $1,300 for his fourteen magazine stories and for *Israel Potter*, the serialized novel that appeared in nine installments in *Putnam's* from July 1854 to March 1855. However, the reviews and magazine notices of Melville's stories, particularly as they appeared individually in *Harper's* and *Putnam's*, were few. That paucity resulted in part from the conventions of reviewing: individual short stories simply did not ordinarily constitute occasions for reviews. But things did not fare much better for *The Piazza Tales*, his collection of five of his magazine tales plus "The Piazza," a story written expressly for the volume. Although Dix and Edwards, which published the collection, distributed 260 copies for review, few took up the opportunity to offer comments. With forty-six reviews and notices, the *Piazza Tales* received less attention than any of Melville's previous books. Sales were especially disappointing; of 2,500 copies printed, only 1,047 sold. Just before its publication, George Curtis, the editor of *Putnam's Monthly*, had cautioned John Dix about the *Piazza Tales*: "I don't think Melville's book will sell a great deal. . . . He has lost his prestige,—& I don't believe the Putnam stories will bring it back up."[96] Both predictions proved correct.

Largely the same situation characterized the reception of *Israel Potter*, both in its serialized and subsequent bound formats. Although reviewers generally were pleased by *Potter*, applying to it such polite adjectives as *charming, delightful,* and *interesting,* they damned with faint praise, since their remarks implied what some reviewers overtly voiced: if *Israel Potter* was good, it was not that good. The *Boston Globe* felt that "Mr Melville has made an interesting book from the facts at his command—a book, not great, not remarkable for any particular in it, but . . . a readable book" (Mar. 15, 1855, *CR* 455). The *Christian Examiner* similarly intoned, "Its style is . . . flowing and graceful, and its tone genial and healthy; and yet the author fails to interest us very much in the fortunes of his hero. His character, in truth, lacks those elements which arrest and enchain the reader's sympathies" (May 1855, *CR* 461). Finding it a pleasant but ultimately tepid novel, a reviewer in *Putnam's Monthly* thought that *Potter* "lacks the animation that pervades those writings of Mr. Melville, which, in other respects, it resembles."[97]

With such remarks, reviewers were telling the fiction-reading public and Melville himself that he was, in effect, in a position comparable to where he had been after *Redburn*, having redeemed himself somewhat with a competent if not very striking book following a problematic novel (i.e., *Mardi*) or a disastrous one (*Pierre*). That was hardly good news to Melville. Moreover, he must have sensed that his position actually was worse than it had been seven years earlier. Fewer people were reading his work, and he was making virtually nothing from the *Piazza Tales* or from *Israel Potter*, once its *Putnam's* run had ceased. In terms of his career as a writer with ambitions for literary greatness and broad audience engagement, such a situation meant that the two novels into which he had poured his greatest creative energy, time, and highest hopes—*Mardi* and *Moby-Dick*—might as well never have existed for his contemporary readers.

Despite the steady decline in his status, however, Melville was not ready to admit defeat by either giving up on fiction or relinquishing his desire to reach a diverse and democratically broad audience. The evidence comes with *The Confidence-Man*, which he began after the reception of *Israel Potter* had largely run its course, and particularly in the title and subject he chose for the novel. For in the mid-1850s, the term *confidence man* possessed currency for many of Melville's readers as a topical reference to a new kind of social huckster and swindler who had appeared in several East Coast cities only a few years before. Coined in 1849 by the *New York Tribune* in reference to one William Tompson, *confidence man* was a term subsequently associated with other sharpers by the *Knickerbocker,* the *Literary World,* the *Merchant's Ledger,* the *Springfield Republican,* and other organs of the popular press. As confidence men became the subject of frequent stories and comments in newspapers and magazines by 1855, Melville no doubt was seeking to tap that broad popular interest with his newest novel.[98] Indeed, his contemporary readers made the topical connection. Evert Duyckinck commented on it in a letter to his brother shortly after the novel's publication,[99] and the *Boston Evening Transcript* specified it publicly for any reader who might have missed the link: "One of the indigenous characters who has figured long in our journals, courts, and cities, is 'the Confidence Man;' his doings form one of the staples of villainy, and an element in the romance of roguery. . . . It is not to [be] wondered at, therefore, that the subject caught the fancy of Herman Melville, an author who deals equally well in the material description and the metaphysical insight of human life" (Apr. 10, 1857, *CR* 489).

Modern Melville critics have tended to take a different view of the *Confidence-Man.* Whatever Melville's original plan may have been, they have characterized the novel as a deliberately enigmatic, fragmented, tautological, experimental, and playfully unreadable text designed (by a bitter but still highly creative author) to challenge, evade, frustrate, and egregiously deceive a contemporary readership that Melville had come to regard as comprised almost entirely of superficial page-skimmers and unappreciative blockheads. It is, in this modern interpretation, the kind of book Melville had described in an 1849 letter to Lemuel Shaw—a book Melville had written for his own artistic satisfaction and designed to "fail" with the public.[100]

A curious dichotomy exists between this twentieth-century critical perspective on the *Confidence-Man* and the clearly popular and topical nature of its subject. For if modern Melvillians have almost unanimously taken it as a complex, self-reflexive, private joke at the expense of an antebellum audience totally befuddled and exasperated by the text, the view of the novel by Melville's contemporaries was both far less dire and more diverse.[101]

For one thing, reviewers quickly seized on and alerted the novel-reading audience to the idea that the *Confidence-Man* featured material that was recognizably American. Not only had the *Evening Transcript* connected the text to the well-known figure of the scam artist; the *New York Day Book* focused on its setting on the Mississippi river to style it "a clever delineation of western characteristics" (Apr. 17, 1857, *CR* 496). Others interpreted the novel by reading its titular character within a motif of disguise that fit audience expectations of what a con man was. Referring to the alternating appearances of the "deaf mute," the "de-formed negro," the "Herb Doctor," and other characters, the *New York Dispatch* explained that "the Confidence Man . . . assumes such a variety of disguises" to get "into the confidence of his fellow-passengers" (Apr. 5, 1857, *CR* 487–88). Other antebellum readers similarly identified such characters as avatars of the confidence man himself, thereby anticipating modern interpretations. The "confidence man and his dupes are presented under a great variety of masks," noted the *Burlington (Vermont) Free Press* (Apr. 25, 1857, *CR* 500); the *Springfield Republican* deduced that "[u]nder various disguises" Melville "introduces the same character who, in some form or another, is engaged evermore in cheating" (May 16, 1857, *CR* 501). The latter reviewer's remark points to the method through which readers made that identification: the principle of character consistency. For the *Republican* reviewer, that consistency resided in the common practice of the avatars, but a reviewer in *Putnam's Monthly* identified a second tell-tale sign: Although Melville's confidence man "comes and goes very mysteriously, and assumes many shapes, . . . he always betrays himself by a certain uniformity in the style of his thoughts and his machinations."[102] The con man's masquerade may fool his dupes in the novel, but antebellum readers were alert to what they saw as Melville's method. Hence, the key question antebellum readers asked themselves was not the one John Bryant has termed the central issue for antebellum readers: "What *is* a confidence man?"[103] Melville's audience already knew the answer as part of the horizon of expectations they brought to the novel. Instead, readers were concerned with another question: What was Melville getting at in his representation?

What the con man's masquerade signified was a point of disagreement among reviewers, and for some a spot where uncertainty or dismay occurred. *Putnam's* called it a book whose purpose "very few [will] understand" (366), while the *Tribune* termed it a novel of "strange vagaries" (Apr. 11, 1857, *CR* 494)—a phrase echoed by the *New York Daily Advertiser* (May 23, 1857, *CR* 504). Exasperation characterized the response in the *New York Journal,* which complained that the book's "dogmatizing, theorizing, philosophising . . . are piled up for forty-five chapters in the most eccentric and incomprehensible manner" (July 1857, *CR* 506). A reviewer in the *Illustrated New Monthly* magazine exemplified this category of response most tellingly: "As to *The Confidence Man,* we frankly acknowledge our inability to understand it. . . . In the course of the voyage the Confidence Man assumes numerous disguises—with what object it is not clear—unless for the sake of dogmatizing, theorizing, philosophising, and amplifying upon every known subject. . . . But the object of this masquerade? None appears" (June 1857, *CR* 504).

Other reviewers, however, hardly agreed. Instead of shrugging their shoulders in bewilderment, they ascribed to the novel various humorous purposes. The *Burlington (Vermont) Sentinel* read it as a Rabelaisan "satire upon American character and society" (Apr. 23, 1857, *CR* 497), and the *Christian Inquirer* agreed, calling the novel "a rattling comic criticism upon the follies of the age" (May 2, 1857: 2). As to the specific target of the satire, some did not know, but others identified various candidates. For the *New York Dispatch* the novel was a regional exposé that sought "to show that the passengers of a Mississippi steamboat are the most gullible people in the world" (Apr. 5, 1857, *CR* 488). The *Berkshire County Eagle* concluded that the "'money-getting spirit which appears to pervade every class of man in the States, almost like a monomania, is vividly portrayed in this satire'" (June 19, 1857, *CR* 504). Indeed, several reviewers took the *Confidence-Man* to be a novel of moral purpose, with "the theme being the confidence or the lack of it in ordinary life," according to the *Salem Register* (Apr. 6, 1857, *CR* 488). A reviewer in the *Boston Advertiser* saw it as a cautionary tale: "The grand *morale* of the book appears to be that the world is full of knaves and fools, and that a man who ventures to believe what is told him, necessarily belongs to the latter class" (Apr. 8, 1857, *CR* 489).

Despite some charges of obscurity, antebellum readers hardly were entirely baffled and exasperated by the *Confidence-Man,* at least in terms of reading its themes and purposes. Rather, reviewers more consistently were troubled by the novel's form and execution—problems that readers had been finding in Melville's novels ever since *Mardi.* The *North American and United States Gazette* felt that the novel's structure was "sketchy" (Apr. 4, 1857, *CR* 487), and the *Troy Budget* agreed, finding the *Confidence-Man* "not a novel" or at least not a well-constructed one, since "[i]t wants the connection, the regular plot and great part of the machinery that is found in the regular novel" (Apr. 20, 1857, *CR* 497). One of the repeated responses was that the book was haphazardly episodic to the point where, as the *Budget* put it, the "various sketches . . . might just as well have appeared anywhere else as in their immediate connection" (497). Even more frequent was the response that the novel lacked a conclusion and even circled back upon itself. The *New York Dispatch* felt that "we close this book—finding nothing concluded" (Apr. 5, 1857, *CR* 487), while the *Times* responded more strongly: "The volume has an end, but there is no conclusion to the book; the last chapter might have been the first" (Apr. 11, 1857, *CR* 494). The reviewer in the *Illustrated New Monthly* was even more chagrined by this open-ended, apparently random structure: "the book ends where it begins. You might, without sensible inconvenience, read it backwards" (June 1857, *CR* 504).

Several reviewers asserted that such abnormal handling of the aesthetics of novel writing constituted a tell-tale sign of artistic incompetence—or worse, carelessness. The *Philadelphia Evening Bulletin* called the *Confidence-Man* "an indifferently digested novel" that, "[l]ike all of Melville's works," is marked by an "artistic or mechanical execution [that] is wretched" (Apr. 11, 1857, *CR* 495). The phrase about Melville's "indifferent" digestion of his materials hinted at a problem that the *New York Atlas* overtly specified: "as regards the general character of the book, we should say it was a remarkably lazy one" (Apr. 19, 1857, *CR* 496). Some reviewers made a connection between what they saw as the novel's formal problems and a rhetorical failure on Melville's part. If Melville was sloppy or even willfully negligent in handling the forms of fiction, he was by extension being careless about his readers and thereby was abandoning his obligations to the fiction-reading audience. By such a light, the *Confidence-Man* struck the *Springfield Republican* as a book that "seems to us like the work of one not in love or sympathy with our kind" (May 16, 1857, *CR* 501), while the *Newark Advertiser* believed that Melville had succeeded in producing only "the most unreadable of books" for the fiction-reading public (May 23, 1857, *CR* 504). Even stronger were the characterizations in the *New York Dispatch* and the *Illustrated New Monthly*. The latter said that with the *Confidence-Man*, "Mr. Melville seems to be bent on obliterating his early successes" among a readership that has the "right to expect something better" (June 1857, *CR* 504). The *Dispatch* was dismayed at the way Melville was now "tir[ing] out the patience of his readers" and added, "It is not right—it is trespassing too much upon the patience and forbearance of the public, when a writer possessing Herman Melville's talents, publishes such puerilities as the Confidence Man [*sic*]" (Apr. 5, 1857, *CR* 488).

Although the reviews of the *Confidence-Man*, when taken as a whole, were far less cutting than the knives of rebuke that had gutted *Pierre*, an important message that novel readers were getting from public discussion of the former was similar to what had come to them since at least 1852: Melville had not developed as a writer, had instead wasted his talents, and in the process had virtually turned his back on his obligations to his readers and their expectations.

Ultimately, it is unclear what impact such an impression had on the sales of the *Confidence-Man* since no record has survived for those figures in the United States, nor even for the number of copies Dix and Edwards printed. We do know, however, that only thirty-seven American reviews of the novel appeared in the antebellum press—fewer even than for the *Piazza Tales* and the lowest number generated by any of Melville's previous books. We also know that the British edition of 1,000 copies sold fewer than 400.[104] Together, that information suggests that antebellum readers and reviewers had little interest in the *Confidence-Man* and that the novel earned Melville virtually nothing in income or reputation.

❧

Melville had to be disappointed in the reception of the *Confidence-Man*. One suggestive clue to his chagrin at this time regarding the relationship between author and audience comes from a marginal notation in his copy of Chapman's translation of the *Iliad*, which Melville received and read in late 1858. In it he underscored and marked with parentheses the lines from the commentaries to book 4 that decry "all the plebeian opinions" that hold that "a man is bound to write to every vulgar reader's understanding." Regarding the craft of fiction itself, Melville's attitude is partly indicated in a letter by his brother-in-law Lemuel Shaw Jr., who reported in June 1857 that "Herman says he is not going to write any more at present & wishes to get a place in the N. Y. Custom House."[105] If Melville did decide in late 1857, following the disappointing reviews of the *Confidence-Man*, to give up, it was not so much by turning his back on his readers as it was by abandoning fiction writing itself.

Not that Melville stopped writing. While he never again entered the literary marketplace by publishing a novel or short story, near the end of his life he composed (and left unfinished) the manuscript of "Billy Budd." Some time in 1859, moreover, Melville turned to writing poetry. His motivation for doing so appears to have arisen from his romantic conception of poetry as a literary art that was primarily private and personal. As Melville conceived it, poetry offered an opportunity to write for himself first and to bracket any questions about the audience and the literary marketplace.[106]

To say this is not to imply that Melville thought of his poetry as completely divorced from readers or from the possibility of finding an audience via print. But after the minimal sales of *Battle Pieces*, his collection of Civil War poems published by the Harpers in a small edition in 1866, Melville treated poetry as an intimate expression suited only for a few select readers.[107] *Clarel*, his epic poem of the Holy Land that was published by Putnam's in 1876 at Melville's expense, only reinforced that idea when a mere 130 copies sold before the remaining 220 in the edition were destroyed three years later to clear Putnam's inventory. One of the few reviews of the poem reached a similar conclusion, calling *Clarel* "one of those works which the author writes for himself, and not for the reader, wherein he simply follows the beat of his own instincts and fantasies" (*New York International Review* Jan. 1877, *CR* 541). For anyone coming upon such a comment, the words would have seemed a final confirmation of the belief that Melville had been turning his back on readers for decades. Significantly, Melville would publish two more collections of poetry, *John Marr and Other Sailors* (1888) and *Timoleon* (1891), but only in privately printed editions of twenty-five copies for presentation to friends and family.[108]

In a very real sense, Melville got his post–Civil War wish to be a writer read only by a select few. After 1857, public discussion of his work grew less and less, narrowing to a trickle following the paltry sales and the few scattered reviews of *Battle Pieces* and *Clarel*. By the 1870s and 1880s he was being referred to in print—when he was mentioned at all—as a forgotten writer. In 1886 the *St. Louis Globe Democrat*, in an article reprinted in the *New York Critic*, made a passing reference to "Herman Melville, once renowned as an author, though seldom mentioned of late." In 1890 the syndicated columnist Edward Bok reported, "There are more people today . . . who believe Herman Melville dead than there are those who know he is living." Added Bok, "Forty-four years ago, when his most famous tale, *Typee*, appeared, there was not a better known author than he, and he commanded his own prices. Publishers sought him, and editors considered themselves fortunate to secure his name as a literary star. And to-day? Busy New York has no idea he is even alive, and one of the best-informed literary men in this country laughed recently at my statement that Herman Melville was his neighbor by only two city blocks. 'Nonsense,' said he, 'Why, Melville is dead these many years!'"[109] By the early 1880s a legend had developed that Melville had lapsed into silence for decades and had fallen into oblivion as a "buried" author.

The former, of course, was literally untrue, given Melville's continued poetic output, but even the characterization of him as "buried" was only partly accurate. Something of a cult following developed in England in the 1880s among a small group of Melville admirers led by the British writer William Clark Russell, who encouraged the group's interest, especially in *Moby-Dick*.[110] Others were claiming that Melville was an important author who deserved more attention than the little he was getting. A letter by William Livingston Alden in the *New York Times* in 1899 asserted, "Herman Melville is far and away the most original genius that America has produced, and it is a National reproach that he should be so completely neglected."[111] Ironically, however, such calls further underscored Melville's greatly diminished status as a writer widely perceived as minor and little worth reading.

When Melville died in 1891, the few obituaries and posthumous comments largely extended that impression. The *North American Review* wrote that "Melville wrote out of his heart" but "[h]is books are now but little read. When he died the other day . . . men who could give you the names of fifty living poets and perhaps a hundred living American novelists owned that they had never heard of Herman Melville." The *Springfield Republican* reported that "Herman Melville . . . has long been forgotten, and was no doubt unknown to the most of those who are reading the magazine literature and the novels of the day." Meanwhile, the *New York Times* claimed that Melville was a "man who is so little known, even by name, to the generation now in the vigor of life that only one newspaper contained an obituary account of him, and that was but three or four lines." Four days later, the *Times* followed up with its own brief memorial article headed, in a kind of ironic self-fulfillment, "The Late Hiram Melville." Outside of a small group of admirers in Britain and the United States, Melville was remembered in the 1890s—if at all—as the writer of a couple of exotic and not-much-read South Sea adventure tales who, as the *New York Mail and Express* phrased it, "wrote as he felt, following out his moods and whims, confessing himself to his readers, of whose condemnation, or absolution, he took no thought."[112]

It would take another three decades for the Melville revival of the 1920s to create a renewed interest in his books—an interest based on fresh interpretations of his fictions, driven largely by reading formations developed under the impact of Modernism.[113] That renewal would transform Melville into the "great American novelist" of the nineteenth century and *Moby-Dick* into an icon of American fiction, but it would also perpetuate the idea that his relation with his contemporary readers consisted of saying "No" in thunder—or simply neglecting them. In his posthumous audience of the twentieth and twenty-first centuries, Melville once again got—and missed—what he had wished for.

CHAPTER 5

Response as (Re)Construction

The Reception of Catharine Sedgwick's Novels

WHATEVER HAPPENED TO Catharine Sedgwick? The question is neither facile nor meant to be rhetorical, if considered through the lens of historical hermeneutics. Instead, the query can be—and needs to be—answered in several different ways, one of which is simply to say that she was forgotten as a fiction writer for most of the twentieth century, until a few scholars rediscovered her as part of the feminist project of recovering "lost" women writers. Certainly such an answer is accurate if we consider that the last twenty-five years have witnessed the republication of three of her novels—*A New England Tale, Hope Leslie,* and *The Linwoods,* all in scholarly editions—following almost a century during which her novels were out of print.[1] Since 1980, critical attention also has picked up noticeably. From 1921 to 1980, according to the *MLA Bibliography,* only five journal articles on Sedgwick were published, with only one before 1963. Since 1980, ninety-three critical articles have appeared.[2] Much of that attention has fallen on *Hope Leslie,* Sedgwick's third novel, originally published in 1827. In its Rutgers University Press edition, *Hope Leslie* is now frequently taught in university courses in nineteenth-century American literature to the point where it could be called hypercanonical, in the mold of Kate Chopin's *The Awakening.*

It would be a mistake, however, to claim that Sedgwick is now firmly established in the American canon. Despite the recent interest, most of her fiction—six to twelve novels, depending on how one counts, and seven collections of short stories—remains out of print. In fact, Sedgwick's position, comparatively speaking, is still at the margins of the canon if scholarly interest serves as the gauge. Contrast the number of critical articles on Sedgwick since 1980 to those over the same period on traditionally canonical antebellum fiction writers: 2,492 for Melville, 1,648 for Hawthorne, 1,793 for Poe, and 517 for Cooper. Among nineteenth-century women fiction writers, Sedgwick lags substantially behind Chopin (470), Harriet Beecher Stowe (422), Louisa May Alcott (229), and Sarah Orne Jewett (210).[3] Even more telling, only three book-length studies devoted to Sedgwick have appeared in the last one hundred years, and only one of those has come as part of the reclamation work on Sedgwick since the 1980s.[4] What needs to be stressed is that there is still a substantial difference between Sedgwick's recovery and the much longer, more intense revival that Melville underwent through most of the twentieth century.

Ironically, the relative rankings of Sedgwick and Melville over the last eighty years—and still today—is nearly the exact inverse of the positions the two authors occupied in the antebellum decades. While Melville began as a popular author with *Typee* and *Omoo* but was largely forgotten by 1860, Sedgwick was one of the most popular American novelists throughout her fiction-writing career and the most successful women writer before the wildly popular debuts of Stowe's *Uncle Tom's Cabin* and Susan Warner's *The Wide, Wide World* in the early 1850s. Moreover, Sedgwick was one of the few women writers in antebellum America to enjoy both popular success and the public acclaim of periodical reviewers and editors. Frequently compared to Walter Scott and Fenimore Cooper as a historical novelist, Sedgwick was also repeatedly linked with Cooper, Washington Irving, and William Cullen Bryant as "founders" of American letters.[5] The *Southern Literary Messenger* asserted that "[o]f America's female writers, we must consider her the first" and admitted no hesitation "in placing her upon a level with the best of our native novelists" (Dec. 1835: 57). The *Ladies Magazine* went so far as to "unhesitatingly place" Sedgwick "as the first and best American novelist" (July 1830: 320), a judgment echoed five years later by the *Museum of Foreign Literature,* which announced that "[b]y the more trained and fastidious of her countrymen, she is considered the first of American novelists" (Nov.–Dec. 1835: 540). While such claims may strike one as quintessential examples of magazine puffery, it is worth noting that in 1834, as a result of her literary reputation and broad popular appeal, Sedgwick was one of only four writers included in the *National Portrait Gallery of Distinguished Americans,* literally a "who's who of statesmen, generals, ministers, and other cultural leaders."[6]

The difference between Sedgwick's antebellum status and her radical devaluation in American literary history for three-fourths of the twentieth century leads back—perhaps inevitably, certainly provocatively—to the question of what happened to cause such a change. How did the virtual erasure of Sedgwick by the mid twentieth century occur? Was it a matter of Sedgwick's falling victim to the patriarchal institutionalization of American literary history in the twentieth century, which conceptualized fiction within a master narrative that Nina Baym has termed a "melodrama of beset manhood"? Or was it less a macrohistorical development of patriarchal prejudices and more a microhistorical phenomenon in which Sedgwick's fate paralleled what Jane Tompkins revealed as the fate of Susan Warner, who fell into literary oblivion because she had the wrong connections—or no significant connections—in the literary marketplace of publishing and reviewing?[7]

The answer to both questions is "no"—or, at least, "not exactly." Unlike Warner and many other nineteenth-century women fiction writers, Sedgwick did not lack professional and social connections with prominent members of the publishing industry and the antebellum literary world. From virtually the beginning of her writing career in the early 1820s, Sedgwick regularly mixed with writers and artists at her brother's and friends' houses in New York City. In the 1840s, the Sedgwick homes in Lenox and Stockbridge, Massachusetts, became a literary center for what would be known as the American Lake District, a region that developed into a gathering place—and in some cases served as the residences—for such literary and publishing luminaries as Bryant, Hawthorne, James Russell Lowell, Oliver Wendell Holmes, Henry Wadsworth Longfellow, and James T. Fields. Sedgwick's short stories and brief nonfiction writings appeared in the leading periodicals of the times, including the *Knickerbocker Magazine,* the *New-Yorker,* the *Southern Literary Messenger, Graham's Magazine,* and *Godey's Lady's Book,* as well as in such prominent annuals as *The Token* (where several of Hawthorne's stories also first appeared). Though her novels were published by several different firms in New York, Boston, and Philadelphia, the majority came out under the cachet of the Harper Brothers, the largest and most prominent U.S. publishing house. Indeed, the Harpers became Sedgwick's main publisher in 1835 because the firm deliberately sought to add her name—and her significant reputation—to its lists.[8]

While the phallocentrism of many twentieth-century literary historians no doubt affected Sedgwick's later demotion, this explanation for

Sedgwick's devaluation as a writer has its limits. For one thing, it cannot account for the consistent canonical status in the twentieth century of women writers such as Emily Dickinson, Edith Wharton, and even Harriet Beecher Stowe. Nor can patriarchal dominance explain how Sedgwick was received so favorably by the interpretive community of antebellum reviewers, a community that was just as phallocentric as the twentieth-century literary historians who read—and wrote—Sedgwick out of the American canon.

Rather than invoke what have become standard assumptions regarding the reputation of nineteenth-century women novelists, we need to look elsewhere in history for answers about Sedgwick's fate. Specifically, was there anything about the way her novels were read and received in antebellum America that not only elevated them but also contributed to their eventual neglect? To ask such a question is to raise in a different way the query about what happened to Sedgwick. In this version, the query becomes part of a broader inquiry regarding what it meant to read Sedgwick in the decades leading up to the Civil War. What did reviewers and other readers make of *A New England Tale, Hope Leslie,* and *The Linwoods,* as well as *Clarence, Live and Let Live, The Boy of Mt. Rhigi,* and her other fictional narratives? What was it about the way her novels were received and interpreted in the public sphere that caused them to be the object of so much praise? In seeking answers to these questions, it is crucial to remember that the work Sedgwick's fiction did on or for her antebellum audience was a function of the work their interpretive practices—particularly the strategies of informed reading—did on her novels.

Although modern critics and historians have directed no attention to questions about antebellum interpretive practices and Sedgwick's fiction, some have addressed other dimensions of her relation to the fiction-reading audience and the literary marketplace. One of the most prominent has been Mary Kelley, who has argued that Sedgwick was one of the earliest examples of antebellum women writers who suffered the angst of authorship as a "literary domestic." According to Kelley, that angst resulted because, in entering the literary marketplace, Sedgwick transgressed social norms by violating the cult of domesticity, with its emphasis on home and private space as the proper female domain. Women writers such as Sedgwick thus "were torn between a desire 'for something out of their condition'" as women and "a conflicting and contradictory desire for 'a right appreciation'" of the domestic sphere as the domain of true womanhood. Finding themselves "private women" on a public stage, these writers experienced not only anxiety but also a "crisis of identity" that "hampered" them throughout their careers. For Sedgwick in particular, Kelley finds that anxiety in the novelist's remarks about authorship in her letters and in the fact that Sedgwick published most of her novels and short story collections anonymously.[9]

More recently, however, one Sedgwick scholar has called this characterization into question, at least in regard to the practice of anonymous publication. For one thing, anonymous publication of fiction was used by such leading male novelists as Scott and the early Cooper. Moreover, while Sedgwick began her career behind the screen of anonymity, by the late 1820s her identity as the author of the anonymously published *New England Tale, Redwood,* and *Hope Leslie* was widely known among reviewers and middle-class readers.[10] Long after it stopped serving as a veil for her identity, Sedgwick continued to maintain the practice of anonymous publication. Indeed, so transparent had the "screen" become by the 1830s that a reviewer in the *American Ladies Magazine* could begin his review of *The Linwoods* by saying that "Miss Sedgwick's name is sufficient to give any work, to which it is prefixed, a passport to public favor," despite the fact that Sedgwick's name appeared nowhere in *The Linwoods* (Nov. 1835: 653). Although one need not go so far as to claim that her continued use of anonymous publication was a market strategy, it clearly was for Sedgwick more of a convention than a symptom of feminine modesty or writerly anxiety.

Whether pseudo anonymity was a strategy or not, it does appear that Sedgwick possessed some savvy about the literary marketplace, including audience expectations. She seems to have been a regular reader of periodical reviews, including those of her own works, and repeatedly attended to the sales figures for her novels. While her family aided her in fiduciary relations with publishers, a letter to her brother Charles reveals she was quite comfortable discussing contracts and marketing issues. Speaking of the publication of her *Poor Rich Man and the Rich Poor Man* in 1836, Sedgwick instructed Charles to "urge upon" the Harpers the "policy of letting it be known to their correspondents ... what sort of thing it is, intended for popular consumption, that it may at once be for sale in the country towns."[11] This is not to imply that Sedgwick was a literary mercenary or panderer to the reading public. Such terms would be no more fitting to describe her interests than they would be for characterizing Melville's desire to reach a broad, popular readership and his meticulous concern for securing publishing contracts in England to prevent pirating of his novels. Indeed, Sedgwick's market awareness was typical of many writers of the time, including not only Poe and Melville but also most women novelists. As Ann Douglas has observed, women writers in antebellum America "showed an extraordinary degree, even by Victorian standards, of market-oriented alertness to their customers." Lawrence Buell has shown, moreover, that antebellum women writers, particularly those who were, like Sedgwick, from New England, preceded men in identifying themselves as professional writers.[12]

Sedgwick's awareness of the literary marketplace and the middle-class audience for fiction was an outgrowth of her conception of what successful authorship entailed—that is, reaching readers broadly for productive social and cultural ends. In part that concept was grounded in assumptions about women and women's roles as defined by the cult of domesticity and its notions of true womanhood. Despite the limitations this ideological construction of gender placed on women, a number of modern feminist scholars have shown how the cult, ironically enough, provided a logic for women to enter the public sphere though writing and publication. As Susan Coultrap-McQuin has pointed out, "Although the ideology of separate spheres could be restrictive to women, it also gave them an area of authority (the home) and an expertise (domesticity and morality)" that some women seized on "to justify an expanded role in society" through authorship.[13] If women were, as the cult said, specially endowed with moral feelings and possessed an intrinsic virtuous authority, it made absolute sense that women were especially fit to help cultivate such attributes in others via the printed word. Who better, in fact, to write the novels that could do more good than harm?

Answering that question by saying "women," the public sphere—led by periodical reviewers—welcomed women writers as fit contributors to the elevation of society. According to *Godey's*, the work of female authors gave "proof that our women are doing their share to promote the moral improvement of society" (Jan. 1837: 48). A review in the *Southern Literary Messenger* claimed that the "[e]levated position assumed by the softer sex in the various departments of elegant literature . . . has been justly deemed an unerring token of the rapid advancement of knowledge and refinement" in America (Sept. 1849: 579). By the early 1850s, an article on "American Female Authorship" in *Godey's* could claim that "the time has gone past when literary tastes or pursuits are admitted as a stigma upon the social relations of any woman. . . . Let the needle and the pen lie side by side, they will not wrangle; for the one induces long, pleasant reveries, and the other can give them expression" (Feb. 1852: 147). Nor were such remarks exceptions to the rule. According to Baym, many reviewers shared this recognition and respect for women writers, treating their works "as serious entrants in the race for literary reputation."[14]

While it is, therefore, necessary to qualify the claim that Sedgwick faced a crisis of identity as an author, it is important not to go to the other extreme and claim that she never experienced anxiety as a writer. On several occasions she expressed dismay over the quality of a novel she was writing and doubts about its possible success. While composing *Hope Leslie* in 1825, she warned her brother Henry, "you *must* moderate your expectation—or you will be sadly disappointed" with the novel, since "my education has been too defective, and my knowledge too circumscribed, to permit the expectation that I can do anything better or half as well as I have done." Five years later, while writing *Clarence*, she lamented to Charles, "I am not satisfied with Clarence [*sic*], and never shall be with any thing that I write."[15] Yet what writers do not have similar doubts about their writing? One need only recall Melville's letter to Hawthorne bewailing his "whale" and lamenting that "all my books are botches" to recognize that Sedgwick's dismay was comparatively mild. Moreover, Sedgwick's remark in 1830 about "never" being satisfied with "any thing that I write" sounds like the expression of a demanding author, who is turning an interrogating eye on her writing and asking tough questions about it.

Similar qualifications need to be made about her comments on literary forms and the profession of authorship, and what such remarks indicate about her self-conception as a writer and her artistic ambitions—or lack thereof. These issues are especially important because several feminist critics have argued that literary women in antebellum America, unlike their male counterparts, did not conceive themselves as artists and thus lacked aesthetic ambition.[16] To be sure, Sedgwick repeatedly made remarks in private, particularly early in her career, that seem to place her within this general pattern. In 1822, she wrote in a letter to Susan Channing, "I protest against being supposed to make any pretension as an author," and five years later, in response to a letter from a reader of *Hope Leslie,* Sedgwick claimed, "[l]iterary occupation is rather a pastime than a profession for me."[17] On literary fame, Sedgwick was even more dismissive. Writing to Henry in the wake of the reception of her second novel, *Redwood,* Sedgwick asserted, "I have always been sincere in my declaration that I did not write for fame—the book has had much more praise and celebrity than I expected."[18] Such a denial Sedgwick repeated throughout her career. In an 1837 letter to William Ellery Channing, she "thank[ed] Heaven that I am not now working for the poor and perishing rewards of literary ambition," and four years later she maintained in a letter to Harriet St. Leger, "I never wrote for fame, never desired it."[19] Sedgwick's comments, however, may well reflect less feminine modesty or a lack or artistic ambition than a distrust of the transience of literary fame and the folly other antebellum writers saw in an ambition for popularity. Again one need only recall Melville's marginal pencilings to find in them echoes of Sedgwick and to recognize them as part of an ambivalence, as Michael Gilmore has shown, shared by a number of male writers, including Hawthorne, Ralph Waldo Emerson, and Henry David Thoreau.[20] Indeed, rather than outright dismissal of artistic ambition, Sedgwick's remarks were part of a similar ambivalence in that, on other occasions, she was quite ready to admit, as she did in 1830, that "I honestly confess that I earnestly desire and hope for success and expect it" with her writing. Or, as she put it in an 1834 journal entry about her fiction, "I have as much pleasure in success & certainly as much in the consciousness of deserving it . . . as others."[21]

Ambivalence about fame and literary ambition hardly indicates that Sedgwick was distraught over her role as a woman in the public literary marketplace. On the contrary, Sedgwick seems to have been comfortable in the public sphere through involvements that were not limited to her writing. Influenced by her family's belief that education and its transmission were obligations and that educated Americans ought to play a leading role in a democratic society, Sedgwick involved herself in social activism through visiting hospitals, establishing schools for immigrant children, and serving for over a decade as president of the New York Women's Prison Association.[22] In her activism, Sedgwick thought of herself as an instrument of the American republic—or even of God—and that idea colored her conception of her fiction and of herself as an author. In a journal entry Sedgwick expressed what she saw as the moral and spiritual instrumentality of her work when she wrote, "When I feel that my writings have made any one happier or better, I feel an emotion of gratitude to Him who has made me the medium of any blessing to my fellow-creatures."[23]

Though admittedly more providential in its conception of her vocation, Sedgwick's view of the fiction writer's role—and of the nature and value of fiction—was very much in line with the assumptions of informed reading. Like most reviewers, Sedgwick valued fiction above all for its ability to instruct while delighting by fusing, in its best manifestations, the aesthetic with the didactic so as to be capable of performing ameliorative cultural work. Expressing the point in an 1830 journal entry, Sedgwick felt that a novel of the highest merit was one that not only interests its audience but also "elevates the feelings, or . . . allies itself . . . to the purest & highest attributes of our nature."[24]

Such ideas, in turn, contributed significantly to Sedgwick's conception of the relation between author and audience, irrespective of gender; however, it was a conception quite different from Melville's and Poe's, despite the fact that all three writers were influenced in this area by the public discussion of fiction in periodicals. Although Sedgwick shared with Poe and Melville a desire to reach common and elite readers, she never conceived that engagement as the acrimonious battle for mastery—via artistic shape shifting and disruption of the audience—that Poe envisioned authorship to be. Nor was it for Sedgwick a matter of seeking to speak to a wide audience because she had something to say and wanted to be sure she was heard, as was the case for Melville. Or rather, it was never just a matter of a expression searching for a wide reach so much as a linkage of Melville's democratic aspirations with Sedgwick's unflagging desire to move readers to thoughts and feelings that would lead to more democratic and ethical social practices. Consequently, while Sedgwick did not conceive of an author's relation to audience as adversarial or unidirectional, neither did it involve for her a mere passive acquiescence to readers' demands. For Sedgwick that relation needed to develop in a cooperative manner, enabling writers to exercise agency in shaping their identity while addressing their readership as bipartisan participants in the experience of fiction. It was a conception of authorship and reader relations to which she would subscribe during her entire career and one that would contribute to the substantial approval her fiction received in antebellum America.

✎

Ironically, Sedgwick began her career with no intention of being a fiction writer. The impetus behind what would become her first novel came from her recent conversion to Unitarianism in 1821, in that Sedgwick originally conceived her book as a religious tract to promote that liberal branch of Christianity. Partly under the encouragement of her brother Henry, to whom she showed a partial version, Sedgwick modified and expanded her draft into a 277-page novel. It was published anonymously in 1822 under the title *A New England Tale; or, Sketches of New England Character and Manners.*[25] Though evidence of its sales is sketchy, it did sell well enough that the publisher quickly issued a second printing, which sold out in two months.[26] Reviews were laudatory, with the *Literary and Scientific Repository* proclaiming that *A New England Tale* was comparable in orientation and merit to Oliver Goldsmith's *Vicar of Wakefield* and the novels of Maria Edgeworth (May 1822: 340). Such public approbation, apparently, was matched by the private reactions of her readers, according to her brother Henry, who reported receiving one day "a large packet of letters . . . from Boston, all of them praising the tale."[27]

Readers sensed that Sedgwick was doing something new even as she was meeting reader desires that had been building in the wake of the heady nationalism that had developed since the American victory in the War of 1812. Seeking to extend that nationalism to the cultural front, the *North American Review* had published a series of articles in 1815 calling for the development of an indigenous American literature that would reflect the national character.[28] Feeding the fire four years later was Sidney Smith's now infamous taunt in the *Edinburgh Review*: "in the four quarters of the globe, who reads an American book?"[29] That remark kicked off discussions in American periodicals that carried through the 1820s.

It was in the midst of such discussions, and the eager expectations they produced, that American reviewers received and positioned Sedgwick's novel. Commenting on the "wide scope which our country affords" for social and historical fiction, the *North American Review* praised *A New England Tale* for its "beautiful little picture[s] of native scenery and manners" (July 1822: 279 n.). The review in the *Literary and Scientific Repository* went a step further, claiming, "of the books that profess to illustrate American society and manners, we have never met with one which so perfectly and agreeably accomplishes the design, to a certain extent, as the little volume before us" (336). No doubt such remarks emanated in part from the campaign to promote an American literature and, thus, rested squarely on ideology and literary politics. Like other formulations in informed reading, these remarks' ideological bearings constituted part of a pattern of response that interpreted *A New England Tale* within a specific horizon of expectations. For the reviewer in the *Literary and Scientific Repository*, that horizon involved not only national pride and topicality but also the interpretive assumption that, to be successful, a novel must fulfill reader expectations in an original way. Hence, the reviewer noted that, while "[o]ur political institutions, the state of learning among us, and the influence of religion upon our national character, have often been discussed and displayed," what set Sedgwick's novel apart was its representation of "domestic manners, the social and moral influences, which operate in retirement . . . and the multitude of local peculiarities, which form our distinctive features" (336).

Amid this view, other readers found Sedgwick addressing expressly one of the areas the *Repository* reviewer had mentioned only in passing: religion and its impact on the national—or at least the New England—character. Certainly, readers could have located any number of places in which religion is both a topic of direct discussion and a factor in Sedgwick's character depictions, particularly that of her protagonist, Jane Elton, and her guardian aunt, Mrs. Wilson, a hypocritical Christian whose "bitter spirit of the Jewish bigot," according to the narrator, "was manifest in the complacency with which she regarded her own faith."[30] Within the codes of informed reading, in fact, *A New England Tale* could be interpreted not only as a religious novel but as a dangerously sectarian attack on Calvinist theology, and a few readers responded to the novel in precisely this manner. The *New York Review* expressed "disgust" at the "narrowness, injustice, and sectarian bitterness" that "marked her 'New England Tale'" (Oct. 1837: 447), while another reviewer—this one in the

Christian Disciple—objected to the novel's depiction of Mrs. Wilson as an embodiment of Calvinist tenets in "their most bold and pernicious forms."[31] A similar dismay marked a letter Sedgwick received from a Daniel James, who, though praising the novel in other ways, nonetheless complained about Sedgwick's depiction of Mrs. Wilson. Citing in particular a scene in chapter 11, when she disparages "some of the sublimest portions of holy scripture," James objected, "Mrs. Wilson is a rank antinomian. She makes religion a mask for all iniquity. And I am extremely sorry" that "the benevolent author has confounded principles with the too common abuse of them."[32] Although it is unclear how widespread such responses were, the *American Ladies Magazine* did summarize the reception of *A New England Tale* with the general comment that "the portraiture of religious hypocrisy which the work contained . . . brought upon its author the charge of sectarianism" (Dec. 1835: 659).

Given such charges and the tendency in informed reading to castigate sectarian and advocacy fiction in general, it is surprising that Sedgwick's first novel was not sweepingly denounced in this area. On the contrary, several commentators defended the novel's treatment of religious issues. A different article in the *American Ladies Magazine,* for example, asserted that, while "[s]ome christians [*sic*] have considered the character of Mrs. Wilson, as an unkind and uncandid caricature of their opinions," such interpretations missed the point. "Had Mrs. Wilson been intended as a representation of the whole body of Calvinists, this [criticism] would unquestionably be just; but as an *individual,* Mrs. Wilson is true to life— most of us have met such in our pilgrimage" (May 1829: 235). Interpreting Mrs. Wilson's character as representative, not of a particular creed, but of an all-too-common pseudo-religious sensibility, this reviewer read *A New England Tale* not as a divisive religious novel but as a form of moral commentary about spiritual hypocrisy. In effect, Sedgwick's characterization of Mrs. Wilson was justified by its verisimilitude, an idea even the otherwise unsettled Daniel James admitted in his letter when he conceded, "of these Mrs. Wilson—I know many of them."

For another reviewer, the charge of sectarianism was equally irrelevant, but not because of the novel's vraisemblance. Rather, according to the *Monthly Review*, "Every character in the tale . . . seems to possess distinct notions on religious subjects; but the author has granted a wide tolerance to all of them," except for the "bigoted" Mrs. Wilson.[33] While interpreting the novel as a critique of religious bigotry, this reviewer did not see it as dangerous advocacy fiction. Rather, his formulation conceived the novel as an expression of nondenominational tolerance grounded in Christian principles. A related interpretation was at work in a remark in a letter from a Mrs. S. S. Wilde to Sedgwick, congratulating the author for "the excellent & Christian principles [that] are maintained in the New England Tale," specifically the "doctrine of love, the forgiveness of injuries, & pity & compassion" to which no "reasonable being can object." Likewise focusing on its nondenominational message of Christian piety and faith in the divine, Eliza Cabot congratulated Sedgwick for the way she "expressed . . . beautifully yourself in the N. E. Tale, the feeling of trust and confidence in the goodness of God."[34]

It is perhaps significant that the last two responses were by women, since women were the leading force, as Douglass has demonstrated, in the cultural shift in antebellum America away from Calvinist theology to a more liberal, even feminine form of Christianity emphasizing divine forgiveness, a loving Christ, and the inherent goodness of humans.[35] If women such as Cabot and Wilde saw no sectarianism in *A New England Tale*, it may have been because the religious sensibilities they ascribed to it accorded so well with their ideas about the oppressive Calvinist creed that American women had started to reject. Given the progressive religious appeal such readers attributed to the novel, combined with what other readers saw as its democratic nationalism, it seems likely that the popularity of *A New England Tale* resulted in part because of the way middle-class women could find in the novel subjects and representations that met both their values and their horizon of expectations.

It would be a mistake, however, to attribute too much of the novel's success to the work of women readers. For one thing, anti-Calvinist feelings were not limited to women—or to liberal ministers. At the time, middle-class antipathy was developing toward what were seen as the limitations of Calvinism in relation to the Christian nurture that were deemed essential to the moral education of children. Since "the saints were powerless to save their progeny," notes G. M. Goshgarian, Calvinism came to be regarded as, in effect, binding the hands of both parents and educators, and "[i]n Jacksonian America, few middle-class parents shared [t]his sense of the limits of parental responsibility." Given such dissatisfaction, it is not surprising that the subject of Calvinism and critiques of its doctrine had entered American fiction as early as 1812—a decade before *A New England Tale*.[36] In this sense, many middle-class readers were not finding anything disturbing in Sedgwick's novel. The linkage of that familiarity and the embrace given the novel for its welcomed nationalism goes far in explaining why some male reviewers also did not take it as a divisive religious novel.

This linkage, however, does not mean that women's reading did not play a role in male reviewers' approval of *A New England Tale*. If Sedgwick's novel was viewed as promoting a religion of the heart founded in the "doctrine of love," that orientation aligned neatly with the assumption within informed reading that women were especially prone to respond emotionally to novels and tales.[37] In that linked logic, *A New England Tale* could be viewed as distinctively valuable for the way it met the needs of women readers. Even the verisimilitude ascribed to Sedgwick's novel had relevance here, since a common assumption of this era, both in England and in the United States, was that women readers paid greater attention to detail than did men.[38] Amid possible connections that readers may have found between a female audience and Sedgwick's novel, however, no reviewer identified *A New England Tale* as primarily or even especially suited for women readers. Instead, reviewers saw the novel's characterization, its verisimilitude, and its distinctive religious flavor as suitable for Americans of both sexes.

Equally interesting is that despite the commercial success of *A New England Tale* and the sheaf of praise it received in public and in private, Sedgwick was dismayed at the novel's reception. To Susan Channing, Sedgwick admitted, "I could not endure the idea that I had written myself out of the affections" of some of her neighbors and fellow New Englanders. Much as Melville did in responding to the reviews of *Mardi*, Sedgwick seems to have been struck most by the few criticisms of the novel as presumptively and offensively sectarian. In another letter to Eliza Cabot, Sedgwick, speaking of the occasional objections to *A New England Tale*, wondered aloud whether "is it not mortifying and shocking Dear Eliza to be held up before the public as an *indelicate & profane* writer?"[39]

Sedgwick, however, was hardly deterred by her dismay or by the comments that had precipitated it. Within a year she was at work on a new book, intended from the start as a novel. It was, moreover, a novel for which she had greater ambitions. In another letter to Eliza Cabot, Sedgwick explained, in what was already becoming for her a characteristic mix of diffidence and determination, that she wanted to "meet the charge of presumption, [by] attempting with my few literary qualifications to write a *real book*" this time.[40] That "real book" was *Redwood*.

When Sedgwick's new novel appeared in 1824, her heightened ambitions for it were quickly validated in the *Atlantic Magazine*, which identified *Redwood* as an advancement in Sedgwick's fiction. "The promise held forth by the 'New England Tale,'" asserted the review, "has been more than abundantly realized in Redwood [*sic*]" in its novelistic craft and greater maturity (July 1824: 239). This sentiment quickly was echoed in other periodicals. Part of the reason for this response lay in the fact that reviewers took *Redwood* as another religious novel, but one in which Sedgwick successfully avoided any tincture of what might be construed as sectarianism. The *United States Literary Gazette* asserted, "Redwood [*sic*] is a religious novel, but there is nothing like bigotry or fanaticism in the opinions of the writer, who displays a spirit of very liberal and rational piety" (Dec. 1, 1824: 254). Reviewers were especially emphatic about praising *Redwood* on this issue when it came to the novel's representation of the Shakers, a community that figures largely in the novel's plot. A review in the *New-York Mirror* noted that in the narrative "that well known [*sic*] religious sect called the Shakers, form a conspicuous group in the picture, and as far as our judgment extends, are painted with fidelity" (June 26, 1824: 380). *Graham's* seconded this interpretation of the novel's accuracy and taste in depicting the Shakers, calling *Redwood* "the best account we have ever read of life among the Shakers," which is "traced with masterly discretion" (Aug. 1850: 135).

Perhaps more important to the view of *Redwood* as an advance in Sedgwick's craft was that reviewers saw additional connections between Sedgwick's first two novels: in their domestic focus and their American character. The *Southern Quarterly Review* boldly proclaimed that Sedgwick's second novel "entitle[s] her to a position among writers second to few" and solidified that claim by forging a link between those two elements—and by implication back to the way *A New England Tale* had been received. According to this review, what gave *Redwood* its imprimatur was its "delineation of household events, the portraitures of the serene, the domestic, even the humble" within a particular regional setting. The novel's domestic sketches of New England life and society "possessed a particularity that," according to this review, made them "highly valuable" (July 1850: 540). Reading the novel for its regional color, in fact, was one of the most common responses to *Redwood*. The review in the *New-York Mirror* praised the novel for the way its "delineations of New England manners is [*sic*] very correct, and form a faithful picture of that part of our country." For the *Mirror*, that authenticity was especially notable in the character of Debby Lennox, a rural healer who plays a key role in the novel's rescue plot. "The character of Debby," intoned the reviewer, "is drawn with a masterly pen. It is replete with sound, but uncultured sense, and Yankee peculiarities" (380). Others made the same claim in responding to Sedgwick's characterization of Debby. The *Atlantic Magazine,* styling Debby a striking "Yankee maiden" whose "peculiarities of . . . dialect are well preserved throughout," called her "the most original [character] in the work" (239). Readers were most struck by what they saw as the regional verisimilitude of Debby. "Who cannot see," asked a reviewer in the *American Ladies Magazine,* "the muscular, gray-haired old woman, with kindly heart, and the blunt freedom of manners, which so peculiarly characterises [*sic*] our good, honest, independent yeoman" of New England? "If there be an artist who hopes to surpass 'Aunt Debby Lenox,'" the reviewer continued, "he may as well lay down his pencil and die." Notwithstanding its hyperbole, the upshot of such a remark, as the reviewer explained in the next sentence, was that Debby, as a fictional character, "was as perfect in its kind as any character Sir Walter Scott ever imagined" (May 1829: 236). Nor were such laudatory responses limited to the public sphere. A letter Sedgwick received from a Mrs. K. Lazarus reported that a reader of *Redwood* had told her that it was "a work of superior talent" and gave special praise to "the character of Aunt Deborah [who] is first rate, in Scott's best manner, yet not an imitation of Scott. It is to America what Scott's characters are to Scotland—valuable as original pictures, with . . . the feeling of reality and life."[41]

Such comparisons to Scott carried larger implications for the way the novel was seen. Its localized setting and what reviews saw as its authentic depiction of regional manners were seized upon as features that made *Redwood* an important contribution to a nascent American fiction. It thereby was given a status similar to Cooper's *The Spy* and *The Pioneers* as America's answers to the novels of Scott. The review of *Redwood* in the

New-York Mirror praised Sedgwick as one of a small but intrepid band of "writers of our own nation, who . . . add to the reputation of this country, by making it the scene of their stories" (380). More explicit was a review in the *Port-Folio*. After grouping *Redwood* with *The Spy* and *The Pioneers* as "filling" a hitherto empty place in the "description of American manners," the *Port-Folio* reviewer went on to call Sedgwick's novel "the first *American* novel, strictly speaking," that offers "a faithful delineation of our fireside" (July 1824: 66). Indeed, intoned the *North American Review*, Sedgwick was a national American novelist in a way quite different than Cooper because *Redwood* provided "a conclusive argument, that the writers of works of fiction, of which the scene is laid in familiar and domestic life, have a rich and varied field before them in the United States" (Apr. 1825: 248).

Such characterizations of the novel both in itself and in relation to the fictions of Cooper and Scott led reviewers to conclude that, despite similarities among the works of the three writers, *Redwood* differed in ways other than its domestic focus. Just as reviewers agreed on what *Redwood* was, they also were in accord that it was not an historical novel. For some reviewers this was a problem. According to the *North American Review*, by setting her story in "the very days in which we live," Sedgwick failed to "avail herself of the . . . abundant resources of interest" for a novel, "the scenes of which should be laid in the United States" (245). Invoking the comparison with Cooper's fictions, the *United States Literary Gazette* found *Redwood* to be a lesser accomplishment precisely because it had "nothing of the historical interest which gives so much value to the works of the latter" (Dec. 1, 1824: 254). The irony here is that a factor in this critique was a feature that reviewers elsewhere identified as an asset of *Redwood*: its domestic focus. For example, while the *New-York Mirror* praised the novel for its depictions of "the humble beauties of a village life," it added that that characteristic made the novel a "plain tale, unadorned by the brilliancy of exuberant figure"; "nor does it take the eagle flight," continued the *Mirror*, "of Mr. Scott" (380).

One notable feature of the comments on *Redwood* as a national novel employing certain American materials (and leaving out others) is the virtual absence of commentary about what Lucinda Damon-Bach has recently called its "complex" treatment and "challenge" to "early-nineteenth-century ideas about gender, class, slavery" and the "relations between Northern and Southern states."[42] What Damon-Bach refers to here regarding the issue of slavery is the book's narrative about Africk, a black slave belonging to the title character and the subject of a brief six-page tale of woe in the novel's third chapter. Only one reviewer—in the *Port-Folio*—mentioned it, merely noting that, while the "episode of Africk is an affecting story, and extremely well told[,] yet we could have dispensed with it, in the fullness of our entertainment" (67). In neither the public nor the private commentary that has survived about the novel did readers indicate that they found in *Redwood* any challenges to ideas about slavery—or gender.

Where they did agree with recent critical comments about the novel was in the idea that, despite the ostensible reference of its title to a male character, Henry Redwood, the novel's most memorable—and laudatory— characters were women.[43] Besides the attention given to Debby Lennox, Ellen Bruce (a young woman who turns out to be Henry Redwood's lost daughter) and Susan Allen (an elderly Shaker) received the most notice from readers. The *North American Review* believed that "next to the character of Debby, that of Susan is sketched with the greatest spirit and originality" (271). In a letter to Sedgwick, William Minot reported that "the book is talked of everywhere" and that "people . . . admire the character of Susan extremely."[44] Of Ellen Bruce, the *New-York Mirror* declared that she is not only the novel's principal character but one from whose "beautiful lips the author seems to delight in speaking the purest sentiments of female virtue." As to those who might think her "too good for reality," the *Mirror* reviewer responded, "we are not of that calculating class, who do not believe" in "her delicacy of sentiment, and purity of thought" (380). Striking in this response is the way it combines antebellum notions of the nature of true womanhood with the interpretive code of fictional vraisemblance to locate the verisimilitude of Ellen's character in the idea that women such as she, though "seldom found in the scenes of real life," are known to exist somewhere (380).

Not every element of *Redwood,* however, came in for praise from readers. Besides chiding the novel for its lack of historical ballast, some reviewers found its plot wanting. The *North American Review* was ambivalent about the novel's plotting, particularly the events that occur at the Shaker village involving Susan Allen, her niece Emily, and Reuben Harrington, a Shaker elder who is in reality a religious hypocrite with salacious designs on Emily. The "episode of Emily, and her adventures among the Shakers," including her rescue from Harrington, said the *North American Review*, "are too extraordinary and romantic, to harmonize well with the general strain of the narrative" (265). This reviewer found a similar "want of perfect verisimilitude" in the novel's plot regarding Ellen Bruce's veiled past and the revelation of her true identity as Redwood's daughter: "There is something a little too strange, for a story of real life, in the obscurity that hangs about Ellen's birth, and the mysterious box containing the miniature of her father. . . . These things remind us too strongly of the machinery of romance" (268). In an otherwise laudatory review, the commentator in the *Atlantic Magazine* expressed dismay not so much at the plot, per se, but with the way Sedgwick handled the narrative design of the plot and its impact on the novel's momentum. In particular, this reviewer was "dissatisfied . . . with the manner in which we are called back so often in the first volume, to a detail of antecedent events, while the progress of the action is suspended" (236). But whether it was a matter of awkwardness or a lack of probability, the irony is that any disruptive or challenging dimensions reviewers found in *Redwood* obtained not in its themes or its representations of race and gender but in the way its structure disrupted readers' expectations of the proper fit between the book's actions and its otherwise realistic profile.

Despite such criticisms, Sedgwick had to be pleased with the otherwise highly positive reader responses to *Redwood*. She also had to be pleased by the general audience reaction as indicated by the book's sales. Shortly after its publication, Henry informed her that "Redwood sells very well; about 1100 [copies] are gone." Moreover, he explained, the "sale is constantly increasing, and the booksellers say that it is now better than Redgauntlet," the Walter Scott novel.[45] The reference and comparison to Scott's success no doubt provided a tonic for Sedgwick in light of the reviewer comments about the novel's failure to tap historical materials in the manner of Cooper and Scott.

Clearly, Sedgwick was affected by those remarks, since she decided to set her next novel, *Hope Leslie*, in seventeenth-century New England. Whether Sedgwick, as Michael Bell has claimed, was actually "inspired" by the comments in the *North American Review* on the subject is far from clear, but a turn to historical subject matter was a logical choice for a writer who was quickly becoming attuned to the dynamics of the literary marketplace.[46] Given the critical and popular success of Scott and Cooper, it seems clear that Sedgwick's choice was a calculated one. Such a turn was especially appropriate for a woman novelist, in light of the assumption in informed reading that historical fiction constituted a particularly suitable genre for women readers and for fulfilling the dual obligation that novels delight and instruct. Indeed, in the same year that *Redwood* had appeared, two other novels were published that demonstrated that historical novels by women could find a ready readership: Harriet Cheney's *A Peep at the Pilgrims in Sixteen Hundred Thirty-Six* and Lydia Maria Child's *Hobomok*. It is difficult not to believe that the seventeenth-century settings of those two novels had an impact on Sedgwick's choice to set *Hope Leslie* in the same period rather then in the eighteenth century of Cooper's *The Spy* and *The Pioneers*.

As noted earlier, among all of Sedgwick's works, *Hope Leslie* has by far received the greatest scholarly attention over the last thirty years. Much of that has come from feminist critics, who have read the novel as a sophisticated, transgressive text that challenges the norms and values of patriarchal culture and its historical narratives. Judith Fetterley, for instance, sees *Hope Leslie* as offering a "radical argument" against antebellum gender ideology that "reifie[d] the separation of public and private by gender"; Lucy Maddox calls the novel a "self-consciously feminist revision of male-transmitted history" in its depiction of a "rebellion of Puritan women against the domination of men"; Barbara Bardes and Susan Gossett declare that *Hope Leslie* "offers a critique of women's place in the Republic under the guise of a historical novel"; Carol J. Singley styles it a "radical frontier romance" that, in "criticizing the 'Law' of the Founding Father," offers "history with a revisionary spirit"; and Elaine Showalter reads it as a critique of the way that "women are the victims of an exchange between men," in which "captivity is part of the female condition." So pervasive has been this interpretation of the novel that even Ann Douglas, who is otherwise extremely critical of antebellum women's novels for their feminization of American culture, attributes to *Hope Leslie* a "revisionist aim" via its "high-spirited heroine," whom Sedgwick uses to wreak "feminine anarchy" and "havoc with official records."[47] With its image of Sedgwick employing *Hope Leslie* as a narrative hammer to smash phallocentric history, such commentary has dominated the criticism of the novel since its recovery, with claims for its subversive-ness being directed, almost as often, to its treatment of race. Kelley calls *Hope Leslie* a "highly critical presentation of the Puritans' subjugation of the indigenous population," while Dana Nelson maintains that the novel "presented a clear challenge to Anglo-American policy toward Native Americans."[48]

There is, however, little if any evidence that antebellum readers experienced *Hope Leslie* as a pyrotechnic challenge to the culture's dominant assumptions about gender and racial norms. Given the differences between the interpretive climates of the antebellum United States and of late twentieth- and early twenty-first-century academic America, such a gap is not unexpected. But the difference in responses cannot be attributed simply to a generalized Foucauldian genealogy of historical rupture or to the acuity of modern critics and the blindness of antebellum readers, who were ostensibly unable to see the transgressiveness of *Hope Leslie*. After all, antebellum readers did see some novels as transgressive, including, as the responses to George Sand and to Melville's *Typee* indicate, fictional treatments of race and gender roles. Antebellum readers, moreover, would have to have been inexplicably dim-witted to miss Magawisca's Native American counter narrative of the Pequot War in *Hope Leslie* and not to have shared with late twentieth-century readers the sense that Sedgwick's novel gives its women characters substantial power and a capacity for bravery and actions outside traditional domestic spaces—actions that sometimes even transgress the law. If antebellum readers responded to such features of the novel without taking them as subversive, it was not, in other words, because of those readers' exceptional obtuseness but because of the way they conceptualized and constructed the novel within a historically specific set of reading conventions that constituted the antebellum interpretive formulations of *Hope Leslie*.

What reviewers pointed to most in Sedgwick's third novel was its profile as historical fiction, but for them, *Hope Leslie* represented more than just another contribution to the form Scott had made famous. Linking *Hope Leslie* to Sedgwick's previous two novels, reviewers saw it as another national novel grounded even more firmly in U.S. materials through its use of America's past. According to a review in *Brother Jonathan*, "'Hope Leslie' is one of the best proofs extant that American writers may find in our own national characteristics and history fresher and more excellent themes for American writers" (Sept. 17, 1842: 90). For a reviewer in the *American Monthly Magazine, Hope Leslie* was not only proof of the value of American fiction based on American materials but also a salutary transformation of historical fiction into a more American genre, since Sedgwick writes "evidently [as] a republican writer, in a department which has hitherto been devoted to glorifying the spirit of feudalism, and its consequent false views" (Jan. 1836: 20). The service Sedgwick provided thus had both aesthetic and sociopolitical value that encompassed, according to a review in *Godey's,* American readers. Claiming that the "best pens among our female writers, we are happy to notice, are chiefly devoted to national subjects," the *Godey's* reviewer lauded *Hope Leslie* for "illustrating the early colonial annals of Massachusetts" and thereby taking on "so patriotic an object as that of increasing the interest of the American people in the history of their own country" (Nov. 1842: 249).[49]

Within this broader formulation, reviewers especially attended to Sedgwick's depiction of the Puritans. Although far from taking the modern view that the novel critiques Puritan society for its patriarchal oppression, antebellum readers nonetheless did not read *Hope Leslie* as a patriotic celebration of those "Founding Fathers" of New England. Rather, readers both in public and private saw the novel as presenting a true-to-life representation of the strengths and flaws of the Puritans. In a letter to Sedgwick, Lucy Aikens noted that "very rarely indeed have the puritans of either hemisphere been drawn with so much impartiality as you display."[50] Periodical reviewers agreed. After noting the seventeenth-century Massachusetts setting of the novel and explaining that the "object of the story is to form a picture of the manners and state of society at that period," a review in the *New-York Mirror* congratulated Sedgwick for the way that "object . . . is admirably accomplished. The stern spirit of liberty for which the settlers of New-England [*sic*] were distinguished, clouded, however, by some dark shadows of fanaticism and misguided zeal, is here presented to our view in lively and glowing colours" (June 23, 1827: 383). Combining a similar view with the response that highlighted the value of the novel for its American readers, the *Baltimore North American* found among the book's "many merits" its capacity to "induce many of all ages to recur to the early history of our country, and to make themselves more thoroughly acquainted with the pure, intellectual and virtuous, *though bigoted,* race of men who settled New England" (Aug. 4, 1827: 95, emphasis added).

In responding to *Hope Leslie* this way, reviewers were not seeing it as revisionist history that sought to counter a cultural filiopiety toward the Puritans. On the contrary, antebellum readers came to the novel already steeped in cultural ambivalence about the Puritan colonists. The antebellum attitude toward the Puritans, as Buell has pointed out, was a mixture of "hostility and filiopietism," and it was a mixture known to virtually every reader of *Hope Leslie* and of the novels about the Puritans that preceded it in the 1820s, including Cheney's *Peep at the Pilgrims* (1824) and Child's *Hobomok* (1824). In those novels, readers would have found confirmation of that ambivalence in that, as Reynolds notes, "admiration for the heroism of the New England forefathers was usually qualified by a distaste for their intolerance, gloom, and logical rigidity."[51] In this regard, Sedgwick's own comments about her object in depicting the Puritans are telling. Explaining to one of her correspondents that "I meant to touch their characters with filial reverence," Sedgwick nonetheless added that "[t]heir bigotry, their superstition, and, above all, their intolerance," especially because of their "thraldom . . . to Calvin's gloomy interpretation of Scripture," were "too apparent on the page of history to be forgotten" or missed by anyone.[52] Such comments suggest that the historical critique Sedgwick saw herself making of the Puritans was directed not so much at their phallocentrism but at their "gloomy" Calvinist creed.

The situation involving the antebellum response to Sedgwick's Indians was, however, a bit more complex. Though generally reviewers viewed the Puritans and other whites as more prominent characters in the novel, Sedgwick's representation of Native Americans received nearly as much attention in the public discussion. Part of the reason lay in the fact that *Hope Leslie* was published amid a wave of popular interest in depictions of Native Americans in historical fiction. These included Child's *Hobomok* and Cooper's widely read *The Pioneers* (1823), *The Last of the Mohicans* (1826), and *The Prairie* (1827). Such interest was fueled by political debates over the status of Indian tribes living east of the Mississippi River, a concern that would shortly culminate in the Indian removal controversy in Georgia. What is interesting is the shape reviewer response took in the face of that growing controversy, given that, as Lucy Maddox has argued, the "widespread public conviction" of the late 1820s was that Indian "presence anywhere in the eastern United States was an obstacle to the national progress of American civilization." In light of such a conviction, how was it that, as one Sedgwick scholar has claimed, "most [readers] applauded Sedgwick's depiction of American Indians" in *Hope Leslie*?[53]

One possible answer is that reviewers and other readers, just as they would do twenty years later with *Typee,* reconciled the novel's sympathetic depiction of Native Americans with the dominant culture's racist ideology by interpreting the text as an elegiac representation of the Indians' regrettable but inevitable fate in the face of white civilization's implacable advance. Certainly readers could have seized on several passages in the novel to construct such a reading, beginning with the book's epigram, an eight-line poem that, in the first stanza, reads:

> Here stood the Indian chief, rejoicing in his glory!
> How deep the shade of sadness that rests upon his story:
> For the white man came with power—like brethren they met—
> But the Indian fires went out, and the Indian sun has set![54]

Readers could well have privileged this image, and combined it with passages in the novel that praise the Puritans for "open[ing] the forests to the sun-beam, and to the light of the Sun of Righteousness," to place the novel within the cultural logic of the "vanishing American," with its assumption that the demise of the Indian, though sad and even deplorable, allows for the admirable advance of Christian civilization.[55]

Such speculation, however, is not really needed to account for reviewer "applause" for Sedgwick's depiction of Native Americans because such broad approval simply did not mark reviewer responses to the novel. Reviewers had little to say about Sedgwick's treatment of Indian culture or of Native Americans as a people, nor did they comment on most of her Indian characters: Mononotto and Monoco, Magwisca's father and mother; Oneco, her brother; and Nelema, an old Indian woman healer whom Hope Leslie rescues from prison. Instead, virtually all reviewer attention, when directed at Sedgwick's Indians, focused on her depiction of Magawisca.

For some, Magawisca was a magnificent creation, admirable in her virtue and deserving of reader sympathy. "There are few nobler creatures than her Indian girl," said the *New Yorker* (Sept. 26, 1840: 24), while a review in the *American Ladies' Magazine* averred that "Magawisca inspires a loftier sentiment" even than Hope Leslie herself because the former, as a "representative of an injured race," "is full of moral grandeur" (Dec. 1835: 661–62). A review in *Littell's Living Age* compared Magawisca to Cooper's Indians and claimed that "her elevated and self-sacrificing heroism" was quite equal to his depiction of Indian courage and "poetical eloquence" (Oct. 19, 1844: 652).

Other reviewers, however, were troubled by what they saw as a lack of verisimilitude in Magawisca. A reviewer in the *North American Review,* while finding her a "charming conception," felt that she "is an Indian maiden only in name. She is the poetical, but not the historical, child of the forest . . . not having a drop of kindred blood with the copper-colored savages of our own primitive woods" (Jan. 1849: 205). An even stronger objection on this principle came in a review in the *Western Monthly Review*. Like the reviewer in *Littell's*, the *Western Monthly's* reviewer also linked Magawisca to Cooper's Indians, but in this case it was to find a common fault: "The authoress has fallen into the error, so prevalent in the works of Cooper and all American novelists, that have anything to do with Indians. They dress a figure in Indian costume; give it a copper skin; make it use extravagantly figurative language; and introduce it with . . . the delicacy of feeling and refinement of civilized life" (Sept. 1827: 294–95). Finding her so idealized, this reviewer dubbed Magawisca "the first Indian angel, that we have met with," a "very pretty fancy; but no more like a squaw, than the croaking of a sand-hill crane is like the sweet, clear and full note of the redbird" (295).

Such a divergence in responses is striking but certainly comprehensible as the product of reviewers' privileging two different criteria within the interpretive repertoire of informed reading: the desideratum of verisimilitude in characterization versus the valuation of inspiring and morally laudable characters. Several reviewers, however, were able to combine and reconcile these two criteria in responding to Magawisca, and they did so in several ways. One method marked the response of a different reviewer in the *North American Review*. Noting that Magawisca "is one of those creations of genius," the reviewer admitted that "[s]ome have questioned her verisimilitude as an Indian. They assert she is too novel, too delicate, too spiritual for an Indian." But in response, this reviewer declared, "This we are disposed to deny. That there were very many Magawiscas, we do doubt ourselves, and therefore, we would not propose her as a fair sample of the Indian character; but that the best features of her character have had a real existence in savage life, that she is a possible Indian, we have no doubt whatsoever; and this is all which is claimed for her in the truly modest preface of our authoress" (Apr. 1840: 418). Following a rule of notice focused on the novel's preface and combining it with a flexible notion of plausibility, this reviewer granted Magawisca verisimilitude as an Indian character because, as an individual within that representation, she possessed enough credibility to enable readers to take her as a "possible Indian."

A different but related interpretive strategy marked the response of other reviewers, who did not stop at the possibility of the existence of a Native American woman like Magawisca. Instead, several reviewers interpreted her character by contextualizing it within American history (or legend) to claim that a person very much like Magawisca had existed. As a reviewer in the *New-York Mirror* put it while citing, in particular, Magawisca's willingness to sacrifice herself to save Everell Fletcher, "[t]o some, the magnanimity and delicacy of feeling discovered in Magawsica may appear unnatural and exaggerated, when attributed to a savage," but such readers must realize that "[i]n drawing the character of this noble child of nature, the author seems to have taken some hints from the celebrated Pocahontas, as, in many respects, they are strikingly similar" (June 23, 1827: 383). Likewise, the review in *Littell's* asserted that Sedgwick "had noble warrant for her creation" of Magawisca "in the well-known incident of the rescue of Captain Smith by Pocahontas" and added that Sedgwick was "only working out the devotion of that noble girl one step further" (Oct. 19, 1844: 653). Both of these reviewers, like the one in the *North American Review*, grounded part of their interpretation in a rule of notice in that Sedgwick's preface had itself brought up Pocahontas as a historical antecedent for the credibility of Magawisca, but it was a matter in both cases of reviewers' combining that move with several others, including a cultural knowledge and conception of Pocahontas widely shared by Sedgwick's audience as a whole. So well known was the story, in fact, that Robert Tilton has claimed that "the nineteenth-century audience for *Hope Leslie* . . . would have made the connection between the heroism of Magawisca . . . and the bravery traditionally identified with Pocahontas even without the aid of the prefatory clues provided by Sedgwick."[56] It is, of course, impossible to say with any certainty whether that was the case, but reviewer comments indicate clearly that some antebellum readers did make the connection in a move that enabled them to ascribe verisimilitude to Magawisca while granting Sedgwick, as the *Mirror* reviewer did, some authorial license in accord with another assumption of informed reading: that accomplished fiction offered well-crafted characters that were both lifelike and artistically enhanced for inspirational effect. Indeed, the Pocahontas legend fit perfectly with this position since both her and Magawisca's nobility could be interpreted within the logic of antebellum assumptions about the values of white ascendancy. That is, if Magawisca, like Pocahontas, could be viewed as an admirable Indian, it was in part because readers could interpret her as an inspirational embodiment of the willingness of the native Other to sacrifice herself for a white man.

In light of these reactions, it is not surprising that the largely laudatory response to Magawisca was part of the broader reception of *Hope Leslie* as a national historical American novel, which reviewers, on the whole, labeled as Sedgwick's best work so far. As a second reviewer in the *American Ladies' Magazine* asserted, "with regard to 'The New England Tale' and 'Redwood' . . . 'Hope Leslie' has more of the glow of vitality of genius" and "is a work of more power," in part because "Magawisca is the noblest conception imagination ever formed" (May 1829: 227–28). Though not according the characterization of Magawisca such hyperbolic ascendancy, the *North American Review* agreed with the overall assessment that "'Hope Leslie' is the last of this lady's three larger works, and, in our judgment, the best" (Apr. 1828: 411).

An interesting feature of the overall response to *Hope Leslie* is what was missing from it in comparison to what reviewers had noted about *A New England Tale* and *Redwood*. Except for the remarks about Magawisca, there were no comments about the vraisemblance of other individual characters or of characterization as a whole in *Hope Leslie*. On the contrary, when the criterion of verisimilitude came up at all, several reviewers directed it to the book's actions and plotting, which they found problematic. The *Western Monthly Review* found a "want of piquancy in this work" owing to the fact that the "parties prosecute their affairs too much," so that events "have not the free, natural movement of voluntary action" (295). According to the review in *Littell's*, "the misconstructions

and adventures in which [Sedgwick] involves Hope Leslie are . . . gratu-
itously puerile," making the novel's "suspense . . . repulsively irritating"
(652). Such disdain for the plotting of *Hope Leslie* echoed what reviewers
had said about *Redwood*, thereby establishing a pattern that would characterize the reception of virtually all of Sedgwick's full-length fictions. It
was a response, as the comments in *Littell's* and the *Western Monthly
Review* indicate, grounded in the paired criteria regarding the effectiveness of a novel's construction and its capacity to handle plotting in a way
that met reader expectations. Given that double imperative, it is striking
that reviewers could fault *Hope Leslie* and *Redwood* in this area yet still
roundly praise her fictions with increasing enthusiasm. Such a pattern
speaks volumes about the assets, both aesthetic and instructional, that
reviewers found in the other elements of her novels.

The success that Hope Leslie enjoyed among reviewers appears to have
been matched by the enthusiasm for the novel among the middle-class
fiction-reading public. Although no overall sales figures have survived,
Hope Leslie outpaced *Redwood* by quickly selling out its first edition of
two thousand copies.[57] The popularity of the novel is also suggested by
the fact that the tag "by the author of *Hope Leslie*" became the lead (or
part of the lead) that Sedgwick and her publishers would use, in lieu of
her name, as the identifying mark of her authorship on the title page of
her novels throughout the 1830s. That strategy enabled her to sustain
the pretense of demure female authorship while wisely making certain
that any informed reader could identify a particular novel as being, in
fact, by Sedgwick, whose name was virtually synonymous with *Hope Leslie* for a decade.

Riding her growing caravan of successes, Sedgwick completed her
next novel, *Clarence*, in 1830 with expectations comparable to those she
had had for *Hope Leslie*. However, she cast those expectations differently because she saw *Clarence* as different, not only from *Hope Leslie*
but also, it seems, from her first two novels. While *Clarence* was still in
press, Sedgwick spoke of it in a letter to Susan Channing as a narrative
that "treats of the present times" by focusing on "the follies of the day."
Noting that the novel is set "chiefly in New York" and deals with "topics
that concern every body," Sedgwick explained that the book's orientation
"seems to me of more popular interest than a tale of the olden time."[58]
Given the popular and critical success of *Hope Leslie,* which was her

"tale of the olden time," Sedgwick's comments suggest she expected even greater results from *Clarence.*

Other comments by Sedgwick in a letter to her brother Charles only a week before her missive to Channing indicate, however, that some dismay accompanied her opinions about her new novel. "I am not satisfied with Clarence," she confessed to Charles. Yet her next sentence indicates that this reaction did not stem from the conventional modesty and self-deprecation expected of women writers. Sedgwick explained that the reason for her dissatisfaction was her "familiarity with fine works, carrying your taste so far ahead of your capacity." Such a remark suggests that Sedgwick's aesthetic and literary sensibilities had developed to a point where she was becoming increasingly demanding and rigorously critical of her own art. Yet even as she questioned the merit of *Clarence,* she qualified her doubts by striking a note that anticipated her comment to Susan Channing: "I do think, nevertheless, that it has a great deal more in it than any thing else I have written, and that it is better adapted to the general taste of novel-readers I am sure."[59] Significantly, if Sedgwick believed that *Clarence* represented an advance over *Hope Leslie,* she did so by linking its novelistic merit to its relationship to her audience in a move well tuned to the assumptions of informed reading.

Sedgwick's guarded optimism about *Clarence* found its echo in the novel's reception. Although modern Sedgwick scholars have asserted that *Clarence* "did not achieve the critical success of its predecessors," particularly *Hope Leslie,* such a characterization is only partly accurate.[60] As one of the leading novel-reviewing organs of the time, the *North American Review* declared that Clarence "has all the fine qualities—of head and heart which have so favorably recommended the former works of the fair author," adding that "had she written nothing but Clarence [*sic*], she would amply deserve our praises" (Jan. 1831: 73–74). This review added, however, that as good as *Clarence* was, it did not quite measure up to one of Sedgwick's previous novels, but the one it cited was not *Hope Leslie.* Instead, the review opined that *Clarence* "is perhaps not so finished as *Redwood*" (73). Such qualifiers, however, were rare. Indeed, one notable feature about the public commentary on *Clarence* is that, unlike the reception of her previous novels, reviewers raised virtually no objections to any part of *Clarence.*

On the whole, reviewers read *Clarence* as a welcomed and representative addition to Sedgwick's oeuvre. For some, that representativeness lay in what they saw as the novel's American character. According to a review in the *Ladies Magazine, Clarence* "effected to prove . . . that American characters, scenes, and circumstances . . . may be wrought into a romance, which shall be intensely interesting, and yet not foreign to our habits of life" (July 1830: 320). The *Literary World* agreed, pointing out in its review that *Clarence* continued the trend that had marked Sedgwick's fiction "since her first entrance into the world of letters," with "literary productions [that] have been mainly, in every sense of the word, American." For this reviewer, moreover, that national character lay not only in the way "her works of fiction have been drawn from the history of their country or its domestic manner" but also in the way *Clarence* and her previous novels "completely reflect the prominent characteristics of the American mind" (Oct. 6, 1849: 297).

When they moved to particulars, reviewers focused, as they had with her earlier fictions, on her characters and especially on Sedgwick's skill at making them true to life. The *North American Review* asserted, "the best part of [the] novel consists of its sketches of character," not only because they are "copies of nature" but also because Sedgwick has "given us a great variety of characters, each of which has the distinctiveness of individuality" (90). A Review in the *New-York Mirror* agreed, noting that "the characters are finely drawn, carefully defined and contrasted. . . . There are no embodied angels. . . ; but in the record of our memories we may find written many a name whose proprietor might have sat for the author's delineations" (June 19, 1830: 394). The *Mirror* reviewer cited in particular Charles Clarence, the novel's title character and father of the tale's female protagonist, Gertrude, as being "a well-drawn personage," not because he is original but because he so faithfully resembles people readers know: "His character may not be new to the reader, for such men are not unfrequent among us, but he will dwell upon it, as upon a good likeness of a valued friend" (394).

Such praise of character verisimilitude was a common response to *Clarence*. A review in the *American Monthly Magazine* found the character of Mr. Layton, the gambling-addicted father of Gertrude's friend Emilie, a "most forcible sketch" because of its "truth to the principles of human nature." For this reviewer the same verisimilitude inhered in Mr. Layton's "heartless sensibility and Gertrude's strong, but perfectly feminine qualities," which are "both so familiar to our commonest experience" (July 1830: 281). Gertrude Clarence, in fact, was singled out most frequently for her resemblance to actual people, and reviewers were not the only ones doing the pointing. Having read the novel for a second time, Ellen Follen informed Sedgwick that "I know not how it is but Gertrude reminds me of you dear."[61] What is interesting is that Follen's remark was not grounded in the interpretive assumption that a novel's narrator was a reflection of the author, since *Clarence* is not told from Gertrude's first-person point of view. Instead, Follen's interpretation appears to have inhered in the assumption in informed reading that characters, and particularly a novel's protagonist, served as an index to or would in some way be a reflection of an author's temperament and mind.

A unique feature of the response to *Clarence* was that, for the first time in the reception of Sedgwick's fiction, reviewers found in the novel's plotting a parallel degree of vraisemblance that was also dramatically effective. In *Clarence* Sedgwick "has a clear and direct manner of telling her story, which leaves an almost irresistible impression of its truth," explained the review in the *Ladies Magazine*, which added, "yet her fancy is so fertile, that none of our novel writers equal her in the involution of plot, in that gradual and as it were incidental unfolding of the web of destiny" (320). The reviewer in the *American Monthly Magazine* found strong plotting to be a new and welcome turn in Sedgwick's craft. Noting that "the good traits" of her previous novels had been their "singular unaffectedness and truth to nature" in their characterizations and domestic scenes, this reviewer explained that the "work before us is quite of another character," but not because it abandoned verisimilitude. "Without abandoning the field, in the selection of which she has done credit . . . , the authoress has brought into her plot . . . a dramatic power which . . . astonishes us" (280). Continuing, the *Monthly Magazine* reviewer found this asset especially in the novel's subplot involving Emilie and Padrillo, the story's "Spanish" villain. Praising Padrillo's characterization as "an uncopied, powerful, yet most natural villain," the reviewer asserted that the "*denouement* of Pedrillo's history is a specimen of the finest dramatic invention." Indeed, in this response it was precisely Sedgwick's success in characterization combined with her expert plotting that marked the singular success of *Clarence*, in that Padrillo's "whole history shows a depth of the study of the human heart, and a maturity . . . in the plot which are not at all common in a modern novel" (280–81).

Although the response to *Clarence* was not seamless in its commendations, reviews did treat the novel as a ringing success, in part because they felt that Sedgwick was doing something new for her art and, perhaps, something "not at all common," as the *American Monthly Review* put it, "in a modern novel." While that newness obtained for some in the novel's effective plotting, other readers concluded that Sedgwick had added topics that her fiction had not before addressed. Pointing out that previously the "scenes and incidents of her works of fiction have been drawn from the history of the country or its domestic manners," the *Literary World* observed that in *Clarence* "her more directly and perhaps most praiseworthy efforts have been in illustration of its social habits and tendencies" (297). Likewise, the review in the *Ladies Magazine* interpreted the "plan of 'Clarence'" to be Sedgwick's design "to display the characters that move in the rich and fashionable circles" (320). Nor was it simply that her audience saw her taking on what was a new area for her: upper-class manners and, as the *North American Review* termed it, the "fashionable society of New-York" (Jan. 1831: 74). Readers interpreted the novel as doing with that subject something fresh and satisfying. In what reads like a fan letter to Sedgwick, one L. T. Osborne explained "how truly I am pleased with the work" because of the way "Fashionable life in N[ew] York is very nicely satirized."[62] The *Ladies Magazine* was even more impressed by what it saw as the novel's comic critique of fashionable society because, ultimately, such satire underscored the broader "moral . . . lessons" of *Clarence*: "to remind the dwellers of this 'bank note world,' that there are objects more elevated, more worthy of pursuit than wealth" (325). In such remarks readers were not crediting Sedgwick with taking the novel, as a form, in a new direction. Rather, reviewers read through what had become, within the interpretive formations of the time, two established sub-genres of fiction, the novel of fashionable life and the satiric novel. In their interpretation of *Clarence*, what readers saw as new was that Sedgwick for the first time was working in these subgenres and successfully combining elements of each without creating a generic cacophony in her novel. As such, *Clarence* was, for a good number of readers, her greatest accomplishment to date.

❧

Although Sedgwick published only short stories over the next four years, when she did return to novel writing, perhaps the largely unchallenged positive response to *Clarence* encouraged her to try something new with her next book, *Home*. Despite that title, which would no doubt have struck antebellum readers as a signifier linking it to Sedgwick's previous domestic fiction, *Home* represented a departure from *A New England Tale*, *Redwood*, *Hope Leslie*, and *Clarence*. For one thing, its genesis was quite different. In 1834 the Reverend Henry Ware, who was in the process of commissioning from several different writers a group of novels that exhibit "Scenes and Characters Illustrating Christian Truth," asked Sedgwick to write a new novel as part of that series. Sedgwick agreed and in the next year composed *Home*, which was published in 1835 and was identified as being "by the author of 'Redwood,' 'Hope Leslie,' etc."[63] As the first and only novel Sedgwick produced under a specific commission, *Home* also differed from *Redwood*, *Hope Leslie*, *Clarence*, and *A New England Tale* by being considerably shorter. At 158 pages, it was slightly over half the length of *A New England Tale* and only a third as long as the other three.

When modern Sedgwick scholars have discussed *Home*, they have identified it as a work altogether different from her first four full-length fictional narratives. Linking it with two of Sedgwick's works of fiction that would follow—*The Poor Rich Man, and the Rich Poor Man* (1836) and *Live and Let Live* (1837)—critics over the last twenty to thirty years have defined *Home* and its two companions as, not full-fledged novels, but "moral tales," "didactic tales," "didactic novellas," "moral tracts," brief "domestic" fictions, "conduct tales," a "didactic trilogy," or fictional versions of domestic self-help manuals such as Louisa Hoare's *Hints for the Improvement of Early Education and Nursery Discipline* (1826).[64]

Such a distinction, however, in no way marked the antebellum response to *Home*. Instead, reviewers linked it to Sedgwick's previous novels as another domestic tale performing valuable cultural work. A review of *Home* in the *New-York Mirror* pointed out that "the amiable authoress of 'Redwood' and 'Hope Leslie,'" who "has not disdained to devote her fine talents and elegant fancy to the illustration of the quiet walks of life" in those books, was doing the same service with *Home*. "Such books are invaluable," continued the review, because they provide a service that all good fiction should, according to one assumption of informed reading: they facilitate reader tranquility by demonstrating the "positive gain . . . to be acquired by being contented in the station in which Providence has placed us" (May 30, 1835: 383). Arguing in more general terms, a review in the *American Monthly Magazine* viewed *Home* as consonant with Sedgwick's fictions to date, since "we see in all her works . . . the marks of a true genius for commencing a literature for the mass of the American people which shall bring up their moral tone to the spirit of their institutions." Identifying *Home* as a work that was both domestic and national, this reviewer interpreted the narrative as another representation of the "peculiar dignity of republicanism," particularly for the way it demonstrates how "naturally this form of society weds Christianity" with the "simple temple of Family" (Jan. 1836: 21).

Besides seeing *Home* as sharing purpose and value with Sedgwick's previous novels, reviewers also found it to be a work of high literary merit, equal—or even superior to—her earlier fictions. Far from demoting *Home* to the level of moral tract, a review in the *Boston Observer* asserted, "Its literary merit is so high, its story so well conducted, the style so beautiful . . . that those who seek in books . . . the gratifications of taste as a relief from the vacuity of idleness, will be eager to read it."[65] The *North American Review* went so far as to proclaim, "We know not a more beautiful example of the faculty and grace" by which the "power of women's intellect" and skill could be expressed "than is presented in Miss Sedgwick's little tale, entitled 'Home,'" the scenes of which, the *Review* felt assured, would "win for their accomplished author a more enduring title . . . and exalted fame" (Oct. 1835: 444).

This ligature between Sedgwick's previous novels and *Home* extended to the marketplace success of the latter, which not only matched but outstripped the popularity of *Redwood* and *Hope Leslie*. In its first two years, *Home* went through twelve editions, and within a decade of its publication, it reached its twentieth edition.[66] It is not hard to see the reason for this success, given reviewers' reactions to it. Like reviewers, readers most likely saw *Home* as a book that gave them more of what they associated with and found attractive about Sedgwick's fictions; they were entertaining and informative, domestic and American in a way that met and reinforced the middle-class horizon of expectations. Sondra Smith Gates has suggested that part of that reinforcing appeal resulted from the economic message antebellum readers could take from the book, particularly in its story of William Barclay, the novel's male protagonist, who rises from poverty to become a successful artisan and businessman as a New York printer. For middle-class readers, Barclay's story may have confirmed the triumphalist American exceptionalism of the time, which viewed penury as a "structural flaw" in European society but believed that "in America it is simply the ground floor upon which the industrious can build happy homes, given the tools of democracy."[67]

Whether readers' responses to Barclay's story or to other elements of *Home* were the cause of its success, Sedgwick was not only pleased by its popularity and notoriety but also admittedly surprised by the extent of her achievement. In an 1836 letter to Louisa Minot, Sedgwick confided that *Home* "has been received with far more favor than I expected—nothing that I have written has seemed so well suited to the *country* market." Quickly and sagaciously sizing up the market for her fiction, Sedgwick added in the next sentence that she had learned something important from the success of *Home*: When she again sat down to "write any thing more than a letter, it will be books of this description which suit the mass of readers."[68] What is interesting, however, is that following *Home* and in the year leading up to her prognosis for success, Sedgwick did not turn to writing the two books that modern scholars have grouped with *Home* as a subgenre trilogy different from Sedgwick's "true" novels. Instead, Sedgwick composed and published later in 1835 her second novel set in America's past: *The Linwoods*.[69]

That move, along with Sedgwick's resolution following the reception of *Home,* are significant in two ways. Her comment to Minot indicates that if Sedgwick herself saw any difference between *Home* and her previous novels, it was one of degree, involving the relation between text and audience. That is, for Sedgwick, *Home* had had an appeal to an even broader readership than the already large audience she had reached with her previous novels. Moreover, her decision to turn next to *The Linwoods,* a book modern Sedgwick critics relate to her first four novels as a different type of work than *Home,* suggests that Sedgwick viewed her new novel, in terms of its relation to her audience, as being in the same mold as *Home.*

The Linwoods, in fact, was received as a novel that had links both to *Home* and to *Hope Leslie,* a connection Sedgwick sought to cultivate by once again—as she had done with the title page of *Home*—identifying her new novel as "by the author of 'Hope Leslie.'" No doubt seizing on that identification and on the book's subtitle, *"Sixty Years Since" in America,* readers opened *The Linwoods* expecting a historical novel set during the American revolution. Engaging in precisely such a rule of notice, a review in the *Boston Pearl* explained that the "title of the book indicates that the time selected is the darkest period in the history of our country . . . not soon to be forgotten by those enjoying the benefits at that time so dearly purchased" (Mar. 12, 1836: 206). Taking the book's subtitle as an echo of one of Scott's while citing, as well, some comments in Sedgwick's preface, the *North American Review* led off its thirty-five page review of *The Linwoods* by identifying it as a historical novel, the "plan" of which evinced "the same general character" as Scott's fictionalized histories (Jan. 1836: 160).

As was the case with the response to *Hope Leslie,* reviewers had high praise for *The Linwoods,* beginning with Sedgwick's decision to set her new historical novel during the American Revolution. The *North American Review* declared, "We think this work the most agreeable that Miss Sedgwick has yet produced" precisely because it "possesses the great additional attraction, that it carries us back to the period of the revolutionary war, the heroic age of our country" (Jan. 1836: 160). A review in the *Museum of Foreign Literature, Science, and Art* agreed, asserting that "the period of American history, which she has chosen for her tale, is, as the title indicates, one that must ever possess unparalleled interest" (Nov.–Dec. 1835: 613). Although the *Museum*'s reviewer believed that *The Linwoods* was "more of a domestic than a historical novel" (613), the initial significance of that remark lay less in the relevant weight it gave to each component than in the way it configured the novel within the prevailing horizon informed reading had established for Sedgwick's novels as a meld of domestic and national/historical materials.

To say this, however, is not to dismiss the qualification raised by the *Museum* reviewer, since it involved an issue other reviewers brought up regarding the genre of *The Linwoods.* That issue was not a matter of readers taking the novel as a problematic generic hybrid that failed to conform to a proper novelistic profile. Virtually all reviewers interpreted Sedgwick's novels as possessing the double dimension of being domestic and nationalistic fictions, and reviewers applauded that duality. What was at stake with *The Linwoods*—and what marked a departure from the responses to her previous novels, especially *Hope Leslie*—was which half of that hybridity dominated. A review in the *Knickerbocker,* for example, agreed with the *Museum* reviewer that *The Linwoods* "cannot be judged as a historical romance" per se because, "while the action of the tale is connected with historical events," the linkage of those events to the novel's plot and main characters is "slight and casual" (Oct. 1835: 368). Such interpretations, in fact, dominated reviewer responses in this area. According to a second review in the *Museum of Foreign Literature, The Linwoods* was not a "strictly historical novel. Washington, and General Putnam, and Governor Clinton, it is true, all of these figure in her pages, but merely as accessories to the true-hearted, noble Isabelle Linwood, and the beautifully gentle and melancholy Bessie Lee" (Nov.–Dec. 1835: 540). Similarly, a review in the *American Ladies' Magazine* asserted that "'The Linwoods' is essentially a domestic story, though the scene is laid during the war of the American Revolution" (Nov. 1835: 653). It is important to understand that none of these comments were couched in critical tones or offered pejoratively. In fact, one of the reviews in the Museum applauded Sedgwick for avoiding a "strictly historical novel," adding that "we are inclined to think that this, her last work, is her best" (540).

Reviewers extended this formulation to the novel's characterization by focusing on its nonhistorical characters, and the ones reviewers most frequently commented on were women. To be sure, occasionally a reviewer did refer to several of the males, though surprisingly little attention went to the two male protagonists, Herbert Linwood and Eliot Lee, both officers in the continental army. Instead, reviewers tended to remark briefly on Kissel, Eliot's comic, feeble-minded sidekick, or Jasper Meredith, a foppish, conniving Tory, who is Eliot's rival. Moreover, despite the fact that Herbert and Eliot take up the greatest percentage of the novel's narrative attention and figure most prominently in its plot, the characters that drew the most notice were Isabelle Linwood and Bessie Lee, the book's female protagonists.

What seem to have been at work here were several assumptions that had come to constitute a frame for interpreting Sedgwick's fictions. Assuming that Sedgwick's novels possessed a strong domestic character and that Sedgwick was at her best in constructing women characters, reviewers came to *The Linwoods* predisposed to interpret the novel much as they had interpreted *Clarence* and *Home* (in which Sedgwick had also placed a male character, William Barclay, at its center)—as a story about the domestic sphere and, thus, a novel about female characters. Moreover, reviewers interpreted Isabelle and Bessie as exemplary female characters.

What the exemplariness consisted of, however, was not the same thing that readers had noted about the women characters of *Hope Leslie, Redwood,* and *Clarence*. Responses to those earlier novels had highlighted Hope Leslie's "enthusiasm" and "gaiety and wit" (*North American Review* Apr. 1828: 420) and called Debby Lennox an "active" and "all-sufficient" woman (*Port-Folio* July–Dec. 1824: 67), who possesses a "mixture of intelligence . . . and decision, of masculine habits with those of her sex" (*North American Review* Apr. 1825: 266). Regarding Gertrude Clarence, the *American Monthly Magazine* enthused over her "strong, but perfectly female qualities" (July 1830: 281), while the *New-York Mirror* forefronted her "energy" and "maturity of intellect" (June 19, 1830: 394). Although an important part of the plot of *The Linwoods* involves, as the other three novels do, women engaged in acts of heroic rescue—with women, in both *Hope Leslie* and *The Linwoods*, rescuing a man—reviewers never highlighted such intrepidity or the intellect and energy of the women in *The Linwoods*. Instead, Isabelle and Bessie were admired for their beauty, affection, loyalty, and vulnerability.

Reviewers particularly focused on Bessie and the subplot of her unrequited love for Jasper Meredith, which leads to a mental and physical breakdown nearly fatal to her. "Seldom has a sweeter creature," intoned one reviewer, "risen upon a novelist's eyes than this frail-minded girl" (*Museum of Foreign Literature* Nov.–Dec. 1835: 540), while the review in the *American Ladies' Magazine* said that Sedgwick's depiction of "the lovely, gentle, melancholy Bessie Lee . . . is one of the most powerful spells of the author" (653). A review in *Godey's* went so far as to proclaim that "Bessie Lee, is one of the most effective presentations to be found in our fictitious literature, and may lay claim to the distinction of originality—no slight distinction where *character* is concerned" (Sept. 1846: 131). What is somewhat puzzling about this last remark is that it came amid observations by several other reviewers that Bessie closely resembled Shakespeare's Ophelia and was, by implication, anything but original. The extensive review of *The Linwoods* in the *North American Review* observed that, owing to Jasper's perfidy, "Bessie . . . loses her reason, and becomes a sort of modern Ophelia." Added the reviewer, "in returning to Meredith certain locks of hair and other presents . . . she seems to copy the example of her fair prototype in Shakespeare" (Jan. 1836: 168–69). Not that this reviewer, or others who noted the parallel, seemed to have been bothered by such a "copy." If anything, they appeared to see it as an accomplishment, testifying to Sedgwick's abilities to match the Bard. Indeed, that logic was behind William Dillingham's remarks in a letter to Sedgwick shortly after the novel's appearance. "We are delighted with your story of 'The Linwoods,'" wrote Dillingham, adding, "I cannot help saying that your 'Bonnie Lee' [*sic*], in pathos, power and beauty, in nature, truth & delicacy, is scarcely inferior to Shakespeare's inimitable Ophelia."[70]

When the novel's other main female character, Isabelle, received attention, it was not as the feisty, bold individual who defies her Tory father and helps concoct the rescue plot of her brother Herbert. Instead, most reviewers interpreted her as an exemplary woman through her devotion, beauty, and high-mindedness. The review in the *Boston Pearl* declared, "We are peculiarly pleased with the high-minded Isabelle Linwood," especially for the way she acts "like a woman" (Mar. 12, 1836: 207). The *New England Magazine* called Isabelle "so gentle; so gifted, yet so simple; so beautiful, yet so unconscious; so majestic, yet so affectionate"—in short, so strikingly yet unassumingly feminine (Nov. 1835: 381). Even when reviewers saw in Isabelle's character a certain strength, as did one of the reviewers in the *Museum of Foreign Literature*, the perception was linked to her feminine "elevation of mind" and "devotion to duty" (Nov.–Dec. 1835: 613).[71]

Clearly, a good part of the popularity of *The Linwoods* lay in what readers saw as its appealing female and feminine characters. And popular it was. Of the 5,000 copies of the novel the Harper Brothers printed in late 1835, nearly 4,300 sold in a little over a year. In the mid-1830s, these were impressive numbers, given that at the time, according to the publisher George Palmer Putnam, sales above 2,000 copies were unusual.[72]

It is important to recognize that readers' engagement with and enthusiasm for Sedgwick's latest narrative involved the way they saw it fulfilling what was coming to be expected of her as a woman novelist, one whose association with the domestic and the womanly had been especially reinforced by readers' experience with *Home*. To be sure, Sedgwick's status as a women writer had colored the response to her novels to some degree since *A New England Tale*. But what the response to *The Linwoods* began to evince was a shift in emphasis that is apparent if we compare an early remark by a reviewer of *A New England Tale* and *Redwood* with one twelve years later on *The Linwoods*. Writing at a time when Sedgwick's authorial identity was not yet fully known, a reviewer in the *United States Literary Gazette* said in 1824, "Common fame has attributed these works—Redwood and the New England Tale—to a lady; if this be so, we can only say we think it surprising." Citing both books' "elegance" and "style," the *Gazettte* reviewer went on to note that "the literary execution of these volumes, would in no degree discredit an author who had disciplined and fortified *his* mind by severer studies than ladies are apt to love" (July 15, 1824: 101 emphasis added). By 1835, however, such characterizations of Sedgwick's style as striking, even somewhat masculine, in its discipline and strength were giving way to comments exemplified by the review of *The Linwoods* in the *Southern Literary Messenger*: "The character of her pen is essentially feminine. No *man* could have written *Hope Leslie*; and no man, we are assured, can arise from the perusal of *The Linwoods* without a full conviction that his own abilities would have proven unequal to the delicate yet picturesque handling. . . . Woman is, after all, the only true painter of that gentle and beautiful mystery, the heart of woman" (Dec. 1835: 57). By such responses, Sedgwick the domestic-national novelist was beginning to be reconfigured by reviewers as the delicate limner of the gentle female heart.

This recasting—and, in effect, typecasting—of Sedgwick's novels as women's fiction did not, however, progress tendentiously in the reception of her next novel, *The Poor Rich Man, and the Rich Poor Man*, which appeared in 1836. Furthermore, although this book and *Live and Let Live*, which followed it a year later, were brief fictional narratives, as *Home* had been, reviewers did not link these two latest novels to *Home* as a "didactic trilogy" distinct from Sedgwick's other "real" novels. In fact, only two reviewers made any overt distinction between Sedgwick's previous novels (including *Home*) and *Poor Rich Man* and *Live and Let Live*, and it was only to remark that the latter two were "shorter" (*Godey's* Sept. 1846: 130).[73]

In contradistinction with even such a minor differentiation, most reviewers responded to both new novels by aligning them within the interpretive formulation they had constructed for Sedgwick's previous novels. Such positioning entailed reading both as quintessentially Sedgwickian American domestic novels. A review in the *Christian Examiner* explained that in *Poor Rich Man* Sedgwick "has more of the character and features of the nation at her disposal than any of the ambitious politicians in this land" because of the book's powerful theme, which the reviewer interpreted as, "Let our families be well ordered, let love and rectitude rule in social intercourse and common affairs, and all will be well. Let domestic economy be perfect, and political economy will take care of itself" (Jan. 1837: 398). Reading the novel as a reassuring reminder of the benevolent partnership among the happy home, the political sphere, and national well-being, this reviewer found in *Poor Rich Man* precisely the idea that antebellum middle-class, patriarchal culture had fashioned as one of its building blocks. In less hyperbolic tones, a review in the *Knickerbocker* said essentially the same thing about *Live and Let Live*, characterizing it as a "charming little book," owing to its "thorough knowledge of American domestic life" and its "spirit of generous kindness toward all" (July 1837: 86).

As they had with Sedgwick's previous books, reviewers also heaped praise on the two works' characterizations. The *North American Review* concentrated on the female characters in *Live and Let Live*, particularly the successful variety Sedgwick gave them, from the "rule-worshiping Mrs. Broadson," the "well-disposed, but inconsiderate, incompetent and always afflicted Mrs. Ardley," and the "lofty, fashion-enslaved and fashion-hardened Mrs. Hartell" to the novel's protagonist, "Lucy Lee, a gentle, patient, bright, heroic creature" (Oct. 1837: 480). The *New York Review* was especially taken with the novel's Mrs. Hyde, in whose "character and house-keeping maxims . . . the writer gives us her *ideal* of a *true lady* and good mistress" of home and hearth (Oct. 1837: 448).

Another parallel between reviewers' responses to *Live and Let Live* and *Poor Rich Man* and the reception of Sedgwick's previous fiction came in interpretations of the two new works as social commentary in the mold of what reviewers had inferred about *Clarence*. Focusing on her depiction of the monied class in *Poor Rich Man*, the *American Quarterly Review* explained that Sedgwick offers some instructive satire. But the review also was careful to warn readers, "let it not be supposed . . . that

Miss Sedgwick joins in the foolish outcry against the rich as such." Sedgwick was no Jacksonian leveler, the review explained, since "it is only against wealth misapplied that her satire is directed" (Mar. 1837: 28). Though not invoking the term *satire*, the reviewer in the *New York Review* described Sedgwick's "graphic sketches ... of the vices and follies that abound in fashionable life" in a way that made clear his assumption that satire was at work in *Live and Let Live*. Indeed, said the reviewer, "the faults and follies of higher life are mirrored" in the novel "to expose and correct the faults of master and mistress" (448).

Yet the responses were not all echoes of the reception Sedgwick's earlier fiction had received. A strain in reviewer commentary on *Live and Let Live* paralleled and thereby continued the slight shift that had started to appear with the public discussion of *The Linwoods*: the interpretive formulation that identified Sedgwick as a womanly writer of domestic fiction designed to be read, in particular, by other women. Identifying the readership it saw as most suited to *Live and Let Live*—and most likely to benefit from it—a reviewer in *Godey's* explained, "We entreat every good lady, and every lady who wishes to learn how to do good, to read this book" (Sept. 1837: 140). Similar interpretations about the novel's audience marked reviewer comments in the *Knickerbocker* and the *North American Review*. The latter "assure[d] our fair readers, the young housekeepers, that here, in the form of an hour's delightful reading, they have a directory for the rule of that world of infinite interests, their home" (480). Ascribing authorial intention and linking it to conceptions of reader engagement, the *Knickerbocker* review proclaimed, "We cannot doubt that the warmest hopes of the benevolent writer, in relation to her work, may be realized; that it *will* rouse female minds to reflection upon the duties and capabilities of mistresses of families" (86).

Besides the explicit gendering of Sedgwick's audience, relatively new was a second strain in reviewer conceptions of *Live and Let Live* and *Poor Rich Man*. Minor at first, this other strain would become an important step in the eventual demotion of Sedgwick's fiction. The *North American Review* was careful to direct *Live and Let Live* not only to women but especially to "young housekeepers." The review in the *New-York Mirror* made a parallel remark in orienting the novel-reading audience to *Poor Rich Man*. While the *Mirror* "strongly recommended this little book to every reader," it specifically drew attention to the novel "to the young for its usefulness, and also for its interest" (Nov. 14, 1836: 151).

I call this strain "relatively" new because it had actually begun in a similarly understated manner in some reviewer comments about *The Linwoods* in 1835. The review in the *American Ladies' Magazine* in November had asserted that the novel "surely will find favor with every young, pure, and innocent heart" (653), and an article on "Caroline Maria Sedgwick" in the same magazine a month later said of *The Linwoods*, "its influence on the young will be most salutary" (665). The review in the *Museum of Foreign Literature* offered a similar identification of the audience for *The Linwoods,* declaring that Sedgwick's "aim has been to give her young American readers a true, if a slight impression of the conditions of their country at the most trying time of its existence" (Nov.–Dec. 1835: 618). Admittedly, reviewers appear to have been responding in this case to a sentence in the preface to the novel, since the *Museum's* comment actually is an unacknowledged quotation of part of that sentence. However, the preface to *Hope Leslie* contained a sentence that had said virtually the same thing about a possible audience of "young people," yet reviewers did not identify that novel as especially suited to a juvenile readership. Conversely, the absence of such an identification in the prefaces to *Poor Rich Man* and *Live and Let Live* did not prevent at least a couple of reviewers from ascribing to those two texts an implied audience of young readers. Such responses, in other words, marked a turn in the reception of Sedgwick's novels that cannot be attributed to the inherent orientation of *The Linwoods, Poor Rich Man,* and *Live and Let Live* or to reader reaction to the subject matter of this trio of novels.

Something else was going on, and part of it may have been that, since the appearance of *Hope Leslie* and *Clarence,* Sedgwick had published several pieces of short fiction and nonfiction in media pitched to a young audience: *The Youth's Keepsake* (an annual) and the *Juvenile Miscellany* (a periodical).[74] Additionally, in the same year that *Live and Let Live* came into print, the Harpers published Sedgwick's *A Love Token for Children,* a collection of seven stories whose readership was announced in its title. The fact that Sedgwick has started in the late 1820s and early 1830s to write and publish short stories geared to younger readers probably played a role in some reviewers' decision to position her three most recent novels as part of a new phase of Sedgwick's authorship. That interpretive decision started a trend that continued with the reception of Sedgwick's next book, *Means and Ends,* published in 1839.

Although most late twentieth- and early twenty-first-century readers would likely call *Means and Ends* a nonfiction conduct book, Sedgwick's contemporaries did not necessarily see it that way.[75] Reviews in the *Expositor* and the *Boston Quarterly Review* identified *Means and Ends* as being of a piece with Sedgwick's other books, with the latter specifically citing its "truly American feeling . . . which breathes through all of Miss Sedgwick's works" (July 1839: 389). Noting that whether Sedgwick "sets her hand to . . . a novel or a moral essay"—a remark that suggests *Means and Ends* was being read as a combination of the two—the reviewer in the *Expositor* identified this volume as once again marking "the character of her mind," which, tellingly enough, the reviewer found "manifested in her writings [a]s essentially feminine" (June 22, 1839: 315). *Graham's* saw *Means and Ends* as typically Sedgwickian in the way it goes about "enforcing truths by anecdote and short story" (July 1842: 60).

What characterized reviewer responses most visibly was their interpretation of *Means and Ends* as a book for juvenile readers. The review in the *Expositor* explained that "the principle object of the work" is to address "the mind of young ladies" (315); "for the formation of the character of the young, the work is addressed," announced a reviewer in the *United States Magazine and Democratic Review* (Aug. 1839: 128). The *New-York Mirror* intoned that the book "is full of excellent and judicious advice . . . interesting to young ladies in their teens" (June 15, 1839: 407). Apparently drawing on a sentence in chapter two in which Sedgwick's narrator explains that the "following pages" of the chapter are "for girls from ten to sixteen years of age," several reviewers, including the one in the *Mirror*, extrapolated from that remark to conclude that "Sedgwick has dedicated this little volume to her young country women" (407).[76] It is little wonder, in light of such associations and interpretive assumptions, that a review in the *New-Yorker* predicted that *Means and Ends* "will be bought by kind fathers and mothers and friends, and will be put into the hands of young Misses to read, with lots of good advice in the bargain" (July 28, 1839: 286).

One of the ironies of these responses on the heels of the reception of *The Linwoods, Poor Rich Man,* and *Live and Let Live* was that just as Sedgwick was being interpretively reconstructed as a different kind of author whose audience was now being more narrowly defined, she enjoyed her greatest popularity to date, even in comparison to *Home* and *Hope Leslie*. While the latter had quickly sold out its first edition of 2,000 copies, the Harpers published *Poor Rich Man* in a first edition of 9,000 copies, and all were sold within six months. By late 1839, the reading public had gobbled up nearly 20,000 copies of that novel. *Live and Let Live* enjoyed comparable success, with a first printing of 8,750 copies and a sales total in two years of nearly 13,000 copies.[77] Even in comparison to *Home*, these two novels performed extraordinarily in the literary marketplace. While *Home* had gone through fifteen editions in six years, *Poor Rich Man* took only three years to go through sixteen editions, and the sales of *Live and Let Live* exhausted twelve editions in less than two years.[78]

In the meantime, the growing conception of Sedgwick as the author of books for the young no doubt was reinforced when the Harpers in 1840 published her collection of short fiction, *Stories for Young People*, which identified itself as "By the author of 'The Linwoods,' 'Poor Rich Man,' 'Love Token,' and 'Live and Let Live.'" Linking the new collection with exactly the four books that had been the site for this new interpretation of Sedgwick, that signature helped reinforce audience perceptions of Sedgwick as a woman author writing primarily for a juvenile readership.

What had begun with *The Linwoods* as a few drops from a spigot turned into a full torrent with the reception of *The Boy of Mt. Rhigi*, published in 1847. Reviewers en masse spoke of Sedgwick's new novel as juvenile fiction. Here is a representative sampling of their remarks: *Sartain's* called the "volume before us . . . an agreeable fiction, designed more especially for the young" (May 1849: 350); *Littell's* observed that "it was written . . . to awaken in those of our young people who have been carefully nurtured, a sense of their duty" (Apr. 14, 1849: 95); and the *Knickerbocker,* quoting part of the preface without acknowledgment, announced that the novel is "designed for the young people of our country" (Nov. 1848: 457). Nor did such characterization of *Boy of Mt. Rhigi* come only in the public sphere. In a letter to Sedgwick, a Reverend Bellows said that after "reading at one sitting—a few pages last evening excepted—of the 'Boy of Mount Rhigi,' . . . I feel it safer to have children . . . when such books are extant, and waiting to throw their mantle of purity and protection over them."[79]

A suggestive feature of Bellows' comment is that his admission of having read the book himself would indicate that, pace reviewer conclusions, adults were drawn to and actually reading *Boy of Mt. Rhigi*. Indeed, calling a work such as *Boy of Mt. Rhigi* juvenile fiction does more than ignore its broader appeal. Such a characterization, as one Sedgwick scholar has argued, "obscure[s] the productive cross-fertilization" of genres in the novel, particularly its "rhetorical techniques" that "overlap . . . literary categories usually dichotomized today (children-adult, straightforward-complex, didactic-aesthetic)."[80] The point here is not that this modern critical view of the book is correct and the antebellum conceptualization is a misreading. What we are looking at are interpretations grounded in different sets of reading codes, and central to the horizon of expectations of Sedgwick's antebellum readers was the assumption, which had become a "fact" by 1848, that Sedgwick was a writer of juvenile fiction.

What was happening to Sedgwick is especially striking if we compare her career to those of other novelists, particularly male ones. Not only did Hawthorne and Dickens write children's fiction without being labeled juvenile authors. As Henry Steele Commager pointed out over five decades ago, "almost every major writer . . . wrote for children as well as adults" in the nineteenth century.[81] Yet few were typecast as writers for the young. Such was not the case for Sedgwick. Rather, as a result of the responses first to *The Linwoods, Poor Rich Man,* and *Live and Let Live,* and then especially to *Means and Ends* and *Boy of Mt. Rhigi,* by the late 1840s Sedgwick's entire corpus began to be reinterpreted in a way that reflected this new formulation. For instance, an article in the *United States Magazine and Democratic Review,* amid discussing Irving, Hawthorne, Cooper, Poe, and Dana, called Sedgwick "pre-eminent among American female writers" because of "her home pictures and tales for children" (June 1846: 472). A reviewer of a new edition of *Redwood* in the *New Englander* took the opportunity to recall how "[y]oung misses" in the 1820s had "languished over the loves of Ellen and Westfall," and then he expressed his hope that "some of the younger generation will be anxious to learn what kind of work pleased their parents" (Aug. 1850: 484). As to the view that *Redwood, Hope Leslie,* and *Clarence* were national American novels suited to the needs and interests of adult readers, that too was being rethought. For example, following the reprinting of *Clarence* in 1849, the *Literary World,* speaking of "Miss Sedgwick's writings" as a whole, denied that "Americanism . . . is their most satisfying ingredient" (Oct. 6, 1849: 297). In the same year, the *North American Review* declared that *Hope Leslie* was not really a historical novel but more of a costume drama that "kept the historical element quite in the background" (Jan. 1849: 205). Even when readers continued to praise the Americanness of Sedgwick's novels, that description took an altered form. According to one commentator, while Sedgwick's novels are "*always* and thoroughly American," her status as a "national writer" depended on the way "Miss Sedgwick says, 'let the little children come unto me.'"[82]

Such remarks might have been less problematic for the status of Sedgwick and her fiction had they not been part of a pattern that unfolded simultaneously with the rise of the conceptualization of juvenile literature as a specific genre with distinct features designed for a particular category of readers with a particular level of intelligence and reading abilities. At this time the American Sunday School Union was taking upon itself the task of codifying standards for children's literature, specifying "adaptation to the understanding of the child" as a desideratum. Soon librarians would begin assembling lists of novels and other books suitable and "recommended" expressly for children.[83] According to Beverly Lyon Clark, this literature came to be viewed, particularly by reviewers, as "being less serious" than adult reading matter.[84] While Clark demonstrates how this view came to prominence especially after the Civil War, such an assumption was already beginning to appear in the late 1830s, as demonstrated by a review of Sedgwick's *Means and Ends* in the *Christian Examiner*. Following up an earlier review in that periodical, which had linked *Means and Ends* with a juvenile readership, this second review explained that "the author of this book, Miss Sedgwick, is favorably known in our country by those who are familiar with lighter literature" (Dec. 1839: 624). The upshot was that juvenile fiction was being conceived as "lighter" literature for a niche market, and Sedgwick was being sutured to both.

What needs to be added is that, as Clark also points out, such a pejorative view of children's literature was inflected by gender ideology, in that it was assumed that the audience for such fiction was primarily girls.[85] That equation was extended to authorship as well, as evidenced by a remark in the *North American Review*. "Such being the importance of juvenile books, who are the best qualified to make them?" asked the reviewer, who then announced the answer: "Women." Subscribing to the logic of the cult of domesticity, this reviewer went on to explain that women writers were especially suited to produce such books since their "natural sympathies unite them most closely with children," which enables women writers to "best know the minds, the wants, and the hearts of children." In what can be taken as an ironic, ominous precursor of what was to come for Sedgwick, these ideas appeared in an 1828 review of *Hope Leslie*.[86]

The publishing regimen the Harpers employed for reissuing Sedgwick's novels in the 1840s further contributed to the perception of Sedgwick as a writer of juvenile fiction pitched to a niche market. With the exception of republishing *Hope Leslie* in 1842, the Harpers throughout the decade concentrated on reissuing *Poor Rich Man* (1840, 1841, 1842, 1843, 1847), *Live and Let Live* (1840, 1841, 1842, 1844), *Love Token for Children* (1844, 1848), *Means and Ends* (1842, 1843, 1844, 1845, 1846), and *Stories for Young Persons* (1841, 1842, 1846).[87] A large part of the firm's motivation was no doubt financial. *Poor Rich Man* and *Live and Let Live* had had the best track records for sales, which provided the greatest promise for future profits. Additionally, in the wake of the panic of 1837, which hit the publishing industry hard and reduced the buying power of middle-class readers, the fact that four of those five books were under 220 pages meant they could be printed more cheaply and sold at a lower price than Sedgwick's slightly older and substantially longer novels—no small consideration for stimulating sales.

A point to stress here is that the popularity of these texts and reviewer conceptions of Sedgwick as a writer of lighter fiction for a juvenile audience did not signal a disparity between the way reviewers and other middle-class readers were responding to her writings. Rather, that popularity resulted because readers acquiesced to the idea, advanced publicly in periodicals, that these fictions were worth buying as reading materials well suited to their children. The irony is that even as Sedgwick continued to have a high public profile and her writings sold well, at work was a subtle but significant devaluation of her fiction as fit primarily for youths.[88]

Reviewers, however, hardly seemed to recognize what was transpiring. Instead, some began to feel in the late 1840s that Sedgwick's novels as a whole were no longer relevant to adult readers. Part of the logic here lay in reviewer conclusions that Sedgwick's novels before 1835 (specifically *Clarence, Hope Leslie, Redwood,* and *A New England Tale*) were out of date, the relics of a simpler time that had been enjoyed by an unsophisticated, callow American audience. An article in the *Literary World,* entitled "Miss Sedgwick's Works," said that *Clarence* belonged to a "class" of novels "which modern improvements in fiction have rather elbowed out of popularity" (Oct. 6, 1849: 297). Responding to Putnam's reissue of *Clarence* in 1849, the *United States Magazine and Democratic Review* commented that in the "twenty years since 'Clarence' first made its appearance . . . the public has undergone considerable change," which has "rendered less attractive . . . the works of Miss Sedgwick" (Nov. 1849: 478). Also asserting that novels and the "public taste" have advanced, the *New York Albion* said of Sedgwick, "Though long since recognized as a standard writer, her works ha[ve] almost gone out of print" (Oct. 1849: 472). Although the remark about her novels being out of print was a patent error, it bespoke a perception of Sedgwick as a writer whose time had come and gone for the broader fiction-reading public.

Some of Sedgwick's letters at this time indicate that she herself believed that she was losing an audience for her earlier novels, partly because her original readers were dying off without being replaced by new ones. Writing to Katherine Minot in 1857, Sedgwick explained how "worried, and anxious, and utterly discouraged" she was when she thought of "all those whose hearts beat for me . . . at the publication of my early books" but who are now "all gone." Such thoughts also shaded Sedgwick's view of the novel she was then working on, *Married or Single?* A month before her letter to Minot, Sedgwick informed Orville Dewey that she was "getting [her] book ready, and working as hard as I dare," but she then asked rhetorically, "Is it not rather a folly . . . to perpetrate a novel without any purpose or hope . . . but only to supply mediocre readers with small moral hints on various subjects that come up in daily life?"[89] The self-deprecating view of her subject as "small" and the conception that her audience now consisted of "mediocre readers" reflect the lowered status that was beginning to envelop Sedgwick and the public perception of both her corpus and her current audience.

In the decade between the publication of *Boy of Mt. Rhigi* in 1847 and Sedgwick's 1857 letter to Minot, that lowering via conceptions of

Sedgwick as a children's author continued, despite the fact that in 1850 Hazard and Mitchell published Sedgwick's *Tales of City Life*, a collection comprised of two long stories that had previously appeared in the adult-oriented magazine *Sartain's*. That volume, however, was overshadowed by the Harpers' continued practice of publishing new editions of Sedgwick's fiction that readers and reviewers had come to view as fiction for the young: *Live and Let Live* (1854), *Means and Ends* (1854), *Stories of Young Persons* (1852, 1855), and *Poor Rich Man* (1856). That pattern and the associations it reinforced were furthered when Crowley and Nichols put out new editions of *Boy of Mt. Rhigi* in 1849, 1850, 1851, 1854, and again in 1857.[90] The last appeared in the same year that Sedgwick published what would be her final novel, *Married or Single?*

Married or Single? could have signaled for antebellum readers a return to Sedgwick's earlier works, in a way analogous to the modern scholarly view that this book belongs with the five other full-fledged novels that Sedgwick published before 1835. Certainly, reviewers might at least have seen it as a novel addressing larger social issues relevant to women and men of all ages: the social status of women, female rights, the relative value of life in and outside of marriage, and the problems of fashionable society. Instead, reviewer responses went in a different direction. The *North American Review* focused on "all the moral axioms and postulates which the story illustrates" to group *Married or Single?* with *Live and Let Live, Home,* and her other briefer works of the 1830s as signature Sedgwickian fictions, among which her latest was "the best of the series" (Oct. 1857: 563). The *Christian Examiner,* after noting that "Miss Sedgwick was one of the most popular writers of a generation which is now fast passing away," suggested whom her current audience consisted of by sandwiching its brief review of *Married or Single?* between reviews of John Browner's *A Child's History of Greece* and Worthington Hooker's *A Child's Book of Nature* (Oct. 1857: 645). What the *Christian Examiner* implied, a review in the *Ladies' Repository* asserted explicitly, declaring that, while some "old people" will enjoy *Married or Single?*, its "moral" is such that "young folks will get as much profit as pleasure" from the novel (Sept. 1857: 564).

What morals and axioms did reviewers find in *Married or Single?* Taking their cue from the novel's title and preface, nearly all concluded, in one form or another, that "the author's prime aim," as the *North Ameri-*

can Review explained, "is to exhibit, as parallel with the holy and benign ministries of the true wife and mother, the no less sacred and lofty sphere open to self-respecting and voluntary maidenhood" (Oct. 1857: 563). But instead of seeing it as a novel that might be challenging the dominant culture's ideas about gender, marriage, and women's place, readers found *Married or Single?* to be an affirmation of wifehood as the true role for young women.[91] The review in the *Ladies' Repository*, for example, observed that the "beginning of the volume gives one the idea that the authoress is about to insist upon the reality of female single blessedness. But the moral—was it accidental and inevitable, or done of a forethought?—is strongly in favor of married life" (Sept. 1857: 564). A review in *Harper's Weekly* agreed and specified a reason: The "moral can scarcely be said to be in favor of single life, since Grace, the heroine, around whom the whole interest of the story moves, like a true woman, loves and marries at last" (July 1857: 470).[92]

Though widely sharing this interpretation, critics disagreed over whether the novel's denouement constituted the book's theme or contradicted it. While the review in the *Ladies' Repository* assumed the former, a review in the *Knickerbocker* declared that, while the "whole moral of the story . . . is that married life is not essential to the cultivation of the warmest affections and noblest traits" of women, "[i]ts force is diminished, however, by the tender relenting of the author, who seems, at the close of the volume, to have departed from her original plan, and after all, marries the heroine" (Oct. 1857: 412). Such a disagreement led reviewers to raise questions about the novel's consistency and, as the *Knickerbocker* implied, Sedgwick's artistic control over her materials. Only hinted at in the *Knickerbocker* review, the problem of ineptitude in this area was more explicitly raised by a reviewer in the *New York Albion*, who groused, "judging from the Preface" of *Married or Single?*, the "tale was designed to plead the cause of Spinster-hood. If this be so, the case is not well pleaded; in fact the object is well-nigh lost sight of." The *Albion* reviewer also found the novel formulaic and even a bit stale, since "the old subject of marriage and giving in marriage is the staple of this, as of ninety-nine out of a hundred kindred works" (Aug. 15, 1857: 393). The irony in these responses is that reviewers came to *Married or Single?* with what had become a standard view of Sedgwick as a safe, domestic writer of novels for the young—and especially young females—but when reviewers found in the novel precisely what they wanted to see, some charged it with being structurally flawed or, worse yet, clichéd.

The damage of familiarity also emerged in a second area of the public response. *Married or Single?* struck most reviewers, in the words of the *Harper's New Monthly Magazine,* as being "of a similar character to that of her previous stories" in that it centers on the "quiet, domestic sphere, where she is particularly at home" (Sept. 1857: 549). For some, however, it was precisely this familiar domesticity that proved disappointing. A review in *Russell's Magazine* found the novel undistinguished because it is "an ordinary domestic tale, meager in incident, and undramatic in action." The *Russell's* reviewer added that such a novel "is not likely to be widely popular" with the "host of novel readers," who desire the "sort of intellectual nutriment" provided by "such skillful artists as the Brontés, Thackeray, [and] Dickens" (Sept. 1857: 572). Displaying a similar impatience with *Married or Single?,* the *Christian Review* found that the book's subject and its treatment resulted not only in an "injured" plot but in a "story spun out to a tedious length" (Oct. 1857: 645). One likely factor in such responses was the publication of a number of highly popular domestic novels in the early 1850s, including Warner's *Wide, Wide World,* Maria Cummins' *The Lamplighter,* and Stowe's *Uncle Tom's Cabin.* Combined with the growing reconceptualization of Sedgwick as a womanly author of mild domestic tales for young females, the public saturation of the genre through such marketplace successes helped provide some reviewers with a ground for reconceiving Sedgwick, not as the author who had pioneered and excelled at writing national novels of the home, but as the author of a tedious and hackneyed narrative in an overworked mode. In the midst of such developments, the *Russell's* reviewer concluded with a remark about *Married or Single?* that would have been unthinkable in the public reception of a Sedgwick novel twenty years earlier: "it should have been better policy to have permitted the book to remain unpublished" (572).

◆

Despite such criticisms and their role in the subtle but significant devaluation and pigeonholing of Sedgwick's novels, her reputation remained surprisingly strong, albeit in a modulated form, right through the Civil War. When Sedgwick died in 1867, the editor of *Harpers's New Monthly Magazine* looked back over her career to remind the audience that "she was the first very noted female author in the United States" (Oct. 1867: 665). Four years later, another article in the same magazine said of Sedgwick, "her career of authorship has classed her, with Irving, among those who first created an American literature worthy the name" (Nov. 1871: 826). Yet even such kudos came with qualifications, as the editor of *Harper's* exemplified in his 1867 remarks when he explained that by the 1850s, "when the more modern school of American writers were [*sic*] becoming known," Sedgwick's "name and fame" had fallen into "comparative retirement" (665).

To the new generation of postbellum American readers, moreover, Sedgwick was known largely during the 1870s as the author of *Live and Let Live, Poor Rich Man, Means and Ends,* and *Love Token for Children*—the books that had come to identify her as a writer for young people and the very ones that the Harpers kept in print throughout the decade.[93] Meanwhile, public discussions of Sedgwick began to reveal a tendency to focus not so much on her fiction, its value, or its artistry, but on the woman herself. This shift is most evident in Mary Dewey's 1872 *Life and Letters of Catharine M. Sedgwick,* in which Dewey characterizes Sedgwick's life not as a writing career built upon a substantial corpus of novels and tales but as a story of "no remarkable occurrences," traced as a genteel "unfolding and ripening amid congenial surroundings of a true and beautiful soul." Besides her own remarks interwoven with excerpts from Sedgwick's letters and journals, Dewey included in the volume several literary reminiscences in which the same emphasis is evident. One by William Cullen Bryant admits that, while Sedgwick's "literary life" was "admirable," "her home life was more so." Bryant adds, "Her unerring sense of rectitude, her love of truth, her ready sympathy, her active and cheerful beneficence" comprised a sterling womanly character that "I would not exchange for any thing in her own interesting works of fiction." In a nineteen-paragraph reminiscence, Orville Dewey devotes a mere three paragraphs to Sedgwick's fiction only to emphasize how "[h]er sweet and graceful nature" repeatedly "was expressed in her writings."[94]

Over the next decade, all of Sedgwick's books except for *Home* would go out of print, and when she was mentioned at all in periodicals, it was almost as a historical relic of an earlier young generation. An article on "The Native Element in American Fiction: Before the War" in the *Century Magazine* admitted that Sedgwick, along with Cooper and James Kirk Paulding, "once held the entire ground of important novelistic literature" early in the century, but in a move that continued the altered conception of Sedgwick, the article added that in her case it was by "charming the youth of New England." Indeed, explained the *Century*, "in 'Redwood,' . . . 'Clarence,' 'The Linwoods,' etc. she took strong hold on the hearts of the New England youth" (June 1883: 288–91).

By 1900 Sedgwick's fiction was starting to be neglected to the point of being completely left out of important literary histories, including Barrett Wendell's path-breaking *Literary History of the United States* (1900). That pattern would continue over the first five decades of the twentieth century. Neither her novels nor Sedgwick herself receives any mention in Richard Burton's *Literary Leaders of America* (1903), John Macy's *Spirit of American Literature* (1913), Percy Boynton's *History of American Literature* (1919), and Carl Van Doren's *What Is American Literature?* (1935). In Arthur Hobson Quinn's *American Fiction: An Historical and Critical Survey* (1936), Sedgwick gets no mention in his chapter on "Washington Irving and Other Pioneers" of antebellum American fiction—a chapter followed, tellingly enough, by one devoted entirely to Cooper, the writer with whom Sedgwick had been most frequently paired in the 1820s and 1830s as leading voices of America's new national literature.[95]

Moreover, even when Sedgwick was referred to in early twentieth-century literary histories, it was in a diminished capacity or by some dismissive remarks. Vernon Parrington, in his *Romantic Revolution* volume in *Main Currents in American Thought* (1927), made a passing reference to Sedgwick's "modest career as a 'lady novelist.'" Fred Lewis Pattee's *The First Century of American Literature* (1935) referred to Sedgwick only as a contributor of short pieces to gift books and annuals. In his *Flowering of New England* (1936), Van Wyck Brooks briefly mentioned Sedgwick as a writer of "stories of New England life" that were "sometimes too-too simple" and concluded, "no one could have supposed that her work could live."[96]

Such disparaging typecasting most frequently took the form that first appeared in the responses to her novels in the mid-to-late 1830s. William J. Long's *American Literature* (1913), in a risible instance of fractured history, claimed that the reviewers of Sedgwick's day dismissed her novels as "weak copies of English originals" and then paired Sedgwick with Louisa May Alcott as the authors of "*Little Women* and other juveniles." Characterizing Sedgwick as a fiction-writing schoolmarm, Walter C. Bronson's *Short History of American Literature* (1902) explained that Sedgwick was "for half a century principal of a young ladies' school at Stockbridge, Mass.," where she "wrote many novels, naturally of a pale hue"—a remark seconded in William B. Cairns's *History of American Literature* (1912), which dismissively smirked that "her novels, *Hope Leslie*, *The Linwoods*, and others have the moral qualities to be expected in the work of a preceptress." In 1917 the monumental *Cambridge History of American Literature* referred to Sedgwick roughly a half dozen times in passing but only to call her an "unread" novelist whose "moral stories" were "obvious" and to mention her fiction amid a discussion of antebellum "books for children." By the 1950s Sedgwick's niche was sealed to the point where even *Hope Leslie* was demoted to the status of a child's book in Ernest E. Leisy's *The American Historical Novel*, which blandly announced, "Miss Sedgwick . . . conceived of her task in *Hope Leslie* as illustrating for juvenile readers domestic manners in the seventeenth century."[97]

And what of the view of *Hope Leslie, Clarence, Redwood,* and *A New England Tale* as striking national novels fit for Americans of all ages? What, too, of the conception of Sedgwick as a fiction-writing pioneer and major novelistic voice in antebellum America? Those interpretations were gone and, it seems, virtually forgotten. For most of the twentieth century, such responses to her novels were replaced by a master narrative built with an interpretive formulation that, at its most "generous," ghettoized Sedgwick as a feminine writer of tepid domestic tales, whose "modest career" was devoted to producing light fiction for the young. Thankfully, it is a formulation from which Sedgwick's fiction has finally started to recover.

CHAPTER 6

Mercurial Readings

The Making and Unmaking of Caroline Chesebro'

ALTHOUGH THE QUESTION "Whatever happened to . . .?" could be as readily asked about Caroline Chesebro' as it could about Catharine Sedgwick, a different preliminary query first needs to be raised. Who *was* Caroline Chesebro'?

Born in upstate New York in 1825, Chesebro' was the author of over a dozen books of fiction from the 1850s to the 1870s. By 1900, however, she was largely forgotten, and she lingered in obscurity throughout the twentieth century. Moreover, unlike Sedgwick—or Elizabeth Stoddard, Susan Warner, Kate Chopin, Mary Wilkins Freeman, or Rebecca Harding Davis—Chesebro' has undergone no recovery and continues to remain outside the canon of American literature—and largely unknown today.

Her obscurity is evidenced in the paucity of scholarly and critical attention to her fiction. Though brief entries for her appear in several standard biographical reference works, such as the *Dictionary of American Biography, American National Biography,* and the *Dictionary of Literary Biography,* since 1925 only one book chapter and two brief scholarly articles have been devoted to her writings.[1] Chesebro' is not even mentioned in most of the important book-length studies of nineteenth-century American women writers published over the last thirty-five years, including Ann Douglas's *The Feminization of American Culture* (1977), Mary Kelley's *Private Women, Public Stage* (1984), Gillian Brown's *Domestic Individualism* (1990), Susan Harris's *Nineteenth-Century American Women's Novels* (1990), Susan Coultrap-McQuinn's *Doing Literary Business* (1990), G. M Goshgarian's *To Kiss the Chastening Rod* (1992), and Lora Romero's *Home Fronts* (1997).[2] Only one master's thesis and no doctoral dissertations have been devoted to her in the last one hundred years.[3] In light of this neglect, it is not surprising that virtually no attention has been paid to the public response to Chesebro's fiction in the nineteenth century.[4]

In her own time, however, Chesebro's reputation and position in the literary marketplace were hardly obscure. Over more than two decades, she published nearly ninety short stories in major periodicals, including *Graham's Magazine,* the *Knickerbocker Magazine,* and *Sartain's* in the 1840s and 1850s and then in *Harper's New Monthly Magazine* and the *Nation* in the 1860s and 1870s.[5] Perhaps more significant, the fact that she published nine novels and four collections of short stories indicates that Chesebro's fiction established sufficient marketplace magnetism to attract publishers, enabling her to maintain a successful string of book publications from 1851 until a year or two before her death in 1873.[6] Nor were her relations with publishers limited to the third-class associations to which many other women fiction writers of the time were relegated.[7] Although she never placed a book with the prestigious Harpers, as both Melville and Sedgwick had done, in her early career Chesebro' published two novels and a collection of short stories with the New York firm of Redfield and Company, which also published William Gilmore Simms and Robert Montgomery Byrd (two of the leading antebellum southern novelists), as well as Edgar Allan Poe and the well-known poet Alice Cary.[8] Chesebro' went on to publish two other collections of tales and her novel *The Fishermen of Gamp's Island* with the firm of Carleton and Porter, a publisher that, according to one historian, was "one of the most successful of the time" and whose list of authors included the highly popular novelists Mary Jane Holmes, Augusta Evans, and Marion Harland.[9]

Nearly all of Chesebro's novels were reviewed in the leading magazines of mid-nineteenth-century America, including *Godey's Lady's Book, Putnam's Monthly,* the *Literary World, Harper's,* the *Nation,* and the *Atlantic Monthly.* Furthermore, the public responses to her fiction were often quite favorable, even laudatory. A reviewer in the *Knickerbocker,* for instance, asserted that "among the numerous candidates for literary fame . . . Miss Caroline Chesebro' has few or no superiors" (Sept. 1856: 303). The *National Era* called her a writer whose "genius . . . is totally unlike [that of] any other author of the age, and promises to make her immortal" (Sept. 11, 1856: 147), while an article in *Holden's Dollar Magazine* placed her among "our most brilliant and popular authors" in whom "we take the most pride" (Jan. 1859: 61). Indeed, thirty years after her death, William Dean Howells would rank her just behind the leading lights of Hawthorne, Emerson, Longfellow, Lowell, and Stowe in his list of American writers of "second brilliance"—a list in which Howells also grouped Henry David Thoreau and Henry James.[10]

Chesebro', accordingly, was hardly one of the many obscure and ephemeral American fiction writers, male or female, of the antebellum and Civil War decades. It is just that she was not a particularly popular novelist, nor did she gain widespread attention in the public sphere. Her books never sold very well, and except for *Peter Carradine* (1863), none of her novels made it to a second edition.[11] Within twenty years of her death, all of her books were out of print. Despite the attention her novels received via reviews in major periodicals, none enjoyed the wide notice that Melville's *Typee* and *Omoo* and Sedgwick's novels of the 1820s and 1830s achieved. Indeed, despite extensive research, I have been unable to uncover more than a dozen reviews of any one of her books. In fact, her two 1865 novels, *Glen Cabin* and *Fishermen of Gamp's Island,* appear to have earned no reviewer notice at all.

This rather unusual reception history makes Chesebro' not only largely unique among antebellum and mid-nineteenth-century American fiction writers. It also offers a fascinating context and scenario for examining in more detail the shape of the contemporaneous response to her fiction and the reasons behind her subsequent modern neglect.

Not a lot is known about Chesebro', and outside her published works of fiction, the archival record is thin. Fewer than fifty of her letters are extant, and none of the correspondence that might have included readers' comments about her fiction has survived. However, the little we do know, along with the public reception of her fiction, indicates that Chesebro' shared affinities with, yet differed markedly from, other nineteenth-century American women fiction writers, particularly in their profile as "literary domestics" and the way they were perceived by nineteenth-century readers.

Like many of the antebellum and mid-nineteenth-century women writers Mary Kelley has focused on, Chesebro' seems to have turned to fiction writing from financial motives. Comments and questions about the economics of publishing and her relation to her publishers frequently punctuate her few surviving letters.[12] Like Sedgwick, Chesebro' could be acute and even unabashed in her dealings with her publishers. At a time when the Duyckinck brothers were not paying most writers for their contributions to the *Literary World,* Chesebro' sent them a story and an accompanying letter in which she asked, "Will you publish the enclosed in your admirable 'World,' and . . . let me contribute to its columns in pay for it?" In another letter to the Duyckincks regarding a different story, Chesebro' boldly asserted, "I trust that it is worth to you, two dollars a page—printed" before adding, "[p]lease let me know if you can afford to pay for this article at that rate—or state *what* sum you are willing to pay for it outright."[13] A letter to William Conant Church of the *Galaxy* reflects her negotiating know-how when it asserts, "I think [?] at the rates I am payed elsewhere, that two dollars a mss sheet . . . may be considered a fair compensation."[14] Chesebro' was also intrepid enough to question her publishers as to the fairness of payment for her fiction. In a letter to the *Atlantic Monthly* she unabashedly pointed out that "[a]ccording to my computation, there are ten dollars yet due on Victor & Jacqueline. I received $50. $30 & $77 on it, but the story filled two pages more than were in the reckoning."[15]

Unlike the literary domestics, however, Chesebro' was closer to Sedgwick in the manner in which she viewed her fiction. Despite her economic motivations and concerns as an author, Chesebro' could see her fiction as valuable in and of itself. As she explained in one of her letters to the Duyckincks regarding a newly submitted short story, "I have written it with uncommon care & feel convinced that it has a worth of its own, which I believe you will recognize."[16] Moreover, at least one of her letters to Church indicates that she approached her writing with the care of an artist—or at least with the care of a skilled craftsperson. Referring to an unnamed story she had sent to the *Galaxy,* Chesebro' explained to Church that the "story is finished but I have only been able to re-read & correct it & do not quite like you to see it, until I have a clearer idea [in] regard to it than I have at the moment."[17]

Yet in her concern for her craft and her sense of the intrinsic value of her fiction, Chesebro' was unlike the Melville painted by modern criticism, who supposedly composed his fiction with an artistic single-mindedness that caused him to ignore his readership. Despite the claim of one modern critic that Chesebro' was oblivious to the impact of her prose on her contemporary audience and thereby "failed to fulfill the expectations of her readers," another of her letters to Church suggests that Chesebro' was, if not keenly attuned to her readership, at least concerned about their reactions to and judgments about her work. Referring to a story entitled "One too Many," which was scheduled to appear in a late 1868 issue of the *Galaxy,* she wrote, "I trust that the good opinion [Church had] expressed in regard to the story to appear in the December number will be seconded by your readers."[18]

In this interest in her audience's responses, Chesebro', of course, shared a concern with many antebellum and midcentury writers, both male and female. And in Chesebro's case, it was a concern well founded, not only because of the lack of strong sales for her books but also because her contemporary reviewers did not respond to her fiction in the way that they reacted to that of other women authors of the time. For one thing, reviewers did not read her novels as domestic or sentimental fiction—the category into which most of her few twentieth-century commentators have placed her work.[19] Moreover, reviewers repeatedly responded to her style with terms seldom used to describe fiction by women. Frequently, as we will see, reviewers demarcated her writing as "masculine," with one magazinist going so far as to label it "cold" and even "obscure" (*Appleton's* Sept. 16, 1871: 330). More reminiscent of the responses to Melville's prose than of reactions to the style of other women writers, such remarks indicate that her fiction presented unique pre-texts for antebellum interpretations of Chesebro' as an author.

Although Chesebro's contemporary audience would come to know her style—and her work as a whole—through her novels, her first book was a collection of short stories. Published in 1851, *Dream-Land by Daylight* consists of twenty-four stories, nineteen of which had already appeared in magazines.[20] The fact that *Dream-Land* was largely a collection of twice-told tales no doubt contributed to the small number of reviews it received. Nevertheless, those previously printed stories, along with the other sixteen tales she had published in the years before *Dream-Land,* served as an asset by making Chesebro' already familiar to her readers and thereby helping to shape a horizon of expectations for her first book. A *Godey's* review of *Dream-Land* claimed, with some hyperbole, that the "name of the author of this volume has long been familiar to American readers . . . as that of one of the most gifted female writers of our country" (Mar. 1852: 231), while a reviewer in *Peterson's* noted that, though Chesebro's fiction "now first appears in a book of her own," her work has "long been known in the magazines" (Feb. 1852: 134). Similar remarks were repeated in *Sartain's* (Feb. 1852: 196), *Harper's* (Jan. 1852: 274), and even the *Scientific American,* which called Chesebro' "an authoress of merit well known to the magazine world for her piquant stories" (Jan. 3, 1852: 128).

What reviewers found in *Dream-Land*—and what they directed the middle-class fiction-reading audience to find there also—largely sat well with their horizon of expectations, both of Chesebro' and of her collection. Most notably—and contrary to what they would say about her novels to come—reviewers characterized her stories as expressions of refined, moral sentiments. Repeatedly, magazinists spoke of the "purity of sentiment and glow of feeling which pervade the entire volume" (*Godey's* 231), of the volume's "great delicacy and beauty of sentiment" (*American Whig Review* Jan. 1852: 89), of its "depth of sentiment and feeling not ordinarily met with" (*Churchman* circa 1852), and of "its relation to the highest moral emotions" (*Albany State Register* circa 1852).[21] A review in the *National Era* singled out the stories "The Phoebe Bird" and "Little Alvah" as especially evincing this element, calling the latter a tale of "plain, homely pathos . . . which goes straight to the heart" (Jan. 29, 1852: 19). Several reviewers even identified the collection as a version of domestic fiction, with the reviewer in *Harper's* calling it one long, interconnected "tale of domestic life" full of "deep feelings [and] delicate sentiment" (Apr. 1853: 715).

No doubt such interpretive positioning of *Dream-Land* shaped reviewers' conceptions about the book's projected audience, for the consensus was that it was especially suited to female readers. The *American Whig Review* claimed that the collection "will be a favorite volume among 'ladies of the land'" (89), while the *Southern Quarterly Review* asserted that *Dream-Land* was "just the sort of volume which a young lady of talent might be expected to write, and which young ladies of taste will be pleased to read" (Jan. 1852: 262). Announced *Peterson's,* "Should any fair lady wish a delightfully readable book, . . . let her purchase 'Dream-Land by Daylight'" (Feb. 1852: 134). For reviewers this was an obvious conclusion related to what they saw as the volume's gendered genre profile. As

Godey's put it, the tales "imparted so great an amount of moral instruction to her readers" (231) that they did important cultural work—work that was intrinsically linked to Chesebro's success as a woman writer "true" to "her moral emotions" (*National Era* 19).

But if reviewers read *Dream-Land* as a conventional, albeit delightful, version of a well-worn genre, they disagreed over the cause of the book's success. *Sartain's* said it was precisely because the stories were not typical in their treatment of emotions. Making a distinction between true and natural sentiment and artificial sentimentality, the *Sartain's* reviewer asserted of Chesebro's tales that the "sentiment that pervades them, is far removed from the false sentimentality and moralistic twaddle, that crowd upon us in these latter days, in a class of compositions" that readers and reviewers greet with "sweeping condemnation" (196). By contrast, one reviewer linked the collection's genre profile with the code of verisimilitude to declare that the stories' "vivid delineation of human feeling" struck a note of realism that rendered Chesebro's "twenty-four tales . . . pictures of life" (*Home Journal* Dec. 21: 1851: [4]). Reviews in both *Harper's* and the *Ontario Messenger* found the book's attraction in a different combination that joined imaginative power to vraisemblance. According to the latter, *Dream-Land* "is a collection of beautiful sketches, in which the cultivated imagination of the authoress has interwoven the visions of Dream-Land with the realities of life."[22] Said the *Harper's* reviewer, "we find in it . . . a rare faculty of seizing the multiform aspects of nature" as found in life, while "giving them the form and hue of imagination" (274).

Another area of divergence in response to the collection involved perceptions of Chesebro's style. Although a handful of modern commentators have characterized that style as severely flawed and have claimed that her contemporary audience responded to it negatively, the actual nineteenth-century reception of her work was more complex.[23] Admittedly, several reviewers were critical of the style of *Dream-Land*. The reviewer in *Harper's*, who was one of the first to call her writing "masculine," found that "[h]er style suffers from want of proportion, of harmony, of artistic modulation," complaining in particular about what he called her tendency toward "fantastic, alliterative" prose (274). Though not as troubled, *Sartain's* felt that Chesebro's "earnest desire to clearly explain her own conceptions, occasionally induces diffuseness in description and weakens her force of expression" (197). More frequently, however, reviewers praised her style in these tales. The *American Whig Review* believed that Chesebro' successfully matched form to content so that "her style is worthy to convey her thoughts" (89). While praising her "richly poetical fancy," the reviewer in the *Home Journal* mentioned that Chesebro' "writes in an easy and graceful style" ([4]). Finding her style more dramatically striking than "easy and graceful," the *National Era* reviewer asserted that "there is a certain intensity in her manner [of writing] which cannot fail to impress her readers" (19).

Despite the differences in responses to *Dream-Land*, the public reaction, in other words, was on the whole quite positive. No doubt in part encouraged by the reception of her first book, Chesebro' next turned to a more ambitious project: a novel that she published in 1852 entitled *Isa, A Pilgrimage*.[24] In their reception of Chesebro's first novel, reviewers once again focused part of their attention on her style as a fiction writer, and once again a minor note of concern emerged in their responses. A *Graham's* reviewer simply felt that the "chief fault" of *Isa* was "its unrelieved intensity" (June 1852: 665), but a review in the *Southern Literary Messenger* was more captious: "As a literary performance the book is barely respectable,—what may be called heavy reading, and is full of affectations and bad English" (May 1852: 319). Interestingly, this remark about *Isa* as stylistically too intense and "heavy," along with the view that its prose was affected, echoed some of the public dismay expressed in response to *Moby-Dick* less than a year earlier. Amid these few objections, however, the majority of reviewers reacted quite positively to the style of *Isa*. A review in the *Knickerbocker* quoted extensively from the work's opening as a "specimen of the directness and vigor of Miss Chesebro's pen" (June 1852: 552), while the *Troy Daily Times* asserted of *Isa* that "the style is flowing and easy, chaste and beautiful."[25] The *New York Tribune* reviewer praised Chesebro's "rare gift of expression" in the novel, adding, "This whole volume is exhibited in a steel-like energy and brightness of style" (Apr. 17, 1852: 7). The *Harper's* reviewer agreed but went a step further to call the style an advance over Chesebro's previous efforts, which marked *Isa* as her best and boldest work to date: "This is a more ambitious effort than the former productions of the authoress, displaying a deeper power of reflection . . . and a more complete mastery of terse and pointed expression. On the whole, we regard it as a successful specimen of a quite difficult species of composition" (May 1852: 853). So impressed by the novel was *Sartain's* that its reviewer boldly proclaimed that "the highest praise will be conceded to 'Isa.' The style is terse and vigorous, yet rhetorical and brilliant. . . . [E]very significant sentence tends sensibly to the development of the author's thoughts" (June 1852: 515). Together with the responses to *Dream-Land,* these paeans to the style of *Isa* call into question the modern view that the texture of Chesebro's prose was somehow problematic and a common target of censure in the antebellum public sphere.

Furthermore, reviewers made much of what they saw as Chesebro's bold and original handling of other elements of fiction. The review in the *New York Tribune* burst into fulsome praise about *Isa*: "A writer must possess a secret consciousness of strength to venture upon an experiment, where the usual common-places of fiction are unavailable. . . . We accordingly wish in the outset to give Miss Chesebro' full credit for the intrepidity which has prompted the present enterprise. No one but a genuine noble thinker . . . would have risked the uncertain chances of success in resting a popular tale upon a purely psychological foundation. No one who had not been conversant from deep experience or from still deeper intuitions . . . could have felt the necessity of recording such a spiritual history as forms the staple of this remarkable story" (7). So impressed was the *Tribune* that it declared the "vigorous originality" of *Isa* all that Chesebro' would need to establish her place in the halls of literary notoriety: "if she shall leave no other memorial of her gifted nature, it is no mean fame to have been the writer of 'Isa's Pilgrimage'" (8).

What sort of "vigorous originality" did the *Tribune* see in *Isa*? A hint lies in its reviewer's reference to the novel's "psychological foundation." A number of reviewers located the book's power and success in its insight into human psychology, passion, and the arcana of the soul. Speaking of Chesebro's development of characters in general, *Graham's* lauded her "insight into the workings of passion" as "remarkably bright and clear" (665), while the *National Era* spoke approvingly of the "earnest thought and analytical power" that this "psychological story" displays (Apr. 22, 1852: 66). The *Albany Argus* declared, "There comes out in this book the evidence of an inventive mind" capable of "deep knowledge of human nature," and a review in the *Christian Freemen* saw *Isa* as proof that Chesebro' "skims not the mere surface of life, but plunges into the hidden mysteries of the spirit, by which she is warranted in making her startling revelations of human passion."[26] *Harper's* described *Isa* as a story "laid in the interior world—the world of consciousness, or reflection, of passion. In this twilight region . . . the author treads with great firmness of step" and with "rare subtlety of discrimination" (853). A significant feature of these responses is that they evince none of the ambivalence that ordinarily marked assumptions within informed reading regarding internal characterization. The main reason for that absence was that reviewers did not find Chesebro's method in *Isa* to be intrusive, which was usually the problem associated with psychological fiction. Indeed, no reviewers saw her approach to psychological characterization as showing the kind of ponderous artlessness that one twentieth-century commentator has ascribed to her method.[27]

Another noteworthy dimension of these overarching reactions to Chesebro's characterization was their relation to responses to the novel's plotting. While reading *Isa* as a psychological character study, the *National Era* also asserted that the novel has "little of plot or incident" (66), an observation repeated almost verbatim by the *New-York Evangelist* (60). Yet reviewers never concluded, as they had in responding to Sedgwick's fiction, that Chesebro's handling of her novel's plot was a problem. According to the *Troy Daily Times*, *Isa's* understated plot gives its events a "naturalness that seem to stamp them as real."[28] For other reviewers, such minimal plotting served as a well-chosen match to the novel's emphasis on character interiority and to its philosophy. Although *Isa,* said the *New York Tribune*, "has barely sufficient incident to serve as the basis of a slight narrative," the novel, "[w]ithout aiming at dramatic effect," offers a striking "record of spiritual experience" (7). The *Sartain's* reviewer concluded that Chesebro' successfully "disdain[s] the accessories of incident, in working out her illustrations of transcendental philosophy, nor does the reader need the usual machinery of the novel to rivet his attention" (515).

When explaining the basis for their view of the novel's effective emphasis on characterization, some reviewers grounded their responses in the conventions of reading for verisimilitude. Speaking of the character of Gansevoort Norton, a "talented" artist and former lover of Mary Irving, one of the novel's two main female characters, the *American Whig Review* claimed that he "is by far the most truthfully drawn" character "of the prominent ones in the book," though the *Whig Review* admitted that Weare Dugganne, an early influence on the novel's eponymous protagonist, possesses "perhaps" as much naturalness (July 1852: 94). Reviewers attended less to verisimilitude alone, however, and more to what Chesebro' did with her characters, especially Isa. According to *Sartain's*, while the "characters, besides Isa, that are introduced . . . are skillfully delineated," the "spell of fascination rests only with the proud, self-relying and gifted heroine" (515). Most frequently, reviewers found her to be a strikingly singular personage, who bespoke Chesebro's imaginative power and insight. The *New York Tribune* called Isa an "exquisite and original creation" whose "spiritual development is traced with singular breadth of outline, betraying knowledge of character that is rare," even in "veteran writers" (7). *Sartain's* beamed that the "deepening phases of her [i.e., Isa's] pilgrimage through life are detailed with a power of thought and imagination that reveals a calm consciousness of strength and mental resources admirable in any writer" and "truly remarkable" for a first novel (515).

Perhaps more significantly, this reaction to Isa involved a set of moves in which reviewers united ideas about characterization and thematic interpretation by repeatedly reading Chesebro's protagonist for her social, philosophical, and moral implications. Such a move entailed, first of all, sorting out exactly what Isa did and who she was. To that end, the *Literary World* and the *Southern Literary Messenger* provided their readers with the following interpretive overviews of the incidents in Isa's life: "Rescued from the poorhouse, at a tender age, by the humanity of a lady residing in Richmond, and brought up as a member of the family, she first falls in love with the son, but crushes the feminine sentiment in the bud, and, when arrived at womanhood, goes off to edit a socialist newspaper in some distant city" (*Messenger* May 1852: 318). The *World* explained that Isa "is a woman of intellect and beauty, who devotes herself to a literary life. Her mind is at an early age corrupted by the perusal of an infidel book, and, afterwards becoming connected with the author of the work in the editorship of a transcendental newspaper, she falls victim to the association—the pair being too transcendental to think of matrimony" (Apr. 17, 1852: 279). Clearly, these remarks function as more than just plot summaries. Within the logic of informed reading, they double as springboards to thematic interpretation.

And interpret reviewers did. The reviewer in the *Knickerbocker* found thematic resonance in Isa's developing philosophy. Explaining that Isa, in her studies, "has come to the conclusion that divinity lies in WILL" and that "the will of man is simply omnipotent," this reviewer claimed that Isa's subsequent relation with Althaus Stuart, her extramarital lover, demonstrates that amid "affection or passion" the "will is simply superfluous." From there the *Knickerbocker* reviewer spun out the philosophical implications he saw arising from these developments in the novel: "People whose affections are greatly satisfied are happy, and are so far discharged from any practical exhibition of the supremacy of the will. . . . The voluntary life is called for only when storms arise, when a conflict takes place between affection and intellect, and we are summoned accordingly to choose or decide between them. Here alone is the province of will. Where our prospects are clear and undisturbed, we have no occasion for it" (551). The review in the *Southern Literary Messenger* took a different view of Isa and her significance, seeing instead of a philosophical theme a political implication involving gender. "The heroine of the story is a sort of Greeley in petticoats," explained the *Messenger*, "who goes about talking obscurely of Women's Rights and Social Reform, and is represented by the authoress as that fearful thing—a woman of strong mind" (318). What clearly disturbed these and other reviewers, even as it appeared to fascinate them, was Isa's position as a thinking, and unsettlingly iconoclastic, woman. The *Messenger* felt that in her mental quest, Isa abandoned her true feminine feelings, while the *Knickerbocker* followed its thematic analysis with the assertion that readers "wish to see how surely and sadly this premature little theologian and philosopher will mismanage life" (552). Concluding that Isa is a proponent of transcendentalism, the *Southern Quarterly Review* claimed that she "would seem to have been drawn from outlines afforded by Margaret Fuller," who had been guilty of "a laborious mystifying of the commonplace" and of writing that was "simply balderdash, and very bad balderdash too" (Oct. 1852: 544).

But how was it possible for reviewers to be fascinated by Isa and drawn to a novel that seemed so disturbing? Within the logic of informed reading, such a book should have been seen as anathema, a danger readers should avoid rather than find compelling. One answer is that some reviewers reached exactly that conclusion. Explaining that Isa's trafficking with "infidel books" and her "guilty" love with Stuart, which includes having an illegitimate child, carried dangerous implications, a review in *Peterson's* declared, "We think the theme badly chosen, and doubt whether such fictions do good" (July 1862: 307). The *Christian Examiner* simply announced that "we cannot approve the moral" of *Isa* (May 1852: 458), and the *Southern Literary Messenger* agreed, giving a slight tip of the hat while wagging a large finger: "'Isa,' by Miss Chesebro', is an anomalous production, of a psychological character, in which the author exhibits considerable but perverted powers." Why "perverted"? Because, according to the *Messenger*, "Miss Chesebro' has little notion of the vicious moral of her subject" (544).

Yet other reviewers saw the novel quite differently, reading it as an engaging and moving cautionary tale about an intellectual, well-intentioned, but flawed woman. Having identified Isa's significance as inhering in her philosophy that "divinity lies in WILL," the *Knickerbocker* added that "the logical scope of the story is to urge the practical fallacy of this conclusion" (551). The *New-York Evangelist* asseverated that the "fate of this strong-minded, earnest, and pure-hearted girl, trusting to herself, and . . . descending through subtle delusions . . . to the cold, depressing depths of utter infidelity, is a theme rather deep," but the "lesson is a powerful and a good one" (60). The *New York Tribune* and *Harper's* agreed that, in the words of the latter, "the story turns on the development of an abnormal spiritual experience, showing the perils of entire freedom of thought in a powerful, original mind" (853). Or as the *Tribune* put it, the "heroine is evidently intended as an awful warning of the perils attendant on freedom of thought" (7). In light of such comments, it is not surprising that the *Troy Whig* could beam that *Isa* "is . . . pervaded by a vein of pure ennobling thought."[29]

Other reviewers, however, were not so certain about what exactly Chesebro' was getting at with her novel and protagonist. *Sartain's* found the narrative to be ambiguous, noting that the "moral aspect of the book may not be so universally agreed upon" (575). "Amid all the trumpery about 'Women's Rights'" in *Isa*, explained the *American Whig Review*, "we can hardly discern what the authoress would teach us. Whether it were better for us to 'dissolve the marriage contract' . . . or whether it were better that we should continue to 'marry, and be given in marriage,' is left almost wholly in the dark" (95). Aware of the interpretive disagreements about the novel, the *National Era* informed its readers that *Isa* "is a book about which many contradictory things are already said, for it is one liable to be misunderstood. . . . The authoress, herself conscientious and high souled, kept the true purpose close before her own mind, but she has not in all places made it clear to the eye of *all* her readers" (66).

But rather than interpreting these ambiguities as an attempt by the novel to provoke questions rather than offer clear-cut answers, several reviewers ascribed the uncertainty they found in *Isa* to Chesebro's mismanagement, the nature of which was articulated at times by those who otherwise interpreted the novel's moral thematics as salutary. The problem, as the *New York Tribune* reviewer saw it, lay in the fact that, while the "heroine is evidently intended as an awful warning of the perils attendant on freedom of thought, and a release from the thrawldom of traditional opinions," Isa is "depicted with such genuine nobleness, such transparent truthfulness of intellect, such a wealth of pure and generous feeling . . . that the reader is often tempted to lose sight of the dangerous tendency of her principles in admiration of the strength and loveliness of her character" (7). The *Knickerbocker* reviewer reached much the same conclusion. Although Chesebro' "aims to portray character . . . of a perverted type," the narrative "does not succeed in arousing the reader's alarm. On the contrary, her sympathy remains with the *pervert* to the close of the volume" (551). According to this interpretive formulation, Chesebro', despite her good intentions, was guilty of committing a cardinal error in the logic of informed reading: encouraging reader sympathy for an ethically suspect character.

The *Knickerbocker*'s comment about the novel's conclusion indicates that it was problematic for readers. Although Isa dies in the company of Stuart, some reviewers invoked the rule of notice to read the ending as lacking something. In the process, several reviewers engaged in what Richard Gerrig has called "participatory responses" or "p-responses," a term that refers to "all non-inferential responses in the [reader's] performance of narration" and includes hopes and preferences and even the mental construction of alternative endings to a story.[30] For example, the *Knickerbocker* reviewer said that readers "wish to see how surely and sadly" Isa will be "cut off from the serene consolations of the affections" (552). "What displeases most of our ideas of propriety" in *Isa*, explained the *American Whig Review*, "is, that evil doing does not meet with its reward. . . . Isa, although she has sinned—and the authoress hesitates not to call it sin—dies peacefully, calmly" and is "launched smoothly, and with love, . . . into the future." Violating expectations about proper poetic justice, *Isa* struck this reader as unfitting at its close because "Isa's death, horrible as it was . . . was not horrible to her" (95). Or, as the *Southern Literary Messenger* observed, the "conclusion of the story presents us with a death-bed (the heroine's) made tranquil by unbelief" instead of with a death scene of suffering or one redeemed by Isa's penitence (319).

Despite these disagreements and feelings of dismay, it should be noted that many of these reviewers were the same ones who praised *Isa* for its originality and called it a stunning accomplishment. It is as if Chesebro' had managed to produce a novel that was strikingly unique yet disturbingly paradoxical, unorthodox yet undeniably fascinating and moving—one that could both disrupt readers' expectations and be disciplined into a narrative that accommodated prevailing interpretive assumptions. To say this is not to claim that the novel was—and is—these things. Rather, in their aggregate, the antebellum responses to *Isa* constructed the narrative that way by operating as a multifaceted, and at times internally contradictory, formulation that gave to the text a multidimensional and textured profile. In the process, that interpretive formulation changed the horizon of expectations of Chesebro's audience and thereby provided a new foundation for responses to her next novel.

Children of Light, which Chesebro' published nearly a year after *Isa*, received attention comparable to that of her previous novel, in the sense that it was reviewed in a number of leading periodicals but did not receive widespread notice and commentary in the press.[31] Moreover, in the wake of the new reading horizon for her fiction, the responses were much more in the mold of what they had been for *Isa* rather than for *Dream-Land by Daylight*. Once again, reviewers saw *Children* as a character-driven novel with minimal plotting. Its "plot is singularly barren of incident," announced the *New York Tribune* review (Jan. 1, 1852: 8), while the review in the *National Era* thought that the "story is a very simple one, and is but the thread on which to string the sentiments of the author" (Dec. 30, 1852: 209).

Seeing *Children* as a relatively plotless novel and responding instead to its characters—a move that paralleled their reading of *Isa*—reviewers nonetheless reacted differently to the characterization in Chesebro's new novel. Although believing that her characters indicated that the "author has evidently studied the human heart, as well as its proudest aspirations," which made *Children* "no common work of fiction," a reviewer in *Godey's* remarked that "these 'Children of Light' appear to us through a mist, rather darkly," as if they lacked clearly defined development (Feb. 1853: 179). Other reviewers also criticized Chesebro's skills at characterization in *Children*. The *Literary World* felt that the "personages of the tale fail to interest because they one and all 'talk like a book.' Ease and nature are wanting," which causes the personages to lack the verisimilitude readers had found in the characters in *Isa* (Dec. 18, 1852: 392). Indeed, the *New York Tribune* expressly saw *Children* as a falling off: "In depth of thought and natural delineation of character, we must regard this work by Miss Chesebro [*sic*] as decidedly inferior to her 'Isa'" (8).

Dissatisfaction with this element of *Children* tended to concentrate especially on Asia Phillips, whom reviewers agreed was the book's protagonist. The *Tribune* reviewer called her "a strange book of being," while describing her story as follows: "Asia Phillips, the heroine of the story, is introduced to us when a child, as the playmate and humble companion of the daughter of a proud, wealthy family, the occupants of Maderon house. A shy, solitary girl, she nourishes her young enthusiasms by the study of the paintings, which the Maderons had collected. . . . The nuns and martyrs in the gallery make a deep impression on her active imagination. She is led to meditate on the purposes of her being—longs to live for some great purpose. . . . Cherishing such visions, Asia grows up to early womanhood without finding the key to the riddle which occupies her thoughts" (8). The *Southern Quarterly Review* interpreted Asia and her story as more than "strange." Its reviewer found them dismaying because of what struck him as inconsistencies in her development: "The portrait of Asia, in this book, rather troubles than satisfies the reader. We are not sure that the author has not made the character to fluctuate with the events, at the same time that she undertakes to show a being superior to events, and with a native will and strength, to control and shape them" (Jan. 1853: 254). This reviewer was responding in particular to Asia's growth as an actress and its relation to her involvement with Aaron Gregorian, her mentor, who later abandons her to what she feels is ignominy. The reviewer asked puzzlingly, "To what end was all the training for the stage? Only to give her villainous tutor his power over her? Could not this have been done without the training? and is the training itself to have no results? The great point to establish was this—that convention cannot make a profession illegitimate, when it is clearly indicated by the natural powers of the individual" (254).

Amid this shift from the kinds of responses generated by reading encounters with *Isa*, this last reaction to *Children* points to a common feature in the reception of the two novels. As they had with *Isa*, reviewers took the characters in *Children* to be inherently yoked to the book's various levels of meaning. The *Tribune* reviewer, for example, read Asia's name as "emblematic of the wild, fierce life that glowed within her" and interpreted her story—and particularly her relationship with Gregorian —as an emblematic tale of "the crushed spirit of the desolate victim" (8). More broadly, *Graham's* asserted that in "this novel, as well as in Isa, the author gives vivid representations of characters who represent the radical ideas of the time in philosophy, government, and theology" (Jan. 1853: 104). The *National Era* saw such philosophical representation via character to be most pronounced in Chesebro's Mr. Borland, a friend of Gregorian. Calling Borland a "high priest of Nature," the *Era* identified one of his speeches in chapter twenty-one as articulating "Miss Chesebro's view of marriage" and the belief that "there is 'better time' coming, 'when men, rejuvenated, regenerated, will no longer worship that ideal MAN . . . but instead, the Truth, NATURE'" (209).[32]

Contrary to the claim of one twentieth-century critic, moreover, reviewers disagreed somewhat in the moral, sociopolitical, and philosophical implications they ascribed to the novel.[33] *Graham's* felt that "we cannot see" Chesebro' as "the champion of the heretics she represents" since "her object is to show the pernicious effect in practice of many opinions which seem beautiful and beneficent in theory," but its reviewer then added that "many of her opinions [in the novel] are exceedingly immature" (104). The *Tribune* reviewer found that while "[m]uch is said in the novel about the mystery of life," readers "are left in the dark . . . as to the convictions of the writer" (8). This reviewer, however, thought that the conclusion of the novel was not as thematically obscure as the rest of the narrative, but, invoking the interpretive code of final authority, he saw a problem even there: "The moral of the close is more obvious than the gist of the philosophising in the progress of the volume. Enforcing the Christian precept of mercy to the erring, it rebukes the ferocity of trampling on the fallen. But the beautiful illustration of this 'twice blessed quality' does not atone, in our opinion, for the absence of definite aim and the blending of irreconcilable elements in the composition of the work" (8). For the *Tribune* reviewer, finally, Chesebro's "taste" for "the extravagant, the distorted, and the unreal" in treating the "enigma of existence" made her novel too eccentric and unpalatable thematically. The reviewer added that he hoped Chesebro' "will find more wholesome lessons" for her readership in other materials in novels to come (8).

This last addendum suggests that part of the concern reviewers had with *Children*—as they had had with *Isa*—was the relation between the novel and its audience's responses. Several reviewers, in fact, were struck by what they saw as disturbing disconnections. Both the *Tribune* and the *National Era* reviewers, invoking the rule of notice, found a puzzling disjunction between the novel and its title. Admitting that *Children of Light* "is certainly an ambitious title," the *Era* reviewer indicated that the audience would find it enigmatic, since "we see no congruity between the title and the contents of the book" (209). The *Tribune* was somewhat more explicit: "A shadowy gloom broods over the history, and we feel during its perusal that the title is a misnomer—for the 'Children of Light' dwell in a region of intolerable darkness" (8).

Partly for this and other mismatches they found in *Children*, reviewers were more critical of the stylistic finish of the novel than they had been with *Isa*. While admitting that Chesebro's second novel "has much of the same vigor and freshness" of her first, *Putnam's Monthly* felt that *Children* lacked "clearness of conception" and representation (Jan. 1853: 106). The *Southern Quarterly Review* maintained that the novel "works spasmodically, and . . . is not sufficiently deliberate of design, and is quite too rash and rapid in execution" (254). By contrast, the review in the *Literary World* found "diffuseness" to be the "main fault" of the novel's style. The "book before us might have been compressed one-third in size," said the *World*'s reviewer, though admittedly, "[i]t would no doubt have taken longer to write" (392).

Considered as a whole, the public reception of *Children* was more critical than it had been for *Isa*. While reviewers did not find Chesebro's new novel as thematically challenging or controversial as her previous one, neither did they respond to it with the kind of impassioned interest and debate about themes and characters that had marked the reception of *Isa*. In fact, except for the reviewer in *Peterson's*, who called *Children* "a better book, in every respect, than its predecessor" (161), reviewers clearly judged it inferior to Chesebro's debut novel.

When antebellum readers encountered Chesebro's work again, it was in a second collection of short stories, entitled *The Little Crossbearers*, which appeared in late 1853 or early 1854.[34] That collection was followed approximately two years later in 1855 by another, *The Beautiful Gate*. These two volumes signaled several new developments in the relation between Chesebro's fiction and her readers and in her position in the literary marketplace.

Unlike most of those in *Dream-Land by Daylight* three years earlier, the ten stories in *Crossbearers* were previously unpublished. More importantly, the book was published not by Redfield, who had put out her previous three, but jointly by the Buffalo, New York, firm of Derby, Orton, and Mulligan and by Derby and Miller of Auburn, New York. Since no information about the reasons for this switch has survived in Chesebro's letters, we can only conjecture as to the cause, but a couple of factors seem to have been at work. The negligible sales of *Dream-Land*, *Isa*, and *Children of Light*, along with reviewer consensus that the last book had not met the quality of *Isa*, may have caused Redfield to decline publishing the new collection. Perhaps, too, Redfield did not print it because volumes of short fiction tended not to sell as well as novels in the first place, and there was no need to put the firm at a disadvantage for a second time with Chesebro's stories. Still, the move to Derby, Orton, and Mulligan and their partner firm was not necessarily a bad choice for Chesebro'. Derby and Miller had published Jared Sparks's well-received *Life of George Washington*, and Orton and Mulligan had put out Fanny Fern's highly popular *Fern Leaves from Fanny's Portfolio* in 1853.[35] Since both firms had thereby achieved some notoriety and financial success, there was nothing to suggest that publishing with them would be unproductive.

The move, however, turned out to be less than propitious, at least in terms of securing public attention for *Crossbearers*. I have been able to locate only one five-line review of the collection—in *Putnam's*—and it is a phantom. Its claim that the book "is a picturesque and touching narrative, quite ingenious in its plot" indicates that the reviewer never opened the volume to discover that it was a collection of ten different narratives (Jan. 1854: 111). Why was this slight glance the only recognition *Cross-bearers* apparently received? Clearly, it was not because the book was merely a collection of twice-told tales. Instead, it appears that Chesebro's two new publishers did little to promote it. Neither firm did much advertising of new titles, and when they did, they tended to publicize their lists of nonfiction. The same seems to have been true of their approach to distributing copies to reviewers—an essential step to securing public notice. Although both firms did do some distributing, they seem to have focused on nonfiction titles or, within their fiction offerings, temperance tales.[36] In all likelihood, few if any copies of *Crossbearers* ever made it into reviewers' hands.

A similar fate seems to have befallen *The Beautiful Gate*, which was published by the newly formed firm of Miller, Orton, and Mulligan two years later, following James Derby's break with Miller in early 1855.[37] One factor for the little attention to *Beautiful Gate* was no doubt that it was almost completely a collection of previously published tales. Except for the title story, in fact, Chesebro's "new" collection was literally a reprint of the ten stories in *Crossbearers*, which virtually guaranteed its neglect in the public sphere. Like their earlier incarnations, moreover, Miller, Orton, and Mulligan appear to have done little to promote *Beautiful Gate*, choosing to favor their nonfiction and works by more recognized authors in their list, including Fanny Fern and Frederick Douglass.[38] Yet the firm must have been a bit more effective in distributing copies to the press, since reviews appeared in at least two publications, the *New York Tribune* and the *Cayuga Chief*.

Both tell us little about the reception of *Beautiful Gate* except for one thing: It was seen as children's fiction. The *Tribune* called it a "collection of juvenile stories" (Oct. 29, 1855: 1) that would position Chesebro' "in an eminent rank as a writer for juvenile minds" (Nov. 24, 1855: 6). That November issue of the *Tribune* quoted the remarks of the reviewer in the *Cayuga Chief,* who wrote that the book should "have interest for children" and expressed the "wish that the book could be read by every child in the land" (3). Whether other antebellum readers responded in the same way in the privacy of their homes is another question, but one index to the response of those readers appears in an inscription in a surviving copy of *Beautiful Gate*. It simply reads, "my dear gra[n]doter hear is a nice buck for you to read from granmother [*sic*]."³⁹ If typical, these remarks from both the public and private spheres indicate that antebellum readers took *Beautiful Gate* as fiction designed expressly for the young.

The paucity of attention and minimal success of these two collections—and particularly *Crossbearers*—did not, however, discourage Chesebro' from continuing to write fiction. Between these two collections, she wrote a new novel, *Susan, the Fisherman's Daughter,* which was published simultaneously by James Derby in New York and by his brother W. H. Derby in Cincinnati in late 1854.⁴⁰ In fact, with this new novel, Chesebro' appears to have decided to redouble her efforts by taking on the most ambitious project of her writing career. Subtitled *Getting Along. A Book of Illustrations, Susan* is Chesebro's longest novel, running to over 600 pages, and is peopled by her largest cast of characters.

Derby seems to have made some effort to promote *Susan,* since it garnered roughly the same degree of attention from major periodicals as had Chesebro's first two novels.⁴¹ Moreover, working from the horizon of expectations built through their encounters with her longer fiction, reviewers responded to *Susan* in a number of ways that paralleled their readings of *Isa* and *Children of Light.*

Once again, reviewers were stuck by Chesebro's style and disagreed about its effects and merits. Like the reviewer of *Children* in the *Literary World,* the reviewer in *Peterson's* found *Susan* diffuse and somewhat turbid: The "novel, on the whole, is inartistic and vague, so much so, indeed, that one continually asks if the author really has any idea half the time what she wishes to bring out. If the story would have been told in half the space . . . the book would have been the best of the season" (Apr. 1855: 317). The *Knickerbocker* reviewer felt the novel was a bit sermonic, in a way that troubled its generic consistency: "The religious tone of the book is far from unpleasant, . . . but it is doubtful whether fiction is the best vehicle for such solemn truths. A sermon in a novel seems as much out of place as adventures related in a sermon" (June 1855: 626). On the other hand, several readers once again called her style "masculine" without finding that trait problematic. According to the *New York Tribune,* Chesebro's "steel-like" imagination in "grappl[ing] with the most perplexing problems . . . gives a substantial masculine character to the work, which . . . will insure it both an elevated rank and a protracted date, beyond the reach of the ephemeral novelties, which flash and fade in a single season (Mar. 30, 1855: 3). Likewise, *Harper's* said of *Susan* that its "style is always sinewy and masculine" and added that "we much prefer the robust and well-compacted phraseology of this work, animated as it always is by the workings of an original and active mind, to the soft and polished sweetness of many of our fashionable sentence-makers" (May 1855: 858). *Peterson's* went so far as to call "its general style . . . a great advance on former efforts," particularly in the way its "thoughts [are] frequently expressed with a felicity that rises to genius" (Apr. 1855: 317). Far more glowing than critical, in fact, reviewer reactions to Chesebro's style in *Susan* were in line with their reception of her prose in *Isa.*

Another carryover was their view of the plot—or more accurately the plots—of *Susan.* Once again reviewers saw plot as a minor element of Chesebro's narrative, the slightness of which, as the *Knickerbocker* explained, contributed to the novel's overall verisimilitude: "The plot . . . is neither intricate nor improbable" (626). The *National Era* indicated that *Susan's* sedate plotting also enabled it to engage its audience without the tumultuous sensationalism on which so many other novels relied. With an extended metaphor that sounds almost as sensual as it does nautical, the *Era* explained that *Susan* "has not the heady flow of the ordinary novel; the reader is not carried upon a current of story, ever swelling with fresh tributaries, driven by fitful winds, tossed by turbulent waves, and then dashed over the denouement into Lake Hymen, to rest after the riot" (Mar. 15, 1855: 43).

In light of its understated plotting, reviewers unsurprisingly interpreted *Susan* as one of Chesebro's character-driven novels. Noting the relative emphasis given to these two elements of fiction in *Susan*, *Harper's* concluded that in "composing the narrative, the writer seems to have aimed at the delineation and development of character, rather than to enchain the reader by a series of exciting outward incidents" (858). Instead of such focusing on "outward" events, reviewers repeatedly explained, *Susan* forefronted the inward unfolding of its characters' minds and temperaments. Reviews in the *New York Tribune* and the *National Era* invoked the rule of notice in reaching this conclusion by interpreting the novel's subtitle as an index to its emphasis on character. Said the *Tribune*, "we find on turning over a few pages, that under the guise of a popular romance, it is devoted to illustrations of character, the story serving merely as a framework to exhibit a variety of portraits" marked by a "fineness of delineation" (3). Although feeling that the "drift of this book is not very well indicated by its first title," the *National Era* added that "it richly deserves its second, for it is a book of Graphics—a sort of moving panorama" in which its cast of characters illustrate and even model various traits. The *Era* then enumerated several examples: "Mr. Horace Chilton [brother of Leah, one of the novel's main female characters] is worthy of the grave consideration of the young gentleman of genius and jerking enterprise. . . . His sister affords a pattern for girls to live and die by, when living is laborious, and dying early inevitable; and Lucia Tree [an illustrator and another of the novel's main women] and Young Vane [a house painter, fellow artist, and kindred spirit of Lucia] are safe instances of artistic enthusiasm for sympathy and emulation" (43). Despite reading these four as virtual character types, the *Era* reviewer agreed with others in interpreting the novel's characters as true to life and marked by psychological depth. The *Era* found in *Susan* evidence that the "author is capable of the largest range of psychical investigation" and that "Hawthorne . . . is the only writer of fiction in this country who outranks the author of Getting Along" in this "vein" (43). Likewise, *Harper's* asseverated that *Susan* evinces "rare insight into character[s]" and their feeling and motivations (858). The *Tribune* found that "the sharp outlines of reality circumscribe . . . every character" in the novel because of the consistency of "their salient individual proportions." Although each character appears in a "singular diversity of relations, their identity is always sacredly preserved" (3). One interesting feature in the responses of the *Tribune* and *National Era* reviewers is that they saw Chesebro's characters as both realistic representations and illustrative patterns for "sympathy and emulation," with no incompatibility in those two qualities.

In dealing with specific characters, reviewers did differ regarding which ones they took to be the novel's main focus. As might be expected, some reviewers, no doubt addressing this question through the rule of notice, took the eponymous Susan to be Chesebro's protagonist. For example, the *National Era* explained that "the most frequently recurring character 'illustrated,' is a fisherman's daughter, Susy, growing up from twelve to eighteen years of age, during the progress of the tale" (43). Instead of privileging Susan, the *Tribune* reviewer focused on Stella Cammon as the novel's center of attention. Noting that a "considerable portion of the work is devoted to the religious experience of a young Catholic maiden, Stella Cammon," who waivers "uncertainly between the nunnery and matrimony," this reviewer felt that the "character of this person is depicted with [such] consummate effect" that she "will, by many readers, be deemed the most valuable feature of the story" (3). The reviewer in *Harper's* concluded that no one character served as the novel's main focus but instead highlighted four as standing out from the "number of subordinate personages": "Leighton, the moody, contemplative student, half lover and half misanthrope—Stella Cammon, vibrating between religious enthusiasm and romantic affection—Falcon, the pure-minded, earnest, but dreaming philanthropist—and Susan Dillon, the noble, self-sacrificing idealist" (858).

This uncertainty about which characters readers were to concentrate on in *Susan* marked a departure from responses to Chesebro's first two novels. But reviewers did agree that, as illustrations, the characters in *Susan* functioned in relation to the novel's themes in characteristic Chesebroesque fashion. None, however, read its characters—and especially its women—as four modern commentators on the novel have seen them: as representations designed to question traditional gender roles and critically investigate marriage as women's proper condition.[42] Instead, reviewers forged connections between characters and ideas to reach other conclusions about the book's themes. For the *Harper's* reviewer, Susan illustrated the philosophy of "wisely attempting to solve the mystery of life by the performance of duty" (858). The *National Era* found the thematic resonance of several characters by reading them not so much as models but as satiric mirrors designed to expose excesses. Hence, the "fashionable Miss Isadore [Baldwin] sits for the picture of her tribe, and there are some of the frivolous who will throw down the book when they see themselves in it, but they will not be able to run quite away from the reflection." Regarding the philanthropical Falcon, the *Era* reviewer interpreted him as a "personage [who] serves, as you take him, as well for honest satire as earnest eulogium" for the part he "plays [as] perpetual chairman" of the "standing committee on public misery" (43).

The conclusion several reviewers reached as a result of such readings was that *Susan* was something of a philosophical fiction—or at least a thinking-person's novel. Employing potable and seduction metaphors, which were commonly used at the time to describe fiction reading, the reviewer in the *National Era* said that *Susan* will not "shock or surprise, or any way seduce, the idleness of the day into . . . solicitudes and indolent intoxications . . . but it will be studied by everyone who reads it, and be appreciated by all who are capable of a good book" and the "truth they meet with" therein (48). The reviewer in the *New York Courier and Enquirer* simply maintained of *Susan* that "[w]e know of no book of the season more worthy of thoughtful minds" (qtd. in *New York Tribune* Apr. 20, 1855: 1).

Reviewers did not all agree on the merit of *Susan,* and some disagreed about Chesebro's management of its plethora of characters. Nonetheless, praise and pleasure far outweighed such reservations in the novel's overall reception. Taken as a whole, in fact, that reception marked *Susan* as the most favorably received and least controversial—and challenging— of Chesebro's full-length fictions thus far. Unfortunately, *Susan* was no more successful than her previous books in garnering a popular readership for Chesebro'.

⌒

Despite the lack of popularity of *Susan* and the two collections of short stories surrounding its publication, Chesebro' no doubt welcomed the favorable reviews of the novel, for within six months of the appearance of *Beautiful Gate,* she published two new books of fiction. The first, which came out in May 1856, was *Philly and Kit,* a volume composed of two novellas.[43] Although she managed to place it with Redfield, her original publisher, the new volume received little attention from reviewers, perhaps because one of its novellas, the "Kit" of the title, was another twice-told tale, having appeared in *Graham's* in March 1855. Only one major periodical, *Godey's,* and one major newspaper, the *New-York Observer,* carried reviews of the volume. Both were brief—and mixed. While the *Observer*'s reviewer asserted that these two tales of "humble life will be found no less redolent of [Chesebro's] sympathies and philosophies than any of the previous productions of her pen" (May 8, 1856: 150), the *Godey's* reviewer could offer no more than back-handed praise in an ironic comment on the verisimilitude of the two stories' characters: "Though we have great confidence in the existence of such curiosities as honest newspaper boys, innocent apple-girls, industrious organ-grinders, and romantic image-sellers, and are extremely sure that beneath the rags and squalor of poverty the noblest virtues and sublimest charities lie hidden, we still think that such stories as the two contained in this volume are at present little needed, however brilliantly composed they may be" (Aug. 1856: 180).

Chesebro's other new work of fiction, which appeared two to three months after *Philly and Kit,* was a novel entitled *Victoria, or the World Overcome,* published by James Derby via his new firm of Derby and Jackson. The book itself marked a departure for Chesebro', since it is a historical novel set in late seventeenth-century Puritan New England. It was, moreover, a change that reviewers, as might be expected, highlighted in their reception of the novel. But they seem to have been somewhat puzzled by *Victoria,* and that difficulty manifested itself in what reviewers both said and did not say about the novel.

In a notable distinction from their reception of Chesebro's previous novels, reviewers said little about the style of *Victoria,* and the few who did found it wanting. The reviewer in the *United States Magazine* quipped that Chesebro' evidently "has been of late reading much of the old 'well of English undefiled,' and it has not improved her style, which is rarely elegant" in the novel (Sept. 1856: 244). A review by Elizabeth Stoddard in the *Daily Alta California* objected to what she saw as a faulty tone in the book, particularly its "external preachment about self-denial." Invoking the standard objection to intrusive narration, in accordance with the codes of informed reading, Stoddard subscribed to the view of that problem as a mark of faulty reader engagement, asserting, "I object to the position she takes in regard to the reader—that of a teacher."[44] Additionally, only one reviewer said anything about the novel's plot as a whole, but it was not to point out that the plot was minimal and avoided melodrama for realistic effect. On the contrary, that reviewer, in an unusual vein in Chesebro's reception, praised *Victoria* for the way its "plot is very absorbing and full of pathos" (*National Era* Sept. 11, 1856: 147). Although this reader did not specify what in the plot made the book such a moving page-turner, other readers did, via responses that were themselves marked by differences and by signs of interpretive perplexity.

A striking feature about other reactions to plot in *Victoria* is that reviewers who responded to it in specific terms repeatedly focused on events in the last third of the novel, involving three of the characters:

Maud Saltonstall, Archibald Kenesett, and Hope Rossiter. Pointing out that their "story is one of witchcraft," the *United States Magazine* described it in detail:

> Maud Saltonstall, a child of genius, glowing with life and beauty, and innocence . . . is attached to Archibald Kensett, who loves her in return with that ardor of youth and romance so little understood in that Puritanic age. Hope Rossiter loves the youth also, and being a godly maiden, learned withall, and, under an apparently cold intellectual character, holding within her the elements of deep passionateness, unknown to herself and unsupposed by others, mistakes her natural human emotions for the action of one acted upon by a wicked, deluded spirit. She is affianced to a Puritan preacher, and bewildered and perplexed by emotions which were alike new and inexplicable, worn by study and hard mental action, she falls ill. Her mind had pondered much the stories of witchcraft, which at that period was the great delusion of the mother country, and with a profound self-delusion, she boldly accuses the beautiful Maud as the cause of her sufferings. (Sept. 1856: 243–44)

The reviewer for the *Knickerbocker* also provided a plot summary only for the final third of the narrative and exclaimed in particular that Maud, "whose poetic nature made her utter thoughts at variance with the Calvinism of the day, was tried, condemned, and executed for a witch!" (Sept. 1856: 303). Both reviewers indicated that they focused on this segment of *Victoria* because they found its plotting especially potent. The *United States Magazine* asserted that "[t]his part of the story is wrought out with genuine power and much artistic skill. It consummates a story" that "lagged heavily in the preceding pages" (244). The *Knickerbocker* compared reading this section to viewing a classic painting of religious suffering: "As we view that master-piece of art, the Martyrdom of Huss, while indignation and pity struggle within us, we are cheered by that faith which makes the fiery trial but the opening of Heaven's gate to the sainted one; so, in reading the volume before us, the fate of the lovely Maud is not without the same consolation" (303). A curious feature of these responses to the plot of *Victoria* is not only their neglect of two-thirds of the novel but also their lack of comment on the other main characters in these events.

Not that reviewers ignored other characters, but in responding to the novel's characterization, reviewers repeatedly treated it not in relation to plot but as a self-contained feature of the book. In one way, this category of reader reaction echoed responses to Chesebro's previous novels. Explaining that Chesebro' "does not aim" at striking narrative movement "so much as at the analysis and development of character," a *Harper's* reviewer found *Victoria* quintessentially Chesebroesque, in that the novel's "persons . . . are all the subject of curious psychological experiment" presented through "the gradual evolution of character" (Oct. 1856: 696). The *New-York Observer* reviewer largely agreed, announcing that the "great power of the writer appears to lie in a delineation of the deep workings of the human heart under the influence of its various passions and sensibilities" (Aug. 7, 1856: 251). This shared sense that development of the characters' interiority was the novel's most salient feature extended to the reviewer in the *Knickerbocker*, who found that in *Victoria* "Miss Chesebro's characters display to us, in a remarkable and interesting manner, the secret springs of action" (303). But as positive—and characteristic— as these responses were, they also pointed to a departure from previous reviewer reaction. In the past, reviewers had seen the minimal plotting of Chesebro's novels as a successful strategy for forefronting character, so that these two elements worked together to enhance verisimilitude. But in reading *Victoria*, reviewers seemed unable to find a relation between its striking plot at the novel's end and the sustained inward development of characters in the book as a whole.

One thing reviewers did agree upon, however, was to find *Victoria*, as they had found Chesebro's earlier novels, to be a story in which theme and idea played major roles. As is the case with *Susan*, moreover, reviewers thematized *Victoria* quite differently than have the novel's few modern commentators, who have read it either as conventional sentimental fiction supporting gender norms or as a feminist novel that questions patriarchal values.[45] Instead, antebellum reviewers interpreted *Victoria* as a novel about religion. Noting that the narrative "is drawn from a melancholy chapter of New England history," the review in the *New-York Observer* explained that "the story is designed to be religious in its character, illustrating the power of fanaticism and the influence of defective views of true religion" (251). The review in the *United States Magazine* took a different tack in articulating the book's religious ideas, focusing not on its criticism but on its salutary ideas: "A vein of religious sentiment, evidently the characteristic of the writer's own mind, divested of cant, and wholesome and healthful, gives a lasting touch of value to a book remarkable in itself" (244).

These thematic interpretations, however, raise a question. Given such a reading, why did 1850s reviewers not take *Victoria* to be a sectarian religious novel and thereby take it to task, within the assumptions of informed reading, as dangerously partisan? The responses to the novel's plot suggest one explanation. That is, reviewer focus on the plot in the last third of the novel as the locus of its theological thematics indicates that antebellum readers did not see the entire novel as a narrative dealing with religious issues. The plot summaries in the *Knickerbocker* and the *United States Magazine* suggest, moreover, that it was not so much the religion of the Puritans—or the residual Calvinism of nineteenth-century America—as much as individual delusion and idiosyncratic religious perversion that reviewers saw as the plot's focus. Hence, reviewers read *Victoria* not as an attack on Calvinism but as an exposé of its abuse, safely removed in history. Such an interpretation prevented reviewers from reading Chesebro's novel as an exercise in divisive sectarianism that promoted an alternative creed at the expense of Calvinism. Just as important was that by the mid-1850s, seventeenth-century New England Puritanism had been the subject of enough criticism in fiction (recall the reception of Sedgwick's *Hope Leslie*) that an additional critique of some of its mistakes—especially such a qualified one—would hardly be taken as culpable of fomenting religious controversy.

Responses to the thematics of *Victoria,* as a function of its plot in the last third of the novel, also help explain why reviewers, despite their apparent difficulty in creating an interpretive gestalt for making sense of the narrative as a whole, praised *Victoria* as much as, if not more than, any of Chesebro's previous novels. The *National Era* quoted an unidentified review to rank *Victoria* with Hawthorne's fiction (Sept. 11, 1856: 147), and several reviewers stoutly declared it Chesebro's best novel to date. "*Victoria,*" proclaimed the *Harper's* reviewer, "is the most finished performance of the gifted authoress," who "has no rival but herself" (696). A review in *Putnam's* announced that "*Victoria, or the World Overcome,* by Miss Caroline Cheseboro [*sic*], is by far her best work, evincing great vigor of conception and rare skill in the execution" (Nov. 1856: 539). A review in the *New York Courier,* moreover, offered praise seldom employed in discussing Chesebro's fiction by ranking *Victoria* as a novel matching the "earnestness" of *Jane Eyre* (qtd. in *National Era* 147).

Despite such praise, nearly eight years would elapse between the reception of *Victoria* and Chesebro's publication of another novel. During that interval, she wrote short stories for the periodical press, returning to the genre and medium she had largely abandoned between 1852, when *Isa* was published, and 1856, when *Victoria* appeared. Though this eight-year span was not as productive as the years between 1849 and 1852, when she had seen thirty-nine stories into print, Chesebro' wrote and published seventeen new tales from 1856 to 1863, with most of them appearing in *Harper's* and the *Atlantic Monthly.*[46] Short stories also composed her next volume of fiction, *Blessings in Disguise,* a collection of five previous unpublished tales, which was put out in 1863 by the New York City firm of Carleton and Porter.

Chesebro's turn to yet another publisher for *Blessings* seems to have resulted, at least in part, from circumstances other than what had produced her previous shifts. Redfield, who had published four of her earlier books, had sold his firm in 1860, and while the new owner, William Widdleton, "inherited" the copyrights to the Poe, Simms, and Byrd volumes that Redfield had put out, Widdleton appears not to have been interested in continuing as Chesebro's publisher.[47] To complicate the matter, three years earlier, Miller, Orton, and Mulligan, who had done Chesebro's previous two collections of stories, had gone out of business. Several years after their failure, George Carleton took over a number of Miller and Orton's authors, and apparently Chesebro' was one of the writers who came over to Carleton.[48] But Chesebro' may have had few other options, not only because of Redfield's departure from publishing but also because Derby and Jackson, which had put out *Susan* and *Victoria,* had dissolved in 1861.[49] Nevertheless, the turn to Carleton and Porter ostensibly was a promising choice for Chesebro', since the firm had recently published an English translation of Victor Hugo's *Les Miserables,* which would go on to sell fifty thousand copies by 1865. Though Carleton was one of New York's smaller publishers, his was an up-and-coming firm that had a knack for latching on to promising American authors and best sellers.[50] The problem was that Carleton was selective in the books he promoted. None of the firm's advertisements in the *New York Tribune* or the *Ameri-*

can *Publishers' Circular*, two of the main venues for promoting books of fiction, included *Blessings* as a touted title, and apparently, much as Miller, Orton, and Mulligan had done with Chesebro's two story collections in the 1850s, Carleton did not distribute copies of *Blessings* to reviewers. Indeed, Carleton and Porter's selective treatment of its authors is reflected in the fact that Elizabeth Stoddard was so upset by the firm's neglect of her novel, *The Morgesons*, that in exasperation she turned elsewhere to publish her next novel, *Two Men*.[51] Nor was Stoddard the only dissatisfied author in Carleton and Porter's stable. A writer named Fannie Bean went so far as to bring suit against the firm, charging that her novel, *Dr. Mortimer's Patient*, "had never been advertised or placed on sale except in the publisher's offices," even though she had paid Carleton a $900 subvention.[52] One consequence of such selectivity, at least in Chesebro's case, was that no reviews of *Blessings* appeared in any major newspaper or magazine.

In the same year that *Blessings* was being neglected, Chesebro' completed a new novel, *Peter Carradine, or the Martindale Pastoral*, published by Sheldon and Company. Chesebro's decision to change publishers yet again was probably motivated in part by Carleton's lack of promotional enthusiasm for *Blessings*, but another factor may have been that Sheldon had taken over several titles originally published by Derby and Jackson following that firm's demise, which made Sheldon something of a logical choice.[53] Happily, her newest firm made an effort to get *Peter Carradine* some notice, placing advertisements for it in the *New-York Observer* and *New York Tribune* and apparently distributing enough copies to gain a degree of reviewer attention somewhat comparable to what Chesebro's four previous novels had earned.[54]

In what had almost become a signature feature of responses to Chesebro's novels, reviewers saw *Carradine* as a true-to-life fiction. But they did not necessarily find its naturalness in minimal plotting. The *New York Tribune*, for instance, located the book's vraisemblance in the way Chesebro' wove the novel's action—and, in a sense, the way she refused to weave it: "The plot is composed of three histories, which although in fact separate, are perhaps sufficiently interwoven with each other for the idyllic character of the story. A more lively artistic ambition might have blended the course of events in each in ingenious complications; but their connection is precisely such as often exists in actual life, where true and vital interests of different persons come into superficial contact with each other, without melting into the cohesion of dramatic unity" (Oct. 21, 1863: 3). As a result, the interest and "sympathy of the reader" get engaged "not so much by any stirring incidents of external condition" but by "unfolding" the "inner life" of characters so "well-rounded" that they seem like "an intimate acquaintance" (3). A reviewer in *Arthur's Home Magazine* offered a parallel assessment in noting that the "narrative is . . . without the sensational element," presenting instead a story "in which the reader's interest is absorbed by the inner life of the characters." Indeed, claimed the *Buffalo Commercial Advertiser*, Chesebro' was at the forefront of novelists both as a portrayer of lifelike characters and as a social realist, since "[s]he has boldly emancipated herself from the entire dependence upon plot which marks most of her contemporaries, and uses incidents as a thread upon which to string" lifelike "delineations of character . . . and social ideas."[55]

Although not quite willing to go that far, virtually all reviewers of *Carradine* were struck by what they saw as its verisimilitude in characterization, though they differed as to the factors behind that achievement. For the *Tribune* reviewer it was that "the personages of her story are always models of dramatic consistency; their identity is admirably preserved" and "they never cease to be true" (3). The review in the *Independent* found the title character, as well as "Mercy Fuller, a cultivated teacher of the school, who marries him" and "Miranda Roy, her unsuccessful predecessor," to be "conceived with much truth, force, and clearness," in part because their "conversation[s] . . . have much that is lifelike" (Oct. 8, 1863: 2). *Harper's* felt that Chesebro's "power of unfolding character" through the "phases of their development" gives readers the impression that "[h]er characters are here persons who might really have lived in this world" (Nov. 1863: 850). A review in the *New-York Observer* discovered verisimilitude in a different vein—the distinct individuality of each character: "There is no danger of ever confounding Peter Carradine with Mr. Collamer, of 'Mandy' with Mercy Fuller or Sally Green . . . each true to life and once seen, always afterward recognizable" (Sept. 24, 1863: 311). Taken in the aggregate, such comments formulated *Carradine*, for all intents and purposes, as Chesebro's most accomplished work of realism, via characterization, to date.

Yet these readings of *Carradine* included a number of subtle but important shifts. Only the reviewers in the *New York Tribune* and *Arthur's Home Journal* found the novel's realistic characterization to be of the kind previously ascribed to Chesebro': development marked by inner depth and, as the *Tribune* put it, "psychological combinations" (3). In fact, the review in *Harper's* argued just the opposite, by declaring that the realism of the characters in *Carradine* was a new departure and by redefining her previous fictions as not realistic at all by comparison, because "her novels have mainly drawn from her own imagination, rather then from observation of the moving world around her" (850).[56]

Just as important was a shift in the way reviewers interpreted the novel's and its characters' significance, not so much in relation to ideas and philosophy, but as a factor in what they saw as the book's purpose— a reading that carried implications for the generic profile of *Carradine*. Reviewers repeatedly saw the novel as engaged in cultural work by promoting human welfare. The *Tribune* approvingly quoted a comment by the *Hartford Courant* that described *Carradine* as "pervaded by spirit of vital philanthropy" (Oct. 2, 1863: 6). The *New-York Observer* announced that the novel was permeated by the "soul of the philanthropist" (Sept. 24, 1863: 311), and that response was echoed verbatim by a review in the *Continental Monthly* (Dec. 1863: 708). The *Independent,* in fact, found the philanthropic purpose of *Carradine* to be so pronounced "as to tinge its whole tone with gravity, and to leave a certain impression of didactic weight upon the reader" (Oct. 8, 1863: 2).

But what was the philanthropic work that readers saw *Carradine* engaged in? A comment by the *Tribune* reviewer provides an indication: "The theme of the story may be described as the influence of woman in the common life,—of woman not as an angel of impossible perfection, but as invested with the natural feminine graces of sympathy, tenderness, and . . . high moral courage . . . as she ministers, with the benignity of a Divine Providence, to the holiest needs of man . . . in the sacred relations of daughter, wife, mother, and friend" (3). In this view, the philanthropy of *Carradine* resides in its cultural work of reinforcing traditional female gender roles grounded in domestic service and self-sacrifice. One interesting feature of this interpretation is that it has been echoed by the few modern critics who have commented on the novel by characterizing it as squarely in the mold of conventional sentimental/domestic fiction—a form that usually is treated as being, if not the antithesis of realism, then at minimum a substantially different genre.[57] The irony, however, is that the relative paucity of antebellum comments about intense emotional characterization in *Carradine* suggests that reviewers as a whole saw the novel as anything but an expression of what the *United States Magazine* called the "Matilda prettiness and sentimentalism" often associated at the time with women's domestic novels (Sept. 1856: 242–43).

But another reading of *Carradine*'s cultural—or philanthropic—work carried different implications for its genre status. Several reviewers saw the novel's contribution to be its accurate portrayal of a particular way of life in the United States. The *New-York Observer* found it especially noteworthy for "bringing out fresh and piquant" views of "rural life" in America (310). The reviewer in the *Continental Monthly* felt that *Carradine* disclosed the "variety of character, motive, and action" otherwise "confined within the limits of a country neighborhood" (708). Likewise, the *New York Tribune*'s reviewer was impressed by the novel's presentation "of the very homeliest details of every-day country life" in upstate New York (3). Precisely which elements of the narrative reviewers were responding to with these comments is unclear, but it may have been the colloquial speech and regional dialect that appear from time to time in the novel. The significance here, however, is not so much what reviewers found "in" the book but how they constituted its true-to-life properties and the implications such an interpretation carried for Chesebro's profile as a fiction writer. For, according to the public response to *Carradine*, Chesebro' was not so much a novelist of ideas working through the psychological depth of her lifelike characters—as she was viewed in the 1850s—but rather a didactic realist depicting the ways and people of a particular segment of rural America. In that formulation, *Carradine* became a regional novel doing the "philanthropic" work of apprising readers about life in rustic upstate New York. In effect, Chesebro's reviewers were now redefining her as a fiction writer through new interpretive categories that were developing in the 1860s as a response to—and as a way of conceptualizing—what was coming to be called local color or regionalist fiction. It was, moreover, a reconceptualization that at once elevated Chesebro' as a novelist at the forefront of a new form and demoted her as a writer whose fiction, owing in part to its regionalist profile, was not quite a full-fledged probing of the inner life of "real" people.[58]

In the same year that reviewers were remaking her in this way through their responses to *Peter Carradine,* Chesebro' published her fourth collection of short stories, *Sparrow's Fall.* For her printers, she returned to Carleton and Porter, and once again the firm apparently neglected to promote the book, for the collection received no public commentary. What is surprising is that the same fate by and large befell her next three novels: *Amy Carr* (1864), *The Glen Cabin* (1865), and *The Fishermen of Gamp's Island* (1865). Of the three, only *Amy Carr* received any attention in the press, and it was minimal, consisting of one notice and one brief review. For these three novels, however, the failure of attention cannot be attributed solely to the practices of Carleton and Porter, since that firm published only *Fishermen. Amy Carr* was published by M. W. Dodd, while *Glen Cabin* was put out by the American Tract Society.

Reviewer neglect of *Amy Carr* is puzzling because Dodd was no small, financially strapped firm that could not afford, or did not know how, to promote its novels. Fifteen years earlier, Dodd had published Susan Warner's *Wide, Wide World,* which not only had become a best seller but had been widely reviewed. The firm, moreover, was thriving by the mid-1860s and would go on to become the prosperous twentieth-century publisher Dodd, Mead, and Company.[59] Hence, why *Amy Carr* languished unnoticed under Dodd's auspices is something of a mystery.

The situation was different for *Glen Cabin* because of the American Tract Society's methods of distributing its titles. The society relied mostly on its large cadre of agents and booksellers around the country to disseminate its books to readers. As Gregory Haynes explains, "none of the [society's] publications reached their audience through conventional book trade outlets," and those eschewed outlets apparently included the review pages in periodicals and newspapers.[60] Nonetheless, the distribution practices of the society would suggest that *Glen Cabin* may have reached a fairly wide readership. The problem is that we have no direct record of how that audience read the novel.

Some evidence nonetheless does exist regarding how *Glen Cabin,* as well as *Amy Carr* and *Sparrow's Fall,* was received by readers and book buyers. That evidence indicates that all three volumes were taken as juvenile fiction designed to inculcate traditional, largely Christian, social and moral values in the minds of young readers. For *Amy Carr* that sense is conveyed both by the notice of the novel in the *Christian Examiner,* which listed the book as a "juvenile" under "New Books Received" (Jan.

1864: 156), and by the brief review in the *American Literary Gazette and Publishers' Circular*, which styled the book an "excellent juvenile" unsullied by "those episodes of reflection and disquisition which young readers are apt to find irksome and dull" (Jan. 1, 1864: 187).[61] For the other two titles, the evidence comes from the same indices that suggest something about the antebellum reception of *Beautiful Gate*: extant copies of those two books. Pasted inside the front cover of one surviving copy of *Sparrow's Fall* is a piece of paper on which is printed "Bell Plaine Methodist Episcopal Sabbath School no. 544," followed by the enjoinment, "Keep this book neatly, read it carefully, and return it promptly to the library in two weeks." Inside the cover of the copy of *Glen Cabin* that I examined is affixed a color illustration of two children pulling a sled. On that copy's flyleaf is a handwritten inscription reading "Amy Smith / From her affectionate / Teacher C. E. C."[62] Such archival markings, when viewed from the perspectives of book history and textual bibliography, suggest that the mid-nineteenth-century audience took these books as belonging to the niche market of children's literature.[63]

Although Chesebro' would follow *Glen Cabin* and *Fishermen of Gamp's Island* with eighteen new stories over the next five years in the *Atlantic, Harper's*, the *Galaxy Magazine*, and *Appleton's Journal*, she published no new novels or story collections during that half decade. However, this drop in productivity does not necessarily indicate that Chesebro', in the wake of the neglect of her three latest novels, suffered from the same type of disappointment that contributed so heavily to Melville's withdrawal from fiction writing in the late 1850s. Rather, other pressing work intruded. In 1865 Chesebro' accepted a teaching position at the Packer Collegiate Institute in Brooklyn, New York, while simultaneously assuming the post of director of composition at that school. While the job did not completely replace her work as a writer, it clearly swallowed enough of her time and energy to cause a significant drop in her literary output.[64]

Nevertheless, in 1871 she published what would be her last—and at 114 pages, her briefest—novel, *A Foe in the Household*.[65] The book was put out by yet another publisher, James Osgood, a former partner in Ticknor and Fields, the firm that had been Hawthorne's publishers and that Osgood bought when Fields had retired in 1870.[66] The pedigree, however, turned out to be less than salutary for Chesebro'. Though Osgood regularly placed announcements and occasionally advertised his new books in the *American Literary Gazette and Publisher's Circular,* not one announcement of *Foe* appeared in that periodical or, as far as I have been able to discover, in any other magazine or newspaper. In spite of this lack of publicity, however, Osgood seems to have made some effort to distribute the novel to reviewers, since at least a half dozen magazines included either reviews or notices of the book. Though small in number, those comments provide some sense of the responses to *Foe,* which constituted the last phase of Chesebro's public reception in her lifetime.

In contradistinction to their reception of Chesebro's early novels but continuing the pattern that had marked their responses to *Victoria* and *Peter Carradine,* no reviewer commented explicitly on the style of *Foe.* It was as if the striking masculine prose that reviewers had found in *Isa* and *Children of Light* had transformed itself in a decade and half into a typical and unremarkable style. Or was it that what had struck reviewers as a distinctive way of writing fiction by a woman in the 1850s had been transformed by interpretive assumptions of the 1860s and 1870s into something that they felt was hardly worth noticing?

The few twentieth-century critics who have remarked on *Foe* have called it Chesebro's best novel and have read it as a critique of patriarchal religion, somewhat akin to some of the modern interpretations of *Victoria.*[67] Readers in the 1870s, however, took a different view. As they had with *Victoria,* none interpreted *Foe* as a censure of phallocentric religion or even, as some had seen *Isa,* as a reproof of more general patriarchal ideology about the nature of womanhood, marriage, and traditional gender roles. In fact, unlike the responses to Chesebro's other novels, the reception of *Foe* did not include any instances of reader interpretations linking plot and/or character with theme and idea.

Where several reviewers agreed with modern commentators was in calling *Foe* Chesebro's best novel. But while this response did parallel what some reviewers had previously claimed about *Victoria,* praise for *Foe* grounded itself in terms that had seldom, if ever, been explicitly applied to Chesebro's fiction. The *Atlantic* first sounded the new note when its reviewer asserted, "No book of our time has combined such high qualities of art and morals with greater success than 'The Foe in the Household.'" In fact, continued the reviewer, *Foe* "deserves to rank with the very best American fictions, and is surpassed only by Hawthorne's romances and Mrs. Stowe's greatest work" (July 1871: 126). What is significant in this remark is not the claim that Chesebro's novel was one of the best of the time or the ranking of her fiction right alongside (or nearly so) that of Hawthorne. Both moves had occurred before. What is new is that Chesebro's novel merited being called "high art." The reviewer for *Appleton's* concurred, exclaiming that *Foe* "is far more artistic" than many a "brilliant rival" and "has many of the high characteristics of art" (Sept. 16, 1871: 330).

For several reviewers that artistry resided in what they repeatedly had identified as one of Chesebro's signature strengths: her representational verisimilitude. The *Appleton's* reviewer itemized the novel's "character-istics of art" as its "fidelity to Nature and probability" and its "accuracy of delineation." Indeed, declared *Appleton's*, the "story, in its probabil-ity, its unity, its coherence, the natural outgrowth of its actions," and "its truthful characterization, seems essentially a history of real things" (330). The reviewer in *Harper's* had a similar reaction. Speaking in par-ticular about the novel's Delia Holcombe (née Rose), the "daughter of a Mennonite bishop," and the plot involving her "secret marriage . . . to an outsider—an act which . . . involves her in difficulties from which it takes many years to extricate her," this reviewer lauded the way these "events . . . are . . . so simply, naturally evolved, one from the other, that all sense of romancing is taken away" (Sept. 1871: 623). Likewise focusing on Delia and the complications involving her marriage first to Edward Rolfe and then to the Reverend Holcombe, the reviewer in the *Atlantic* warned that even informed, experienced novel readers needed to be alert because of the subtle artistic verisimilitude of *Foe*: "It is so very quietly and decently wrought, that perhaps the veteran novel-reader, in whom chords of feeling have been rasped and twanged like fiddle-strings by the hysterical performance of some of our authoresses, may not be at once moved by it; but we believe that those who feel realities will be deeply touched. Delia Holcombe, in the lifetime expiation of her girlish error, is a creation as truthful as she is original" (126). A review in the *New York Tribune* offered an interesting riff on this note in the reception of *Foe*. Instead of linking Chesebro's characterization to art, the *Tribune* review decoupled the two by claiming that "the singular reality of all her charac-ters," grounded as it is in the "record of their experiences, . . . reads more like personal biography than a creation of art," and that quality gives her writing "the air of a rehearsal of facts, rather than of artistic invention."[68]

Despite this overt decoupling, however, what the *Tribune* review seemed to imply is that the art of *Foe* lay in Chesebro's ability to craft her verisimilitude so effectively that it subtly disguised the novel's artistry.

However, as was the case with *Peter Carradine*, reviewers did not invoke this view of Chesebro's vraisemblance to interpret her writing as the work of a full-fledged realist. Despite their view of *Foe* as art, reviewers in the *Nation* and *Harper's* indicated that they saw the novel primarily as regionalist fiction. *Harper's* yoked its remark on Chesebro's verisimilitude to the stipulation that the "scene is laid in Pennsylvania" with a specificity that marks the characters as "thoroughly American" (623). Citing the characters Father Trost, the Mennonite deacon August Ent, and Friend Holcombe, and the novel's depiction of the Mennonite community as a whole, the *Nation's* reviewer explained that of this "local coloring . . . there will be praise, we imagine, from those whose knowledge qualifies them to speak." As if to cement this idea in readers' minds, the *Nation's* reviewer added that, rather "than by trying to describe this aspect of Miss Chesebro's works, we can illustrate our meaning by saying that as a novelist she [is] of a kin to a better known anatomist . . . Mrs. Rebecca Harding Davis" (Feb. 27, 1873: 150). By linking Chesebro' to Davis and extending this profile to Chesebro's "works" as a whole, this reader implied that "as a novelist" Chesebro' had actually always been a painter of "local coloring."

Although Chesebro' followed *Foe in the Household* with half a dozen new short stories in *Appleton's, Harper's,* and the *Nation*, she published no new book of fiction before she died in 1873. Following her death, only a few obituaries appeared in newspapers and magazines, and most were brief. After giving the date of her death as February 16, *Harper's* simply identified her as a "well-known writer, and often a contributor to the pages of this magazine" (Apr. 1873: 794). The obituary in the *New York Tribune* ticked off the titles of her work in eight lines that ended by nonchalantly remarking that "the most important perhaps were 'Victoria, or the World Overcome,' 'Peter Carradine,' 'The Foe in the Household,' and others" (Feb. 19, 1873: 1). The *New York Times* merely listed her with twenty others under the heading "Died," noting only that she expired "On Sunday morning, Feb. 16, at her residence near Piermont, N.Y." (Feb. 18, 1873: 5). Although *Appleton's* was a bit more generous, with a sixteen-line obituary acknowledging that her "art was admirable" and "her style smooth and choice," that journal also pointed out that Chesebro' "has died almost without public notice or comment" (Mar. 8, 1873: 348).

Appleton's remark was both accurate and prescient. By the turn of the century, Chesebro' was hardly remembered at all, and when she was, it was as a diminished author of attenuated reputation. William Dean Howells's 1907 "Recollections of an Atlantic Editorship," while grouping her among writers of "second brilliancy," also noted that she was among those whose names "are faded or fading beyond recall." Though an entry for her was included in Oscar Fay Adams's 1904 *Dictionary of American Authors,* it consisted of a mere fifteen lines, which listed the titles of her books and described her as a "writer of stories and sketches who was during the later part of her life a teacher in the Packer Institute in Brooklyn."[69] Chesebro' was not mentioned in Barrett Wendell's 1900 *Literary History of America,* Walter Bronson's 1902 *Short History of American Literature,* Richard Burton's 1903 *Literary Leaders of America,* or, for that matter, any of the standard American literary histories and surveys discussed at the close of this book's chapter on Sedgwick. Not even those who mentioned Sedgwick only to reduce or dismiss her bothered to say anything about Chesebro'. By the 1930s and 1940s, she was, in effect, off the radar to the point where her name, unlike Sedgwick's, did not come up even once in Robert Spiller's *Literary History of the United States,* which remained the most authoritative reference work on American literary history for decades following its 1946 publication. Even today, as noted earlier, Chesebro's fiction continues to be largely ignored and, for all intents and purposes, forgotten.

Why did Chesebro' end up in such dismal obscurity? Certainly it was not because, like Sedgwick, Chesebro' was redefined—and then demoted—by readers as a writer whose fictions were suited primarily for children—despite the fact that Chesebro' published four to five books that nineteenth-century readers took to be juvenile literature. Nor can Chesebro's neglect be attributed solely or even primarily to her demotion as a writer of local-color fiction. Though that reduction no doubt was a factor, such a designation did not, after all, keep Bret Harte or Sarah Orne Jewett out of the canon or prevent the twentieth-century recrudescence of Mary Wilkins Freeman and Rebecca Harding Davis. The modern view that Chesebro's style and plots were the culprits—and that nineteenth-century readers found her stories tedious and shopworn—is equally problematic.[70] As we have seen, mid-nineteenth-century reviewers overwhelmingly found her style noteworthy and engaging and repeatedly praised her plotting as well suited to her novels' verisimilitude.

Offering a different rationale, a couple of modern critics have suggested that Chesebro's obscurity in the twentieth and twenty-first centuries resulted because her fiction in its form and content was conventionally sentimental—or an inferior version of sentimental/domestic fiction—and thus indistinguishable from the hundreds of other run-of-the-mill and equally forgotten novels by women in the 1800s.[71] However, both the claims of other modern commentators that her novels—particularly *Isa, Children of Light,* and *Victoria*—are bold feminist works and the absence of mid-nineteenth-century comments linking her novels to domestic/sentimental fiction suggest that her writing was anything but that.[72] Indeed, there is something paradoxical about this last modern explanation because neither feminist boldness nor conventional sentimentality—as traits of nineteenth-century American women's fiction—have prevented the recovery of Kate Chopin on the one hand and Susan Warner and Maria Cummins on the other.

The point here is not so much the inadequacy of any one of these explanations but the problems that result from any attempt to explain Chesebro's nineteenth-century status and twentieth- and early twenty-first-century obscurity by pointing to her texts themselves and their supposedly intrinsic traits. Chesebro's fiction was not and is not inherently iconoclastic or conventional, neither stylistically problematic nor regionalist or realistic by its nature. Rather, whatever her fiction "is" has been the product of what readers have made and continue to make of her texts. Indeed, if we want to understand what happened to Caroline Chesebro', we have to turn to the history of her reception both as a function of readers' responses and as a product of the literary marketplace.

In that light, Chesebro's relation with her publishers appears to have had some effect. Although her publishers included several of the leading firms that handled writers who either achieved popular success in the nineteenth century or have become part of the modern canon, albeit sometimes at its margins, the fact that she was never in a position to develop a reliable, ongoing relation with a publisher who promoted her books throughout her career or kept them in print after her death—as Harpers had done for Sedgwick—no doubt was a factor in her fate.

But more important, I would argue, are the shape and diversity that marked public conceptions of her fiction—and of Chesebro' as a writer— in her own time and that have continued among modern commentators. What did that diversity have to do with the (de)valuation of Chesebro'? Pierre Bourdieu provides a relevant clue in his assertion that "the value of the arts, genres, works and authors depends on the . . . marks attached to them," which entails a "particular case of the 'labeling' effect." That is, "the capacity to recognize" a body of works' "legitimacy and perceive them as worthy of admiration in themselves . . . is inseparable from the capacity to recognize in them . . . traits appropriate to characterizing them in their singularity."[73] Bourdieu's point here is related to Barbara Herrnstein Smith's argument that axiology and taxonomy are closely related. As Smith has pointed out, "When we allude to a work as great, good, bad, or middling, we usually employ great, good, bad or middling . . . *as* something." That is, "judgment of the work will also be part of . . . the *classification* of the work."[74] What is true for individual works, moreover, is true for a writer's entire corpus. Valuation depends on such a corpus being classified *as* something in a way that is recognizable as such by an interpretive (and axiological) community. Such a requirement suggests that when a recognizable classification does not materialize—or when readers construct a corpus in such a diverse way that its "something" is amorphous—valuation gets short-circuited. To put this matter in terms of literary history, such dependencies, in conjunction with the dynamics of literary interpretation and history, suggest that for a writer to achieve notoriety and popularity in his or her own time and/or to gain an ongoing place in that history and its canon(s), readers have to construct a fairly consistent topographical profile of that author's corpus, which audiences can share as a horizon of expectations and an agreed-upon landscape of recognition (as has been the case for Poe as the haunted genius of Germanic/gothic fiction) or which becomes a basis against which readers construct an alternate interpretive horizon and axiology (as was the situation for Melville—and even Sedgwick—in the twentieth century).

For Chesebro', however, nothing like a consistent conception of her corpus of fiction developed during her lifetime or in the 130 years after her death. Was she, after all, a full-fledged realist *avant la lettre* or an early practitioner of the more minor genre of regionalist fiction? Do her novels offer controversial challenges to nineteenth-century ideas of womanhood, or are they philanthropical narratives promoting traditional values, especially about women's social place? Are her novels marked by the conventional, unrealistic ideals and characters of sentimental romances or by the verisimilitude that represented the truth of inner lives? Are they sermonically didactic or thematically ambiguous? Were those qualities a product of Chesebro's mercurial genius or of her artistry—or are they marks of her lack of art as a fiction writer? Was her style extravagant and at times obscure, in the mold of Melville's? Or was it unusually masculine, awkward and uncontrolled, femininely chaste, or nondescript and unremarkable? Is her fiction all—or none—of those things? Or are we looking at a swirling set of variations composed of a medley of nineteenth- and twentieth-century interpretive formulations that, in the aggregate, have constituted Chesebro's corpus as a protean puzzle? If the last is the case—and the history of her reception suggests that it is—then the absence of a consistent authorial profile and of an overarching interpretive paradigm for making sense of Chesebro's fictions goes a long way in explaining her limited success in her own century and her continued neglect in our own.

To point to these developments as factors in Chesebro's ongoing obscurity is not to argue that critics and literary historians need to develop a single, uniform profile for Chesebro's fiction that would claim for it a particular, inherent set of characteristics, which in turn could serve as the basis for reclaiming her texts. Although such a move would no doubt be useful, it would also be as misleading as any one of the many interpretive formulations that already exist for her novels and tales, not because such a profile would reduce the "intrinsic" complexity of that fiction, but because it would ascribe to her texts themselves what is, instead, a product of interpretive practices. What we need to recognize, rather, is that recovery can take a number of forms and that, in Chesebro's case, turning to the history of her reception can be an important component of that work. Such a turn can also be a prod for helping us understand that her fiction, like the novels and tales of any writer, is ineluctably linked to the work readers have done—and will continue to do—on her texts.

American Literary History and the Historical Study of Interpretive Practices

B^{Y THE LAST TWO DECADES} of the nineteenth century, when Mel-ville, Sedgwick, and Chesebro' were all but forgotten, a new genera-tion of fiction writers, readers, and magazine reviewers had come to the fore in the United States. My point in referencing that change is not to open the way for a detailed discussion of the shape of reading formations and the reception of fiction after the Civil War, which would require an-other book. Nonetheless, one facet of postbellum interpretive practices merits some attention here for two reasons. First, it enables us to see the way historical hermeneutics can offer a fresh perspective on a particular diachronic dimension of nineteenth-century American literary history. Second, and more broadly, such reconsideration discloses the potential of reception study in general and of historical hermeneutics in particular to serve as a perspicacious tool for examining issues of genre, periodiza-tion, and the relation between the two.

One of the most important and long-lasting paradigms in narratives of American literary history has been the claim that romances and sen-timental/domestic fictions dominated the antebellum literary market-place, but that after the Civil War, realism, and to a lesser extent nat-uralism, developed and soon became the leading forms of postbellum fiction in the United States. Although Michael Davitt Bell has pointed out that "ever since Howells declared his so-called Realism War in the 1880s, it was been a staple of literary history that the great development in American fiction after the Civil War was the rise of 'realism,'" it was the 1930s and after that witnessed the growing centrality of the romance-to-realism paradigm in academic literary histories of nineteenth-century American fiction.[1] To be sure, some twentieth-century literary critics challenged that paradigm, most notably with the claim inaugurated by

299

Richard Chase and continued by Joel Porte and others that the American novel throughout the nineteenth century tended toward romance.[2] Conversely, Alfred Habegger and others have argued that realism was already in its early stages of development before the Civil War via the protorealistic domestic fiction of the 1840s and 1850s.[3] A third challenge has even claimed that nineteenth-century American fiction was actually a hybrid "in which mythic and quotidian time, realism and romanticism, the natural and the supernatural, the realistic and the fantastic . . . compete and negotiate with one another.[4] Despite such challenges, however, the antebellum romance/postbellum realism paradigm has continued in many cases to shape late twentieth- and early twenty-first century conceptions of nineteenth-century American fiction, as evident in major course anthologies, literary histories, and critical studies.[5] Part of the reason for this continued impact no doubt is the usefulness of the paradigm for genre study and for traditional formalist conceptions about fiction. But the power of the paradigm—particularly in its claim about the postbellum rise of realism—also inheres in the way it embodies what Warner Bertoff called "fundamental motives to expression"—a phrase that Bell has amplified by explaining that the "terms 'realism' and 'naturalism' matter . . . for the simple reason that they have been used by generations of American fiction writers, from the 1880s to the present, to describe what they were doing—or at least what they wished others to think they were doing."[6]

I will return to and significantly extend the last part of Bell's suggestive comment in a moment, but for now it is worth mentioning that the romance-to-realism paradigm was neither Howells's creation nor a manifestation only of the 1880s and 1890s. An article in the *North American Review* in 1853 was already making a distinction between the "romance proper" of fiction in the early nineteenth century, which "dealt with an ideal world," and the trend of fiction "nowadays," in which "there is no truth but literal truth" and in which "troubles, to touch our hearts, must be every-day troubles."[7] Nevertheless, by the 1880s, Howells had taken the lead among a group of novelists, magazine reviewers, and early literary historians—a group that included George Curtis, Hjalmer Boyesen, Brander Matthews, James Herbert Morse, Henry Beers, Anna Dawes, Henry James, and Frank Norris—to claim that the 1870s, 1880s, and 1890s were witnessing a salutary outpouring of American realistic and naturalistic fiction to displace the now outdated romances of earlier decades. Morse made the point perhaps most explicitly (and with specific invocation of the Civil War as the pivot point) in a pair of 1883 articles in the *Century Magazine*, in which he asserted that "in the early half of the present century the novelist was left free to range ... in romance," but "the war brought a change in the dispensation of the intellectual forces of America," which "forced the romance out" and witnessed the rise of fictions that "show American life by its facts."[8] One irony in such formulations was that the claim for and championing of the rise of American realism in the 1870s and after was hardly unanimous. For this was the time when the self-styled "realism war," which was waged largely in magazines and periodicals, was driven in part by what was seen—and celebrated by its defenders—as a "romantic revival" in American fiction.[9]

The point here is not that this romantic revival, as Nancy Glazener has pointed out, has been virtually erased from American literary histories over the last century or even that claims about its development tacitly call into question the neat historical dichotomy of the romance-to-realism paradigm.[10] The point, rather, is that the shifting critical claims and the occasional silences about the generic profiles of nineteenth-century American fiction begin to reveal the effect of interpretive practices on the ostensible shape of that fiction and our conception of its literary history.

The role of reading strategies in that conception has not been limited to modern literary historians and critics. It was central to nineteenth-century formulations about U.S. fiction. In fact, its importance to the romance-to-realism paradigm that developed after the Civil War as a way of conceiving American fiction is especially visible in the differences between antebellum and postbellum responses to the fiction of James Fenimore Cooper and Nathaniel Hawthorne. At first blush, such a claim may seem odd, given that Hawthorne called himself a romancer and that both his and Cooper's novels were repeatedly described by antebellum reviewers as romances—or in Cooper's case, "historical romances." Yet what troubles these historical givens is that before the Civil War "romance," as a genre marker, was not necessarily opposed to true-to-life fiction, nor did it preclude in readers' eyes a strong degree of verisimilitude in a novel or tale. That is, romance and the realistic—like the related duo "romance" and "novel"—were hardly clear cut, stable, mutually exclusive categories in antebellum informed reading.[11] My concern here, however, is not with the instability of those distinctions before the Civil War but, instead, with a series of shifts in nineteenth-century thinking about—or more accurately, reading for—realism, which involved changes in some assumptions about what constituted realism in fiction and a variety of conceptualizations—and reconceptualizations—about what texts warranted the "realist" label.

These reconceptualizations were central to the response to Cooper's fictions. Despite the romance label attached to many of his novels, antebellum reviewers repeatedly described them as true-to-life narratives. An 1824 review in the *New-York Mirror,* for example, said that in *The Pilot* Cooper "confers reality on all of his descriptions. We hear the roar of the waves—the splash of the oars—the hoarse language of the seamen" to the point where it seems "we actually take part in the proceedings and conversations of the crew."[12] So different is our view of Cooper today that we forget, as John Anderson pointed out over five decades ago, that "contemporary reviewers overwhelmingly shared the opinion of Cooper's fidelity to naval life" in his sea novels and spoke with "considerable praise (and no overt criticism) of the realism of his sailor characters."[13] Yet not only his sea fiction did reviewers view as natural and true to life. A reviewer in the *Port Folio* counseled the novel reader that in *The Pioneers* "[h]is feelings will not be excited by any romantic traits." Instead, Cooper has written a novel in which "the historian can scarcely find a more just and vivid delineation of the first settlements of our wilderness" (Mar. 1823, *FCCH* 69–70). A *Graham's* reviewer made a similar claim about *Wyandotté,* asserting that the novel "gives a narrative of fictitious events, similar, in nearly all respects, to occurrences which actually happened during the opening scenes of the Revolution" and possesses a "Robinson-Crusoe-like detail" in its representations (Nov. 1843, *FCCH* 207–8). Another review in the *Mirror* said that in *The Deerslayer,* Cooper's "descriptions . . . are in his best style, that is, remarkably clear and minute and exquisitely true to nature. We can almost fancy ourselves looking down on the unruffled surface of Otsego" (Sept. 1841, *FCCH* 205). Even Cooper's Native Americans, which on occasion came under censure for being "romanticized" and unreal, were defended for their verisimilitude. A review of *The Last of the Mohicans* pointed out that in depicting "north American Indians" Cooper "has interwoven with his vision more of what actually belongs to the aboriginal character than any other writer" (*North American Review* July 1826, *FCCH* 112). Such views continued for a decade after Cooper's death. A retrospective overview of his novels in the *Atlantic Monthly* in 1862 asserted that "no one has caught and reproduced more broadly and accurately . . . the character of our people." Singling out *The Spy* for having the "charm of reality" and *The Chainbearer* for being "true to human nature," the *Atlantic* went on to state that "everywhere" in Cooper's fiction "we recognize the substantial truth of his pictures" (June 1862, *FCCH* 52–58).

In the decades after the Civil War, however, public responses to Cooper's novels performed a virtual about-face. Instead of verisimilitude, readers found the idealized and the improbable. An article in the *Critic* in 1889 said that the dialogue between Cooper's characters "is frequently stilted or unnatural" and that a marked development in the current "realistic novel has been . . . in a direction far away from Cooper's" (Sept. 18, 1889: 125–26). An article on "Fenimore Cooper's Rank as a Novelist" announced that it is difficult to imagine a "more preposterous plot than that of 'The Pilot' and that "his Indians and his sailors never had their prototypes on sea or land" (*Literary Digest* Mar. 25, 1899: 339). An article on "The Centenary of Fenimore Cooper" contrasted the "outline drawing of Cooper" with the characterizations of "our contemporary realists" and admitted that "we cannot say that Cooper sketched the . . . real sailor in fiction" (*Century Magazine* Sept. 1889: 796–97). Postbellum biographers and literary historians largely agreed with such assessments. In his 1882 biography of Cooper, Thomas Lounsbury explained, "in all of Cooper's novels . . . the incidents are more than improbable, they are impossible." Readers "are continually exasperated . . . by the unnatural if not ridiculous conduct of the characters." A decade and a half later, Henry S. Pancoast's *Introduction to American Literature* berated Cooper's "romances" for "plots [that] are crudely constructed and improbable" and concluded that Cooper "was incapable of presenting human nature."[14]

Of course, the best known and most devastating reading of Cooper as a bumbling, unrealistic romancer came in Mark Twain's 1895 article in the *North American Review*. Leaving little doubt about his view by entitling his essay "Fenimore Cooper's Literary Offenses," Twain dismantled *The Deerslayer* for violating eighteen of the "nineteen rules governing literary art," the most comically desolating of which was Cooper's failure to understand "that the personages in a tale shall be alive, except in the case of corpses, and that the reader shall always be able to tell the corpses from the others" (*FCCH* 277).[15] Interestingly, some twentieth-century Cooper scholars have sought to rescue him from Twain's eviscerating satire by claiming, in a move echoing antebellum responses, that Cooper's novels are, in fact, quite realistic.[16] Yet as James Wallace has pointed out, such defenses may be missing the point in that "the object of Twain's attack is not Cooper, after all, nor his works. . . . Rather, Twain was attacking the audience that Cooper had created and that inexplicably continued to prefer the novels of Cooper and his literary heirs to those of the realists" of Twain's own era.[17]

Although hyperbolic in its claim for Cooper's single-handed creation of his audience, Wallace's point carries broader significance. Twain and other proponents of postbellum realism not only were seeking to create an audience but were modeling a way for that audience to read for realism—or its absence—in previous fiction as well as in their own. They were, in other words, promoting a particular interpretive agenda that constituted the generic profiles of novels through the way they were read.

In light of such moves, it is not surprising to find similar divergences between antebellum and postbellum responses to Hawthorne's fiction. As they did with Cooper, antebellum commentators repeatedly pointed to the historical accuracy and vraisemblance of Hawthorne's novels. An article in *Church Review,* for example, applauded the *Scarlet Letter* for the manner in which "its scene-painting is in a great degree true to the period of our Colonial history," while an essay in the *Southern Literary Messenger* claimed that "in developing bravely and justly the sentiment of life it depicts, it is as true to humanity as Dickens."[18] The *Messenger* review said much the same about the *House of the Seven Gables,* styling it a novel whose "tone and personages . . . are imbued with a local authenticity" so "life-like . . . that they are daguerreotypes in the reader's mind" (*HCH* 217). With a similar take, *Harper's New Monthly Magazine* called the characters in *Seven Gables* "living realities" drawn with such a "genuine expression of flesh and blood, that we can not doubt we have known them" (May 1851, *HCH* 196). Comparable responses greeted the *Blithedale Romance* and the *Marble Faun* in the 1850s in such magazines as the *Christian Examiner, Graham's, Brownson's Quarterly Review,* and the *Atlantic Monthly.*[19]

Despite such responses, after the Civil War Hawthorne's novels frequently became a point of contrast for characterizing postbellum realistic fiction. As early as 1869, an article in the San Francisco based *Overland Monthly* complained that Hawthorne "never presents what we commonly call a natural character" (Feb. 1869, *HCH* 455), a view echoed a year later by the *Southern Review,* which concluded that Hawthorne "did not depict . . . nor even conceive of men or women as such, but only certain attributes" garbed in "shadowy, unreal" forms (Apr. 1870, *HCH* 465). Such responses continued through the 1870s, during which time the *Springfield Republican,* claiming to quote one of Hawthorne's friends, said, "His characters are not drawn from life."[20] In the same decade an article in the *North American Review,* locating Hawthorne's unique "genius" in anything but realistic fiction, affirmed that "in no American writer is to be found the same preponderance of weird imagination as in Hawthorne" (Sept. 1879, *HCH* 515). It was, of course, Henry James who most markedly and repeatedly identified Hawthorne as the consummate romancer—an interpretive formulation by which James could position Hawthorne as a central figure in a developing American literary canon, while simultaneously using Hawthorne's fiction as a counterpoint to define his own realistic methods. That dual purpose is most evident in his 1879 book on Hawthorne. There James praises the *Scarlet Letter* as one of the finest American novels ever produced only to then explain that its "historical coloring is rather weak than otherwise; there is little of the modern realism of research." Concluding that "the faults of the book are, to my sense, a want of reality," James likewise finds that the "fault" of the *Marble Faun* "is that the element of the unreal is pushed too far." Again and again James locates "the absence of the realistic quality" as the distinguishing feature of Hawthorne's fiction. As if seeking to give his point the force of a finely filed blade, James asserts, "It cannot be too often repeated that Hawthorne was not a realist."[21] Clearly, the Hawthorne of James and other postbellum readers is a very different Hawthorne from the one antebellum reviewers saw.

If these shifts were limited to the reception of Hawthorne and Cooper in nineteenth-century America, it might be possible to dismiss them as aberrations or at least bracket them as exceptions that prove the rule. But they were neither. The reconceptualizations of Cooper and Hawthorne, which transformed the verisimilitude of their novels into romantic improbabilities and idealizations, marked postbellum responses to Melville and other fiction writers. *Typee* and *Omoo*, which antebellum reviewers profiled as "romances of real life," became for an *Atlantic* commentator in 1892 simply "romance[s] of the South Sea Islands" (Apr. 1892: 499), comparable, in the words of the *Springfield Republican* to "the vivacious ventures of Robert Louis Stevenson, whose scenes are laid in the same region of 'lotus eating.'"[22] It mattered little that antebellum readers had found *Redburn* and *White-Jacket* brimming with verisimilitude or that others had felt *Moby-Dick* to be grounded in the true-to-life details of the whaling industry. Rare postbellum comments on Melville's novels after *Omoo* simply noted that in reading them we feel that "everything about us is wonderful, is marvelous . . . but nothing is tangible, real" (*New York Mail and Express* Oct. 8, 1891, *MCH* 424). Rebecca Harding Davis's fiction experienced a similar fate. Although "Life in the Iron Mills," as Glazener points out, had "drawn praise for its verisimilitude" when it appeared in the *Atlantic* in 1861, James would later dismiss it and her other stories as "all disfigured by injudicious straining . . . which leaves nature and reality at an infinite distance behind and beside them."[23] And then there was *Uncle Tom's Cabin*, the changing status of which was epitomized in an article in the *Critic* from 1886: "Not long ago 'Romola' and 'Uncle Tom's Cabin' were offered . . . as instances showing the highest power of realism; but Mrs. Stowe's great story is a picture of slavery idealized down to the lowest terms, not of slavery as it really was. . . . The 'imaginative lift' is the dark romance of Uncle Tom" (July 10, 1886: 20).

These genre reclassifications were not limited to responses to fiction written by Americans. Also reread as part of the shifting conceptualizations of realistic fiction were British authors such as Dickens and Scott. Like some of his American counterparts, but even more strongly, Dickens was regularly identified by antebellum American reviewers as a writer whose novels were marked by truth to nature and verisimilitude, particularly in their lifelike characters. As early as 1867, however, Dickens started to be read quite differently via genre distinctions. An article on "The Genius of Dickens" in the *Atlantic Monthly* admitted that Dickens did, indeed, draw on observations for his materials but added, "he always modifies these materials, and often works them up into the most fantastic shapes." Instead of realism, this reader found "a strong infusion of the melodramatic element" in *Oliver Twist* and *Barnaby Rudge* (May 1867: 549–50). By the 1870s, American journalists, with those from the *Atlantic* leading the way, were regularly labeling Dickens's novels as "specially wanting in that power of real characterization" and locating the fault in his narrative method.[24] According to an article on the "Growth of the Novel," "in proportion as the novelist intervenes, visibly, between the reader and the characters of his story, he detracts from the realness of the latter." Because such intrusive narration "is a prominent defect in Dickens," his fiction "never seems to have clearly taken the direction of clearly outlined truth of character" (*Atlantic* June 1874: 688–89). Howells and James were especially critical of what they saw as Dickens's tendency toward the melodramatic, the fantastic, and the unnatural. In a review of John Forster's *Life of Dickens,* Howells underscored Dickens's "failure" as a novelist owing to "the unnaturalness of his situations" and "the crudity of his treatment of characters" in "his romances" (*Atlantic* Feb. 1873, *DCH* 580–81). By the close of the century, Dickens's novels had been so redefined as the virtual polar opposite of realism that Howells could unabashedly identify Dickens as a "romanticist" and James could rhetorically ask, "Who could pretend that Dickens was anything but a romantic?"[25]

Scott provides an even more telling index of such rereadings because his fictions came to embody for some postbellum proponents of realism a particularly pejorative influence on American fiction. Before the Civil War, Scott, like Hawthorne, had been repeatedly described as a romancer whose novels were, nonetheless, true to life. A review of *Rob Roy* in the *North American* averred that Scott's historical fictions are "supported in some measure by fact, and all are faithful sketches of society and nature at different periods. . . . They have the truth, . . . for men here are grouped and at work, very much as they are in life."[26] As late as 1858, a review of the *Waverley Novels* in the *Atlantic* was claiming that Scott "has succeeded in domesticating his creations in the general heart and brain, and thus obtained the endorsement of human nature as evidence of their genuineness. His characters are the friends and acquaintances of everybody . . . as though they were natural beings" (May 1858: 889). But after the war, Scott's novels came to stand for everything that was wrong with fiction in the first half of the century. Twain was the most strident here, lamenting that American fiction "forty years ago" was "filled with wordy, windy, flowery, 'eloquence,' romanticism, sentimentality—all imitated from Sir Walter, and sufficiently badly done too."[27] Howells could be almost as caustic, claiming that "the art of fiction . . . declined . . . through Scott," who made his characters "talk as seldom man and never women talked," which turned them into "stage players" straight out of "melodrama" and devoid of "verity."[28]

For some, the damage Scott had done extended beyond literature. Twain, of course, went so far as to blame Scott for the delusions of Southern chivalry, which Twain believed had helped foment the Civil War, but Hjalmer Boyesen saw the effects as a contemporary threat to American democracy. In an article on "The Great Realists and the Empty Story-Tellers," Boyesen warned that the "romantic fiction" of "Sir Walter Scott and his successors" was contributing to the promotion of the "recent aristocratic development in the United States, with its truly medieval inequality between the classes" (*Forum* Feb. 1895: 730). Through such remarks the postbellum response to Scott became tied to questions of national well-being in a way that enabled defenders of realism to define American fiction after the Civil War as more true to life, more mature, and more egalitarian.

It might be argued at this point that there is nothing particularly troubling in these postbellum rereadings of Scott, Cooper, Dickens, Melville, Hawthorne, Stowe, and Davis, that they can be explained within the romance-to-realism paradigm or at least at the juncture of that paradigm and reception criticism. That is, postbellum reviewers and fiction writers were simply responding to what was there all along in the texts of these earlier writers but had simply been invisible to the strategies of antebellum informed reading. In this logic, the interpretive formulations of postbellum realists were made possible by a more accurate and precise sense of what realism was, what texts had it, and thus which ones belonged to that genre.

Besides the dubious textual essentialism of such a claim, however, two historically specific problems tax its viability. As Bell has pointed out, "it is pretty much a truism that late nineteenth-century discussions of 'realism' . . . were far from rigorous and generally rather slipshod."[29] Even more troubling are the numerous disputes and variations that marked postbellum attempts to define the generic profile of a particular text or a particular writer's oeuvre. Nowhere is this phenomenon more striking than in the substantial interpretive disagreements over the genre profiles of fiction by writers (both American and European) who were often taken as practitioners of the new realism. For instance, to Howells, Ivan Turgenev was an exemplary realist, but James spoke of that "author's closely commingled realism and idealism."[30] Among continental authors, Emile Zola received the most variform responses in terms of genre placement. On the one hand, some maintained, in the words of the *Overland Monthly*, that "Zola . . . writes realism in large letters" (May 1889: 510). According to an article on "Further Aspects of Realism" in the *Dial*, Zola was a realist because he was an empiricist, and "the method of realism is on the whole the empirical method" (Mar. 16, 1893: 171). For some, the honesty of his gritty depictions of the brutal side of everyday life earned him that status. For others, however, such grittiness was a mark not of realism but of its failure, since, according to a *North American Review* article on "Profligacy in Fiction," the "seamy side of things is no more real than the other, and its delineation no more 'realistic'" (July 1880: 82). Extending this logic, a review of *Nana* in the *Atlantic* claimed that Zola "exhibits most unscientific inexactness in overlooking . . . whatever is honorable in humane nature." Hence, he is not a realist but simply "vulgar" (May 1880: 696–97). Indeed, for some, such vulgarity stamped Zola as, more than anything else, a disreputable purveyor of sensational romances. As an article on "The Decadence of Romance" put it in a farrago of terminology, "Romance, finding little romance in the real world, has taken two different lines in the desperate effort to amuse us somehow. . . . The disreputable line is Zolaesque beastiality, and forced, unreal, unlovely hysterical sensationalism" (Apr. 1893: 222). Though more tolerant of the "indecent" and the "disgusting" in Zola's fiction, Howells could nevertheless announce that "Zola was never a realist in the right sense" because "the fever of romanticism is in his blood; the taint is in his work."[31] Seizing on these conflicting interpretations of the genre of Zola's fiction, Frank Norris used them to promote his own agenda by claiming that the Frenchman's novels combine the "accuracy" of realism and the "truth" of romance to yield a new, preeminent form of fiction: the naturalist novel.[32]

When it came to determining the genre profiles of postbellum American writers, the same kind of interpretive variation obtained. Consider the case of Twain. Although he was repeatedly called a writer whose stories were authentic and "vividly realistic," and as Huck Finn put it, "told the truth mainly," the labels "romance" and "romantic" were also invoked in postbellum remarks on his novels.[33] Howells identified *A Connecticut Yankee in King Arthur's Court* as a "romance" and by 1900 was quite willing to style Twain "our greatest romancer."[34] Nor was Howells alone in applying that genre epithet to Twain's fiction. An *Atlantic* reviewer labeled *Prince and the Pauper* a "novelty in romance" (Dec. 1881, *MTCR* 200), an interpretation echoed by the *New York Tribune* and the *Boston Herald* (*MTCR* 215). The *Saturday Review* termed *Huckleberry Finn* a novel from which "the boy of today may get his fill of fun and romance" (Jan. 1895, *MTCR* 260); *Connecticut Yankee* earned the moniker of "romantic tale" from the *Utica Herald* (Dec. 1889, *MTCR* 285) and the *Keokuk (Iowa) Constitution-Democrat* (Feb. 21, 1890, *MTCR* 314), and the *Hartford Times* blithely announced that, on the whole, "probability, inherent and extraneous, is as soon to be looked for in Mr. Twain's stories as in the *Arabian Nights* (Feb. 1895, *MTCR* 370).

A similar variation in generic profiling marked the postbellum reception of Henry James's novels. In his responses, Howells epitomized that divergence, calling James a realist revolutionary in an 1882 *Century Magazine* essay but then going on in the same piece to declare, "Mr. James stands at the dividing way of the novel and the romance, and I am sometimes sorry that he declared even superficially for the former. His best efforts seem to me those of romance."[35] An essay on American literature in the "First Century of the Republic" in *Harper's* grouped James with Melville, William Gilmore Simms, and Louisa May Alcott as "writers of romantic narratives" (Mar. 1876: 529), and a reviewer of *Portrait of a Lady* in the *Atlantic,* though not invoking a label, made clear what genre he believed James's fiction fit by complaining that, while his "people walk, and sit, and talk," they "are not bodily shapes, for the most part, but embodied spirits," whose artificiality makes a reader feel that he is watching them "upon a stage" (Jan. 1882: 128).

Perhaps surprisingly, the novels of even that ostensible arch realist, Howells himself, earned similar characterizations. In a letter to Howells, James remarked, almost in a cautionary manner, that while "I regard you as the great American naturalist . . . you are haunted with romantic phantoms."[36] Meanwhile, an article in the *Critic* entitled "The Analysts Analyzed" asked, "Is Mr. Howells a realist to the total exclusion of the romantic element of art?" But instead of claiming that Howells's novels were a generic hybrid, the analyzer took the dean to task as a poser, announcing that, in actuality, "Romance *disguised* as realism . . . constitutes a large part . . . of Mr. Howells's fiction" (July 10, 1886: 21, my emphasis).

Taken together, these widely divergent responses to both antebellum and postbellum fiction call into question the idea that nineteenth-century America witnessed a marked shift in genre forms that depended on a correct way of seeing what realism actually entailed. That is, it was not a matter of postbellum readers and writers developing a set of reading strategies that enabled them to determine accurately the genre profile of any fictional text as romance, realism, naturalism, or sentimentalism, based on its intrinsic qualities. But what, then, was going on? In light of such variations, we might be inclined to evoke a different formalist—or, more accurately, textualist—explanation: what Jacques Derrida called the "law of genre." According to Derrida, "a text cannot belong to no genre" under that law, which also says that "genres are not to be mixed." But "within the heart of the law itself" lurks "a law of impurity or principle of contamination . . . decomposing, perversions," which turns every text into a generic melange that "never amounts to belonging."[37] As enticing as this deconstructive principle is, there are, however, several problems with it. In continuing to attribute generic features—or what might be called generic heteroglossia—to texts themselves, it subscribes to a problematic textual essentialism that historical hermeneutic theory severely questions. Moreover, by treating all texts as inherently multigeneric, the poststructuralist law of genre divorces genre from the contextually specific, historically changing ways texts are interpreted within shifting conceptions of genre categories. Consequently, such a move severs the analysis of genre from other poststructuralist positions relevant to questions about genre and their relations to reading and interpretive practices.

Those questions are precisely the ones Tony Bennett and John Frow have taken up and addressed in offering a more historically informed conception of genre. Bennett has argued that genres are not so much entities as they are "definitions" that engage in "the tracing of boundaries rather than the discovery of an essence." As part of that tracing, "a text's generic belongingness . . . is determined not by its semiotic properties but by its uptake in particular reading practices." Because such uptake operates through "culturally specific knowledges, associations and assumptions which inform and animate particular reading practices," particular genre categories and "genre distinctions which are operative in one society may not be so in another, with the consequence that the same text may be subject to different genre classifications in different social and historical contexts."[38] Frow has made a similar point is his recent book-length study of the nature of genre. Unlike "traditional genre theory," which "turns genre into something really existent," Frow's position identifies genres as interpretive heuristics or protocols that "systematically form the objects of which they speak." In other words, "genre is not a *property* of a text but is a function of reading"; it "is the category we [as readers] impute to texts, and under different circumstances this imputation may change." Reconceptualizing genre as a function of reception, Frow argues that "in dealing with questions of genre, our concerns should not be with matters of taxonomy ('which classes and subclasses are there? To which class does this text belong?') . . . but rather with questions of use: 'What models of classification are there, and how have people made use of them in particular circumstances?'"[39]

What are the consequences of such a reception-oriented view of genre for the romance-to-realism paradigm? Conjoined with the kaleidoscopic whirls in nineteenth-century American claims about the generic profiles of specific fictional texts and their authors, a reception-based conception of genre lets us see the postbellum era as one marked by a shift not so much in genre forms as in reading formations. Let me make clear here that to reconceptualize the romance-to-realism paradigm in this way is not to claim that there was not a realist movement or that writers such as Howells, James, Chopin, Jewett, Twain, and others did not believe that they were writing realistic fiction. A realist agenda did develop after the Civil War, but at its core were public patterns of reading by reviewers, essayists, and fiction writers such as Howells, James, Twain, and Norris, who sought for various reasons to pull the puppet strings of that agenda by reshaping the interpretive practices of magazine- and fiction-reading audiences. Such a view of the postbellum "rise of realism" offers an important reconceptualization of the history of nineteenth-century American fiction by incorporating changing reading and interpretive strategies as a central, contouring component of that history.[40]

To speak of this as a "change" may, however, be the wrong word because postbellum reading for realism constituted less a rupture with antebellum strategies of informed reading and more of a redeployment of many of those interpretive codes. These included identifying a text as true to life and realistic if it privileged—or more precisely, was read as privileging—character over plot; employed a geographically specific setting; possessed authenticity of historical representation and a recognizable typicality in its characters; and avoided narrative intrusion by showing rather than telling.[41] It is just that these and other assumptions were given a new emphasis and redeployed for purposes that fit the realist agenda. For instance, as Bell and Glazener have explained, a primary function of privileging such elements after the Civil War involved gender identifications, since such elements were repeatedly singled out as markers of authentic, masculine writing as opposed to effeminate artistry and feminine romance.[42] Additionally, in the 1870s and after, realism and the realistic went from being a trait defining particular elements of a work of fiction (and thus interpretable as vraisemblance, naturalness, or truth to life), as was the case in the antebellum era, to being a mark of a text's defining generic status and of authorial identity, as manifested in one's overall practice as a fiction writer.

If we ask why these alterations and redeployments developed in the 1870s and after, several answers are possible. One was the changing literary marketplace after the Civil War, which witnessed the professionalization of reviewing in the United States and a backlash by male writers against what they saw as the excessive dominance of women in the production of fiction. Other factors were the sobering effect of the war, the struggles of Reconstruction, and the acceleration of urbanization, industrialization, and national expansion (along with regional differentiations) that followed the war. That is, many of the same economic, political, and cultural developments that literary historians have identified in the traditional narrative about the rise of realism as a genre form could be cited as factors in the rise of the realist agenda as an historically altered interpretive formation.

An exploration of this complex subject of causes would, like a detailed discussion of the strategies of this formation, be impossible in—and in fact, extraneous to—a comparatively brief final chapter of a book about the reception of antebellum fiction and informed reading. Instead, in the remainder of this chapter, I want to return to the problem about historical hermeneutics that I raised in chapter 1.

Among the criticisms that have been leveled against response and reception study, the most problematic has been the charge that it is incoherent or self-contradictory. While reception *theory*—particularly in the version that I have called historical hermeneutics—calls into question positivist and essentialist assumptions of intrinsic textual essences and attributes structures and meaning not to texts themselves or to authorial intentions but to historically specific responses within particular interpretive formations, reception *practice* examines evidence of those responses that are encoded "in" texts as their authors' (i.e., the readers') intended meanings. Seeking to counter essentialist claims about what texts supposedly say and do, reception study turns out to be, in Dominick LaCapra's words, a "neopositivitic . . . return to a narrowly documentary mode of knowledge" that is not on all fours with its own principles.[43] Such a critique raises, in effect, a question about historical hermeneutics that might be phrased as follows: How does it account for the authority, the accuracy, the veridicality of its historical analysis of reception practices in the face of its anti-essentialist claim that texts are not ontological essences but the creations of interpretations? To put the query another way, are not its historical accounts of interpretive activity trapped in the hermeneutical circle—or more accurately, in the infinite regress of historically specific acts of interpretation?

The issues raised here, we should recognize, are not unique either to reception study in general or historical hermeneutics in particular. Rather, they are a specific version of a larger question historians have been grappling with in the face of what has been called the "linguistic turn" in historiographical theory—that is, the issue of the status and nature of history and historical inquiry in the wake of poststructuralist theory.[44] In that wake, it is no longer possible to invoke history as an authoritative register that provides an unmediated pathway to knowledge. Derrida's oft-cited assertion that there is nothing outside textuality, that all is constructed discourse, has led to the recognition—to use the formulation that has become the virtual calling card of New Historicism—that all history is itself textual and all textuality, including that of historical practice, is historical. Since history is what the present seeks to make of the past, Paul Rabinow and William Sullivan, among others, have called this formulation the "interpretive turn" in history—a turn that, as Mary Fulbrook has pointed out, "indicates that historical interpretations are essentially constructions in the present, not—as traditional historians would claim—reconstructions of the past." The interpretive nature of history extends even to supposed historical "facts," in that the doing of history, as Hayden White has observed, "hinges on conceptions of membership in communities" that "control . . . not only 'what are the facts' but also and most important 'what counts as a fact.'"[45] To do history is thus already to be embedded within a system of interpretive strategies that constitute the thing they purport to describe.

Despite such a recognition, however, historians have disagreed about its consequences for historical practice. Michel de Certeau has asserted that the linguistic/interpretive turn in historiography has "transformed the search for meaning unveiled in objective reality into an analysis of the options or organizations of meaning implied in interpretive operations."[46] More frequently, other historians, including LaCapra and Keith Windschuttle, have asserted that poststructuralism has created a "crisis in history" that some have lamented because, in Windschuttle's words, it is "murdering our past."[47] Others have pointed out that this crisis is hardly a fault of poststructuralism, since the problems it raises have their own history reaching back to the 1930s relativist arguments of Carl Becker and Charles Beard, which themselves developed in part out of the "crisis in history" that had been materializing in Europe since the late nineteenth century.[48] That pedigree, however, hardly alters the fact that poststructuralist theory has given strong pause to the assumption that a turn to history can provide an avenue out of the regress of interpretation or a space outside presentism. In light of that recognition, we are left with the question of what kinds of claims history can legitimately make and what justifies the continuation of historical practice. Or, to ask the question differently, why bother to do history—and more specifically, a historical version of response-and-reception study—in the first place?

One answer is that despite poststructuralist theory, histories continue to be produced. That is, as several historians have pointed out, despite the linguistic/interpretive turn in historiographical theory, in practice historians continue to make claims about the past as an entity that can be discovered and described. Hans Kellner, for instance, has observed that, while it "is difficult to find any proponents of naive realism in historical practice," who believe histories can "present the past as it actually was, . . . historians just as routinely behave as though their research were into the past, as though their writing were 'about' it, and as though 'it' were as real as the text which is the object of their labors."[49] Indeed, as Nancy Partner notes, the linguistic/interpretive turn in historiography seems to have been a "revolving door" through which "everyone went around and around and got out exactly where they got in. For all the sophistication of the theory-saturated part of the profession, . . . [t]he theoretical destabilization of history achieved by language-based modes of criticism has had no practical effect on academic practice because . . . all historians—Marxist, feminist, old historicist, new historicist, empiricist—still speak the same basic language of evidentiary syntax, logical grammar, and referential semantics."[50] Though the claim that poststructuralism has had absolutely no impact on historical practice is questionable, it is clear that even those who have approached the question of history through poststructuralist theory have continued to make historical claims. Hence, even as he deconstructed history, Derrida could assert that "the history of the West, is the history of . . . metaphors and metonomies."[51] Likewise, Hayden White could produce poststructuralist metahistories of historical discourse by making referential assertions about that discourse. We can find the same thing in the writings of the New Historicists, from Stephen Greenblatt and Louis Montrose to Amy Kaplan and Donald Pease.

What all these instances provide are concrete manifestations of a theoretical point Stanley Fish articulated two decades ago when commenting on the New Historicists and the warrant for historical inquiry itself. According to Fish, the fact that history is an interpretation all the way down does not preclude our ability to ask and answer the question "What happened?" because the principle of "'wall to wall' textuality"—and the constructed status of all historical facts—operates on a metacritical level that is different from the level on which questions about historical occurrences are answered. Consequently, the metacritical principle of historical constructedness can have no practical consequences for historical practice.[52]

Fish's argument is, of course, a version of the theoretical "against theory" position, but a version that does not deny the power of theory by undermining its claim to govern practice from the outside. Instead, Fish claims that theory is so powerful that it must be declared irrelevant if investigation of the past is to proceed. Such an argument is not only functionally attractive; it is also reasonably convincing, particularly in its claim that no matter how much we may believe in the constructedness of all historical interpretations and all historical facts as products of particular contextual conditions, the knowledge produced by those interpretations remains cogent for us as long as those particular conditions are not challenged. Furthermore, even when such a challenge occurs, "the result will not be an indeterminacy of fact, but a new shape of factual firmness underwritten by a newly, if temporarily, settled perspective."[53] What is unsatisfying about Fish's argument is the claim that the principle of historical constructedness has no consequences for practice. The danger of such a position is that it becomes a warrant for doing business as usual without concern for the theoretical implications of the way practice is pursued. Its implacable differentiation between theory and practice also ignores the fact that practice is always informed by a set of assumptions that function as theory. The interconnections between theory and practice, along with the recognition that our histories are inherently interpretive and textual—and thus inevitably the products of our own contemporary perspectives—leads, however, back to the question of why do history at all.

Several answers are possible. One is to recognize that the constructed nature of history is perhaps less a liability than a strength. Here a remark by Raymond Williams is relevant. In the *Long Revolution,* Williams pointed out that "we tend to underestimate the extent to which the cultural tradition" and our collective sense of the cultures of the past are "not only a selection but an interpretation. We see most past work through our own experience, without even making the effort to see it through the original terms. What analysis can do is . . . to make the interpretation conscious" by creating "historical alternatives; to relate the interpretation"—both our own and that constructed in the past—"to the particular contemporary values on which it rests."[54] The value of such analysis lies in its potential to defamiliarize our own ways of reading, through alternatives that constitute an otherness by which we can test and redefine our relation to texts from the past.

Such a claim, it seems to me, is especially attractive because it suggests that there is something supreme about invoking history to study interpretation. In fact, in addressing the question of the warrant for and value of the historical study of reception a number of years ago, I made precisely that claim while arguing that, whether we realize it or not, we cannot avoid constructing texts and producing readings from within a historically particular interpretive formation. But in light of that recognition, I asserted, what makes historical reception study a superior activity is that it deliberately incorporates that principle as part of its analytical practice. By this logic, accepting the metacritical principle of the historicity of textuality makes the investigation of response as an historical activity our most viable critical strategy. I no longer, however, find this claim tenable, primarily because it asserts as fact what is itself an interpretation formed within a particular reading formation—that of historical hermeneutics itself. That is, such a defense now strikes me as tautological, since it enlists its own position to justify that position.

I want, therefore, to offer a different answer by arguing that historical hermeneutics provides not a superior form of analysis but a form that is valuable in its own right because of the distinctive advantages it holds. More specifically, historical hermeneutics has the virtue of demonstrating, both by what it says about the past and in its own practice, the contextual and historically specific conditions of reading, response, and interpretation—a situation that applies to the method's own claims as historically conditioned acts of historiographical interpretation. From this angle, reception study in general and historical hermeneutics in particular could be said not to reveal—or claim to reveal—the past as an unmediated thing in itself, but to stage versions of the past via representations of how reading and interpretation may be said to have transpired. The value of such historical representations is that they offer us a different way of seeing the past and of seeing reading as contextual interpretive encounters—a way that is distinct from what other theoretical perspectives and critical practices offer. In this sense, the value and justification of historical hermeneutics resides in its utility as a unique method that takes into account and focuses on the centrality of response and reception as historically specific components of the way texts work on readers by virtue of the work readers do on texts.

Such work is valuable, in part, because thinking—and interpreting—

historically is unavoidable. That is, "historical consciousness," as Fulbrook reminds us, "is not a choice; it is an inevitable part of the human condition," because we "act, as human beings, in the knowledge or perception of what we think has gone before and in the light of what we think of it. We inhabit human worlds which are intrinsically suffused with a sense of history and a placement within webs of historical significance."[55] Recognizing the unavoidable historical dimension of our consciousness also means recognizing that the historical study of reception can function as a discourse of intervention for understanding ourselves as subjects embedded in our own histories.

In that sense, Frederick Jameson's well-known injunction to "always historicize" can be seen less as a call to action than as a fait accompli. As readers and discourse users we always already historicize because we cannot escape our own historical embeddedness. The question, then, is not whether we *will* historicize but whether we do so rigorously and self-consciously—whether we approach the historicity of reading, response, and reception in a way that seeks to address the manner in which that history includes our own practices as historical readers. Such a potential is what historical hermeneutics offers in that, unlike the unacknowledged, muffled presentism of response and reception criticism of the last quarter of the twentieth century—as well as much of the scholarship over the last two decades in the history of reading—a theoretically informed historical hermeneutics has the capacity to enhance our awareness of our present and of our presence as interpreters of our own constructed histories.

What such self-conscious reflection might consist of can be neither proscribed nor prescribed. It might take the form, as it has in the last several paragraphs of this chapter, of seeking to unpack the theoretical premises and problematics that underscore and constitute a particular method, such as historical hermeneutics. Or it might involve an analysis of otherwise unacknowledged dimensions of the strategies of a practice, its rhetorical moves, and its hidden assumptions. For example, for this study I might point out that I can now see each of my four case-study chapters as having a shape that I did not intend nor one that I recognized until I had written all four, in that each tells a common story. That is, the chapters on the antebellum receptions of Poe, Melville, Sedgwick, and Chesebro' offer narratives colored by repeated failures, disappointments, and frustration in those four writers' relationships with their contemporary readerships. I might also point out that this feature of these chapters may be an unacknowledged function of my own sense of the unavoidable nature of author-audience relations—specifically, that writers can never shape, yet alone control, those relations and that as a result they will always involve interpretive disruptions and authorial failures.

I could continue such analysis by invoking White's four-fold modal and tropological model to describe my four histories of antebellum reception as ironic narratives emplotted as tragedies. Or I might acknowledge that my entire approach has been driven not only by my belief in the centrality of interpretation and reading to nearly everything we do but also by my desire—professional and personal—to construct something new and to re-cognize something not previously seen, a desire rooted at once in private satisfaction, disciplinary conventions, professional and institutional expectations, and a sincere commitment to the goal of creating new knowledge. Ultimately, however, whatever form my and other self-conscious gestures might take, they will always consist of a further interpretation that must itself be interpreted by other readers, whose readings of readings of (my) readings must themselves be interpreted as historically specific ways of interpretation.

To make this point is not to claim some timeless longevity for this study or for historical hermeneutics as a practice. It is, instead, to offer one final reminder that reading and response—including our own interpretations of our own interpretive premises and practices—are historically constituted activities and that historical approaches to the hermeneutical practices of reception mark out analytical pathways that criticism and scholarship can ill afford to ignore—or even avoid.

CHAPTER ONE: *Historical Hermeneutics, Reception Theory, and the Social Conditions of Reading in Antebellum America*

1. *North American Review* Oct. 1844: 435.

2. Elizabeth Freund, *The Return of the Reader: Reader-Response Criticism* (London: Methuen, 1987); Terry Eagleton, *Literary Theory: An Introduction* (Minneapolis: U of Minnesota P, 1983) esp. 74–75. For a recent, useful—though at times tendentious—overview of the interest in readers, response, and audience in a variety of critical areas over the last fifty years—as well as in Western thought over the last two millennia—see Karin Littau, *Theories of Reading: Books, Bodies, and Bibliomania* (Cambridge, UK: Polity, 2006). On the place of such work in cognitive linguistics, see Gilles Fauconnier, "Methods and Generalizations," *Cognitive Linguistics: Foundations, Scope, and Methodology*, ed. Theo Jenssen and Gisela Redeker (New York: Gruyter, 1999) 95–127. On the relation between reading study and the New Historicism, see Edward Pechter, "The New Historicism and Its Discontents: Politicizing Renaissance Drama," *PMLA* 102 (1987): 292. For a typology of orientations and approaches to audience and reading in the history of the book, see David D. Hall, "Readers and Reading in America: Historical and Critical Perspectives," *Proceedings of the American Antiquarian Society* 103 (1993): 337–57; Jonathan Rose, "How Historians Study Reader Response," *Literature and the Marketplace: Nineteenth-Century British Publishing and Reading Practices*, ed. John O. Jordan and Robert L. Patten (Cambridge: Cambridge UP, 1995) 195–212; Jennifer Anderson and Elizabeth Sauer, "Current Trends in the History of Reading," *Books and Readers in Early Modern England*, ed. Jennifer Anderson and Elizabeth Sauer (Philadelphia: U of Pennsylvania P, 2002) 1–20; and Leah Price, "Reading: The State of the Discipline," *Book History* 7 (2004): 303–20. Whether the recently developed field of the history of reading is a subfield of the slightly older field of book history or a separate "offspring" is a point of disagreement among scholars. Anderson and Sauer, e.g., subscribe to the first view; holding the second is H. J. Jackson, "Marginal Frivolities: Readers' Notes as Evidence for the History of Reading," *Owners, Annotators and the Signs*

of Reading, ed. Robin Meyers, Michael Harris, and Giles Mandelbrotte (New Castle, DE: Oak Knoll; London: British Library, 2005) 149.

3. Wolfgang Iser, *The Act of Reading: A Theory of Aesthetic Response* (Baltimore: Johns Hopkins UP, 1978) 3. This phenomenon was prevalent in the practice of most reader-response and other reader-oriented critics who worked either from formalist premises or from what Steven Mailloux has called a "social" model of reading (*Interpretive Conventions: The Role of the Reader in the Study of American Fiction* [Ithaca: Cornell UP, 1982] 40–65). See, e.g., Stanley Fish, *Surprised by Sin: The Reader in* Paradise Lost (London: St. Martin's, 1967); Walter Slatoff, *With Respect to Readers: Dimensions of Literary Response* (Ithaca: Cornell UP, 1970); Gerald Prince, "Introduction to the Study of the Narratee," *Poetique* 14 (1973): 177–96; Walter J. Ong, S.J., "The Writer's Audience Is Always a Fiction," *PMLA* 90 (1975): 9–21; Judith Fetterley, *The Resisting Reader: A Feminist Approach to American Fiction* (Bloomington: Indiana UP, 1978); Umberto Eco, *The Role of the Reader: Explorations in the Semiotics of Texts* (Bloomington: Indiana UP, 1979); Iser, *Act of Reading*; Wolfgang Iser, *The Implied Reader: Patterns of Communication in Prose Fiction from Bunyan to Beckett* (Baltimore: Johns Hopkins UP, 1974); and Susan Suleiman and Inge Crosman, eds., *The Reader in the Text: Essays on Audience and Interpretation* (Princeton: Princeton UP, 1980).

4. For versions of this critique of 1970s and early 1980s reader-oriented practice, see Susan Suleiman, "Introduction: Varieties of Audience-Oriented Criticism," Suleiman and Crosman 3–45; Frank Lentricchia, *After the New Criticism* (Chicago: U of Chicago P, 1980) 105–12; Mary Louise Pratt, "Interpretive Strategies / Strategic Interpretations: On Anglo-American Reader-Response Criticism," *boundary 2* 10 (1982): 201–31; Robert Holub, *Reception Theory: A Critical Introduction* (London: Methuen, 1984) 84, 135–53; Steven Mailloux, *Rhetorical Power* (Ithaca: Cornell UP, 1989) 3–33; Stanley Fish, "Why No One Is Afraid of Wolfgang Iser," *Doing What Comes Naturally: Change, Rhetoric, and the Practice of Theory in Literary and Legal Studies* (Durham: Duke UP, 1989) 68–86; and Littau 107. A common shortcoming of such critiques, however, is that even as they were offered, they have perpetuated a gap between theory and practice in one of two ways. In the most frequent instances (Suleiman, Lentricchia, Holub, Pratt, and Littau), the recognition of history remains at the theoretical level, with little if any move toward reader-oriented praxis. In the second case, epitomized by Fish, the theoretical recognition simply drops out when practice begins, thus duplicating the problem of the reader-oriented approaches cited in note 3 above (see Fish, "Things and Actions Indifferent: The Temptation of Plot in *Paradise Regained*," *Milton Studies* 17 [1983]: 163–85; and more recently *How Milton Works* [Cambridge: Belknap Press of Harvard UP, 2001]). One of the few theo-

rists who has attempted to unite theory and practice has been Mailloux, who has proposed that critics give up trying to forge a "general theory" of reading and turn instead to "rhetorical hermeneutics," which would "provide histories of how particular theories and critical discourses have evolved" by tracing the rhetorical practices of interpretation as "historical sets of topics, arguments, tropes, ideologies, and so forth" (*Rhetorical Power* 15–17). In taking this turn, however, Mailloux opens up a different gap by neither explaining nor demonstrating how such rhetorical histories could provide—or intersect with—accounts of particular reading practices and the dynamics of reception as products of historically specific interpretive strategies.

5. These problematic tendencies of 1970s reader-oriented criticism did not extend in the same way to psychological reader-response critics such as David Bleich and Norman Holland, primarily because their work dealt with contemporary reading strategies and contemporary readers (mostly college students) and thus had no methodological implications for the issue of reading as a historical act. The same applies to the vast majority of reception study in cultural studies and mass communication because of its contemporaneous orientation. Hence, the question of history is a moot point even in the strongly contextualized ethnographic and active-audience work that began with David Morley's *The "Nationwide" Audience: Structure and Decoding* (London: British Film Institute, 1980) and Janice Radway's *Reading the Romance: Women, Patriarchy, and Popular Literature* (Chapel Hill: U of North Carolina P, 1984) and has continued with such works as Jacqueline Bobo's *Black Women as Cultural Readers* (New York: Columbia UP, 1995); Janet Staiger's *Perverse Spectators: The Practices of Film Reception* (New York: New York UP, 2000); and Kimberly Chabot's *Postmodern Texts and Emotional Audiences* (West Lafayette, IN: Purdue UP, 2007). For a discussion and representative examples of reception study in cultural studies, see the critical introduction and accompanying essays in the fourth section of James L. Machor and Philip Goldstein, eds., *Reception Study: From Literary Theory to Cultural Studies* (New York: Routledge, 2001) 203–317.

6. Hans Robert Jauss, *Aesthetic Experience and Literary Hermeneutics*, trans. Michael Shaw (Minneapolis: U of Minnesota P, 1982); *Toward an Aesthetic of Reception,* trans. Timothy Bahti (Minneapolis: U of Minnesota P, 1982); and *Question and Answer: Forms of Dialogic Understanding,* trans. Michael Hays (Minneapolis: U of Minnesota P, 1989). Early U.S. examples include Gary Taylor, *Reinventing Shakespeare: A Cultural History from the Restoration to the Present* (London: Weidenfeld and Nicholson, 1989); and Peter Widdowson, *Hardy in History: A Study in Literary Sociology* (London: Routledge, 1989). In treating Jauss and reception aesthetics in a different category from Iser and 1970s response criticism as a whole, I am following a distinction made by others, includ-

ing Holub and Mailloux, but it is a distinction somewhat problematized by the fact that Iser and Jauss developed their methods as members of the Konstance school, which has led some critics to group them together (e.g., Freund 134–51). Despite their affinity, however, a differentiation seems warranted in that Iser himself sought to distinguish his method from reception aesthetics (see *Act of Reading* x, 151).

7. This characterization of a "turn" toward history in audience studies of the 1980s needs some qualification because the dichotomy was not as sharp as that term implies. Indeed, one common feature of a major segment of audience-oriented criticism from the 1970s through the 1990s involved the continual problematic reliance on an unchanging, achronic, textualized notion of the reader, particularly in criticism that sought to outline a transhistorical poetics of reading: see, e.g., Horst Ruthrof, *The Reader's Construction of Narrative* (London: Routledge and Kegan Paul, 1981); W. Daniel Wilson, "Readers in Texts," *PMLA* 96 (1981): 848–63; Patrocinio P. Schweickart, "Reading Ourselves: Toward a Feminist Theory of Reading," *Gender and Reading: Essays on Readers, Texts, and Contexts*, ed. Elizabeth A. Flynn and Patrocinio P. Schweickart (Baltimore: Johns Hopkins UP, 1986) 31–62; Peter Rabinowitz, *Before Reading: Narrative Conventions and the Politics of Interpretation* (Ithaca: Cornell UP, 1987); Inge Crosman Wimmers, *Poetics of Reading: Approaches to the Novel* (Princeton: Princeton UP, 1988); Paul B. Armstrong, *Conflicting Readings: Variety and Validity in Interpretation* (Chapel Hill: U of North Carolina P, 1990); Lillian R. Furst, *Through the Lens of the Reader: Explorations in European Narrative* (Albany: State U of New York P, 1992); Jean Marie Goulement, *Forbidden Texts: Erotic Literature and Its Readers in Eighteenth-Century France*, trans. James Simpson (Philadelphia: U of Pennsylvania P, 1994); and George N. Dove, *The Reader and the Detective Story* (Bowling Green, OH: Bowling Green State UP, 1997). The same tendency has marked discussions of readers and reading in narratology; see, e.g., Lillian R. Furst, *All Is True: The Claims and Strategies of Realist Fiction* (Durham: Duke UP, 1995); and, more recently, James Phelan, *Experiencing Fiction: Judgment, Progressions, and the Rhetorical Theory of Narrative* (Columbus: Ohio State UP, 2007). Several commentators on audience and reception studies from the 1980s and 1990s, including Jauss's work, have noted this problem, as well as other theoretical and methodological blind spots: Holub, *Reception Aesthetics* 134–53; Jonathan Culler, *The Pursuit of Signs: Semiotics, Literature, Deconstruction* (Ithaca: Cornell UP, 1984) 54–57; David Shepherd, "Bakhtin and the Reader," *Bakhtin and Cultural Theory*, ed. Ken Hirschkop and David Shepherd (Manchester: Manchester UP, 1989) 103; Mailloux, *Interpretive Conventions* 167–70; and David Perkins, *Is Literary History Possible?* (Baltimore: Johns Hopkins UP, 1992) 25–27. Mailloux, for instance, points out how

"in reconstructing the horizon of social norms for a group of French lyrics in 1852 [an analysis contained in *Toward an Aesthetic of Reception*], Jauss discusses the effect of their reception on . . . bourgeois society; but his 'horizon analysis' leaves completely unexplained the interpretive work of readers that would have to be performed *before* such a socialization effect could take place"; in other words, notes Mailloux, "[l]ike traditional literary history . . . *Rezeptionäesthetik* tends to cover over the [contextually specific] interpretive work of readers . . . that underlies all literary history" (170, 11).

8. See, e.g., Jane Tompkins, *Sensational Designs: The Cultural Work of American Fiction, 1790–1860* (New York: Oxford UP, 1985); Jon P. Klancher, *The Making of English Reading Audiences, 1790–1832* (Madison: U of Wisconsin P, 1987); Michael Denning, *Mechanic Accents: Dime Novels and Working-Class Culture in America* (London: Verso, 1987); Susan Harris, *Nineteenth-Century American Women's Novels: Interpretive Strategies* (Cambridge: Cambridge UP, 1990); Tom Keymer, *Richardson's* Clarissa *and the Eighteenth-Century Reader* (Cambridge: Cambridge UP, 1992); Lucy Newlyn, Paradise Lost *and the Romantic Reader* (Oxford: Clarendon Press, 1993); Richard H. Brodhead, *Culture of Letters: Scenes of Reading and Writing in Nineteenth-Century America* (Chicago: U of Chicago P, 1993); Garrett Stewart, *Dear Reader: The Conscripted Audience in Nineteenth-Century British Fiction* (Baltimore: Johns Hopkins UP, 1996); Deidre Lynch, *The Economy of Character: Novels, Market Culture, and the Business of Inner Meaning* (Chicago: U of Chicago P, 1998); Paul Magnuson, *Reading Public Romanticism* (Princeton: Princeton UP, 1998); Diana Holmes, *Romance and Readership in Twentieth-Century France: Love Stories* (Oxford: Oxford UP, 2006); Melissa Frazier, *Romantic Encounters: Writers, Readers, and the* Library for Reading (Stanford, CA: Stanford UP, 2007); and Joe Bray, *The Female Reader in the English Novel: From Burney to Austen* (New York: Routledge, 2009).

9. Representative examples of this work from the mid-1980s to the turn of the century include James D. Wallace, *Early Cooper and His Audience* (New York: Columbia UP, 1986); Ezra Greenspan, *Walt Whitman and the American Reader* (Cambridge: Cambridge UP, 1990); Tillotama Rajan, *The Supplement of Reading: Figures of Understanding in Romantic Theory and Practice* (Ithaca: Cornell UP, 1990); Stephen Railton, *Authorship and Audience: Literary Performance in the American Renaissance* (Princeton: Princeton UP, 1991); Eugene R. Kintgen, *Reading in Tudor England* (Pittsburgh: U of Pittsburgh P, 1996); Nancy Glazener, *Reading for Realism: A History of a U.S. Literary Institution, 1850–1910* (Durham: Duke UP, 1997); Lucy Newlyn, *Reading, Writing, and Romanticism: The Anxiety of Reception* (Oxford: Oxford UP, 2000); Lisa Gordis, *Opening Scripture: Bible Reading and Interpretive Authority in Puritan New*

England (Chicago: U of Chicago P, 2003); and Suzy Anger, *Victorian Interpretation* (Ithaca: Cornell UP, 2005).

10. The number of reception studies with this orientation has grown over the last two decades to the point that a complete listing of articles, essays, and books would be impossible here. As far as full-length studies go, important and/or representative works since the 1990s are Michael Bérubé, *Marginal Forces/Cultural Centers: Tolson, Pynchon, and the Politics of the Canon* (Ithaca: Cornell UP, 1992); K. P. Van Anglen, *The New England Milton: Literary Reception and Cultural Authority in the Early Republic* (University Park: Pennsylvania State UP, 1993); Seth Lerer, *Chaucer and His Readers: Imagining the Author in Late-Medieval England* (Princeton: Princeton UP, 1993); William Kolbrener, *Milton's Warring Angels: A Study of Critical Engagements* (Cambridge: Cambridge UP, 1997); Jonathan Arac, Huckleberry Finn *as Idol and Target: The Function of Criticism in Our Time* (Madison: U of Wisconsin P, 1997); Marianne L. Nouy, *Engaging with Shakespeare: Responses of George Eliot and Other Women Novelists* (Iowa City: U of Iowa P, 1998); Stephen Gill, *Wordsworth and the Victorians* (Oxford: Oxford UP, 1998); Steven Mailloux, *Reception Histories: Rhetoric, Pragmatism, and American Cultural Politics* (Ithaca: Cornell UP, 1998); Ronald Paulson, Don Quixote *in England: The Aesthetics of Laughter* (Baltimore: Johns Hopkins UP, 1998); Barbara Hochman, *Getting at the Author: Reimagining Books and Reading in the Age of American Realism* (Amherst: U of Massachusetts P, 2001) esp. 16–26, 70–116; Philip Goldstein, *Communities of Cultural Value: Reception Study, Political Differences, and Literary History* (Lanham, MD: Lexington-Rowman and Littlefield, 2001); Eliza Richards, *Gender and the Poetics of Reception in Poe's Circle* (Cambridge: Cambridge UP, 2004); Dayton Haskin, *John Donne in the Nineteenth Century* (Oxford: Oxford UP, 2007); Craig Kallendorf, *The Other Virgil: "Pessimistic" Readings of the* Aeneid *in Early Modern Culture* (New York: Oxford UP, 2007); and Kate Loveman, *Reading Fictions, 1660–1740: Deception in English Literature and Political Culture* (Aldershot, UK: Ashgate, 2008). A noteworthy exception to this orientation is Nicola Diane Thompson's *Reviewing Sex: Gender and the Reception of Victorian Novels* (New York: New York UP, 1996), which looks at reviewers' responses to nineteenth-century British fiction. But Thompson's book is limited to the public reception of only four novels and is cripplingly narrow in its examination of only one factor in British reviewers' horizon of expectations: gender assumptions.

11. The term *interpretive community* was conceived most prominently, of course, by Stanley Fish (*Is There a Text in This Class?* [Cambridge, Harvard UP, 1980] esp. 167–73), though it has antecedents, particularly in Charles Sanders Peirce's discussion of the communal intersubjectivity of semiosis (on this point in Peirce, see Umberto Eco, *The Limits of Interpretation* [Bloomington: Indiana UP, 1990] 40–41). The term *reading formation* comes from Tony Bennett,

"Texts, Readers, and Reading Formations," *Bulletin of the Midwest Modern Language Association* 16, no. 1 (Spring 1983): 3–17. Fish has defined interpretive communities differently on different occasions: at one point he has said that an interpretive community consists of "those who share interpretive strategies" and "a structure of interests and understood goals" (*Is There a Text in This Class?* 14, 333). Elsewhere, he has explained that "the idea of an interpretive community [designates] not so much a group of individuals who share a point of view, but a point of view or way or organizing experiences that share[s] individuals in the sense that its assumed distinctions, categories of understanding, and stipulations of relevance and irrelevance [are] the content of the consciousness of community members" (*Doing What Comes Naturally* 141). Bennett characterizes a reading formation as "a region of discourse that is specifically concerned with the production of readings, with the operation of a hermeneutic," and therefore consists of beliefs, interpretive strategies, and other activities that vary from one formation to another within "the variety of material, social, institutional, and ideological contexts" in which they are formed (14). Since Bennett's reading formation and Fish's interpretive community, in the second definition, work out to be much the same thing, the two terms are, in effect, interchangeable and even redundant. But I want to retain both terms to make an important distinction. That is, I will be using *reading formation* (and *interpretive formation*) to refer to any set of interrelated interpretive codes, ideologies, and beliefs, while *interpretive community* will designate any group of people, not limited by geographical proximity, who share a particular reading formation within a historically specific set of social conditions.

12. For a discussion of this issue, see James L. Machor and Philip Goldstein, "Reception Study and the History of the Book," Machor and Goldstein, *Reception Study* 155–59.

13. Jonathan Rose, "Rereading the English Common Reader: A Preface to the History of Audiences," *Journal of the History of Ideas* 53 (1992): 51. Such a definition, it should be noted, is not without its problems. According to it, teachers, lawyers, doctors, nurses, and historians could never be "common readers" no matter what they read, since all depend to a substantial degree on book reading for their livelihood. This definition also begs the question as to whether, say, professional films reviewers, who do not necessarily rely on reading books for their living, are "common" readers when they review.

14. Examples of historical studies looking at the reception of single works include Sylvia Huot, The Romance of the Rose *and Its Medieval Readers: Interpretation, Reception, Manuscript Transmission* (Cambridge: Cambridge UP, 1993); Peter Burke, *The Fortunes of* The Courtier (Cambridge, UK: Polity, 1995); Nicholas von Maltzahn, "The First Reception of 'Paradise Lost' (1667)," *Review*

of *English Studies* 47 (1996): 479–99; Leon Jackson, "The Reader Retailored: Thomas Carlyle, His American Audiences, and the Politics of Evidence," *Book History* 2 (1999): 46–72; James A. Secord, *Victorian Sensations: The Extraordinary Publication, Reception, and Secret Audience of* Vestiges of the Natural History of Creation (Chicago: U of Chicago P, 2000); Kenneth Roemer, *Utopian Audiences: How Readers Locate Nowhere* (Amherst: U of Massachusetts P, 2003); and Cree LeFavour, "*Jane Eyre* Fever: Deciphering the Astonishing Popular Success of Charlotte Brontë in Antebellum America," *Book History* 7 (2004): 113–41. Work in book history that has looked at a single reader began with Carlo Ginzburg's groundbreaking *The Cheese and the Worm: The Cosmos of a Sixteenth-Century Miller* (London: Routledge and Kegan Paul, 1980), a fascinating but problematic study that explores the life and mind of a sixteenth-century miller known as Menocchio. Subsequent studies of single readers, which have rectified some of those problems—though not the one involving the question of the representativeness of such readers—include Robert Darnton, "Readers Respond to Rousseau: The Fabrication of Romantic Sensitivity," *The Great Cat Massacre and Other Episodes in French Cultural History* (New York: Basic Books, 1984) 215–56; Lisa Jardine and Anthony Grafton, "'Studied for Action': How Gabriel Harvey Read His Livy," *Past and Present* 129 (1990): 30–78; William H. Sherman, *John Dee: The Politics of Reading and Writing in the English Renaissance* (Amherst: U of Massachusetts P, 1994); John Brewer, "Reconstructing the Reader: Prescriptions, Texts and Strategies in Anna Larpent's Reading," *The Practice and Representation of Reading in England,* ed. James Raven, Helen Small, and Naomi Tadmor (Cambridge: Cambridge UP, 1996) 226–45; Kevin Sharpe, *Reading Revolutions: The Politics of Reading in Early Modern England* (New Haven: Yale UP, 2000); Alison A. Scott, "'This Cultivated Mind': Reading and Identity in a Nineteenth-Century Reader," *Reading Acts: U.S. Readers' Interactions with Literature, 1800–1950,* ed. Barbara Ryan and Amy M. Thomas (Knoxville: U of Tennessee P, 2002) 29–52; Daniel Wakelin, *Humanism, Reading, and English Literature, 1430–1530* (Oxford: Oxford UP, 2007) 93–125; and Susan M. Stabile, "Female Curiosities: The Transatlantic Female Commonplace Book," *Reading Women: Literacy, Authorship, and Culture in the Atlantic World, 1500–1800,* ed. Heidi Brayman Hackel and Catherine E. Kelley (Philadelphia: U of Pennsylvania P, 2008) 217–43.

15. Representative, important full-length studies in this vein include David Cressy, *Literacy and the Social Order: Reading and Writing in Tudor and Stuart England* (Cambridge: Cambridge UP, 1980); James Smith Allen, *Popular French Romanticism: Authors, Readers, and Books in the 19th Century* (Syracuse: Syracuse UP, 1981); Robert Darnton, *Literary Underground of the Old Regime* (Cambridge: Harvard UP, 1982); Cathy N. Davidson, *Revolution and the Word: The*

Rise of the Novel in America (New York: Oxford UP, 1986); Roger Chartier, *The Cultural Uses of Print in Early Modern France*, trans. Lydia G. Cochrane (Princeton: Princeton UP, 1987); William Gilmore, *Reading Becomes a Necessity of Life: Material and Cultural Life in Rural New England, 1780–1835* (Knoxville: U of Tennessee P, 1989); Michael Warner, *The Letters of the Republic: Publication and the Public Sphere in Eighteenth-Century America* (Cambridge: Harvard UP, 1990); Ronald J. Zboray, *A Fictive People: Antebellum Economic Activity and the American Reading Public* (New York: Oxford UP, 1993); Harry Y. Gamble, *Books and Readers in the Early Church: A History of Early Christian Texts* (New Haven: Yale UP, 1995); Charles Johanningsmeier, *Fiction and the American Literary Marketplace: The Role of Newspaper Syndicates, 1860–1900* (Cambridge: Cambridge UP, 1997); William Beatty Warner, *Licensing Entertainment: The Elevation of Novel Reading in Britain, 1684–1750* (Berkeley and Los Angeles: U of California P, 1998); Jacqueline Pearson, *Women's Reading in Britain, 1750–1835: A Dangerous Recreation* (Cambridge: Cambridge UP, 1999); Brian Richardson, *Printing, Writers, and Readers in Renaissance Italy* (Cambridge: Cambridge UP, 1999); Martyn Lyons, *Readers and Society in Nineteenth-Century France: Workers, Women, Peasants* (Basingstoke, UK: Palgrave, 2001); Lori Humphrey, *Reading Popular Romance in Early Modern England* (New York: Columbia UP, 2002); Elizabeth Long, *Book Clubs: Women and the Uses of Reading in Everyday Life* (Chicago: U of Chicago P, 2003); William St. Clair, *The Reading Nation in the Romantic Period* (Cambridge: Cambridge UP, 2004); Ronald Zboray and Mary Saracino Zboray, *Literary Dollars and Social Sense: A People's History of the Mass Market Book* (New York: Routledge, 2005); Joan Shelley Rubin, *Songs of Ourselves: The Uses of Poetry in America* (Cambridge: Harvard UP, 2007); and Matthew P. Brown, *The Pilgrim and the Bee: Reading Rituals and Book Culture in Early New England* (Philadelphia: U of Pennsylvania P, 2007).

16. See Ronald Zboray and Mary Saracino Zboray, "Transcendentalism in Print: Production, Dissemination, and Common Reception," *The Transcendent and the Permanent: The Transcendental Movement and Its Contexts*, ed. Charles Capper and Conrad Edick Wright (Boston: Massachusetts Historical Society, 1999) 310–81; William Galperin, "Austen's Earliest Readers and the Rise of the Janeites," *Janeites: Austen's Disciples and Devotes*, ed. Deidre Lynch (Princeton: Princeton UP, 2000) 85–114; Jonathan Rose, *The Intellectual Life of the British Working Classes* (New Haven: Yale UP, 2001), chaps. 1, 3–4, 9–10, and 13; Joad Raymond, "Irrational, Impractical, and Unprofitable: Reading the News in Seventeenth-Century Britain," *Reading, Society, and Politics in Early Modern England*, ed. Kevin Sharpe and Steven N. Zwicker (Cambridge: Cambridge UP, 2003) 185–212; LeFavour; H. J. Jackson, *Romantic Readers: The Evidence of Marginalia* (New Haven: Yale UP, 2005); Ronald Zboray and Mary Saracino

Zboray, *Everyday Ideas: Socioliterary Experience among Antebellum New Englanders* (Knoxville: U of Tennessee P, 2006) 245–74; Annika Bautz, *The Reception
of Jane Austen and Walter Scott: A Comparative Longitudinal Study* (London:
Continuum, 2007) 15–113; and Amy Blair, "Main Street Reading *Main Street*,"
New Directions in American Reception Study, ed. Philip Goldstein and James L.
Machor (Oxford: Oxford UP, 2008) 139–58. Again, the history of this work is
more complex than my linear sequence suggests, since disclosures of interpretive moves by historical readers, as evidenced in notebooks, diaries, letters, and
marginalia, did form a small but important element in some reception and book
history studies as far back as the early 1990s; see, e.g., Huot; James Smith Allen,
In the Public Eye: A History of Reading in Modern France (Princeton: Princeton
UP, 1991), chaps. 8–10; and Barbara Johnson, *Reading* Piers Plowman *and* The
Pilgrim's Progress (Carbondale: Southern Illinois UP, 1992) 148–59.

17. For these caveats, see Kintgen 63–65, 214; Rose, "How Historians Study
Reader Response" 206; Raymond 190; Jackson 38; Rubin 253; Rose, *Intellectual
Life* 2; St. Clair 5–6; William Sherman, "What Did Renaissance Readers Write
in Their Books?" Anderson and Sauer 130–31; Scott E. Casper, "Antebellum
Reading Prescribed and Described," *Perspectives in American Book History: Artifacts and Commentary*, ed. Scott E. Casper, Joanne D. Chaisson, and Jeffrey D.
Groves (Amherst: U of Massachusetts P, 2002) 160; Price 312–13; Wakelin 17;
and Loveman 13. One problem with the use of marginalia, letters, and memoirs
not noted in these critiques is that historians who have employed such evidence
have repeatedly turned to readers who were intellectuals and scribes, members
of the British aristocracy or of the publishing industry, or themselves novelists
and poets, which calls into question the claim that such records provide evidence
of the activities of "common" or "typical" readers. Studies exemplifying this pit-
fall include Jackson; Bautz; Wakelin; Sharpe; Rubin; and Zboray and Zboray,
Everyday Ideas.

18. This problem is apparent, for example, in Huot; Johnson; Allen; and
Rose, *Intellectual Life*.

19. Kevin Sharpe and Steven N. Zwicker, "Introduction: Discovering the Renaissance Reader," Sharpe and Zwicker 9.

20. Patrocinio Schweickart, "Understanding an Other: Reading as a Receptive Form of Communicative Action," Goldstein and Machor, *New Directions in
American Reception Study* 3. Sharpe has noted a similar disjunction between
response-and-reception criticism and historians of reading and of the book in
that "historians have not for the most part been attracted to the programme of a
historical reception theory or historical reader-response criticism" (37).

21. My use of the designation *historical hermeneutics* needs some explanation,
since *hermeneutics* is a term that itself carries implications of an engagement with

history. As it originally developed within theological discourse, hermeneutics was a method of reading distinguishable from exegesis and interpretation. According to Paul Achtmeier, "exegesis normally meant determining what meaning the text had for its own author and intended readers, interpretation sought the meaning the text could have for the current age, and hermeneutics concerned the rules to apply in order to get from the former to the latter" (*An Introduction to the New Hermeneutic* [Philadelphia: Westminster, 1969] 13–14). In the twentieth century, however, the meaning of *hermeneutics* began to be expanded to include first exegesis and then interpretation, so that hermeneutics has come to designate loosely any activity concerned with the explanation and understanding of texts (see Robert Marsh, "Historical Interpretation and the History of Criticism," *Literary Criticism and Historical Understanding*, ed. Phillip Damon [New York: Columbia UP, 1967] 1). By *hermeneutics*, however, I mean something more specific that draws on Paul Ricoeur's assertion that hermeneutics is "the theory of the operations of understanding in their relation to the interpretation of texts" ("The Task of Hermeneutics," *Hermeneutics and the Human Sciences*, ed. and trans. John B. Thompson [Cambridge and Paris: Cambridge UP and Éditions de la Maison des Sciences de L'Homme, 1981] 43). That is, I take hermeneutics to refer to a theoretically informed practice that studies both the act of interpretation—the making sense of a text—and the reading formation that produced it. Historical hermeneutics, therefore, is concerned with the dynamics of response and reception as the products of historically specific reading formations shared by particular interpretive communities. Conceived this way, historical hermeneutics differs from what Hans-Georg Gadamer means when he uses that same term, in that for Gadamer, historical hermeneutics signifies something closer to the traditional idea of hermeneutics as an activity seeking to contextualize a text to discover the historically specific meaning it contains. Gadamer's historical hermeneutics is thus concerned, not with the process of interpretation by which a text's original historical audience(s) made sense of it, but with the method by which subsequent readers can, within their own horizon of assumptions, come to an understanding of a text's original and intrinsic meaning (Gadamer, *Truth and Method*, 2nd rev. ed., trans. Joel Weinsheimer and Donald G. Marshall [New York: Crossroad, 1990] esp. 165–379).

22. Jonathan Culler, "Prolegomena to a Theory of Reading," Suleiman and Crosman 56–66.

23. The designations "positive" and "negative" belong to Suleiman, "Introduction: Varieties of Audience-Oriented Criticism"; "idealist" and "realist" are distinctions employed by Mailloux, *Rhetorical Power* 3–14.

24. Michael Berubé, *Rhetorical Occasions: Essays on Humans and the Humanities* (Chapel Hill: U of North Carolina P, 2006) 97–110.

25. Suleiman, "Introduction: Varieties of Audience-Oriented Criticism" 43–46. Fish first posed this question and his answer in *Critical Inquiry* in an essay later incorporated in *Is There a Text in This Class?* 147–73, esp. 165. Fish also went on to anticipate the claim of Suleiman and others by asserting that the question and its nonanswer had no relevance for critical practice (370–71)—an assertion he would later echo in *Doing What Comes Naturally* 315–41.

26. The first of these is most closely associated with E. D. Hirsh (*Validity in Interpretation* [New Haven: Yale UP, 1967]; and *The Aims of Interpretation* [Chicago: U of Chicago P, 1976]), while the plenitude argument is espoused both within and outside of response and reception criticism and includes among its proponents Eco, Rabinowitz, Furst, Ruthrof, Iser, Jauss, Paul Armstrong, Robert Scholes (*Protocols of Reading* [New Haven: Yale UP, 1989]), and those who use statistical approaches (see, e.g., Elaine F. Nardocchio, ed., *Reader Response to Literature* [Berlin: Mouton de Gruyter, 1992], esp. the essays by David S. Miall, Rosanne Potter, and Teresa Snelgrove). The positing of textual gaps found its strongest proponent, of course, in Wolfgang Iser (*Act of Reading* and *Implied Reader*). Despite his later turn from reader-response criticism to "literary anthropology," Iser continued to invoke his theory that gaps are inherent features of texts in *The Fictive and the Imaginary: Charting Literary Anthropology* (Baltimore: Johns Hopkins UP, 1993) and *The Range of Interpretation* (New York: Columbia UP, 2000). Those who attribute to texts intrinsic formal features or properties include most response and reception critics and historians of reading, though this position is hardly limited to those working in reception and audience study. In fact, many of the leading poststructuralist theorists also fall into this category. See, e.g., Paul Ricoeur, *Time and Narrative*, vol. 3, trans. Kathleen McLaughlin and David Pellaver (Chicago: U of Chicago P, 1988) 170–71; and J. Hillis Miller, "Theory and Practice," *Critical Inquiry* 6 (1980): 611.

27. Mailloux, *Rhetorical Power* 9.

28. Eco, *The Limits of Interpretation* 1–5. Subsequent citations appear in the text. For a similar argument, see Steven Knapp and Walter Benn Michaels, "Against Theory 2: Hermeneutics and Deconstruction," *Critical Inquiry* 14, no. 1 (Autumn 1987): 54–56. The example of the car and the school children that I discuss next is a modified version of an example Knapp and Michaels use.

29. Regarding the issue of "normal" circumstances, see also Fish, "Normal Circumstances and Other Special Cases," *Is There a Text in This Class?* 268–92.

30. Jacques Derrida, *Limited, Inc.* (Evanston, IL: Northwestern UP, 1988) 132, 137.

31. On the hierarchical arrangement of interpretive assumptions, see also the brief comments by Mailloux, *Interpretive Conventions* 193; and Fish, *Doing What Comes Naturally* 146. In arguing for the "foundational" or "more funda-

mental" status of some interpretive codes, I do not mean that some codes are foundational in any totalizing manner—i.e., foundational to all interpretive activity. My point is that such foundations exits only as a result of and in regard to particular interpretive communities at particular times. My argument here is less radical than it may at first appear in that over a decade ago the semiotician William Rogers also asserted that "interpretation interprets itself" and can do so "only within the boundaries of some interpretive system" (*Interpreting Interpretation: Textual Hermeneutics as an Ascetic Discipline* [University Park: Pennsylvania State UP, 1994] 2, 9). A major difference between his claim and mine, however, is that, as a follower of Charles Sanders Peirce, Rogers did not attribute this self-deciphering to the work of readers or interpretive communities but instead claimed that "the nature of the sign is to interpret itself in interpreting its object" (13).

32. Of course, recognizing a pre-text *as* pre-text—i.e., particular signs that warrant an interpretive act—is itself an interpretation grounded in a reading code that consists of at least an elementary linguistic competency. But it seems necessary to assume such competency as a given before formalist or semantic interpretation begins. That is, the basic ability to recognize a pre-text as *parole* within a "natural" language system (or *langue*) will be shared by all interpretive communities working within that language, irrespective of historical context. Regarding the role of interpretation in determining when the interpretive act is warranted in the first place and thus "what counts as an interpretable object," see Miguel Tamen, *Friends of Interpretable Objects* (Cambridge: Harvard UP, 2001) 3.

33. The principle that intention is involved in reading is held by many contemporary critics and theorists, a number of whom maintain that reading for meaning inherently involves reading for authorial intention: e.g., Steven Knapp and Walter Benn Michaels, "Against Theory" (1982), rpt. in *Against Theory: Literary Studies and the New Pragmatism*, ed. W. J. T. Mitchell (Chicago: U of Chicago P, 1985) 11–30; Eco, *Limits of Interpretation* 59; Michael Steig, *Stories of Reading: Subjectivity and Literary Understanding* (Baltimore: Johns Hopkins UP, 1989) xi–xv; Fish, *Doing What Comes Naturally* 99–101, 116–17; Patrick Colm Hogan, *On Interpretation: Meaning and Inference in Law, Psychoanalysis, and Literature* (Athens: U of Georgia P, 1996) 45; and James Phelan, "Reading Across Identity Borders," *Reading Sites: Social Difference and Reader Response*, ed. Patrocinio Schweickart and Elizabeth Flynn (New York: Modern Language Association, 2004) 40.

34. Michel Foucault, "What Is an Author?" *Textual Strategies: Perspectives in Post-Structuralist Criticism*, ed. Josué V. Harari (Ithaca: Cornell UP, 1979) 141–60.

35. Diana Goodrich, *The Reader and the Text: Interpretive Strategies for Latin American Literature* (Amsterdam: Benjamins, 1986) 16.

36. For an analysis of the way reprinting and repackaging can both have an impact on and serve as a form of reception, see Barbara Hochman, "Sentiment without Tears: *Uncle Tom's Cabin* as History in the 1890s," Goldstein and Machor, *New Directions in American Reception Study* 255–76.

37. Rabinowitz 21.

38. Jauss, *Toward an Aesthetic of Reception* 34–35.

39. Bureau of the Census, *Historical Statistics of the United States: Colonial Times to 1957* (Washington, DC: GPO, 1960), 8; *Eighth Census of the United States: 1860*, 4 vols. (Washington, DC: GPO, 1864) 1: lii, 337, 432.

40. Helmut Lehmann-Haupt, Lawrence W. Wroth, and Rollo G. Silver, *The Book in America: A History of the Making and Selling of Books in the United States*, 2nd ed. (New York: Bowker, 1951) 120; Peter Dzwonkoski, ed., *American Literary Publishing Houses, 1638–1899* (Detroit: Gale, 1986) 192; Per Gedin, *Literature in the Marketplace*, trans. George Bisset (Woodstock, NY: Overlook Press, 1977) 36–39. Besides the gargantuan Harpers, J. B. Lippincott of Philadelphia, as Michael Winship has noted, was "described as possibly the largest book distributing house in the world" in the 1850s ("Distribution and Trade," *The Industrial Book, 1840–1880*, vol. 3 of *The History of the Book in America*, ed. Scott E. Casper, Jeffrey D. Groves, Stephen W. Nissenbaum, and Michael Winship [Chapel Hill: U of North Carolina P, 2007] 121).

41. John Tebbel, *The Creation of An Industry, 1630–1865*, vol. 1 of *A History of Book Publishing in the United States*, 4 vols. (New York: Bowker, 1972) 13, 221; Lehmann-Haupt, Wroth, and Silver 123; *American Bibliography of Charles Evans: A Chronological Dictionary of All Books, Pamphlets and Periodical Publications Printed in the United States of America from the Genesis of Printing in 1639 Down to and Including the Year 1800*, vol. 13 (1903; Worcester, MA: American Antiquarian Society, 1955–59); Orville A. Roorbach, *Bibliotheca Americana: Catalog of American Publications Including Reprints and Original Works from 1820 to . . . 1861*, vols. 1 and 3 (1852–61; New York: Peter Smith, 1939), 4 vols.; "Our Books—Their Abundance and Its Causes," *Ladies' Repository* Sept. 1869: 546; Richard H. Shoemaker, Gayle Cooper, Carol Rinderknecht, and Scott Bruntjen, comps., *A Checklist of American Imprints for 1820–1844*, 26 vols. (Metuchen, NJ: Scarecrow, 1964–93).

42. Oscar Weglin, *Early American Fiction, 1774–1830*, 3rd ed. (New York: Peter Smith, 1929); Lyle Wright, "A Statistical Survey of American Fiction," *Huntington Library Quarterly* 2 (1939): 309; Dzwonkoski 76, 84, and throughout; "Works Published in 1855," *Ladies' Repository* July 1856: 441. John Tebbel sets the figures for fiction even higher, asserting that among the approximately 2,000

titles published in the United States in 1855, 1,200 were original or reprinted novels (224).

43. David Vincent, *Bread, Knowledge, and Freedom: A Study of the Nineteenth-Century Working Class Autobiography* (London: Europa, 1981) 116; Sidney P. Moss, *Poe's Literary Battles* (Durham: Duke UP, 1963) 21.

44. Richard Altick, *English Common Reader: A Social History of the Mass Reading Public, 1800–1900* (Chicago: U of Chicago P, 1957) 8, 264; Davidson 17. See also Tebbel 222; James Hart, *The Popular Book in America: A History of America's Literary Taste* (New York: Oxford UP, 1950) 93, 111–12; and Lee Erickson, *The Economy of Literary Forms: English Literature and the Industrialization of Publishing, 1800–1850* (Baltimore: Johns Hopkins UP, 1996) 5, 143.

45. Hart 46; *New-York Mirror* May 31, 1828: 375; Charles Sellers, *The Market Revolution: Jacksonian America, 1815–1846* (New York: Oxford UP, 1991) 370; J. D. B. DeBow, *Statistical View of the United States . . . Being a Compendium of the Seventh Census* (Washington, DC: Beverley Tucker, 1850) 155–56; *Eighth Census of the United States* 4: 320; Anthony Smith, *The Newspaper: An International History* (London: Thames and Hudson, 1979) 139.

46. Frank Luther Mott, *A History of American Magazines*, 4 vols. (Cambridge: Harvard UP, 1938) 1: 341–42, 2: 4; *Ladies' Repository* Apr. 1861: 248; "Newspaper Men," *Ladies' Repository* Mar. 1854: 103; "Journalism in France," *British Quarterly Review*, rpt. in *Littell's Living Age* July 1846: 67–89. These cumulative numbers, however, only hint at the magnitude of periodical publication in the United States between 1825 and 1850, since many ephemeral periodicals that began after 1825 disappeared by 1850 and thus were not part of the total for that year. Mott calculates that more than 4,000 periodicals appeared over those twenty-five years in the United States.

47. Tebbel 257–62; Robert Escarpit, *The Book Revolution* (London: Harrap; Paris: United Nations Educational, Scientific, and Cultural Organization, 1966) 23; William Charvat, *The Profession of Authorship in America, 1800–1870* (1968; New York: Columbia UP, 1992) 46; Zboray, *Fictive People* 9–11, 131, 145; Lehmann-Haupt et al. 63–98; David S. Reynolds, *Beneath the American Renaissance: The Subversive Imagination in the Age of Emerson and Melville* (New York: Knopf, 1988) 182, 281; Altick, *English Common Reader* 300; Michael Winship, "Manufacturing and Book Production," Casper et al., eds., *The Industrial Book, 1840–1880* 42–48, 53–58.

48. Frank Luther Mott, *Golden Multitudes: The Story of Best Sellers in the United States* (New York: Macmillan, 1947) 67; James Gilreath, "American Book Distribution," *Proceedings of the American Antiquarian Society* 95 (1985): 552; Mott, *History of American Magazines*, 2:7; Zboray, *Fictive People* 6; Zboray and Zboray, *Literary Dollars* xviii.

49. On the growth of the transportation infrastructure in antebellum America, the seminal source remains George Rogers Taylor, *The Transportation Revolution, 1815–1860* (New York: Rinehart, 1957): for canals, see 32–55; for steamboats, 56–73; for railroads, 74–103. On railroads, see also John F. Stover, *American Railroads* (Chicago: U of Chicago P, 1961) 11–56; and "The Railroads of the World," *Littell's Living Age* Apr.–June 1862: 109. On the impact of transportation advances, and of the railroad in particular, on book distribution, see Zboray, *Fictive People* 55–68.

50. Zboray, *Fictive People* 212, n. 4, raises a similar cautionary note.

51. Lee Soltow and Edward Stevens, *The Rise of Literacy and the Common School in the United States: A Socioeconomic Analysis to 1870* (Chicago: U of Chicago P, 1981) 34, 153–55; Carl F. Kaestle, "The History of Literacy and the History of Readers," *Review of Research in Education* 12 (1985): 26, 30; Zboray, *Fictive People* 83, 96; Tebbel 207, 257–59; Richard D. Brown, *Modernization: The Transformation of American Life, 1600–1865* (New York: Hill and Wang, 1976) 139; Allen, *In the Public Eye* 59; Richard Altick, "English Publishing and the Mass Audience in 1852," *Studies in Bibliography* 6 (1954): 6; Roger S. Schofield, "Dimensions of Illiteracy in England, 1750–1850," *Literacy and Social Development in the West: A Reader,* ed. Harvey J. Graff (Cambridge: Cambridge UP, 1981) 201–13; Carlo M. Cipolla, *Literacy and Development in the West* (Harmondsworth, UK: Penguin, 1969) 115.

52. Allen, *In the Public Eye* 56, 61.

53. Carl Bode, *The Anatomy of American Popular Culture, 1840–1861* (Berkeley and Los Angeles: U of California P, 1959) 111–12; Zboray, *Fictive People* 15, 79.

54. Elmer D. Johnson, *A History of Libraries in the Western World* (New York: Scarecrow, 1965) 312–17; Hart 85; *Seventh Census of the United States* (Washington, DC: Robert Armstrong, 1853) lxiii; Soltow and Stevens 81; *Eighth Census of the United States* 4: 505; Kenneth E. Carpenter, "Libraries," Casper et al., eds. *The Industrial Book, 1840–1880* 306. Commercial and subscription libraries open to the public appear to have been substantially more numerous in the United States than in Britain. According to Altick, for instance, an 1849 English report documented the "appalling lack of public library facilities [i.e., libraries open to general public access] in Great Britain as contrasted with those in . . . United States" (*English Common Reader* 224).

55. Edgar Martin, *The Standard of Living in 1860* (Chicago: U of Chicago P, 1942) 296–97; Brown, *Modernization* 138–39; Soltow and Stevens 105.

56. Harry G. Good, *A History of American Education,* 2nd ed. (New York: Macmillan, 1962) 41; Soltow and Stevens 36; Paul Monroe, *Founding of the American Public School System: A History of Education in the United States from*

the Early Settlement to the Close of the Civil War Period (New York: Macmillan, 1940) 59, 202–90, and 309.

57. Ira Katznelson and Margaret Weir, *Schooling for All: Class, Race, and the Decline of the Democratic Ideal* (New York: Basic Books, 1985) 79. This distrust was true even in England, where such resistance was less pronounced than it was in other European nations. Hence by 1850, there were 80,000 public schools in the United States with enrollments of 3.3 million, in comparison to Britain's 15,000 public schools with 1.4 million students (*Seventh Census of the United States*, lx, lxiii).

58. Sellers 366–67; Soltow and Stevens 24; Samuel Bowles and Herbert Gintis, *Schooling in Capitalist America: Educational Reform and the Contradictions of Economic Life* (New York: Basic Books, 1976) 151–58; Carl F. Kaestle, *Pillars of the Republic: Common Schools and American Society, 1780–1860* (New York: Hill and Wang, 1983) 62–74.

59. Zboray, *Fictive People* 14–15; Faye E. Dudden, *Serving Women: Household Service in Nineteenth-Century America* (Middleton, CT: Wesleyan UP, 1982) 129; Lawrence S. Cook, *Lighting in America: From Colonial Rushlight to Victorian Chandeliers* (New York: Main Street, Universe Books, 1975) 52–80; Harold F. Williamson and Arnold R. Drum, *The American Petroleum Industry*, 2 vols. (Evanston, IL: Northwestern UP, 1959) 1:38–39, 312–14.

60. Marlene Stein Wortman, "Domesticating the Nineteenth-Century American City," *Prospects: An Annual of American Cultural Studies* 3 (1977): 535; Zboray, *Fictive People* 13, 74; Charvat, *Profession of Authorship* 299; Steven Mintz, *A Prison of Expectations: The Family in Victorian Culture* (New York: New York UP, 1983) 34–35; Martin 345; Julie A Matthaei, *An Economic History of Women in America: Women's Work, the Sexual Division of Labor, and the Development of Capitalism* (New York: Schocken; Brighton: Harvester, 1982) 107; Gary Cross, *A Social History of Leisure Since 1600* (State College, PA: Venture, 1990) 123.

61. Soltow and Stevens 17, 58–192; John Higham, "Hanging Together: Divergent Unities in American History," *Journal of American History* 61 (1974): 13–14. On the role of religion in promoting literacy and reading in antebellum America, see David Paul Nord, *Faith in Reading: Religious Publishing and the Birth of Mass Media in America* (Oxford: Oxford UP, 2004); Nathan O. Hatch, *The Democratization of American Christianity* (New Haven: Yale UP, 1989) 125–45 and throughout; and David S. Reynolds, *Faith in Fiction: The Emergence of Religious Literature in America* (Cambridge: Harvard UP, 1981).

62. Richard D. Brown, *Knowledge Is Power: The Diffusion of Information in America, 1700–1865* (New York: Oxford UP, 1989) 163; David Tyack and Elizabeth Hansot, *Managers of Virtue: Public School Leadership in America, 1820–*

1860 (New York: Basic Books, 1982) 65; Mary Beth Norton, "The Evolution of White Women's Experience in Early America," *American Historical Review* 89 (1984): 593–619; Jo Anne Preston, "Domestic Ideology, School Reformers, and Female Teachers: Schoolteaching Becomes Women's Work in Nineteenth-Century New England," *New England Quarterly* 66 (1993): 531–51. How far the combination of the cult of domesticity and the ideology of reading affected actual reading practices in the home is unclear, but based on an examination of book ownership by married and unmarried women in America from 1790 to 1859, Soltow and Stevens conclude that "the data support the contention that the mother was a key figure in teaching reading" (169).

63. Carl F. Kaestle, *The Evolution of the Urban School System* (Cambridge: Harvard UP, 1973); Carl F. Kaestle and Maris A. Vinovskis, *Education and Social Change in Nineteenth-Century Massachusetts* (Cambridge: Cambridge UP, 1980) 119–20, 250, 262; Soltow and Stevens, 39, 170–72; Zboray, *Fictive People* 95. On the connection between urbanization and the domestic ideal, see Wortman. Elizabeth Fox-Genovese has demonstrated that the cult of domesticity had a comparatively weaker hold on the plantation and rural South (*Within the Plantation Household: Black and White Women in the Old South* [Chapel Hill: U of North Carolina P, 1988] 37–99).

64. On bookstores as a predominately urban institution in antebellum America, see Bode 111–12; and Zboray, *Fictive People* 136–55. Zboray 37–54, also provides an extensive discussion of the predominant urban itinerary of book peddlers. Regarding the connection between population density and number of libraries, Soltow and Stevens note that in 1850 counties of 10,000 or more inhabitants averaged 2.86 libraries, while counties of 1,000 or fewer averaged .37, or one library for every three rural counties (82).

65. Martin 248–54; Zboray, *Fictive People* 12, 66. One index to the urban character of print consumption is the few surviving subscription lists of antebellum periodicals, such as the *Southern Quarterly Review*. In the list of paid subscribers that magazine included in its July 1846 issue, urban inhabitants comprised 75 percent of the names.

66. Review of *Ruth Hall*, by Fanny Fern, *Southern Quarterly Review* Jan.–Apr. 1855: 440. Important studies of the development of an urban middle class in antebellum America include Burton Bledstein, *The Culture of Professionalism: The Middle Class and the Development of Higher Education in America* (New York: Norton, 1976); Mary P. Ryan, *Cradle of the Middle Class: The Family in Oneida County New York, 1790–1865* (Cambridge: Cambridge UP, 1981); Karen Halttunen, *Confidence Men and Painted Women: A Study of Middle-Class Culture in America, 1830–1870* (New Haven: Yale UP, 1982); Sellers 364–95; Cindy S. Aron, "The Evolution of the Middle Class," *A Companion to Nineteenth*

Century America, ed. William L. Barney (Maldon, MA: Blackwell, 2001) 178–91; and esp. Stuart M. Blumin, *The Emergence of the Middle Class: Social Experience in the American City, 1760–1900* (Cambridge: Cambridge UP, 1989). Although urging caution, Blumin argues that if we approach this designation, not in terms of ownership of the means of production or solely in terms of income categories, but through structures of shared social and cultural experiences that constitute "class consciousness," the descriptor "middle class" becomes a viable category for differentiating a segment of American society that developed and grew in the forty years before the Civil War.

67. Soltow and Stevens 129, 152; Sellers 367–68; Ryan, *Cradle of the Middle Class* 162–65; and Paul G. Faler, *Mechanics and Manufacturers in the Early Industrial Revolution: Lynn, Massachusetts, 1760–1860* (Albany: State U of New York P, 1981) 195–203.

68. On the multiroom home as a predominantly middle-class and urban development, see Mintz 34–35; and Sam Bass Warner Jr., *The Private City: Philadelphia in the Three Periods of Its Growth* (Philadelphia: U of Pennsylvania P, 1968) 66.

69. For working-class wages in antebellum America, see "Social Statistics," ms. schedules, New York County, 1850, microfilm AFM-95, box 25, New York State Library; *Hunt's Merchants' Magazine* 42 (1860): 752; Robert A. Margo, *Wage and Labor Markets in the United States, 1820–1860* (Chicago: U of Chicago P, 2000) 11–14, 45; and Martin 177. The penurious condition of working-class women was even worse. Most piecework laborers, a class composed mostly of women, earned in the 1830s about $2 a week, while women factory workers did only slightly better at $3 per week (Mary Ryan, *Womanhood in America: From Colonial Times to the Present*, 2nd ed. [New York: New Viewpoints, 1979] 122–23). On the slow growth in free public libraries before the Civil War, see Carpenter 311. On the cost of subscription and social libraries, see Jesse H. Shera, *Foundations of the Public Library: The Origins of the Public Library Movement in New England, 1629–1855* (1949; Hamden, CT: Shoe String Press, 1965) 77.

70. Zboray, *Fictive People* 11–12, 145; Charvat, *Profession of Authorship* 75; Tebbel 243; Johanningsmeier 13; Louise Stevenson, "Homes, Books, and Reading," Casper et al., eds. *The Industrial Book, 1840–1880* 320. The problem of working-class access to books and periodicals went beyond a mere percentage of cost to wages. It was also a function of discretionary income, which was significantly lower among the working class (Blumin 109–14). To underscore these disparities, however, is not to imply that the antebellum working classes were barred from access to print in general and fiction in particular. Besides the availability of some used books, the advent of inexpensive story newspapers in the 1840s provided working-class readers an avenue into print culture. On

this new medium and working-class improvisational strategies for securing access to reading materials, see Ronald Zboray, "Technology and the Character of Community Life in Antebellum America: The Role of Story Papers," *Community and Change in American Religious History*, ed. Leonard I. Sweet (Grand Rapids, MI: Eerdmans, 1993) 185–215; Isabelle Lehuu, *Carnival on the Page: Popular Print Media in Antebellum America* (Chapel Hill: U of North Carolina P, 2000) 44–46, 67–68; Zboray and Zboray, *Everyday Ideas* 116–17, 225–26; and Johanningsmeier 14.

71. Dudden 60–65; Christine Stansell, *City of Women: Sex and Class in New York, 1789-1860* (New York: Knopf, 1986) 272, n. 6; Jeanne Boydston, *Home and Work: Housework, Wages, and the Ideology of Labor in the Early Republic* (New York: Oxford UP, 1990) 17, 77–79. For a general discussion of the difference in leisure time among classes in nineteenth-century America, see Cross 75–76, 124 and throughout.

72. Dudden 144–45.

73. On the increase in leisure time of middle-class women and its reconfiguration as a new kind of labor under the cult of domesticity, see Barbara Welter, "The Cult of True Womanhood, 1820–1860," *American Quarterly* 18 (1966): 51–74; Stansell 159 and throughout; Dudden 7, 127–29, and throughout; Matthaei 157, 178; and Cross 103. On the cult of domesticity as primarily a middle-class urban development, see Nancy Cott, *The Bonds of Womanhood: "Woman's Sphere" in New England, 1780-1835* (New Haven: Yale UP, 1977) 9–13, 50–51, 92–93; Ryan, *Cradle of the Middle Class* 155–65; Fox-Genovese 37–79; and Blumin 179–91.

74. R. Laurence Moore, "Religion, Secularization, and the Shaping of the Culture Industry in Antebellum America," *American Quarterly* 41 (1989): 216–42; Pierre Bourdieu, *Distinction: A Social Critique of the Judgement of Taste*, trans. Richard Nice (Cambridge: Harvard UP, 1984). On the importance of books and reading as cultural capital for the creation of bourgeois identity and the "symbolic ecology" of the middle-class home, see Richard L. Bushman, *The Refinement of America: Persons, Houses, Cities* (New York: Knopf, 1992); Ronald J. Zboray and Mary Saracino Zboray, "Books, Reading, and the World of Goods in Antebellum New England," *American Quarterly* 48 (1996): 587–622; and Lehuu 18, 30.

75. Zboray, *Fictive People* 122, 205.

76. Zboray, *Fictive People* 163, table 15. The question of the representativeness of the holdings of the New York Society Library is also germane. For instance, Caritat's Circulating Library in New York City in the early 1800s listed over a thousand works of fiction among the several thousand volumes in its catalog, figures that put its holdings for fiction closer to 20 percent (Johnson, *History of Libraries* 318).

77. Review of *Ruth Hall*, 440. Literary critics and historians who have assumed a predominantly female audience for antebellum fiction include Nina Baym, *Women's Fiction: A Guide to Novels by and about Women in America, 1820-1870* (Ithaca: Cornell UP, 1978) 12–21; and Ann Douglas, *The Feminization of American Culture* (New York: Knopf, 1977) 227–55.

78. David Leverenz, *Manhood and the American Renaissance* (Ithaca: Cornell UP, 1989) 138; Zboray, *Fictive People* 163–64. Zboray notes, moreover, that although women tended to favor sentimental fiction while men were more likely to read novelists such as Cooper, the library records show that women repeatedly charged novels by Cooper while men regularly checked out sentimental and "feminine" novels (164). On men as an important part of the antebellum reading audience for fiction and periodicals, including those designed primarily for women, see also Mary Lynn Stevens Heininger, *At Home with a Book: Reading in America, 1840-1940* (Rochester: Strong Museum, 1986).

79. *Home Journal* Dec. 23, 1848: 2; *Ladies' Repository* Feb. 1860: 125. Subsequent citations to antebellum periodicals will be given parenthetically in the text. On the hostility toward fiction in the colonial era and in the early republic, see Davidson 38–54; and Terence Martin, *The Instructed Vision: Scottish Common Sense Philosophy and the Origins of American Fiction* (Bloomington: Indiana UP, 1961) 57–76. On the changed attitude toward and acceptance of fiction, see also Baym 26–29.

80. John Frow, "After Life; Texts as Usage," Reception Study Society Second Biannual Conference, University of Missouri, Kansas City, Sept. 29, 2007; Culler, "Prolegomena" 56. See, too, Kintgen 13; and John Fiske and Robert Dawson, "Audiencing Violence," *The Audience and Its Landscape*, ed. James Hay, Lawrence Grossberg, and Ellen Wartella (Boulder, CO: Westview Press, 1996) 297–316.

81. It should be noted that few book historians have taken this attitude toward reviews vis-à-vis letters, memoirs, and marginalia; in fact, most hold the contrary view that the latter are superior as a window into "common" and everyday readers. A few book historians, however, have questioned that supposed advantage, pointing out that letters, memoirs, and even marginalia are hardly unalloyed avenues into readers' private reading practices but are, like reviews, public performances designed to be viewed by others—performances shaped by their own sets of conventions (Rubin 253; Jackson, *Romantic Readers* 301; Kintgen 63–65; Raymond 190; Rose, "How Historians Study Reader Response" 206; and Scott E. Casper, "Antebellum Reading Prescribed and Described," *Perspectives on American Book History: Artifacts and Commentary*, ed. Scott E. Casper, Joanne D. Chaison, and Jeffrey D. Groves [Amherst: U of Massachusetts P, 2002] 160). Others have questioned the typicality of remarks in letters and memoirs as

representative of the practices of the vast majority of historical readers who never self-consciously recorded their responses (e.g., Kintgen 214; Rose, *Intellectual Life* 2; St. Clair 5–6).

82. Wallace 26. The work of Ronald and Mary Zboray is relevant here because, while it questions, it also reinforces my argument about the affinities between periodical reviewers and the middle-class audience for fiction. In their study of reading practices of middle-class families in antebellum Boston, the Zborays argue that these readers had "limited critical vocabularies" for talking about books and that "these readers certainly do not seem to have acquired such a vocabulary from critics" ("'Have You Read. . . ?': Real Readers and Their Responses in Antebellum Boston and Its Regions," *Nineteenth-Century Literature* 52 [1997]: 148). However, the responses the Zborays discover cause them to admit, in a note following their claim about a lack of reviewer influence, that there are substantial "commonalities between the discourse of reviewers and readers" in their sample. Indeed, in another study of antebellum New England readers, the Zborays write that "[i]n an effort to learn more about works . . . readers often turned to reviews" ("Transcendentalism in Print").

83. On the middle-class "ethos" of antebellum periodicals and their roles in the formation of bourgeois culture, see Cheryl D. Bohde, "'Magazines as a Powerful Element of Civilization': An Exploration of the Ideology of Literary Magazines, 1830–1859," *American Periodicals* 1 (1991): 34–45. On the connection between periodicals and the "cultural universe" of the middle class in nineteenth-century America, see also Denning 46.

84. In designating the interpretive practices of reviewers and magazine essayists as components of a "public sphere" of interpretation, I am using that term somewhat analogously to the way Jürgen Habermas has employed it to designate a social or cultural (not physical) space in which access (in theory) is guaranteed to all (*The Structural Transformation of the Public Sphere: An Inquiry into a Category of Bourgeois Culture,* trans. Thomas Burger and Frederick Lawrence [Cambridge: MIT Press, 1989]). Originally developed in the seventeenth century to encompass "the *lecteurs, spectateurs,* and *auditeurs* as the addressees and consumers, and the critics of art and literature" (31), the public sphere had grown and increased in power via the mass culture of print in the nineteenth century. The manner in which that culture was demographically coded by class and location, however, indicates that the public sphere in antebellum America was hardly guaranteed to all.

85. Charvat, *Profession of Authorship* 314, 3.

86. *Edgar Allan Poe: Essays and Reviews,* ed. G. R. Thompson (New York: Library of America, 1984) 1118.

CHAPTER TWO: *Interpretive Strategies and Informed Reading in the Antebellum Public Sphere*

1. On the fear among antebellum educators about the dangerous ramifications of literacy, see Lee Soltow and Edward Stevens, *The Rise of Literacy and the Common School in the United States: A Socioeconomic Analysis to 1870* (Chicago: U of Chicago P, 1981) 60–61. This concern about the social dangers of reading—and particularly novel reading—was shared outside the public sphere as well. For example, Scott E. Casper quotes the following from an 1835 diary entry of one Michael Floy, a resident of Bowery Village, New York: "I fully believe novels and romances have made a greater part of the prostitutes of the world, to say nothing of the many miserable matches" ("Antebellum Reading Prescribed and Described," *Perspectives on American Book History: Artifacts and Commentary*, ed. Scott E. Casper, Joanne D. Chaison, and Jeffrey D. Groves [Amherst: U of Massachusetts P, 2002] 145–46).

2. In this formulation of purpose, American reviewers mirrored the practice of British magazinists and critics, who, as Patrick Parrinder points out, "saw themselves as middlemen in an essentially corporate process of production and consumption" (*Authors and Authority: English and American Criticism, 1750–1900* [New York; MacMillan, 1991] 121).

3. In analyzing the public forum of periodical responses to fiction, I treat reviewers and critics as one group even though at times in this period a distinction was made between the two. An 1853 article in *Putnam's Magazine*, e.g., defined reviewing as an examination of a specific work or works but designated criticism as a more theoretical or general treatment of literary genres or literature as a whole. However, John Paul Pritchard points out that "this distinction . . . was almost completely ignored in general practice" (*Literary Wise Men of Gotham: Criticism in New York, 1815–1860* [Baton Rouge: Louisiana State UP, 1963] 85).

4. William Charvat was one of the first to define antebellum literary criticism, especially in periodicals, as exercising a self-appointed "watchdog" function (*The Origins of American Critical Thought, 1810–1835* [1936; New York: Russell and Russell, 1968] 7–26 and 107). Hazel Dickson-Garcia has applied the same term to antebellum journalism as a whole, arguing that from 1830 to 1850 "the emphasis on the press's 'watchdog' function . . . grew" as a result of a shift in the press's role from overt political partisanship to an "information or news role," which "emphasized . . . providing the individual with information useful in life's conduct" (*Journalistic Standards in Nineteenth-Century America* [Madison: U of Wisconsin P, 1989] 106–7). On the regulatory tendency of ante-

bellum periodicals in general and reviews in particular and their self-conception as conservators of civilization, culture, and literature, see also Cheryl D. Bohde, "'Magazines as Powerful Element of Civilization': An Exploration of the Ideology of Literary Magazines, 1830–1860," *American Periodicals* 1 (1991): 34–45; Nina Baym, *Novels, Readers, and Reviewers: Responses to Fiction in Antebellum America* (Ithaca: Cornell UP, 1984) 30; and Terence Martin, *The Instructed Vision: Scottish Common Sense Philosophy and the Origins of American Fiction* (Bloomington: Indiana UP, 1961) 11–12 and throughout.

5. *New York Mirror,* qtd. in Pritchard 87.

6. A number of previous studies have shed substantial light on the practices of antebellum critics and reviewers, and I have found much of their work useful in my discussion in this chapter of the public codes of interpretation. This foundational work includes Charvat's *Origins of American Critical Thought*; Pritchard's *Literary Wise Men of Gotham*; Martin's *The Instructed Vision*; John Stafford's *The Literary Criticism of "Young America": A Study in the Relationship of Politics and Literature, 1837–1850* (Berkeley and Los Angeles: U of California P, 1952); Richard H. Fogle's "Organic Form in American Criticism: 1840–1870," *The Development of American Literary Criticism,* ed. Floyd Stovall (Chapel Hill: U of North Carolina P, 1955), 75–111; Perry Miller's *The Raven and the Whale: The War of Words and Wit in the Era of Poe and Melville* (New York: Harcourt Brace, 1956); Sidney Moss's *Poe's Literary Battles: The Critic in the Context of His Literary Milieu* (Durham: Duke UP, 1963); and, as the most wide-ranging and sustained work in this group, Nina Baym's *Novels, Readers, and Reviewers.* Several of the general categories I focus on to examine the interpretive strategies of reviewers—particularly plot, character, narrative, morality, and instruction— parallel categories discussed in several of these studies, primarily because these *were* the areas to which reviewers repeatedly turned their attention, both as formal elements they ascribed to fiction and as categories in which their interpretive moves were played out. While building on these previous studies, however, my analysis seeks to move in a different direction or pursue substantially different ends. For one thing, while this scholarship has concentrated on particular critical battles, the intellectual basis of antebellum criticism, or the poetics of reviewers, my focus is on reviewers' interpretive strategies as they entailed assumptions about the way reading should proceed, the type of fiction readers that existed, the ways fiction engaged the audience, and the roles it implied for its readers. Only Baym has addressed briefly the second and third of these four dimensions of antebellum reviewing, but it has been in the form of examining reviewers' conceptions of the work fiction did or should do on its readers. While that element inevitably is part of my concern, my emphasis is on reviewers' ideas about the work readers should do on fiction. Moreover, in my study as a whole, I am

less interested in the interpretive practices of reviewers in and of themselves than in the way this antebellum reading formation constituted fictional texts that have come down to us (whether as well known or neglected) in forms that owe their shape and significance, in one degree or another, to reception events in the antebellum public sphere.

7. Baym extensively discusses reviewers' emphasis on the primacy of entertainment as a function of their conception that plot was the defining feature of the novel (*Novels, Readers, and Reviewers* 24, 63–82).

8. These three functions, according to Steven Mailloux, mark the categories in which all communicative conventions fall (*Interpretive Conventions: The Reader in the Study of American Fiction* [Ithaca: Cornell UP, 1982] 126–39).

9. On this characterization of fiction readers in eighteenth-century English reviews, see Joseph F. Bartolomeo, *A New Species of Criticism: Eighteenth-Century Discourse on the Novel* (Newark: U of Delaware P; London: Associated U Presses, 1994) 114–16. Regarding the broader impact of British periodicals on antebellum reviewers in the United States, see Charvat 28 ff.

10. On nineteenth-century working-class Americans and fiction reading, the best study remains Michael Denning's *Mechanic Accents: Dime Novels and Working-Class Culture in America* (London: Verso, 1987).

11. An interesting implication of this assumption is that antebellum reviewers, though not invoking the term, anticipated Gerald Prince's 1970s concept of the "narratee" ("Introduction to the Study of the Narratee," *Poetique* 14 [1973]: 177–96).

12. Pritchard, *Literary Wise Men of Gotham*; Baym, *Novels, Readers, and Reviewers*. See also the other studies cited in note 6.

13. On this point, see Pritchard 78–81; and Baym, *Novels, Readers, and Reviewers* 24, 65–69. Pritchard points out, however, that this assumption about the primacy of plot was being challenged in this period through increased emphasis on character as equally important.

14. Roland Barthes, *S/Z*, trans. Richard Miller (New York: Hill and Wang, 1974) 19, 75. Although Barthes identifies this code as a function of the text itself, it is more accurate to say that it is a strategy readers bring to bear to decipher the discourse of the text. The same is true of Barthes's other codes.

15. For antebellum reviews of *The Scarlet Letter*, see J. Donald Crowley, ed., *Hawthorne: The Critical Heritage* (London: Routledge and Kegan Paul, 1970) 155–64.

16. On this terminological morass, see Michael Davitt Bell, *The Development of American Romance: The Sacrifice of Relation* (Chicago: U of Chicago P, 1980) 3–36; and Nina Baym, "Concepts of the Romance in Hawthorne's America," *Nineteenth-Century Fiction* 38 (1984): 426–43. For a contrary view of antebel-

lum genre designations, particularly as they involve a "notable consistency" in reviewer distinctions between romance and novel, see G. R. Thompson and Eric Carl Link, *Neutral Ground: New Traditionalism and the American Romance Controversy* (Baton Rouge: Louisiana State UP, 1999) 85–104.

17. On these three as common categories in antebellum reviews, see Baym, *Novels, Readers, and Reviewers* 196–223, 235–41. Baym also includes as antebellum genre categories metropolitan novels and highly wrought novels, but my own research indicates that *metropolitan novel* was a designation rarely used. By contrast, *highly wrought* was less an adjective for designating a genre category and more a judgmental descriptor applicable to any novel that was viewed as sensational, excessively melodramatic, or morally suspect. That is, one could have highly wrought historical fiction or a highly wrought advocacy novel.

18. For related and in some cases parallel discussion of reviewers' conceptions of advocacy novels, see Baym, *Novels, Readers, and Reviewers* 213–23.

19. Baym, *Novels, Readers, and Reviewers* 61. Recently, Suzy Anger has made a similar claim about British reviewers in the first half of the nineteenth century (*Victorian Interpretation* [Ithaca: Cornell UP, 2005] 132). By contrast, John Paul Pritchard asserted, almost twenty years before Baym's remark, that New York magazinists of this era believed "the proper way of telling a story, however it might be stated, required that it have some degree of meaning" (65).

20. In reading for meaning and idea, reviewers were engaging in a form of response that antebellum readers as a whole may well have shared. On this parallel, a remark by Ronald and Mary Zboray about antebellum New Englanders is especially telling. Based on data from over a thousand letters, diaries, and other manuscripts, the Zborays assert, "Few populations have made literature and the ideas they got from it as much a part of their daily lives" (*Everyday Ideas: Socioliterary Experience among Antebellum New Englanders* [Knoxville: U of Tennessee P, 2006] xvi).

21. Wolfgang Iser, *The Act of Reading: A Theory of Aesthetic Experience* (Baltimore: Johns Hopkins UP, 1978) 173.

22. Antebellum periodical readers could have gained a familiarity with such emblematic reading of flowers from magazines themselves. See, e.g., the articles on the "Language of Flowers" in the *Home Journal* May 9, 1846: 4 (no pag.) and July 12, 1851: 4 (no pag.). For a relevant discussion of the widespread familiarity with "flower symbolism" (or more accurately, the emblematic use of flower imagery) among antebellum readers and its relevance to fiction reading, see Susan Harris, *Nineteenth-Century American Women's Novels: Interpretive Strategies* (Cambridge: Cambridge UP, 1990) 80–82.

23. Roland Barthes, *Mythologies*, trans. Annette Lavers (1957; New York: Hill and Wang, 1972) 155.

24. Pritchard 64–68; Baym, *Novels, Readers, and Reviewers* 124–28.

25. Baym, *Novels, Readers, and Reviewers* 119. Over the last seven to eight years, other scholars also have pointed out this antebellum equation of—or tendency to conflate—authors and fictional narrators: Barbara Hochman, *Getting at the Author: Reimagining Books and Reading in the Age of American Realism* (Amherst: U of Massachusetts P, 2001) 12–15; Cree LeFavour, "*Jane Eyre* Fever: Deciphering the Astonishing Success of Charlotte Brontë in Antebellum America," *Book History* 7 (2004): 115–27; and Susan S. Williams, "Authors and Literary Authorship," *The Industrial Book, 1840–1880,* vol. 3 of *The History of the Book in America,* ed. Scott E. Casper, Jeffrey Groves, Stephen W. Nissenbaum, and Michael Winship (Chapel Hill: U of North Carolina P, 2007) 105–6.

26. Although *auto-biographical* was the common antebellum designation, occasionally the more modern term *first-person* was employed. Poe, e.g., used it in one of his New York Literati sketches in *Godey's.* See *Edgar Allan Poe: Essays and Reviews,* ed. G. R. Thompson (New York: Library of America, 1984) 1209.

27. This claim is made by Baym, *Novels, Readers, and Reviewers* 147–48. One reason for the absence among reviewers of the very term *unreliable narrator* may be that it was not invented until the second half of the twentieth century, according to Wayne Booth, who has asserted that he coined that descriptor in the "late fifties" ("Narrative Theory: Two Stories," "Looking Backward, Looking Forward: MLA Members Speak," *PMLA* 115 [2000]: 1992–93).

28. On the early-to-mid-nineteenth-century assumption that reading (through) fiction involved getting to know the author, see Hochman 11–28.

29. Pritchard 84, 87–88, and throughout. The founding document for this method of response appears to have been George Allen's "Reproductive Criticism," *New York Review* 1838: 49–75. Regarding the alternative designations for this form of response, as well as its prominence among magazinists and critics of the "Young America" movement, see Stafford 39–53.

30. For this idea among reviewers, see also Pritchard 72, who briefly discusses similar reminders in the *New York Mirror* and the *Knickerbocker Magazine.*

31. For related discussion of antebellum valorization of verisimilitude in conceptions of fictional characterization, see Pritchard 71–76; and Baym, *Novels, Readers, and Reviewers* 90, and throughout. I should note here that the remainder of my discussion of strategies shaping informed response to character in antebellum America parallels several of Baym's and Pritchard's points. What I have sought to emphasize, however, are different dimensions of these principles and, especially, the way they functioned as interpretive strategies for guiding and promoting the public formation of "informed" response at that time.

32. Regarding nineteenth-century magazinists' efforts to empower, rather than discipline, women readers, see Jennifer Phegley, *Educating the Proper*

Woman Reader: Victorian Family Literary Magazines and the Cultural Health of the Nation (Columbus: Ohio State UP, 2004) 2, 27, and 31–69.

33. Daniel R. Schwarz, *The Humanistic Tradition: Critical Theories of the English Novel from James to Hillis Miller* (Philadelphia: U of Pennsylvania P, 1986).

CHAPTER THREE: *"These Days of Double Dealing"*

1. *Writings in the* Broadway Journal, vols. 3 and 4 of *The Collected Writings of Edgar Allan Poe*, ed. Burton Pollin (New York: Gordian, 1986) 3: 25. Poe reiterated this idea in one of his Marginalia pieces in *Graham's* in Dec. 1846 (*Edgar Allan Poe: Essays and Reviews*, ed. G. R. Thompson [New York: Library of America, 1984] 1414, hereafter cited parenthetically as *ER*). On Poe's conception of the importance of periodicals, see also Kevin J. Hayes, *Poe and the Printed Word* (Cambridge: Cambridge UP, 2000) 93, 115. Regarding Poe's career as a magazinist within the antebellum literary marketplace, see Jonathan Hartmann, *The Marketing of Edgar Allan Poe* (New York: Routledge, 2008) 2–10.

2. Poe to J. P. Kennedy, June 21, 1841, *The Letters of Edgar Allan Poe*, ed. John Ward Ostrom, 2 vols. (New York: Gordian, 1966) 1: 164. Poe repeated this claim in letters to Irving, Longfellow, and Fitz-Greene Halleck (*Letters* 1: 162–70).

3. See also the review of Cooper's *Wyandotté*, in which Poe equates popularity in fiction with the ephemeral and a feeling of "something very nearly akin to contempt" (*ER* 480).

4. Classic studies of Poe as critical maverick include Perry Miller, *The Raven and the Whale: The War of Words and Wits in the Era of Poe and Melville* (New York: Harcourt, Brace, 1956); Sidney P. Moss, *Poe's Literary Battles* (Durham: Duke UP, 1963); and Robert D. Jacobs, *Poe: Journalist and Critic* (Baton Rouge: Louisiana State UP, 1969).

5. Poe's public battles with reviewers, particularly from New England, began as early 1836 with his Drake-Halleck review in the *Southern Literary Messenger* (see *ER* 505–39). But his plan for the critical component of the aborted Folio Club Tales, which he explained in 1833 was "intended as a burlesque upon criticism," indicates that at the very start of his career Poe conceived himself in a fight with the critical "establishment" (Poe to Joseph T. Buckingham and Edwin Buckingham, May 4, 1833, *Letters* 1: 52).

6. J. Lasley Dameron, "Poe, Plagiarism, and American Periodicals," *Poe Studies* 30, no. 1/2 (June 1997): 40. See also Meredith McGill, *American Literature and the Culture of Reprinting: 1834–53* (Philadelphia: U of Pennsylvania P, 2003) 199.

7. On the currency of this idea among antebellum reviewers, see Nina Baym,

Novels, Readers, and Reviewers: Responses to Fiction in Antebellum America (Ithaca: Cornell UP, 1984) 35–36, 40.

8. *Writings in the* Broadway Journal 3: 67; *Complete Works of Edgar Allan Poe*, ed. James A. Harrison, 17 vols. (New York: DeFau, 1902) 8: 71. On Poe's belief that magazinists were to serve as guides and mediators for the reading public, see James M. Hutchisson, *Poe* (Jackson: UP of Mississippi, 2005) 110.

9. *Complete Works* 15: 200.

10. *Complete Works* 10: 98.

11. Poe's objections to immoral and sensational fiction also have been pointed out by David S. Reynolds, *Beneath the American Renaissance: The Subversive Imagination in the Age of Emerson and Melville* (New York: Knopf, 1988), who observes that "dismay at the wildness and repulsiveness" of some American fiction "is a common thread running through much of Poe's literary criticism" (227–28).

12. *Complete Works* 8:42. Regarding Poe's view on didacticism in fiction, Michael Allen in his study of Poe and English periodicals pointed out that "Poe's essentially conservative tendency" caused him "to see fiction as a species of learning" (*Poe and the British Magazine Tradition* [New York: Oxford UP, 1969] 84.

13. Although Poe articulated his theories about effect and aesthetic power in the 1840s, even earlier in his career he espoused those principles. See, e.g., his review of Dickens in the *Southern Literary Messenger* in June 1836 (*ER* 204–7). For a parallel concern with effect among antebellum reviewers, see Baym 141. One reason for this convergence between Poe and other reviewers may have been that all were drawing on a common source: August Wilhelm Schlegel. Arthur Hobson Quinn has suggested that articles on Schlegel in the *North American Review* "may well have given Poe direction" for his theory of effect (*Edgar Allan Poe: A Critical Biography* [Baltimore: Johns Hopkins UP, 1941] 243). For discussions of Schlegel as a source for Poe's ideas, see Jacobs 115–16; Kenneth Silverman, *Edgar Allan Poe: Mournful and Never-Ending Remembrance* (New York: Harper Collins, 1991) 166; and Thomas S. Hansen and Burton R. Pollin, *The German Face of Edgar Allan Poe* (Columbia, SC: Camden House, 1995) 91–94.

14. Stephen Railton, *Authorship and Audience: Literary Performance in the American Renaissance* (Princeton: Princeton UP, 1991) 133, 138. In also noting that Poe's conception of authorship "suggests a man who raged above all for control," James Hutchisson speculates that such an idea was "as much a cover-up as anything else for Poe's lack of control" (169–70).

15. On Poe's concern over the way audience activities within the new mass market of fiction threatened mastery over the writer, see Michael J. S. Williams, *A World of Words: Language and Displacement in the Fiction of Edgar Allan Poe* (Durham: Duke UP, 1988) 45–49. Williams argues that Poe located the danger

in the nature of language itself, specifically in the "potential surplus of meaning that threatens to overflow the constraints of intention" (48). Though such a conclusion is partially accurate, it does not account for the way Poe sought to produce surplus, slippery, and unstable meanings as a means of maintaining his ascendancy over the audience. An analogous argument to Williams's appears in Jonathan Auerbach, "Poe's Other Double: The Reader in the Fiction," *Criticism* 24 (1982): 343.

16. Over the last two decades, several important studies have explored the anxiety antebellum authors, both popular and canonical, felt in depending upon audience demands and fulfilling audience expectations in the new literary marketplace. See Michael Newbury, *Figuring Authorship in Antebellum America* (Stanford: Stanford UP, 1997); Kenneth Dauber, *The Idea of Authorship in Antebellum America: Democratic Poetics from Franklin to Melville* (Madison: U of Wisconsin P, 1990); and Railton. An earlier benchmark study of this issue for antebellum women writers is Mary Kelley's *Private Women, Public Stage: Literary Domesticity in Nineteenth-Century America* (New York: Oxford UP, 1984). For a discussion of similar anxieties among early nineteenth-century British writers, see Lucy Newlyn, *Reading, Writing, and Romanticism: The Anxiety of Reception* (Oxford: Oxford UP, 2000).

17. Several critics have read Poe's tales as thematizations or allegories of his battles with the reader. See, esp., Williams; Railton 132–51; and J. Gerald Kennedy, *Poe, Death, and the Life of Writing* (New Haven: Yale UP, 1987) 116–17. For a different but parallel view, see Hartmann, who argues that Poe conceived the writer's relation with readers not so much as a battle but as a two-pronged engagement, which involved overtly pleasing and covertly "diddling" the audience (31–33).

18. Terence Whalen, *Edgar Allan Poe and the Masses: The Political Economy of Literature in Antebellum American* (Princeton: Princeton UP, 1999) 91–92; Benjamin Fisher, *Cambridge Introduction to Edgar Allan Poe* (Cambridge: Cambridge UP, 2008) 57. Other proponents of this second argument include Louis A. Renza, "Poe's Secret Autobiography," *The American Renaissance Reconsidered,* ed. Walter Benn Michaels and Donald Pease (Baltimore: Johns Hopkins UP, 1985) 67; David R. Saliba, *A Psychology of Fear: The Nightmare Formula of Edgar Allan Poe* (Lanham, MD: UP of America, 1980) 4; Peter Garrett, *Gothic Reflections: Narrative Force in Nineteenth-Century Fiction* (Ithaca: Cornell UP, 2003) 37; and Allen 191. Interestingly, earlier in his study (36) Allen also espouses the former argument about specific texts targeted to each audience.

19. Poe's growing conviction about the union of imagination and analysis as a desideratum of the artistic experience is discussed in David Ketterer, *The Rationale of Deception in Poe* (Baton Rouge: Louisiana State UP, 1979) 238.

20. Williams 65.

21. *Southern Literary Messenger* May 1835, *Baltimore Republican* July 10, 1835, and *Baltimore Gazette* Aug. 7, 1835, qtd. in Dwight Thomas and David K. Jackson, *The Poe Log: A Documentary Life of Edgar Allan Poe, 1809–1849* (Boston: Hall, 1987) 155, 169, 164, respectively. Subsequent citations to reviews reprinted or excerpted in the *Poe Log* are given parenthetically by their original dates, followed by *PL* and the corresponding pages in the *Log*. For quotations directly from magazines, this and all subsequent chapters follow the method used in chapter 2 by providing parenthetical citations by periodical date and original page numbers.

22. *New York Corsair* Dec. 1839, rpt. in *Edgar Allan Poe: Critical Assessments*, ed. Graham Clarke, 4 vols. (Mourtfield, UK: Helm, 1991) 2: 102.

23. On the absence of the term *gothic* in the lexicon of antebellum reviewers' comments on fiction, see Baym 201. Michael Gamer has pointed out that in early nineteenth-century Britain, *gothic* had also not taken on its modern meaning as a genre category (*Romanticism and the Gothic: Genre, Reception, and Canon Formation* [Cambridge: Cambridge UP, 2000] 2, 49.

24. *Compiler* remark as reprinted in *Southern Literary Messenger* Apr. 1836: 345.

25. These characters are from, respectively, "Duc de L'Omlette," "A Tale of Jerusalem," "Loss of Breath," "Lionizing," and "King Pest."

26. Such parallels were well documented by modern Poe scholars during the time when source-and-influence studies were central to the profession. Most of those parallels are included in the notes to the tales in *Tales and Sketches*, vols. 2–3 of *Collected Works of Edgar Allan Poe*, ed. Thomas Ollive Mabbott, 3 vols. (Cambridge: Belknap Press of Harvard UP, 1978).

27. On the subgenre of Germanic satire and its extent in the early nineteenth century, see Bruce I. Weiner, "Poe and the *Blackwood's* Tale of Sensation," *Poe and His Times: The Artist and His Milieu*, ed. Benjamin Franklin Fisher IV (Baltimore: Poe Society, 1990) 56–57; and G. R. Thompson, *Poe's Fiction: Romantic Irony in the Gothic Tales* (Madison: U of Wisconsin P, 1973) 73. Although Thompson refers to this subgenre by the modern designation of "gothic satire," Weiner calls such tales "burlesques of . . . the kind of sensationalism *Blackwood's* promoted" in its tales of "German metaphysics."

28. Mabbott, *Tales and Sketches* 2:18. All subsequent references to Poe's tales will be to this edition and will be given parenthetically in the discussion.

29. Thompson 55–56, 64–65.

30. Critics who have read "Metzengerstein" as a spoof or gothic hoax include Thompson 52–65; Edward H. Davidson, *Poe: A Critical Study* (Cambridge: Belknap Press of Harvard UP, 1957) 137–38; and Stuart Levine and Susan Levine,

"Slapstick Gothic," *The Short Fiction of Edgar Allan Poe,* ed. Stuart Levine and Susan Levine (Indianapolis: Bobbs-Merrill, 1976) 294–95. For contrary arguments for the seriousness of the story as gothic fiction, see Quinn 192–93; Edd Winfield Parks, *Edgar Allan Poe as Literary Critic* (Athens: U of Georgia P, 1964) 24; and Benjamin Franklin Fisher, "Poe's 'Metzengerstein': Not a Hoax," *American Literature* 42 (1971): 487–94.

31. *Courier and Enquirer* remark as reprinted in *Southern Literary Messenger* Dec. 1835, *PL* 180.

32. Paulding to White, Mar. 3, 1836, *The Letters of James Kirk Paulding,* ed. Ralph M. Aderman (Madison: U of Wisconsin P, 1962) 173–74.

33. *Southern Literary Messenger* June 1835: 335, rpt. in *Edgar Allan Poe: The Critical Heritage,* ed. Ian Walker (London: Routledge, 1986) 81. Philip Cooke, one of Poe's correspondents, pointed to the same trait in a letter to Poe years later (Cooke to Poe, Aug. 4, 1846, *Complete Works* 17: 262).

34. Kennedy to Poe, Feb. 9, 1836, *Complete Works* 17: 28.

35. James M. Garnett to Thomas Willis White, June 22, 1835 *PL* 159; on the Harpers' judgment, see Quinn 250–51.

36. Poe to Kennedy, Feb. 11, 1836, *Letters* 1: 84; Poe to Hill, Sept. 2, 1836, *Letters* 1: 103.

37. Poe to White, Apr. 30, 1835, *Letters* 1: 57–58.

38. Kent P. Ljungquist, "Poe in the Boston Newspapers: Three More Reviews," *English Language Notes* 31, no. 2 (Dec. 1993): 45.

39. Poe to Snodgrass, Nov. 11, 1839, *Letters* 1: 121.

40. "Preface," *Tales of the Grotesque and Arabesque,* Mabbott, *Tales and Sketches* 2: 473–74. Quotations in the next paragraph are also from these pages.

41. McGill 198.

42. The two other stories with major revisions, mostly in the form of deletions, were "A Decided Loss" (retitled as "Loss of Breath") and "The Bargain Lost" (retitled as "Bon-Bon"). For the changes in these two stories as well as detailed information about alterations in the other twenty-three stories collected in *Tales of the Grotesque and Arabesque,* see the bibliographical notes in Mabbott, *Tales and Sketches* 2: 18–471.

43. This narrative as the central paradigm for Poe's career goes back at least as far as Fred Lewis Pattee's discussion of Poe's fiction in *The Development of the American Short Story* (New York: Harper, 1923) 124–37. For this paradigm and its prevalence, see also William Howarth, introduction, *Twentieth-Century Interpretations of Poe's Tales,* ed. William Howarth (Englewood Cliffs, NJ: Prentice-Hall, 1971) 7. In his recent *Cambridge Introduction to Edgar Allan Poe,* Benjamin Fisher subscribes to the view that Poe began as a writer of comic fiction, but Fisher also admits that these early tales "elicited mixed responses from

readers, who were puzzled by the mix of comic and Gothic elements" (50–58). My conviction is that readers before 1839 were not puzzled but instead interpretively privileged the comedic as the distinguishing mode of Poe's tales.

44. For "Hans Pfaall," see Ketterer 84–85; for "Metzengerstein" see the works cited in note 32 above. Those who view "The Assignation" as serious include Pattee 123, 128–29; Daniel Hoffman, *Poe Poe Poe Poe Poe Poe Poe* (Garden City, NY: Doubleday, 1972) 218; Benjamin Franklin Fisher, "To 'The Assignation' from 'The Visionary' (Part Two): The Revisions and Related Matters," *Library Chronicle* 40 (1976): 221–51; and Mabbott, *Tales and Sketches* 2: 149. Comic readings of the tale include Davidson 500; Richard Benton, "Is Poe's 'The Assignation' a Hoax?" *Nineteenth-Century Fiction* 18 (1963): 193–97; and Thompson 126–30. For the double view of "Ms. Found in a Bottle," see Fisher, "To 'The Assignation' from 'The Visionary'" 221; and Donald B. Stauffer, "The Two Styles of Poe's 'Ms. Found in a Bottle,'" *Style* 1 (1967): 107–20. Other modern scholars who have contributed to the debate over whether the Folio Club Tales are all comic or a mixture of serious and comic include Allen 124–26; J. S. Wilson, "The Devil Was in It," *American Mercury* 24 (1931): 215–20; Jay B. Hubbell, "The Literary Apprenticeship of Edgar Allan Poe," *Southern Literary Journal* 2 (1969): 99–105; Fisher, *Cambridge Companion to Edgar Allan Poe* 52–55; and Hartmann 59–81. Hartmann coins the term *light gothic* to designate the genre of the Folio Club tales (59).

45. Hoffman 210. See also Sidney Lind, "Poe and Mesmerism," *PMLA* 62 (1947): 1094; and Bernard Drabek, "'Tarr and Fether'—Poe and Abolitionism," *ATQ* 14 (1972): 177–84. About these diametrically opposed interpretations, Benjamin F. Fisher recently observed that "[d]ebates over what is serious, what comic, in Poe's fiction continue to the present day" ("Poe and the Gothic Tradition," *Cambridge Companion to Edgar Allan Poe*, ed. Kevin J. Hayes [Cambridge: Cambridge UP, 2002] 80).

46. Benjamin Franklin Fisher, "Playful 'Germanism' in 'The Fall of the House of Usher,'" *Ruined Eden of the Present: Hawthorne, Melville, Poe*, ed. G. R. Thompson and Virgil L. Lokke (West Lafayette, IN: Purdue UP, 1981) 355–74; George S. Soule Jr., "Byronism in Poe's 'Metzengerstein' and 'William Wilson,'" *ESQ: A Journal of the American Renaissance* 24 (1978): 158–61; Clark Griffith, "Poe's 'Ligeia' and the English Romantics," *University of Toronto Quarterly* 24 (1954–1955): 8–25; and James M. Cox, "Edgar Poe: Style as Pose," *Virginia Quarterly Review* 44 (1968): 67–89.

47. The most sustained case for such readings of Poe's tales is by Thompson, who claims that "the burlesque, or ambiguously burlesque, intent is constant in Poe's fiction" (137). See also Williams, who asserts that "almost all his texts are shot through with what we might call parodic self-criticism" (66).

48. Stuart Levine, introduction, Levine and Levine, *The Short Fiction of Edgar Allan Poe* xix.

49. On the decline in popularity of gothic fiction, see Allen 139. More telling are the statistics of Oral Sumner Coad, "The Gothic Element in American Literature Before 1835," *Journal of English and Germanic Philology* 24 (1925): 72–93. Despite his claim that gothic literature enjoyed "one of the most prolific periods in America before reaching its apogee in the hands of Poe and Hawthorne," Coad's data tell a different story: Of the sixty poems, works of fiction, and plays he lists, only ten appeared after 1830.

50. Greg Laderman, *Sacred Remains: American Attitudes Toward Death, 1799–1883* (New Haven: Yale UP, 1996) esp. 24, 74–76.

51. On increases in urban violence, particularly in the form of riots during this time, see Michael Feldberg, *The Turbulent Era: Riot and Disorder in Jacksonian America* (New York: Oxford UP, 1980) 4–5. For the convergence of this rioting and the effects of the 1837 panic, see Thomas R. Heitela, *Manifest Design: Anxious Aggrandisement in Late Jacksonian America* (Ithaca: Cornell UP, 1985) 109.

52. M. J. Heale, *American Anticommunism: Combating the Enemy Within, 1830–1970* (Baltimore: Johns Hopkins UP, 1990), 8.

53. The link among fear of Catholic conspiracies, concerns about Irish and German immigration, and "Gothic alarmism" in the United States in the late 1830s and early 1840s is discussed in Jenny Franchot, *Roads to Rome: The Antebellum Protestant Encounter with Catholicism* (Berkeley and Los Angeles: U of California P, 1994) 101–2.

54. Clarke, *Edgar Allan Poe: Critical Assessments* 2: 78, 81, 76, 77.

55. See, e.g., the *Saturday Courier* Aug. 4, 1838, *PL* 250.

56. For the *Knickerbocker* review, see Clarke, *Edgar Allan Poe: Critical Assessments* 2: 76. On reviewer uncertainty over how to read *Pym*, see also Fisher, *Cambridge Introduction to Edgar Allan Poe* 114. For a more detailed discussion of the antebellum reception of *Pym*, see Burton Pollin, "Poe's *Narrative of Arthur Gordon Pym* and the Contemporary Reviews," *Studies in American Fiction* 1 (1974): 37–56.

57. *Complete Works* 8: 231.

58. Heath to Poe, Sept. 12, 1839, *PL* 270; Irving to Poe, Nov. 6, 1839, *PL* 275.

59. Cooke to Poe, Dec. 19, 1839, *PL* 283.

60. Charles Sellers, *The Market Revolution: Jacksonian America, 1815–1846* (New York: Oxford UP, 1991) 251 ff.

61. This expression of Glanville's idea by the narrator occurs only in the initial 1839 version of the tale (see Mabbott, *Tales and Sketches* 2: 318 n.).

62. Twentieth-century interpretations of the narrator of "Ligeia" as unreliable have been common, beginning with Roy Basler, "The Interpretation of 'Ligeia,'" *College English* 5 (1944): 363–72. See, e.g., Joel Porte, *The Romance in America* (Middleton, CT: Wesleyan UP, 1969); James W. Gargano, "Poe's 'Ligeia': Dream and Destruction," *College English* 23 (1962): 335–42; Terry Heller, *The Delights of Terror: An Aesthetics of the Tale of Terror* (Urbana: U of Illinois P, 1987) 114–26; and Thompson 80–82.

63. Cooke to Poe, Sept. 16, 1839, *Complete Works* 17: 49–50.

64. Several Poe critics have argued for a formalist version of this match by asserting that the disoriented narrators of "Ligeia," "Usher," and "William Wilson" serve as textual models for Poe's ideal reader: e.g., Heller 170; and Ronald Bieganowski, "The Self-Consuming Narrator in Poe's 'Ligeia' and 'Usher,'" *American Literature* 60 (1988): 185.

65. Poe to Cooke, Sept. 21, 1839, *Letters* 1: 118. For these revisions and continuities in "Ligeia," see the variorum edition in Mabbott, *Tales and Sketches* 2: 308–34.

66. Poe to Cooke, Sept. 21, 1839, *Letters* 1: 118; Poe to Thomas, Nov. 23, 1840, *Letters* 1: 148.

67. Hoffman 197. Hoffman's claim, however, may be less than definitive, given the number of different targets modern critics have put forward as the object of the story's satire. Cf. Reynolds 527; William Whipple, "Poe's Political Satire," *University of Toronto Studies in English* 35 (1956): 81–95; Ronald T. Curran, "The Fashionable Thirties: Poe's Satire in 'The Man That Was Used Up,'" *Markham Review* 8 (1978): 14–20; Richard Alekka, "'The Man That Was Used Up': Further Notes on Poe's Satirical Targets," *Poe Studies* 12 (1979): 36; and Gary Lindberg, *The Confidence Man in American Literature* (New York: Oxford UP, 1982) 53–54.

68. Silverman points out that "Julius Rodman," which appeared over six issues in the *Broadway Journal*, succeeded "well enough as a hoax . . . to have been cited as factual in an 1840 U.S. Senate document on the Oregon Territory" (*Edgar Allan Poe* 147).

69. Poe to Joseph E. Snodgrass, Sept. 19, 1841, *Letters* 1: 183. For a reading of "Never Bet the Devil Your Head" as a parody of reform literature, see Reynolds 528.

70. Poe to Philip Cooke, Aug. 9, 1846, *Letters* 2: 328.

71. *American Review* Sept. 1845, Clarke, *Edgar Allan Poe: Critical Assessments* 2: 162–63.

72. Poe to Philip Cooke, Aug. 9, 1846, *Letters* 2: 328–29.

73. Norman Dain, *Concepts of Insanity in the United States, 1789-1865* (New Brunswick, NJ: Rutgers UP, 1964) 75, but see also 49–50, 73–74. A more recent

discussion of these developments and their relation to narratives of crime in antebellum America comes in Karen Halttunen, *Murder Most Foul: The Killer and
the American Gothic Imagination* (Cambridge: Harvard UP, 1998) 215–17.

74. On the relation among the Mercer trial, Poe's familiarity with the insanity
defense, and these two stories, see John Cleman, "Irresistible Impulses: Edgar
Allan Poe and the Insanity Defense," *American Literature* 63 (1991): 623–40.
Although Cleman's analysis is substantially different from mine, in that he uses
this historical context to argue that Poe's two stories *are about* these issues, his
discussion has aided my thinking about the context for the antebellum reception
of these tales.

75. On the growth of crime fiction on the 1840s, see David Brion Davis, *Homicide in American Fiction, 1790–1860: A Study in Social Values* (Ithaca: Cornell UP, 1957) 259.

76. *Graham's* Sept. 1845, Clarke, *Edgar Allan Poe: Critical Assessments* 2:
166.

77. Reynolds 176.

78. Ketterer 102.

79. Jonathan Elmer, *Reading at the Social Limit: Affect, Mass Culture, and
Edgar Allan Poe* (Stanford: Stanford UP, 1995) 129.

80. Halttunen 145.

81. On the temperance movement as a development of bourgeois ideology for
promoting social discipline, particularly to meet the needs of capitalist transformation, see Sellers 259–68.

82. On the advent of the sympathetic view of the alcoholic in the 1840s, see
T. J. Matheson, "Poe's 'The Black Cat' as a Critique of Temperance Literature,"
Mosaic 19, no. 3 (Summer 1986): 70.

83. *Literary Annual Register* 1845, Walker, *Edgar Allan Poe: The Critical
Heritage* 199.

84. *Blackwood's* Nov. 1847, Walker, Edgar *Allan Poe: The Critical Heritage*
220.

85. Poe to Cooke, Aug. 9, 1846, *Letters* 2: 236.

86. Poe to Duyckinck, Mar. 8, 1849, *Letters* 2: 433.

87. Poe to Duyckinck 433; *ER* 1367; Poe to an unnamed correspondent in
London, circa Apr. 1846, *PL* 631.

88. On the public responses, see "Edgar Allan Poe," *Southern Literary Messenger* Jan. 1848: 36; *PL* 468, 567; and Robert C. Fuller, *Mesmerism and the
American Cure of Souls* (Philadelphia: U of Pennsylvania P, 1982) 37–38. For the
inquiries by Whitman and Eveleth, see, respectively, *PL* 619; and Thomas Ollive
Mabbott, ed., "The Letters of George W. Eveleth to Edgar Allan Poe," *Bulletin of
the New York Public Library* 26 (1922): 174. Among those writing to Poe was a

Robert H. Collyer of Boston, who told him, "Your account of M. Valdemar's case has been universally copied in this city, and has created a very great sensation. It requires from me no apology, in stating, that I have not the least doubt of the *possibility* of such a phenomenon" (Collyer to Poe, Dec. 16, 1845, *Complete Works* 17: 225).

89. Poe to Arch Ramsey, Dec. 30, 1846, *Letters* 2: 337. For Poe's public gloating, see *Writings in the* Broadway Journal 3: 254 and *ER* 1430–31.

90. Sidney Lind, "Poe and Mesmerism," *PMLA* 62 (1947): 1094.

91. *Tribune*, qtd. by Poe, "Editorial Miscellany," *Writings in the* Broadway Journal 3: 340; *PL* 587, 621.

92. *Courier*, qtd. in Esther F. Hyneman, "The Contemporaneous Reputation of Edgar Allan Poe with Annotated Bibliography of Poe Criticism: 1827–1967," diss., Columbia U, 1968, 45; *Southern Patriot*, Clarke, *Edgar Allan Poe: Critical Assessments* 2: 28.

93. *Knickerbocker*, qtd. in Burton Pollin, "Poe 'Viewed and Reviewed': An Annotated Checklist of Contemporary Notices," *Poe Studies* 13, no. 2 (Dec. 1980): 25.

94. *Harbinger* July 1845, Clarke, *Edgar Allan Poe: Critical Assessments* 2: 154; *Compiler* June 1845, rpt. in Burton R. Pollin, "The Richmond *Compiler* and Poe in 1845: Two Hostile Notices," *Poe Studies* 18, no. 1 (June 1985): 6.

95. See *Knickerbocker* May 1846: 421; and *PL* 624, 633–35. For brief discussions of these responses and of libelous representations of Poe (in both fiction and nonfiction) in the 1840s, see Hyneman 47–48; and Ian Walker, "The Poe Legend," *Companion to Poe Studies*, ed. Eric W. Carlson (Westport, CT: Greenwood, 1996) 22–23. Stories of Poe's dissolute habits had apparently surfaced as early as 1840, circulated by William Burton, proprietor of *Burton's Gentlemen's Magazine*, at the termination of Poe's editorship of that periodical (see Quinn 301–3).

96. Eveleth to Poe, Jan. 11, 1846, *PL* 716.

97. That impact resulted in part because within weeks of its Oct. 9, 1849, appearance in the *New York Daily Tribune*, Griswold's defamatory article was reprinted in whole or in part in at least a dozen periodicals and newspapers around the country, including the *National Anti-Slavery Standard*, the *Chicago Weekly Democrat*, the *New York Evening Mirror*, the *Oregon Spectator*, the *Cleveland True Democrat*, the *Richmond Enquirer*, and the *Philadelphia Dollar Newspaper* (Burton Pollin, "A Posthumous Assessment: The 1849–1850 Periodical Press Response to Edgar Allan Poe," *American Periodicals* 2 [1992]: 6–50).

98. *Model American Courier* Oct. 1849, Clarke, *Edgar Allan Poe: Critical Assessments* 1: 85.

99. *National Magazine* Mar. 1853, qtd. in Burton Pollin, "The Temperance

Movement and Its Friends Look at Poe," *Costerus* 2 (1972): 138. Pollin notes that "one of the oft-reprinted sermonizing notices of Poe's death was entitled 'Genius and Gin'" ("Posthumous Assessment" 8). One of the few antebellum readers to question such reading from text to author was one of Poe's defenders, George Graham, who asserted that Poe's character and temperament "were in no way reflected in or connected with his writings" (*Graham's Magazine* Feb. 1854: 219).

100. Sarah Helen Whitman, *Edgar Allan Poe and His Critics*, rpt. in Clarke, *Edgar Allan Poe: Critical Assessments* 1: 174, 172. The fact that Whitman was for a short time engaged to Poe may well have played a role in her romanticized version of him as the misunderstood, troubled genius.

101. Recent examples of the scholarly tendency to equate Poe and his narrators—or at minimum, to read Poe's life (and death) through the phantasmagoric events and characters of his fiction—include Jeffrey Meyers, *Edgar A. Poe: His Life and Legacy* (New York: Scribners, 1992) 253 ff.; Kenneth Silverman, introduction, *New Essays on Poe's Major Tales*, ed. Kenneth Silverman (Cambridge: Cambridge UP, 1993) 1–26; and Hutchisson 49–53, 78–79, 88–89, 95–96, 164–65, and 235–36. On twentieth-century popular conceptions and mass-culture representations of Poe as the obsessive, alcoholic, drug-addled writer whose stories reflect his own macabre perversity, see Mark Neimeyer, "Poe and Popular Culture," Hayes *Cambridge Companion to Poe*, 205–16, 219–20.

CHAPTER FOUR: *Multiple Audiences and Melville's Fiction*

1. This dimension of Melville's writing has been repeatedly noted by Melville critics beginning with Eleanor Melville Metcalf, *Herman Melville: Cycle and Epicycle* (1953; rpt. Westport, CT: Greenwood, 1970), 173; and William Charvat, *The Profession of Authorship in America, 1800–1870*, ed. Matthew J. Bruccoli (New York: Columbia UP, 1958) 266–67. See also Ann Douglas, *The Feminization of American Culture* (New York: Knopf, 1977) 293; Warwick Wadlington, *The Confidence Game in American Literature* (Princeton: Princeton UP, 1975) 424–46; John Bryant, *Melville and Repose: The Rhetoric of Humor in the American Renaissance* (New York: Oxford UP, 1993) ix; and, more recently, Sheila Post, "Melville and the Marketplace," *Historical Guide to Herman Melville*, ed. Giles Gunn (Oxford: Oxford UP, 2005) 105–32.

2. Melville's oral story-telling experiences and abilities, both aboard ships and amid family members, are discussed in Metcalf 172; Leon Howard, *Herman Melville: A Biography* (Berkeley and Los Angeles: U of California Press; London: Cambridge UP, 1951) 91–92; Laurie Robertson-Lorant, *Melville: A Biography* (New York: Clarkson Potter, 1996) 134; and Hershel Parker, *Herman Melville: A*

Biography, 2 vols. (Baltimore: Johns Hopkins UP, 1996–2002) 1: 264, 309–11, and 354–55.

3. Brian Higgins and Hershel Parker, introduction, *Herman Melville: The Contemporary Reviews,* ed. Brian Higgins and Hershel Parker (Cambridge: Cambridge UP, 1995) ix. Regarding Melville's relation to the periodical milieu and its editors, particularly via his friendship with Evert Duyckinck, see Perry Miller, *The Raven and the Whale: The War of Words and Wits in the Era of Poe and Melville* (New York: Harcourt Brace, 1956) 260–79 and throughout.

4. See, e.g., Parker, *Herman Melville* 1: 835; F. O. Matthiessen, *The American Renaissance: Art and Expression in the Age of Emerson and Whitman* (1941; New York: Oxford UP, 1974) 415; Michael Gilmore, *American Romanticism and the Marketplace* (Chicago: U of Chicago Press, 1985) 57, 62, and 91; Richard Brodhead, *The School of Hawthorne* (New York: Oxford UP, 1986) 23; and Watson Branch, Hershel Parker, Harrison Hayford, and Alma A. MacDougall, "Historical Note," *The Confidence-Man,* ed. Harrison Hayford, Hershel Parker, and G. Thomas Tanselle, vol. 10 of *The Writings of Herman Melville,* ed. Harrison Hayford, Hershel Parker, and G. Thomas Tanselle, 15 vols. (Evanston, IL: Northwestern UP and Newberry Library, 1968–93) 269.

5. The idea that Melville had developed a quarrel with his readers and, by the time of *Pierre,* sought to alienate his audience was first raised in modern Melville criticism by William Braswell, "The Satirical Temper of Melville's *Pierre,*" *American Literature* 7 (1936): 424–38. Later advocates of this version of Melville as an adversarial writer via-à-vis audience include Charvat 204-09, 271, and 281; Douglas 296 and 304; Gilmore 17; Parker, *Herman Melville* 2: 163; Bryant, *Melville and Repose* 230–43; Stephen Railton, *Authorship and Audience: Literary Performance in the American Renaissance* (Princeton: Princeton UP, 1991) 157–60; Elizabeth Renker, *Strike Through the Mask: Herman Melville and the Scene of Writing* (Baltimore: Johns Hopkins UP, 1996) 72; Michael Newberry, *Figuring Authorship in Antebellum America* (Stanford: Stanford UP, 1997) 54–57; Carol Colatrello, *Literature and Moral Reform: Melville and the Discipline of Reading* (Gainesville: UP of Florida, 2002) 77; Edgar A. Dryden, *Monumental Melville: The Formation of a Literary Career* (Stanford, CA: Stanford UP, 2003) 33; Andrew Delbanco, *Melville: His World and His Work* (New York: Knopf, 2005) 142–43; and Wyn Kelley, *Herman Melville: An Introduction* (Malden, MA: Blackwell, 2008) 48. At least one Melvillian has claimed that that agonistic relationship with readers obtained from the beginning of Melville's career as a novelist: John Evelev, "Made in the Marquesas: *Typee,* Tatooing, and the Critique of the Literary Marketplace," *Arizona Quarterly* 48, no. 4 (1992): 19–45.

6. Melville to Alexander Bradford, May 23, 1846; Melville to Duyckinck, Dec.

14, 1849; Melville to Hawthorne, Nov. 17, 1851; all in *Correspondence,* ed. Lynn Horth, vol. 14 of *The Writings of Herman Melville,* 38, 149, and 212, respectively.

7. Lawrence Buell, "Melville and the Question of America's Decolonization," *Melville's Evermoving Dawn,* ed. John Bryant and Robert Milder (Kent, OH: Kent State UP, 1997) 96, n. 6. Despite subscribing to the standard narrative, Bryant periodically raises a similar point in *Melville and Repose* (e.g., 27, 185, and 264).

8. Wai-chee Dimock, *Empire for Liberty: Melville and the Politics of Individualism* (Princeton: Princeton UP, 1989) 7.

9. Dimock 8 and throughout; Parker, *Herman Melville* 1: 59 and 348. Suggestive in this regard is a June 1851 letter to Hawthorne, in which Melville confesses, "I can well perceive, I think, how a man of superior mind can . . . bring himself, as it were, into a certain spontaneous aristocracy of feeling" (*Correspondence* 190).

10. Melville, "Hawthorne and His Mosses," The Piazza Tales *and Other Prose Pieces, 1839-1860,* ed. Harrison Hayford, Alma A. MacDougall, and G. Thomas Tanselle, vol. 9 of *The Writings of Herman Melville* 245. Subsequent citations to "Hawthorne and His Mosses" will be to this edition and will appear parenthetically. An interesting discussion of Melville's "doubts about the masses" is provided by Larry J. Reynolds, *European Revolutions and the American Literary Renaissance* (New Haven: Yale UP, 1988) 101–6.

11. In this regard William G. Rowland Jr. has made a relevant but ultimately misguided remark in stating, "During Melville's working lifetime, two conceptions of literary work were common: the American writer could be either a professional working for the growing reading public or a romantic genius working to satisfy his own impulses. Every student of Melville knows that he felt pressed to choose one conception over the other" (*Literature and the Marketplace: Romantic Writers and their Audiences in Great Britain and the United States* [Lincoln: U of Nebraska P, 1996] 145). Such a simple dichotomy, I believe, never pressed itself upon Melville as a fiction writer, because he sought to avoid the choice by embracing both roles.

12. Renker xix, 37, and throughout; Melville to Hawthorne, Apr. 16, 1851, *Correspondence* 186. On Melville's "democratic imagination" as a product of his experiences in New York City, see Delbanco 119.

13. Douglas 303.

14. Sheila Post-Lauria, *Correspondent Colorings: Melville and the Marketplace* (Amherst: U of Massachusetts P, 1996). Despite the major differences between my approach and Post-Lauria's formalistic study, her arguments have been instrumental in my thinking about Melville and his conception of audience.

For a brief and partial anticipation of her argument, see Douglas Anderson, *A House Undivided: Domesticity and Community in American Literature* (Cambridge: Cambridge UP, 1990) 132. Modern critical discussion of the heterogeneity of modes, forms, and genres in Melville's novels include, besides Post-Lauria, Richard Brodhead, *Hawthorne, Melville, and the Novel* (Chicago: U of Chicago P, 1976), 134–62; Nina Baym, "Melville's Quarrel with Fiction," *PMLA* 94 (1979): 909–23; and Kelley.

15. Review of *The Confidence-Man, Westminster and Foreign Quarterly Review* July 1857, rpt. in Higgins and Parker, *Herman Melville: The Contemporary Reviews* 505. Subsequent quotations from reviews of Melville that are reprinted in this edition will be designated *CR* and will be cited parenthetically by the original date of the review, followed by the pages in the Higgins and Parker collection.

16. Jay Leyda, *The Melville Log: A Documentary Life of Herman Melville*, 2nd ed., 2 vols. (New York: Gordian, 1969) 1: 227; G. Thomas Tanselle, "The Sales of Melville's Books," *Harvard Library Bulletin* 17 (1969): 206. Figures for the British edition were also strong, with 5,000 copes printed and 4,104 sold in less than two years (*Melville Log* 265). Some critical disagreement exists about the "best-seller" status of *Typee*. Parker, for instance, argues that the novel "had not been a best seller by the standards of the time" (*Herman Melville* 1: 452–53), but Post-Lauria asserts that its sale of 6,000 copies in the United States would qualify it as such since "nineteenth-century publishers continually pointed out [that] a best-seller during the 1840s referred to a work that sold between three and ten thousand copies" (42).

17. Sylvester Stevens, *American Expansion in Hawaii, 1842-1898* (Harrisburg, PA: Archives, 1945), 4–5; Thomas R. Hietala, *Manifest Design: Anxious Aggrandizement in Late Jacksonian America* (Ithaca: Cornell UP, 1985) 59–62. Several previous Melville scholars have also discussed the topical appeal of *Typee*: Hugh H. Hetherington, *Melville's Reviewers: British and American, 1846-1891* (Chapel Hill: U of North Carolina P, 1961) 64; and Charles Roberts Anderson, *Melville and the South Seas* (1939; New York: Dover, 1966) 77 ff.

18. The reviews in the *United State Magazine* and the *Anglo American* are reprinted in Higgins and Parker, *Herman Melville: The Contemporary Reviews* 8 and 20, respectively.

19. *Literary World* Aug. 4 and 11, 1849, rpt. in Watson Branch, ed., *Melville: The Critical Heritage* (London: Routledge and Kegan Paul, 1974) 165.

20. Howard, *Herman Melville* 92. On the vogue and audience for travel literature, esp. about the South Pacific, see also Post 109–10; and Parker, *Herman Melville* 1: 208 and 267. For periodical attention to this genre and its connections

to American expansionist ideology, see William E. Lenz, "Narratives of Explora-tion, Sea Fiction, Mariners' Chronicles, and the Rise of American Nationalism," *American Studies* 32, no. 2 (1991): 41–61.

21. The reviews for the *Tribune* June 26, 1847; *Mirror* Apr. 4, 1846; *Morning Herald* Apr. 3, 1846; and *National Intelligencer* Dec. 16, 1851, are reprinted in Higgins and Parker, *Herman Melville: The Contemporary Reviews*, 130, 42, 38, 399, respectively. For the *Richmond Enquirer* July 7, 1849, see Sonja Krusic and Kevin J. Hayes, "Melville Reviewers South and West," *Melville Society Extracts* 86 (1991): 6.

22. Hetherington, in his useful overview of seventeen British reviews of *Typee*, offers the conclusion about the generally positive response (31–32). My own examination of twenty-three British reviews reprinted in Higgins and Park-er's *Herman Melville: The Contemporary Reviews* has convinced me of the ac-curacy of Hetherington's claims. Hetherington also (3–4) concisely explains the conditions and nature of the effects of British reviews on the American reception of Melville's novels. For a brief discussion of that impact on American reviews of *Typee* in particular, see Parker, *Herman Melville* 1: 410. Both Hetherington (21, 31, and throughout) and Parker (410–15) point out important parallels be-tween the British and American reviews of *Typee* and offer useful overviews of the prominent issues addressed by each.

23. For this strain in the British responses, see Hetherington 21–25.

24. Duyckinck qtd. in Leyda, *Melville Log* 211 and 264.

25. Specifically, these were the *Evangelist* and the *Christian Parlor Magazine* in New York and the *Universalist Review* and the *Christian Observatory* in Bos-ton, though the review in the *New Haven New Englander* also responded to *Typee* in kind. For a discussion of this response as limited to a few religious periodicals, see Hetherington 47–48; and Parker, *Herman Melville* 1: 431–33.

26. Elizabeth Elkins Sanders, *Remarks on the "Tour Around Hawaii," by the Missionaries, Messrs. Ellis, Thurston, Bishop, and Goodrich* (Salem, 1848), 34, 41. The pages on *Typee* from the *United States Catholic Magazine* are reprinted in Higgins and Parker, *Herman Melville: The Contemporary Reviews* 172–76. The denominational variation in magazine responses to *Typee* is discussed in Mentor L. Williams, "Notices of Melville's Novels in Religious Publications," *American Literature* 22 (1950): 119–27. For antebellum opposition to missionary activi-ties, see Bertram Wyatt-Brown, "The Antimission Movement in the Jacksonian South," *Journal of Southern History* 36 (1970): 501–29.

27. Sophia Hawthorne qtd. in Metcalf 91.

28. For a useful discussion of the relation between *Typee* and earlier accounts, see Charles Anderson 90 ff. and 117–78.

29. John Coward, *The Newspaper Indian: Native American Identity in the*

Press, 1820–1890 (Urbana: U of Illinois P, 1999) 69 and throughout. See also Richard Slotkin, "Frontier Myth as a Theory of Development," *The Fatal Environment: The Myth of the Frontier in the Age of Individualism, 1800–1890* (New York: Athenaeum, 1985) 33–47. On the cult of the vanishing or doomed aborigine, see Brian W. Dippie, *The Vanishing American: White Attitudes and U.S. Indian Policy* (Middletown, CT: Wesleyan UP, 1982).

30. Bryant, *Melville and Repose* 168, discusses and provides the omitted passage. Melville refers to the Lory-Lory account in his letter to Murray, Jan. 29, 1847, *Correspondence* 78. Whether Melville eliminated this passage on his own or at Murray's insistence is unclear. The comment about "intellectual advancement" is quoted in Leon Howard, "Historical Note," *Typee*, ed. Harrison Hayford, Hershel Parker, and G. Thomas Tanselle, vol. 1 of *The Writings of Herman Melville* 280. For a detailed, albeit somewhat speculative, account of Melville's composition of *Typee*, see John Bryant, *Melville Unfolding: Sexuality, Politics, and the Versions of Typee* (Ann Arbor: U of Michigan P, 2008), 21–26, 31–43, and 58–248.

31. Melville to John Murray, July 15, 1846, *Correspondence* 56.

32. Geoffrey Sanborn, *The Sign of the Cannibal: Melville and the Making of a Post-Colonial Reader* (Durham: Duke UP, 1998), 75–76.

33. For this growth in Melville through his reading, see, Charvat 232; Howard, *Herman Melville* 115–16; and Parker, *Herman Melville* 1: 573–74.

34. The review in the *American Whig Review*, which appeared in July 1847, is also reprinted in Higgins and Parker, *Herman Melville: The Contemporary Reviews* 131–42. For discussions of both these reviews and the responses they generated in defense of Melville in the periodical press, see Hetherington 85–90; Miller 21–28; and Parker, *Herman Melville* 1: 529–40.

35. On this principle within antebellum reviewing, see Nina Baym, *Novels, Readers, and Reviewers: Responses to Fiction in Antebellum America* (Ithaca: Cornell UP, 1984) 250–51.

36. Melville to John Murray, Mar. 25, 1848; Melville to Murray, Jan. 29, 1849, *Correspondence* 106 and 114–15, respectively. For a full discussion of the antebellum reception of *Omoo* and its impact on Melville's reconception of his craft with *Mardi*, see James L. Machor, "Reading the 'Rinsings of the Cup': The Antebellum Reception of Melville's *Omoo*," *Nineteenth-Century Literature* 59 (2004): 53–77.

37. These are the most common critical views of *Mardi* in Melville scholarship, exemplified in Parker, *Herman Melville* 1: 609, from which the "declaration" remark comes, and Railton 156, which offers the other quoted characterization. See also Charvat 217 and Dimock 43. A notable voice of dissent that somewhat anticipates my claim is Post-Lauria, who asserts, "By demonstrating how popular

materials can be used for aesthetic purposes" in *Mardi,* Melville curried the "allegiance of literary readers who sought writers able to transform the democratic materials of popular culture into art" (66–67).

38. Melville, *Mardi,* ed. Harrison Hayford, Hershel Parker, and G. Thomas Tanselle, vol. 3 of *The Writings of Herman Melville* xvii.

39. Melville to John Murray, Jan. 1, 1848, *Correspondence* 100.

40. Melville made the request for a larger advance in at least two letters to Murray, one on Oct. 29, 1847, and the second on Jan. 28, 1848 (*Correspondence* 98–99 and 114–115). For the argument that *Mardi* was a novel in which Melville was "narrowing" his readership, see John Evelev, *Tolerable Entertainment: Herman Melville and Professionalism in Antebellum New York* (Amherst: U of Massachusetts P, 2006), 72–73.

41. Higgins and Parker, introduction, *Herman Melville: The Contemporary Reviews* xiv.

42. Hetherington 101–12 provides an excellent discussion of these British reviews of *Mardi.*

43. See, e.g., Higgins and Parker, introduction, xv; Howard, *Herman Melville* 131; Renker 66; Railton 156; Miller 248 ff.; and Dryden 10.

44. Hetherington 131. Other sources for the sales figures of *Mardi* include Tanselle 210; Leyda, *Melville Log* 313; and Elizabeth Foster, "Historical Note," *Mardi* 671.

45. On the cost of *Mardi,* see Foster 664; for the British printing and sales figures, see Tanselle 198.

46. Charvat 233. Other Melville scholars expressing the same view include Branch 2; and Leland Person, "*Mardi* and the Reviewers: The Irony of (Mis) reading," *Melville Society Extracts* 72 (Feb. 1988): 3–4.

47. *Putnam's Monthly* Feb. 1853, rpt. in Branch 328.

48. Qtd. in Metcalf 61.

49. *Putnam's Monthly* Apr. 1857, rpt. in Branch 364.

50. Melville to Evert Duyckinck, Dec. 14, 1849; Melville to Richard Bentley, June 5, 1849, *Correspondence* 149 and 131, respectively; Hetherington 133.

51. *Correspondence* 131.

52. This view is held by most critics who have addressed the question of Melville's conception of audience relations in 1849, e.g., Charvat 232–33 and 271; Dimock 109–10; and Parker, *Herman Melville* 1: 654.

53. Melville to Evert Duyckinck, Apr. 3, 1849, *Correspondence* 128; Melville, "Journal 1849–1850," *Journals,* ed. Howard C. Horsford and Lynn Horth, vol. 15 of *The Writings of Herman Melville* 12.

54. Melville to Lemuel Shaw, Apr. 23, 1849, *Correspondence* 130; Brodhead, *School of Hawthorne* 28.

55. Melville to Evert Duyckinck, Dec. 14, 1849; Melville to Lemuel Shaw, Oct. 6, 1849, *Correspondence* 149 and 139, respectively.

56. Melville to Hawthorne, circa Nov. 17, 1851, *Correspondence* 212.

57. *Springfield Republican* Nov. 19, 1849, qtd. in Hetherington 145.

58. Qtd. in Parker, *Herman Melville* 1: 670.

59. Tanselle 210–14.

60. On flogging as an issue in the legislature and the popular press in 1848–49 and before, see Howard, *Herman Melville* 243; Charles Anderson 430; and Myra C. Glenn, "The Navy Reform Campaign Against Flogging: A Case Study in Changing Attitudes Toward Corporal Punishment," *American Quarterly* 35 (1983): 408–25. Further stoking public interest were the links reformers made between corporal punishment in the navy and the slavery issue by arguing that flogging turned white sailors into the equivalent of black slaves (Richard Brodhead, *Cultures of Letters: Scenes of Reading and Writing in Nineteenth-Century America* [Chicago: U of Chicago P, 1993] 15; Glenn, 419–22; and Samuel Otter, *Melville's Anatomies* [Berkeley and Los Angeles: U of California P, 1999] 67–77).

61. For further discussion of support in the popular press for the reformist position in *White-Jacket*, see Hetherington 174–80.

62. These phrases appear respectively in the *Boston Zion's Herald* Apr. 14, 1850: 58; *Boston Christian Register* Apr. 6, 1850; *New York Knickerbocker* May 1850; and *New Bedford Mercury* Apr. 4, 1850. The last three are reprinted in Higgins and Parker, *Herman Melville: The Contemporary Reviews* 330, 344, and 328, respectively.

63. Hennig Cohen, introduction, *White-Jacket*, by Herman Melville (New York: Holt, Rinehart, and Winston, 1967) xxvi. For *White-Jacket* as a tail-end participant in what was virtually a fait accompli of naval reform, see Hetherington 183–84 and Charles Anderson 431.

64. Willard Thorp, "Historical Note," *White-Jacket*, ed. Harrison Hayford, Hershel Parker, and G. Thomas Tanselle, vol. 5 of *The Writings of Herman Melville* 408.

65. Melville to Evert Duyckinck, Feb. 12, 1851, *Correspondence* 181.

66. Dimock 109–10. Besides Dimock's extended discussion of Melville's connection to an imperial conception of authorship throughout his career, Ellen Weinauer explores its relevance to Melville in 1851 and calls it a "profound shift" in Melville's conception of authorship ("Plagiarism and the Proprietary Self: Policing Boundaries of Authorship in Herman Melville's 'Hawthorne and His Mosses,'" *American Literature* 69 [1997]: 711).

67. *Correspondence* 191, Charvat 240.

68. *Correspondence* 160.

69. Weinauer, "Plagiarism and the Proprietary Self" 708.

70. For a somewhat related but different account of "Hawthorne and His Mosses" as a repository of Melville's ambivalence about audience, see Railton, who calls the essay Melville's "fullest statement" of himself as a writer "performing for an audience that has come to seem his bitterest foe, even while it remains the only possible friend to his hopes for a literary career" (188).

71. Melville to Hawthorne, June 1, 1851, and Nov. 17, 1851; Melville to Sarah Morewood, Sept. 1851, *Correspondence* 193, 212, and 206, respectively.

72. Melville to Nathaniel Hawthorne, Nov. 17, 1851; Melville to Sophia Hawthorne, Jan. 8, 1852, *Correspondence* 213 and 219. Regarding reviewer assumptions about the gendered propriety or impropriety of some novels, see Baym, *Novels, Readers, and Reviewers* 183–85. It is relevant to note that among Melville scholars, *Pierre* "is commonly viewed as Melville's failed attempt to attract female readers of the sentimental mode" (Post-Lauria 127).

73. Melville to Richard Bentley, Apr. 16, 1852, *Correspondence* 226. On Melville's goal of making *Pierre* a popular novel, see also Charlene Avallone, "Calculations for Popularity: *Pierre* and *Holden's Dollar Magazine*," *Nineteenth-Century Literature* 43 (1988–89): 82–110. Brian Higgins and Hershel Parker speculate about another factor in Melville's conceptualization of *Pierre*, which seems at least indirectly relevant to his thinking about audience: Hawthorne's popular and critical success with the *House of the Seven Gables*. That success may have induced Melville to believe that he could achieve the same results by creating his own "Gothic-flavored romance" with a domestic American setting (*Reading Melville's* Pierre; or, the Ambiguities [Baton Rouge: Louisiana State UP, 2006] 4–5).

74. On the early British reviews and their negative impact, see Parker, *Herman Melville* 2: 19–21; and Harrison Hayford, Hershel Parker, and G. Thomas Tanselle, "Historical Note," *Moby-Dick*, ed. Harrison Hayford, Hershel Parker, and G. Thomas Tanselle, vol. 6 of *The Writings of Herman Melville* 701. It is worth mentioning that scholars disagree substantially over whether the British reviews of *The Whale* were largely negative or positive. Those who hold to the former include Hetherington 201–3, Charvat 242, and Matthiessen 251. Support for the latter comes from Higgins and Parker, introduction xviii; and Parker, *Herman Melville* 2: 106.

75. The dominant critical view that the American reception of *Moby-Dick* was captious is represented in Matthiessen 251; Howard Vincent, *The Trying-Out of* Moby-Dick (Boston: Houghton Mifflin, 1949) 3; Steven Mailloux, *Interpretive Conventions: The Reader in the Study of American Fiction* (Ithaca: Cornell UP, 1982) 171; and Parker, *Herman Melville* 2: 17–30. One of the few exceptions is Hetherington 215–19.

76. *Boston Daily Bee,* Nov. 19, 1851, rpt. in Hershel Parker and Harrison Hayford, Moby-Dick *as Doubloon: Essays and Extracts* (New York: Norton, 1970) 38–39; *Literary World* Nov. 15, 1851, rpt. in Higgins and Parker, *Herman Melville: The Contemporary Reviews* 375–76. On the topicality of whaling, the whaling industry, and marauding whales, see Howard, *Herman Melville* 45; Charles Anderson 62; and Delbanco 40.

77. *American Literary Gazette* Nov. 16, 1863, rpt. in Branch 382.

78. *Daily Gazette* Nov. 19, 1851, rpt. in Parker and Hayford 39.

79. Charvat 139. The variety of reviewers' reactions to Ahab also belie Robert Milder's claim that the narrative of *Moby-Dick* structures reader response so that at first "the reader, like Ishmael, has identified with Ahab's hunt" but that the structure later turns Ahab into a character "who absorbs the reader's cosmic anger and who is repudiated, expelled from the moral community of the audience" ("*Moby-Dick*: The Rationale of Narrative Form," *Approaches to Teaching* Moby-Dick, ed. Martin Bickman [New York: MLA, 1985] 45). Antebellum responses to Ahab cannot be reduced to such a lockstep, uniform pattern.

80. Leyda, *Melville Log* 438 and 446; Hetherington 221.

81. *United States Magazine* Jan. 1852 and *To-Day* Jan. 10, 1852, rpt. in Higgins and Parker, *Herman Melville: The Contemporary Reviews* 410–11 and 412–13, respectively. It is important to distinguish this factor from Charvat's claim that *Moby-Dick* did not sell well because the reviews were horrible (241–42). As I have demonstrated, such a characterization of the reviews simply is not accurate. There is also no evidence to support Charvat's other conjectured factor: that *Moby-Dick* suffered from a lack of "word-of-mouth recommendations" by women readers, who did not buy or read the novel because there were no women in it (242).

82. Hawthorne to Evert Duyckinck, Dec. 1, 1851, *Correspondence,* ed. Thomas Woodson, L. Neal Smith, and Norman Holmes Pearson, vol. 15 of *Centenary Edition of the Works of Nathaniel Hawthorne,* ed. William Charvat, Roy Harvey Pearce, and Claude M. Simpson, 23 vols. (Columbus: Ohio State UP, 1962–85) 508.

83. Bentley to Melville, May 5, 1852, *Correspondence* 620.

84. Melville to Evert Duyckinck, Feb. 14, 1852, *Correspondence* 222–23. Melville repeated the request in a letter of Apr. 16, using the impersonal salutation "Editors of the Literary World" (*Correspondence* 225). Despite the rift, Melville wrote to Evert on at least seven occasions afterward and clearly continued to value Duyckinck's literary judgment and advice.

85. Douglas 302. For a similar characterization, see Kenneth Dauber, *The Idea of Authorship in America* (Madison: U of Wisconsin P, 1990) 209. The view of *Pierre* as a product of Melville's disappointment and anger over the recep-

tion of *Moby-Dick* is held by, among others, Howard, *Herman Melville* 190–92; Charvat 253–56; Hershel Parker, "Why *Pierre* Went Wrong," *Studies in the Novel* 8 (1978): 7–23; Railton 158 and 185; and Higgins and Parker, *Reading Melville's* Pierre.

86. Leon Howard and Hershel Parker, "Historical Note," *Pierre; or, The Ambiguities*, ed. Harrison Hayford, Hershel Parker, and G. Thomas Tanselle, vol. 7 of *The Writings of Herman Melville* 372–77.

87. *North American Review* Apr. 1856: 368. On this protocol in informed reading, see chapter 2 of this study.

88. *Putnam's Monthly* Feb. 1853, rpt. in Branch 328.

89. Interestingly enough, several critics from the first generation of modern Melville scholars agreed with this view of *Pierre*, holding that the novel is a satire of antebellum sentimental fiction: William Braswell, "The Sentimental Temper of Melville's *Pierre*," *American Literature* 7 (1936): 424–38; and Edward R. Rosenberg, *Melville and the Comic Spirit* (Cambridge: Harvard UP, 1955) 159. Occasionally more recent Melville critics have acceded: e.g., Robert Milder, "Melville's Intentions in Pierre," *Studies in the Novel* 6 (1974): 193; Brian Higgins and Hershel Parker, "The Flawed Grandeur of Melville's *Pierre*," *New Perspectives on Melville*, ed. Faith Pullin (Edinburgh: Edinburgh UP, 1978), 167; Michael Davitt Bell, "Women's Fiction and the Literary Marketplace in the 1850s," *The Cambridge History of American Literature*, ed. Sacvan Bercovitch, vol. 2 (Cambridge: Cambridge UP, 1995) 122; and Otter 174.

90. *Hunt's Merchants' Magazine* Oct. 1852, rpt. in Brian Higgins and Hershel Parker, eds., *Critical Essays on Herman Melville's* Pierre; or, the Ambiguities (Boston: Hall, 1983) 54.

91. *Putnam's Monthly* Feb. 1853, rpt. in Branch 329.

92. Leyda, *Melville Log* 468; Howard and Parker, "Historical Note," *Pierre* 379; Higgins and Parker, *Reading Melville's* Pierre 184. On the deleterious impact of the reviews of *Pierre* on the sales of *Moby-Dick*, see Hayford, Parker, and Tanselle, "Historical Note," *Moby-Dick* 728. Compounding the problem with *Pierre* were its debilitating economic consequences. Not only were sales low, but unlike his previous contracts with Harpers, which allotted Melville half the profits after manufacturing costs, his contract for *Pierre* specified a 20 percent royalty only after 1,190 copies were sold (Susan S. Williams, "Authors and Literary Authorship," *The Industrial Book, 1840–1880*, vol. 3 of *The History of the Book in America*, ed. Scott E. Casper, Jeffrey D. Groves, Stephen W. Nissenbaum, and Michael Winship [Chapel Hill: U of North Carolina P, 2007] 92).

93. *National Magazine* Nov. 1852, rpt. in Higgins and Parker, *Critical Essays* 68.

94. Qtd. in Parker, *Herman Melville* 2: 142. Regarding Melville's conception

of a successful writing career as one marked by a "consistent movement upward," see Evelev, *Tolerable Entertainment* 17.

95. Merton M. Sealts Jr., "Historical Note," Piazza Tales *and Other Prose Pieces* 484 and 493; Parker, *Herman Melville* 2: 163. Eleven of the fourteen stories Melville published in *Harpers* and *Putnam's* appeared either anonymously or under a pseudonym: "Bartleby," "Cock-a-Doodle-Doo!," "The Encantadas," "Poor Man's Pudding and Rich Man's Crumbs," "The Happy Failure," "The Lightening-Rod Man," "The Fiddler," "The Paradise of Bachelors and the Tartarus of Maids," "The Bell-Tower," "Benito Cereno," and "Jimmy Rose" (Sealts 458).

96. Tanselle 196; Dix, Edwards, & Co. to Melville, Aug. 28, 1856, *Correspondence* 649; Curtis qtd. in Leyda, *Melville Log* 510. For an analysis of the antebellum response to Melville's short stories, see James L. Machor, "The American Reception of Melville's Short Fiction in the 1850s," *New Directions in American Reception Study*, ed. Philip Goldstein and James L. Machor (New York: Oxford UP, 2008) 87–98.

97. *Putnam's Monthly* Apr. 1857, rpt. in Branch 365.

98. Johannes Dietrich Bergman, "The Original Confidence Man," *American Quarterly* 21 (1969): 560–77. On Melville's knowledge about and motivations in centering his last novel on this well-known figure, see Post-Lauria 215–19; and Robertson-Lorant 361.

99. Duyckinck letter of Mar. 31, 1857, rpt. in Leyda, *Melville Log* 563.

100. Melville to Lemuel Shaw, Oct. 6, 1849, *Correspondence* 139. This modern view of *The Confidence-Man* is so widespread that a full citation would need to include almost every article and book chapter that has treated the novel. In lieu of that, see Matthiessen 411–12; Railton 189–94; Dimock 207–12; Nina Baym, "Melville's Quarrel with Fiction," *PMLA* 94 (1979): 909–23; and Dauber 221–22. One of the few exceptions to this position is Leon Howard, who asserted over fifty years ago, "there is no evidence of any sort that Melville anticipated the failure of his new book" (*Herman Melville* 232).

101. The modern critical view of the antebellum reception of *The Confidence-Man* as marked by "hostility and bafflement" is exemplified in Renker 71; and Higgins and Parker, introduction xxi. Compare Kelley, who asserts that antebellum "readers saw it as an improvement over *Pierre*" (129). While that response is closer to the novel's actual reception, there is little evidence to support Kelley's claim that those same readers likened the novel to *Mardi* and *Moby-Dick* (129).

102. *Putnam's Monthly* Apr. 1857, rpt. in Branch 366.

103. Bryant, *Melville and Repose* 236.

104. Tanselle 198.

105. Walker Cowen, *Melville's Marginalia,* 2 vols. (New York: Garland, 1987) 2: 27; Shaw letter, June 2, 1857, qtd. in Metcalf 165–66.

106. On Melville's conception of poetry as a private form of writing and the role of that view in his decision to turn to that genre, see Post-Lauria 229; Robertson-Lorant 503; Dryden 148–66; and Kelley 138.

107. Regarding Melville's conception of the audience for his poetry as a select group or "coterie," see Matthew Giordono, "Public Privacy: Melville's Coterie Authorship in *John Marr and Other Sailors*," *Leviathan: A Journal of Melville Studies* 9, no. 3 (2007): 65–78. For a related discussion of Melville's relation to his poetic audience, see William Spengemann, "Melville the Poet," *American Literary History* 11 (1999): 583.

108. For publication figures for *Clarel, John Marr,* and *Timoleon,* see Parker, *Herman Melville* 2: 839 and 879.

109. "Bok's Literary Leaves," *Publisher's Weekly* Nov. 15, 1890, rpt. in Branch 417–18.

110. On Melville's British admirers in the 1880s, see Hetherington 270–83; Robertson-Lorant 574; Melville *Correspondence* 744; and Hayford, Parker, and Tanselle, "Historical Note," *Moby-Dick* 338–39.

111. *New York Times* Aug. 5, 1899, qtd. in Parker, *Herman Melville* 2: 923.

112. *North American Review* Feb. 1892; *Springfield Republican* Oct. 4, 1891; *New York Times* Oct. 2, 1891; and *Mail and Express* Oct. 8, 1891, rpt. in Branch 429, 421, 418, and 424, respectively. For the botched headline in the Oct. 6, 1891, *New York Times,* see Leyda, *Melville Log* 788. The gaff in the *Times* may, however, have been a typesetter's error rather than a mistake by the writer (see Parker, *Herman Melville* 2: 921).

113. For a useful discussion of the Melville revival from the 1920s to the 1950s, see Sanford E. Merovitz, "The Melville Revival," *Companion to Melville Studies,* ed. Wyn Kelley (Malden, MA: Blackwell, 2006) 515–31. Paul Lauter discusses Melville's revival in relation to Modernism in "Melville Climbs the Canon," *American Literature* 66 (1994): 1–24.

CHAPTER FIVE: *Response as (Re)Construction*

1. *Hope Leslie* appeared as a Rutgers UP edition in 1987; *A New England Tale* was published in 1995 by Oxford UP; and the UP of New England published *The Linwoods* in 2002. A fourth novel, *Redwood,* was also briefly available as a Garret Press reissue in 1969.

2. *MLA International Bibliography of Books and Articles on the Modern Languages and Literature* (New York: MLA, 1921–).

3. On the positive side, Sedgwick, with 98 articles devoted to her, is ahead of other marginally canonical antebellum women novelists such as Susan Warner (54), Sara Payson Willis / Fanny Fern (49), E.D.E.N. Southworth (25), and

Maria Cummins (17) (*MLA International Bibliography*). For an earlier statistical comparison of articles on Sedgwick and on other nineteenth-century American writers, see Dana Nelson, "Rediscovery," *Catharine Maria Sedgwick: Critical Perspectives*, ed. Lucinda L. Damon-Bach and Victoria Clements (Boston: Northeastern UP, 2003) 286–93.

4. The one post-1980 work is the Damon-Bach and Clements collection cited in the previous note. The two other studies were Mary Welsh, *Catharine Maria Sedgwick* (Washington, DC: Catholic U of America P, 1937); and Edward Halsey Foster, *Catharine Maria Sedgwick* (New York: Twayne, 1974).

5. On those links made by antebellum commentators, see Rebecca R. Saulsbury, "Catharine Maria Sedgwick," *Nineteenth-Century American Women Writers: A Bio-Bibliographical Sourcebook*, ed. Denise D. Knight (Westport, CT: Greenwood, 1997), 353, 356; and Foster 20. Foster also claims that "until Harriet Beecher Stowe published *Uncle Tom's Cabin*, Miss Sedgwick was the *only* woman who was widely considered a major American writer" (21).

6. Lucinda L. Damon-Bach and Victoria Clements, introduction, Damon-Bach and Clements, eds., *Catharine Maria Sedgwick* xxiii. Melissa J. Homestead has argued that antebellum praise of Sedgwick as a national American author transpired within, and as part of, a particular economic and legal context: the debate over international copyright (*American Women Authors and Literary Property, 1822–1869* [Cambridge: Cambridge UP, 2005] 77–78 ff.).

7. Nina Baym, "Melodramas of Beset Manhood: How Theories of American Fiction Exclude Women Authors," *American Quarterly* 33 (1981): 123–39; Jane Tompkins, "Masterpiece Theater," *Sensational Designs: The Cultural Work of American Fiction, 1790–1860* (New York: Oxford UP, 1985) 3–39.

8. Eugene Exman, *The Brothers Harper: A Unique Publishing Partnership and Its Impact upon the Cultural Life of America from 1817 to 1853* (New York: Harper and Row, 1965) 30. For Sedgwick's involvement in New York City literary society, including the Knickerbocker group and the salon culture that included Edgar Poe and Margaret Fuller, see Charlene Avallone, "Catharine Sedgwick and the Circles of New York," *Legacy* 23 (2006): esp. 116–17, 120–21, and 124–25. On Sedgwick's prominence in the Lenox-Stockbridge region and her literary relations in New York, see Foster 19–39.

9. Mary Kelley, *Private Woman, Public Stage: Literary Domesticity in Nineteenth-Century America* (New York: Oxford UP, 1984) xi, 111, 129–30. For a related discussion of the cult of true womanhood and its restrictive implications for women writers in antebellum American, see Susan Coultrap-McQuin, *Doing Literary Business: American Women Writers in the Nineteenth Century* (Chapel Hill: U of North Carolina P, 1990) 11. Kelley's argument, as it relates specifically to Sedgwick, has been echoed by T. Gregory Garvey, "Risking Reprisal: Catha-

rine Sedgwick's *Hope Leslie* and the Legitimation of Public Action by Women," *American Transcendental Quarterly* 8 (1994): 287–98; Victoria Clements, introduction, *A New England Tale,* by Catharine Maria Sedgwick, ed. Victoria Clements (New York: Oxford UP, 1995) xxi–xxii; and Elaine Showalter, *A Jury of Her Peers: American Women Writers from Anne Bradstreet to Annie Proulx* (New York: Knopf, 2009) 41.

10. Melissa J. Homestead, "Behind the Veil? Catharine Sedgwick and Anonymous Publication," Damon-Bach and Clements, eds., *Catharine Maria Sedgwick* 23–27. Homestead claims that Sedgwick's use of anonymous authorship actually was a "market strategy for constructing an authorial persona" (20) as a "reluctant" women author, through which, as Homestead explains elsewhere, Sedgwick "positioned herself in the literary field as a producer responding to readers' needs" and expectations (*American Women Authors* 70).

11. Catharine Sedgwick to Charles Sedgwick, July 22, 1836, *Life and Letters of Catharine M. Sedgwick,* ed. Mary Dewey (New York: Harper, 1871) 254. Sedgwick's knowledge about and dealings with the literary marketplace are also discussed in Sarah Robbins, "Periodizing Authorship, Characterizing Genre: Catharine Maria Sedgwick's Benevolent Literary Narratives," *American Literature* 76 (2004): 5–6; C. Deirdre Phelps, "American Authorship and New York Publishing History, 1827–1842: The Market Experience of Catharine Maria Sedgwick and William Cullen Bryant," diss., Boston U, 1993, 83–89, 121–22, and throughout; and Homestead, *American Women Authors* 63–104.

12. Ann Douglas, *The Feminization of American Culture* (New York: Knopf, 1977), 9; Lawrence Buell, *New England Literary Culture: From Revolution to Renaissance* (Cambridge: Cambridge UP, 1986) 375–92.

13. Coultrap-McQuin 8. On the authority of the cult of domesticity and its ideology of privatized womanhood in justifying female authorship in nineteenth-century America, see also Linda M. Grasso, *The Artistry of Anger: Black and White Women's Literature in America, 1820–1860* (Chapel Hill: U of North Carolina P, 2002) 24; and Michael Newbury, *Figuring Authorship in Antebellum America* (Stanford: Stanford UP, 1997) 68. That justification of a connection between public and private cultural spaces, it should be added, was one of a series of linkages in gender formations within antebellum ideology and culture that historians have recently pointed to in revising earlier scholarly ideas about the supposedly fixed and unbreachable division of gender-coded separate spheres in nineteenth-century America. For an excellent overview of this revisionist historiography on the notion of separate spheres, see Dana D. Nelson, "Women in Public," *The Cambridge Companion to Nineteenth-Century American Women's Writing,* ed. Dale M. Bauer and Philip Gould (Cambridge: Cambridge UP, 2001) 38–68.

14. Nina Baym, *Novels, Readers, and Reviewers* (Ithaca: Cornell UP, 1984) 23.

15. Catharine Sedgwick to Henry (Harry) Sedgwick, June 1, 1825, qtd. in Kelley 202–3; Catharine Sedgwick to Charles Sedgwick, Mar. 7, 1830, Dewey 205.

16. Kelley 219; Nina Baym, *Women's Fiction: A Guide to Novels by and about Women in American, 1820–1870* (Ithaca: Cornell UP, 1978) 16.

17. Sedgwick to Susan Channing, June 15, 1822, Dewey 156; Sedgwick to "Dear Sir," Nov. 6, 1827, qtd. in Kelley 203.

18. Catharine Sedgwick to Henry Sedgwick, Oct. 18, 1824, Catharine Maria Sedgwick Papers III, Massachusetts Historical Society.

19. Sedgwick to William Channing, Aug. 24, 1837, Dewey 271; Sedgwick to St. Leger, July 4, 1841, Catharine Maria Sedgwick Papers I, Massachusetts Historical Society; Sedgwick to Susan Channing, Apr. 6, 1857, Catharine Maria Sedgwick Papers I, Massachusetts Historical Society.

20. Michael Gilmore, *American Romanticism and the Marketplace* (Chicago: U of Chicago P, 1985).

21. Sedgwick to Lydia Child, June 13, 1830, qtd. in Kelley 204; Sedgwick, Journal 1834–1835, Oct. 1, 1834, Catharine Maria Sedgwick Papers I, Massachusetts Historical Society.

22. Saulsbury 352–54.

23. Sedgwick, Journal, Dec. 17, 1835, Dewey 249–50.

24. Sedgwick, Journals 1827–1830, June 7, 1830, Catharine Maria Sedgwick Papers I, Massachusetts Historical Society.

25. Foster 15, 45; Sedgwick to Mrs. Frank Channing, "Sunday evening, 1822," Dewey 153–54.

26. Saulsbury 352. Widely divergent—and largely unsubstantiated—claims have been made by modern scholars regarding the sale of Sedgwick's first novel. Saulsbury, for instance, asserts that it "was a best seller in Britain and America" (352). By contrast, Helen Papashvily writes that the novel "did not rank among the best sellers of the decade" (*All the Happy Endings: A Study of the Domestic Novel in America, the Women Who Wrote It, the Women Who Read It, in the Nineteenth-Century* [New York: Harper, 1956] 41).

27. Henry (Harry) Sedgwick to Catharine Sedgwick, May 25, 1822, Dewey 152.

28. See, esp., "Essays on American Language and Literature," *North American Review* Sept. 1815: 307–14; "Reflection on the Literary Delinquency of America," *North American Review* Nov. 1815: 33–43; and William Tudor, "An Address Delivered to the Phi Beta Kappa Society," *North American Review* Nov. 1815: 13–32.

29. Smith qtd. in Richard Gravil, *Romantic Dialogues: Anglo-American Continuities, 1776–1862* (New York: St. Martin's, 2000) 51.

30. Sedgwick, *A New England Tale* 24.

31. *Christian Disciple* (1823) qtd. in David Reynolds, *Faith in Fiction: The Emergence of Religious Literature in America* (Cambridge: Harvard UP, 1981) 115.

32. James to Sedgwick, May 17, 1822, Catharine Maria Sedgwick Papers III, Massachusetts Historical Society.

33. *Monthly Review* (1823) qtd. in Patricia Larson Kalayjian, "Her 'Classic Pen': Critical Politics and the Reputation of Catharine Maria Sedgwick," diss. Duke U, 1991, 25.

34. Wilde to Sedgwick, Oct. 25, 1852, Catharine Maria Sedgwick Papers II, Massachusetts Historical Society; Cabot to Sedgwick, Nov. 16, 1822, Catharine Maria Sedgwick Papers III, Massachusetts Historical Society.

35. Douglas, esp. 6–8, 13, 17–19.

36. G. M. Goshgarian, *To Kiss the Chastening Rod: Domestic Fiction and Sexual Ideology in the American Renaissance* (Ithaca: Cornell UP, 1992) 38; Reynolds 73.

37. On the assumption in informed reading linking emotional response and women readers, see chapter 2.

38. Kate Flint, *The Woman Reader, 1837–1914* (Oxford: Clarendon Press, 1993), 66, n. 4; Susan Williams, *Reclaiming Authorship: Literary Women in America, 1850–1900* (Philadelphia: U of Pennsylvania P, 2006) 30–31.

39. Sedgwick to Susan Channing, Aug. 17, 1822, Dewey 157; Sedgwick to Cabot, Oct. 22, 1822, Catharine Maria Sedgwick Papers I, Massachusetts Historical Society.

40. Sedgwick to Cabot, June 2, 1824, Catharine Maria Sedgwick Papers I, Massachusetts Historical Society.

41. Lazarus to Sedgwick, July 16, 1826, Catharine Maria Sedgwick Papers II, Massachusetts Historical Society.

42. Lucinda Damon-Bach, "To 'Act' and 'Transact': *Redwood*'s Revisionary Heroines," Damon-Bach and Clements, eds., *Catharine Maria Sedgwick* 57.

43. For this view of *Redwood*'s characters among modern readers, see Baym, *Women's Fiction* 58.

44. William Minot to Catharine Sedgwick, July 16, 1824, Catharine Maria Sedgwick Papers III, Massachusetts Historical Society.

45. Henry Sedgwick to Catharine Sedgwick, Aug. 24, 1824, Dewey 168.

46. Michael Bell, "History and Romance Conventions in Catharine Sedgwick's *Hope Leslie*," *American Literature* 22 (1970): 214.

47. Judith Fetterley, "'My Sister, My Sister!': The Rhetoric of Catharine Sedgwick's *Hope Leslie*," *American Literature* 70 (1998): 495–97; Lucy Maddox, *Removals: Nineteenth-Century American Literature and the Politics of Indian Affairs* (New York: Oxford UP, 1991) 103; Barbara Bardes and Susan

Gossett, *Declarations of Independence: Women and Political Power in Nineteenth-Century American Fiction* (New Brunswick: Rutgers UP, 1990) 13; Carol J. Singley, "Catharine Maria Sedgwick's *Hope Leslie*: Radical Frontier Romance," *Desert, Garden, Margin, Range: Literature on the American Frontier*, ed. Eric Heyne (New York: Twayne; Toronto: Maxwell Macmillan, 1992) 110–13; Showalter 38; Douglas 184–85. Other examples of this view of *Hope Leslie* include Christopher Castiglia, "In Praise of Extra-Vagant Women: *Hope Leslie* and the Captivity Romance," *Legacy* 6, no. 2 (1989): 3–16; Philip Gould, *Covenant and Republic: Historical Romance and the Politics of Puritanism* (Cambridge: Cambridge UP, 1996) 132; and Mark G. Vasquez, "'Your Sister Cannot Speak to You and Understand You as I Do': Native American Culture and Female Subjectivity in Lydia Marie Child and Catharine Maria Sedgwick," *American Transcendental Quarterly* 15 (2001): 173–90.

48. Mary Kelley, "Legacy Profile: Catharine Maria Sedgwick," *Legacy* 6.2 (1989): 47; Dana Nelson, "Sympathy as Strategy in Sedgwick's *Hope Leslie*," *The Culture of Sentiment: Race, Gender, and Sentimentality in Nineteenth-Century America*, ed. Shirley Samuels (New York: Oxford UP, 1992) 192. Others have argued that the novel combines a two-pronged attack on patriarchy and white racism: Sandra A. Zagarell, "Expanding 'America': Lydia Sigourney's Sketch of Connecticut, Catharine Sedgwick's *Hope Leslie*," *Tulsa Studies in Women's Literature* 6 (1987): 225–45; Gustav Stadler, "Magawisca's Body of Knowledge: Nation-Building in *Hope Leslie*," *Yale Journal of Criticism* 12 (1999): 41–56; and Castiglia.

49. For a brief comment on the appeal of *Hope Leslie* to the patriotic and nationalistic ideology of the antebellum audience, see also Bardes and Gossett 25.

50. Aikens to Sedgwick, Sept. 15, 1827, Catharine Maria Sedgwick Papers II, Massachusetts Historical Society.

51. Buell 194, 230; Reynolds 106. Baym makes a relevant point on this issue by arguing that Sedgwick "perform[s] no culturally subversive acts when deplor[ing] Puritan shortcomings" because she was operating within a Unitarian notion of cultural progress, in which "the Puritans need not—should not—be presented as history's culmination" but only as an important but flawed step in the "long road traveled from the seventeenth to the nineteenth century" (*American Women Writers and the Work of History, 1790–1840* [New Brunswick: Rutgers UP, 1995] 157).

52. Sedgwick to M. Sismondi, Mar. 15, 1828, Dewey 192–93.

53. Maddox 97. The claim about antebellum readers' applause is from Singley 111.

54. Sedgwick, *Hope Leslie; or, Early Times in Massachusetts*, ed. Mary Kelley (New Brunswick: Rutgers UP, 1987) 1.

55. Sedgwick, *Hope Leslie* 73. One modern critic, it should be noted, has, in fact, interpreted the novel as an elegiac expression of the antebellum racist conception of the "vanishing" Indian (Nelson 202).

56. Robert Tilton, *Pocahontas: The Evolution of an American Narrative* (Cambridge: Cambridge UP, 1994) 81.

57. On the brisk early sales of *Hope Leslie*, see Kelley, *Private Woman* 12.

58. Sedgwick to Susan Channing, Mar. 14, 1830, Dewey 207.

59. Catharine Sedgwick to Charles Sedgwick, Mar. 7, 1830, Dewey 205.

60. Saulsbury 357.

61. Follen to Sedgwick, Dec. 25, 1837, Catharine Maria Sedgwick Papers II, Massachusetts Historical Society.

62. Osborne to Sedgwick, July 29, 1830, Catharine Maria Sedgwick Papers III, Massachusetts Historical Society.

63. Reynolds 118; Foster 117.

64. For these characterizations of *Home*, as well as *Live and Let Live* and *Poor Rich Man*, see Saulsbury 353, 357; Kelley, "Legacy Profile" 43; Nancy Cott, *The Bonds of Womanhood: "Woman's Sphere" in New England, 1780-1835* (New Haven: Yale UP, 1977) 63; Sondra Smith Gates, "Sedgwick's American Poor," Damon-Bach and Clements, eds., *Catharine Maria Sedgwick* 177; Susan Harris, "The Limits of Authority: Catharine Maria Sedgwick and the Politics of Resistance," Damon-Bach and Clements, eds., *Catharine Maria Sedgwick* 284, n. 7; Charlene Avallone, "Catharine Sedgwick and the 'Art' of Conversation," Damon-Bach and Clements, eds., *Catharine Maria Sedgwick* 199; and Homestead, *American Women Authors* 90–97.

65. *Boston Observer* Apr. 30, 1836, rpt. in part in Damon-Bach and Clements, eds., *Catharine Maria Sedgwick* 171.

66. Lyle H. Wright, *American Fiction, 1774-1850* (San Mateo, CA: Huntington Library, 1948) 253.

67. Gates 178.

68. Sedgwick to Louisa Minot, Nov. 26, 1836, Sedgwick Family Papers, qtd. in Phelps 133.

69. In the same year, Sedgwick also published a volume of short stories, *Tales and Sketches*, but the eleven stories that composed it had all been previously published in periodicals and gift books (Lucinda L. Damon-Bach, "Chronological Bibliography of the Works of Catharine Maria Sedgwick," Damon-Bach and Clements, eds., *Catharine Maria Sedgwick* 298, 302–5.

70. Dillingham to Sedgwick, Nov. 12, 1835, Catharine Maria Sedgwick Papers II, Massachusetts Historical Society.

71. Cf. such remarks to the interpretation of Isabelle by modern Sedgwick readers. For example, in her introduction to *The Linwoods* Maria Karafilis as-

serts that in the course of the novel not only is Isabelle transformed "from Tory to Rebel" but that "[i]n the process, Isabelle rebels against . . . the institutions of slavery, gender norms, and patriarchal authority" (*The Linwoods or, "Sixty Years Since" in America*, by Catharine Sedgwick, ed. Maria Karafilis [Hanover, NH: UP of New England, 2002] xv).

72. George Haven Putnam, *George Palmer Putnam: A Memoir* (New York: Putnam's, 1912) 22. The printing and sales figures for *The Linwoods* were recorded by Sedgwick on an informal accounting sheet dated Nov. 25, 1841, Catharine Maria Sedgwick Papers I, Massachusetts Historical Society.

73. The other review to remark on length was in the *American Quarterly Review* Mar. 1837: 18–28.

74. Between the publication of *Hope Leslie* in 1827 and the appearance of *The Linwoods* in 1835, Sedgwick published a total of ten pieces in these two venues with eight of those appearing in the *Juvenile Miscellany* (Damon-Bach, "Chronological Bibliography" 303–5). Interestingly, two years before *Hope Leslie* Sedgwick had published a freestanding novella, *The Travellers. A Tale*, that was "Designed for Young People," as its title page announced, but that volume had no impact on reviewer responses to *Hope Leslie* and *Clarence* or on their conceptions of the audiences of those two novels.

75. For such a modern characterization of *Means and Ends* see, e.g., Maria Lamonica, "'She Could Make a Cake as Well as Books . . .': Catharine Maria Sedgwick, Anna Jameson, and the Construction of the Domestic Individual," *Women's Writing* 1 (1995): 236.

76. Sedgwick, *Means and Ends, or Self-Training* (Boston: Marsh, Capen, Lyon, and Webb, 1839), 12.

77. The sales figures for the two novels are from Sedgwick's Nov. 25, 1841, accounting sheet, Catharine Maria Sedgwick Papers I, Massachusetts Historical Society.

78. Foster 117.

79. Rev. Dr. Bellows to Sedgwick, undated but probably between July 1848 and Jan. 1849, Dewey 310–11.

80. Robbins 5.

81. Henry Steele Commager, "When Majors Wrote for Minors," *Saturday Review* May 10, 1952, qtd. in Beverly Lyon Clark, *Kiddie Lit: The Cultural Construction of Children's Literature in America* (Baltimore: Johns Hopkins UP, 2003) 48.

82. Undated ms. review, circa 1841, Catharine Maria Sedgwick Papers II, Massachusetts Historical Society.

83. Richard Darling, *The Rise of Children's Book Reviewing in America, 1865–1881* (New York: Bowker, 1968) 46. Sarah Wadsworth points out that by the 1840s a market for books and other reading materials specifically designed

for children had been "well established" by Samuel Goodrich, the American Tract Society, and other publishers (*In the Company of Books: Literature and Its "Classes" in Nineteenth-Century America* [Amherst: U of Massachusetts P, 2006] 30).

84. Clark 69. Telling in this regard is Hawthorne's own attitude toward the fiction he had written for the juvenile market and its young readership in that, according to Sarah Wadsworth, Hawthorne's "correspondence suggests that he regarded these early juvenile stories as a kind of hackwork" (*In the Company of Books* 31).

85. Clark 113. On the gendered segmentation of children's literature and its audience in mid-nineteenth-century America, see also Wadsworth 44–69.

86. *North American Review* Apr. 1828: 407.

87. Damon-Bach, "Chronological Bibliography" 295–301.

88. One index to Sedgwick's continued prominence is that among the seventy-two writers Rufus Wilmot Griswold included in his 1847 *Prose Writers of America*, Sedgwick was one of only five women in that assembly (Fred Lewis Pattee, *The Feminine Fifties* [New York: Appleton-Century, 1940] 50).

89. Sedgwick to Katherine Minot, Apr. 2, 1857, Dewey 370; Sedgwick to Orville Dewey, Mar. 1857, Dewey 369.

90. Damon-Bach, "Chronological Bibliography," 298–301.

91. For a modern critical view of *Married or Single?* as a novel that "questions the commonplace assumption that any marriage is preferable to a single life for women, and intersects with the discourse of women's rights," see Deborah Gussman, "Equal to Either Fortune: Sedgwick's *Married or Single?* and Feminism," Damon-Bach and Clements, eds., *Catharine Maria Sedgwick* 257.

92. Interestingly enough, at least two modern Sedgwick scholars have reached the same conclusion about the ending of *Married or Single?:* Foster 130; and Gussman 260.

93. The Harpers reissued *Poor Rich Man* in 1872 and 1876, *Live and Let Live* in 1876, *Means and Ends* in 1870, and *Love Token for Children* in 1871. The one exception to this pattern was the Harpers' 1872 reissue of *Hope Leslie* (Damon-Bach, "Chronological Bibliography" 295–301).

94. Dewey 10, 446, 430.

95. Barrett Wendell, *A Literary History of America* (New York: Scribner's, 1900); Richard Burton, *Literary Leaders of America: A Class-book on American Literature* (New York: Chautauqua, 1903); John Macy, *Spirit of American Literature* (Garden City, NY: Doubleday, Page, 1913); Percy Boynton, *A History of American Literature* (Boston: Ginn, 1919); Carl Van Doren, *What Is American Literature?* (New York: Morrow, 1935); Arthur Hobson Quinn, *American Fiction: A Historical and Critical Survey* (New York: Appleton-Century, 1936).

96. Vernon Parrington, *The Romantic Revolution in America*, vol. 2 of *Main Currents in American Thought* (New York: Harcourt Brace, 1927) 241; Fred Lewis Pattee, *The First Century of American Literature, 1770-1870* (1935; New York: Cooper Square, 1966) 381, 387, 399, 405; Van Wyck Brooks, *The Flowering of New England, 1815-1865* (New York: Modern Library, 1936) 188.

97. William J. Long, *American Literature: A Study of the Men and the Books That in the Earlier and Later Times Reflect the American Spirit* (Boston: Ginn, 1913) 175, 282, n. 2; Walter C. Bronson, *A Short History of American Literature: Designed Primarily for Use in Schools and Colleges* (Boston: Heath, 1902) 172; William B. Cairns, *A History of American Literature* (New York: Oxford UP, 1912) 206; William Peterfield Trent, John Erskine, Stuart P. Sherman, and Carl Van Doren, eds., *The Cambridge History of American Literature*, 4 vols. (New York: Putnam's; Cambridge: Cambridge UP, 1917), 1: 310, 324, 2: 396–98, 406; Ernest E. Leisy, *The American Historical Novel* (Norman: U of Oklahoma P, 1950), 43. A late nineteenth-century predecessor to this scholarly typecasting of Sedgwick's fiction was Charles F. Richardson, *American Literature, 1607-1885* (New York: Putnam, 1885) 1: 409–10.

CHAPTER SIX: *Mercurial Readings*

1. The lone chapter appears in Nina Baym, *Women's Fiction: A Guide to Novels by and about Women, 1820-1870* (Ithaca: Cornell UP, 1978) 208–30. Both articles are thumbnail overviews by Lucy Freibert and are nearly identical: "Caroline Chesebro' (Caroline Chesebrough) (1825–1873)," *Nineteenth-Century American Women Writers: A Bio-Bibliographical Critical Sourcebook*, ed. Denise D. Knight (Westport, CT: Greenwood, 1997), 36–41; and "Caroline Chesebro' (1825–1873)," *Writers of the American Renaissance*, ed. Denise D. Knight (Westport, CT: Greenwood, 2003), 51–55. Besides entries in the standard biographical dictionaries mentioned, entries for Chesebro' appear in Lina Mainiero, ed., *American Women Writers: A Critical Reference Guide from Colonial Times to the Present* (New York: Ungar, 1979–1994) 1: 346–48; and Lucy Freibert and Barbara A. White, eds., *Hidden Hands: An Anthology of American Women Writers, 1790-1870* (New Brunswick, NJ: Rutgers UP, 1985) 322–23. The Freibert and White anthology also includes thirteen pages of excerpts from Chesebro's first novel, *Isa, a Pilgrimage*.

2. This lack of attention to Chesebro' has continued in more recent book-length studies of nineteenth-century American women writers, including Linda Grasso, *The Artistry of Anger: Black and White Women's Literature in America, 1820-1860* (Chapel Hill: U of North Carolina P, 2002); Melissa Homestead, *American Women Writers and Literary Property* (Cambridge: Cambridge UP,

2005); Susan S. Williams, *Reclaiming Authorship: Literary Women in America, 1850–1900* (Philadelphia: U of Pennsylvania P, 2006); and Laura Laffrado, *Uncommon Women: Gender and Representation in Nineteenth-Century U.S. Women's Writing* (Columbus: Ohio State UP, 2009). Two exceptions are Anne E. Boyd, *Writing for Immortality: Women and the Emergence of High Literary Culture in America* (Baltimore: Johns Hopkins UP, 2004); and Joyce Warren, *Women, Money, and the Law: Nineteenth-Century Fiction, Gender, and the Courts* (Iowa City: U of Iowa P, 2005). Warren, however, includes only a two-sentence dismissal of Chesebro's *Isa, a Pilgrimage* (227). Likewise, Boyd mentions Chesebro' only briefly, treating her as a stalking horse who typified the pious, conventional feminine writers against whom true women artists, such as Elizabeth Stoddard, defined themselves (322, 325–26).

3. See Marjorie Jane Hunt, "The Short Stories of Caroline Chesebro'," M.A. thesis, George Washington U, 1970. The scholarly neglect of Chesebro' is reflected as well in the early covers of *Legacy*, the official journal of the Society for the Study of American Women Writers. Those covers list the names of individual women writers in changing orders, but among the more than two hundred names—which include Fanny Fern, Caroline Lee Hentz, E.D.E.N. Southworth, and Ann Stephens—Chesebro's never appears.

4. Beyond a passing sentence on this topic in one of her biographical dictionary entries, Freibert devotes in her other entry two half-pages of discussion to Chesebro's nineteenth-century reception (38–39), while Baym briefly quotes comments about *Isa* from a *Harper's* review and from John Hart's 1854 *Female Prose Writers of America* (210–11).

5. When *Harper's* began compensating American authors for their contributions, several of Chesebro's short stories—along with Melville's—were among the first to appear. For an extensive, though slightly incomplete, bibliography of Chesebro's magazine fiction, see Hunt 31–84.

6. Chesebro' may have been working on—and possibly completed—a tenth novel at her death, according to the entry for her in the 1886 *Appleton's Cyclopedia of American Biography*, but if so, the novel was never published (Hunt 8).

7. On this problem faced by nineteenth-century women writers and by Susan Warner in particular, see Jane Tompkins, *Sensational Designs: The Culture Work of American Fiction, 1790–1860* (New York: Oxford UP, 1985) 23–34.

8. James C. Derby, *Fifty Years among Authors, Books and Publishers* (New York: Carleton, 1884) 585.

9. Timothy D. Murray, "G. W. Carleton," *American Literary Publishing Houses, 1638–1899*, ed. Peter Dzwonkoski, vol. 49 of *Dictionary of Literary Biography*, 336 vols. to date (Detroit: Gale, 1986) 84–85.

10. William Dean Howells, "Recollections of an Atlantic Editorship," *Atlantic Monthly* Nov. 1907: 594.

11. Although no sales figures of Chesebro's novels appear to have survived, there is general agreement about her lack of popularity and broad sales. See Derby 586; Baym 208; and Tess Lloyd, "Caroline Chesebrough," *American National Biography*, ed. John H. Garraty and Mark C. Carnes (New York: Oxford UP, 1999) 4: 783. Regarding *Peter Carradine*, the *New York Tribune* announced that the novel was "out of print" shortly after its publication but that a second edition "is now ready" (Oct. 2, 1863: 6).

12. See, e.g., her letters to R. H. S., Apr. 4, 1859, Anthony Collection, New York Public Library, and to William Conant Church, Jan. 29, 1867, *The Galaxy* Correspondence, William Conant Church Mss., New York Public Library. In the former, Chesebro' bluntly asks, in regard to several stories she has submitted, "will you let me know what price you would pay for them." Of Church she inquires when she can expect him to "remit payment" for a story that appeared in the Feb. 1867 issue of the *Galaxy*.

13. Chesebro' to "Messrs. E. & G. Duyckinck," Nov. 26, 1849, Literary Correspondence, Duyckinck Collection, New York Public Library; Chesebro' to "Messrs. Duyckinck," 1851, Literary Correspondence, Duyckinck Collection.

14. Chesebro' to William Conant Church, Nov. 2, 1868, The *Galaxy* Correspondence.

15. Chesebro' to the *Atlantic Monthly*, Dec. 4, 1860, Correspondence with the Publishers, Cairns Collection of American Women Writers, Special Collections, Memorial Library, University of Wisconsin, Madison. Of additional interest in this letter is Chesebro's claim that she is owed $10 more for two printed pages of the story. If her calculations were correct, they indicate that the *Atlantic* was paying her at the same rate of $5 per page that Melville received from *Harper's* and *Putnam's* in the mid-1850s.

16. Chesebro' to "Messrs. Duyckinck," 1851. In this area, Chesebro' provides a specific instance of Susan William's recent claim that, contrary to the standard division literary historians have often invoked between authors (usually female) who wrote for the marketplace and authors (usually male) who wrote for artistic purposes, male and female authors in nineteenth-century America often wrote "to achieve 'high art'" just as both frequently wrote for economic gain ("Authors and Literary Authorship," *The Industrial Book, 1840–1880*, vol. 3 of *The History of the Book in America*, ed. Scott E. Casper, Jeffrey D. Groves, Stephen W. Nissenbaum, and Michael Winship [Chapel Hill: U of North Carolina P, 2007] 90).

17. Chesebro' to William Conant Church, circa 1870, The *Galaxy* Correspondence.

18. S. J. Wolfe, "Caroline Chesebro," *Nineteenth-Century American Fiction Writers*, ed. Kent P. Ljungquist, vol. 202 of *Dictionary of Literary Biography* (Detroit: Gale, 1999), 77; Chesebro' to William Conant Church, Nov. 2, 1868, The *Galaxy* Correspondence.

19. See, e.g., Wolfe 78; Juliann E. Fleenor, "Caroline Chesebrough," Mainiero 346; Lloyd 783; Herbert Ross Brown, *The Sentimental Novel in America, 1790-1860* (New York: Pageant, 1959) 281; and Sheryl L. Meyering, "Caroline Chesebrough," *Oxford Companion to American Women's Writing in the United States*, ed. Linda Wagner-Martin and Cathy N. Davidson (New York: Oxford UP, 1995) 164.

20. *Dream-Land* included Chesebro's first published story, "An Exhausted Topic," which had appeared originally in *Graham's* in December 1848. Eight of the nineteen previously published stories in the collection had been published in that periodical, with the remainder having appeared in *Holden's Dollar Magazine* (six), the *Knickerbocker* (four), and *Sartain's* (one).

21. *Churchman* and *Albany State Register* qtd. in Redfield advertisement in *Isa, a Pilgrimage*, by Caroline Chesebro' (New York: Redfield, 1852) 321.

22. Qtd. in Redfield advertisement, *Isa* 321.

23. For this characterization and claim, see, e.g., Baym 209 and Wolfe 77.

24. It should be mentioned that Chesebro' was probably deep into writing *Isa* when the reviews of *Dream-Land* came out in January and February, since her publisher announced the novel as available for purchase only a month later in an advertisement in the Mar. 6, 1852, *New York Tribune* (1).

25. Qtd. in Redfield advertisement in *Children of Light* by Caroline Chesebro' (New York: Redfield, 1853) 381.

26. *Albany Argus* and *Christian Freemen* qtd. in Redfield advertisement, *Children of Light* 381.

27. See Baym 209.

28. Qtd. in Redfield advertisement, *Children of Light* 381.

29. Qtd. in Redfield advertisement, *Children of Light* 381. This view of *Isa* as ultimately a conventional novel that subscribes to traditional gender values is held by at least one modern critic; see Warren 227. For a contrary modern interpretation of *Isa* as a narrative that supports its protagonist and critiques patriarchal culture, see Baym 214–15.

30. Richard Gerrig, *Experiencing Narrative Worlds: On the Psychological Activities of Reading* (New Haven: Yale UP, 1993) 27, 69. According to Pierre Macherey, responses involving preferences and invoked alternatives are an inherent part of axiological reading and of criticism as "appreciation (the education of taste)" (*A Theory of Literary Production*, trans. Geoffrey Wall [London: Routledge and Kegan Paul, 1978] 3, 15).

31. Although the publication year of *Children* was officially 1853, the *New York Tribune* announced the novel as published "this day" in its Nov. 24, 1852, issue (1).

32. The part of Borland's speech about true worship, quoted by the *National Era* reviewer, is in *Children of Light* 273.

33. Freibert asserts that *Children* "met no criticism for its morality" (38). Curiously, Freibert also declares that Chesebro's second novel is actually more iconoclastic than *Isa* because of what she sees as its homosexual character relations and "the lesbian overtones of the ending" (37–38).

34. The publication date listed in *Little Crossbearers* is 1854, but the *New York Tribune* announced it in early December 1853 as available for a price of fifty cents (Dec. 6, 1853: 1).

35. John Tebbel, *The Creation of an Industry, 1630–1865,* vol. 4 of *A History of Book Publishing in the United States,* 4 vols. (New York: Bowker, 1972) 342–43, 484.

36. The *New York Tribune,* one of the major outlets for publishers' advertising, regularly listed "books received," often as a prelude to upcoming reviews. In the two years following its publication, *Crossbearers* never appeared in the paper's list of receipts from Derby, Miller, Orton, and Mulligan. Instead, the *Tribune* announced, for instance, receipt of those firms' *Life of Mary Queen of Scots* and *The Three Colonies of Australia* (Mar. 2, 1854: 6–7) and their temperance tales entitled *Dick Wilson, the Rum-seller's Victim* and *Minnie Brown: The Landlord's Daughter* (Jan. 6, 1855: 1).

37. Tebbel 342–43. Derby sold Miller his half of their partnership at about the time that *Crossbearers* came out (Dzwonkoski, ed., *American Literary Publishing Houses* 116).

38. Miller, Orton, and Mulligan regularly advertised Fern's *Fern Leaves* and Douglass's *My Bondage and My Freedom* in the *American Publishers' Circular and Literary Gazette* (see, e.g., Oct. 6, 1854: 94, and Oct. 13, 1855: 107) and the *New York Tribune* (e.g., Jan. 3, 1855: 1, and July 21, 1855: 1). The firm also must have distributed review copies of their nonfiction titles, since in 1855 Miller, Orton, and Mulligan ads in the *Tribune* started including excerpts from reviews of *My Bondage and My Freedom* as well as *Memoirs of the Court and Reign of Catherine the Second, Empress of Russia* and the biography *Henrietta Robinson* (Dec. 22: 1855: 1). Compounding the problem for Chesebro' was that the firm went out of business because of mismanagement two years after *Beautiful Gate* came out (Dzwonkoski 117). It should be noted, however, that Chesebro's third collection did make it into one Miller, Orton, and Mulligan ad in the *Tribune,* which described the volume as "a gem for little folks" (Dec. 18, 1855: 1).

39. The copy of the original 1855 edition of *Beautiful Gate* with this inscription is in Special Collections, Hale Library, Kansas State University.

40. An interesting side fact is that during the time between *Crossbearers* and *Susan* Chesebro' largely abandoned publishing short fiction in periodicals.

41. More specifically, ten major periodicals and newspapers carried reviews of *Children of Light,* while seven did so for *Susan.* I have also found a fragment of an eighth review from the *Worcester Palladium.*

42. Baym 221–22; Freibert and White 322; Lloyd 783.

43. *Philly and Kit* was announced that month in the *American Publishers' Circular and Literary Gazette* as a "new work" priced at $1 (May 10, 1855: 282).

44. Elizabeth Stoddard, "Our Lady Correspondent," *Daily Alta California* Aug. 3, 1856, The Morgesons *&* *Other Writings, Published and Unpublished,* ed. Lawrence Buell and Sandra A. Zagarell (Philadelphia: U of Pennsylvania P, 1985) 325–26.

45. For the view of *Victoria* as a conventional sentimental novel, see Brown 285. Brief interpretations of the book as a feminist critique appear in Wolfe 79 and Baym 223, 226.

46. Eleven of the seventeen appeared in *Harper's,* in whose pages Chesebro' averaged roughly a story a year until 1863, when, in that one year, *Harper's* published five of her tales.

47. Tebbel 361.

48. Derby 46; Tebbel 348.

49. Tebbel 350.

50. Tebbel 344, 348, 544. Carleton's savvy as a publisher did fall short in one notable case, however. In 1867 he turned down the opportunity to publish Mark Twain's *Celebrated Jumping Frog of Calaveras County and Other Sketches* (Justin Kaplan, *Mr. Clemens and Mark Twain: A Biography* [New York: Simon and Schuster, 1966] 26–27).

51. Lawrence Buell and Sandra Zagarell, introduction, The Morgesons *&* *Other Writings* 3.

52. Madeleine B. Stern, "G. W. Carleton," *Publishers for Mass Entertainment in Nineteenth Century America,* ed. Madeleine B. Stern (Boston: Hall, 1980) 86.

53. Tebbel 350.

54. Although reviews of *Carradine* appeared in five major periodicals and newspapers, which was slightly less than what each of her previous novels had secured, several smaller regional publications ran reviews of the book, making its overall total approximately equal to the numbers for her first four books.

55. *Commercial Advertiser* qtd. in advertisement for *Peter Carradine, New York Tribune* Nov. 7, 1864: 6.

56. Interestingly enough, seven years earlier a reviewer in the *United States Magazine* had reached just the opposite conclusion, claiming that her fictional techniques indicate that "Miss Cheseboro [*sic*] is deficient in imagination" (Sept. 1862: 243).

57. Freibert and White 322; Wolfe 79; Baym 230. The differences—as well as the relations and even overlappings—between realistic and domestic/sentimental fiction have, of course, been the subject of substantial discussion and disagreement. See, e.g., Tompkins, 149, 152–53; Harold H. Kolb, *Illusion of Life: American Realism as a Literary Form* (Charlottesville: U of Virginia P, 1969), 137–38; Alfred Habegger, *Gender, Fantasy, and Realism in American Literature* (New York: Columbia UP, 1982); Philip Fisher, *Hard Facts: Setting and Form in the American Novel* (New York: Oxford UP, 1987); Michael Davitt Bell, "Women's Fiction and the Literary Marketplace in the 1850s," *Prose Writing 1820–1865*, vol. 2 of *The Cambridge History of American Literature,* ed. Sacvan Bercovitch (New York: Cambridge UP, 1995) 118; Nancy Glazener, *Reading for Realism: A History of a U.S. Literary Institution, 1850–1910* (Durham: Duke UP, 1997) 38, 121–29; Nancy Bentley, "Women and Realist Authorship," *Prose Writing 1860–1920*, vol. 3 of *The Cambridge History of American Literature,* ed. Sacvan Bercovitch (Cambridge: Cambridge UP, 2005) 151–52; and Richard Lehan, *Realism and Naturalism: The Novel in an Age of Transition* (Madison: U of Wisconsin P, 2005) 112, 199.

58. On the status of local-color and regionalist fiction as inferior to realism (or as an inferior version of full-blown realism) in the 1860s and after, see Glazener 198–99, 214–15, and 249; Richard Brodhead, *Cultures of Letters: Scenes of Reading and Writing in Nineteenth-Century America* (Chicago: U of Chicago P, 1993) 166–67; and Donna M. Campbell, *Resisting Regionalism: Gender and Naturalism in American Fiction, 1885–1915* (Athens: Ohio UP, 1997) 22, 59–146.

59. Tebbel 312–15.

60. Gregory Haynes, "American Tract Society," Dzwonkoski, ed., *American Literary Publishing Houses* 19.

61. The *American Publishers' Circular and Literary Gazette* inverted its title when it moved from New York to Philadelphia in 1863 to become the *American Literary Gazette and Publishers' Circular.*

62. These copies of *Sparrow's Fall* and *Glenn Cabin* are in Special Collections, Hale Library, Kansas State University.

63. Such reception indices may help explain Chesebro's motivation for turning to the American Tract Society for the publication of *Glen Cabin*. The society was already a prominent publisher of books for children, and with *Sparrow's Fall* and *Amy Carr,* Chesebro' had demonstrated that she could write fiction that could be marketed to and have some appeal for a juvenile audience. Hence, she

may have seen the society as a good match that also offered a promising opportunity for national distribution—and possibly successful sales—of *Glen Cabin*.

64. Freibert 37; Hunt 4–6.

65. Some evidence suggests that Chesebro' may have finished at least a partial draft of *Foe* as early as 1863, for in February of that year she informed Robert Bonner that "I have a story, a novel, in Mister Miller's hands ... of life in the Pennsylvania Coal Mines, amongst the Mennonites," which is the scenario of *Foe* (Chesebro' to Bonner, Feb. 9, 1863, Correspondence, Robert Bonner Papers, New York Public Library).

66. Tebbel 401–2, 445.

67. Freibert 38; Wolfe 80.

68. Qtd. in James S. Hart, *A Manual of American Literature: A Text-Book for Schools and Colleges* (Philadelphia: Eldredge, 1873) 502.

69. Howells, "Recollections" 594; Oscar Fay Adams, *Dictionary of American Authors*, 5th ed. (Boston: Houghton Mifflin, 1909) 60.

70. Baym 209; Wolfe 77.

71. Wolfe 76; Lloyd 784; Fleenor 348.

72. See, e.g., Freibert 37; and Sheila Post-Lauria, *Correspondent Colorings: Melville in the Marketplace* (Amherst: U of Massachusetts P, 1996) 128.

73. Pierre Bourdieu, *Distinction: A Social Critique of the Judgement of Taste*, trans. Richard Nice (Cambridge: Harvard UP, 1984) 86, 26.

74. Barbara Herrnstein Smith, *Contingencies of Value: Alternative Perspectives for Critical Theory* (Cambridge: Harvard UP, 1988), 13–14.

CONCLUSION: *American Literary History and the Historical Study of Interpretive Practices*

1. Michael Davitt Bell, *The Problem of American Realism: Studies in the Cultural History of a Literary Idea* (Chicago: U of Chicago P, 1993) 1. On the development of the romance-to-realism paradigm in academic criticism in the 1920s, see David Shumway, *Creating American Civilization: A Genealogy of American Literature as an Academic Discipline* (Minneapolis: U of Minnesota P, 1994) 136–37, 168. A variation of this paradigm has marked studies of nineteenth-century American women's authorship over the last thirty years, which has tended to posit a dichotomy in women's fiction between an emphasis on "sentimental and domestic fiction in the antebellum period and on regionalism in the postbellum period" (Susan Williams, *Reclaiming Authorship: Literary Women in America, 1850–1900* (Philadelphia: U of Pennsylvania P, 2006) 1–2.

2. Richard Chase, *The American Novel and Its Tradition* (New York: Gord-

ian, 1957); Joel Porte, *The Romance in America: Studies in Cooper, Poe, Hawthorne, Melville, and James* (Middleton, CT: Wesleyan UP, 1969).

3. Alfred Habegger, *Gender, Fantasy, and Realism in American Literature* (New York: Columbia UP, 1982). Other proponents of this position include Lucy M. Freibert and Barbara A. White, introduction, *Hidden Hands: An Anthology of American Women Writers, 1790–1870*, ed. Lucy M. Freibert and Barbara A. White (New Brunswick, NJ: Rutgers UP, 1985) 4.

4. G. R. Thompson and Eric Carl Link, *Neutral Ground: New Traditionalism and the American Romance Controversy* (Baton Rouge: Louisiana State UP, 1999) 60. Eric Sundquist, who curiously reaffirms the traditional paradigm even as he questions it, makes a related though somewhat different argument by claiming that "from the Civil War to W.W. I," American "realist fiction—like the literature of romance that preceded it . . . kept spilling over into the 'neutral territory' of romance that Hawthorne had made emblematic of American fiction" ("Introduction: The Country of the Blue," *American Realism: New Essays*, ed. Eric J. Sundquist (Baltimore: Johns Hopkins UP, 1982) 7.

5. Recent examples are Gregg Crane, *Cambridge Introduction to the Nineteenth-Century American Novel* (Cambridge: Cambridge UP, 2007) 31, 148–64; and Richard Lehan, *Realism and Naturalism: The Novel in an Age of Transition* (Madison: U of Wisconsin P, 2005). Current anthologies subscribing to the paradigm include the 7th edition (2007, vol. C) of the *Norton Anthology of American Literature*, the 10th edition (2002, vol. 2) of the McGraw-Hill *American Tradition in Literature*, the *Bedford Anthology of American Literature* (2008, vol. 2), and the Penguin-Pearson Longman *American Literature* (2004, vol. 2).

6. Warner Bertoff, *Ferment of Realism: American Literature, 1884–1919* (New York: Free Press; London: Collier-Macmillan, 1965) 3; Bell 2.

7. "Novels and Novelists," *North American Review* Jan. 1853: 105.

8. "Native Element in American Literature," *Century Magazine* June 1883: 288, July 1883: 362–63.

9. On the romantic revival, the realist wars, and the impact of the former upon the latter, see Edwin Cady, *The Realist at War: The Mature Years 1885–1920 of William Dean Howells* (Syracuse, NY: Syracuse UP, 1959), 28–55; Eric Carl Link, "The War of 1893; or, Realism and Idealism in the Late Nineteenth Century," *American Transcendental Quarterly* 11 (1997): 309–21; and Nancy Glazener, *Reading for Realism: A History of a U.S. Literary Institution, 1850–1910* (Durham: Duke UP, 1997) 145–75.

10. Glazener 157.

11. It should be mentioned that the stability—or lack thereof—of the ro-

mance/novel distinction in antebellum America has itself been the subject of interpretive disagreement among late-twentieth-century critics. Two of the strongest critiques of the stability and consistency of the dichotomy before the Civil War include Nina Baym, "Concepts of the Romance in Hawthorne's America," *Nineteenth-Century Fiction* 38 (1984): 426–43; and John McWilliams, "The Rationale for 'American Romance,'" *The New Americanists: Revisionist Interpretations of the Canon,* ed. Donald Pease, special issue of *boundary 2* 17 (1990): 71–82. By contrast, Glazener has maintained that "polemics about the novel, which contrasted it most frequently with the 'romance,' coursed through the 1850s and 1860s" in American periodicals (47). Thompson and Link argue more forcefully and at great length for this position, claiming that the novel versus romance distinction "directly reflect[ed] the dominant understanding in mid-nineteenth-century America of the two main varieties of modern prose fiction" (14–15).

12. Review of *The Pilot, New-York Mirror* Dec. 1824, rpt. in *Fenimore Cooper: The Critical Heritage,* ed. George Dekker and John P. McWilliams (London: Routledge and Kegan Paul, 1973), 74. Subsequent citations to reviews in this collection will be given parenthetically as *FCCH.*

13. John Anderson, "Cooper's Sea Novels Spurned in the Maintop," *Modern Language Notes* 66 (1951): 389.

14. Thomas Lounsbury, *James Fenimore Cooper* (Boston: Houghton, Mifflin, 1882), 51, 276; Henry S. Pancoast, *Introduction to American Literature* (New York: Holt, 1900) 138–39.

15. Not surprisingly, perhaps, there has been some disagreement among critics as to what exactly Twain is claiming about Cooper's novel. Everett Carter, for example, read the essay as an attack upon Cooper as a romancer and as an argument for realism (*Howells and the Age of Realism* [Philadelphia: Lippincott, 1954] 72), but Chase felt that Twain was faulting Cooper for producing an incompetent romance (*American Novel and Its Tradition* 147–48). Thompson and Link argue that Twain "is not rejecting the romance but advocating a form of it in which improbabilities do not subvert realistic attention to detail" (*Neutral Ground* 144).

16. See, e.g., Richard Abcarian, "Cooper's Critics and the Realistic Novel," *Texas Studies in Literature and Language* 8 (1966): 33–41.

17. James D. Wallace, *Early Cooper and His Audience* (New York: Columbia UP, 1986) 181.

18. *Church Review* Jan. 1851 and *Southern Literary Messenger* June 1851, both rpt. in *Hawthorne: The Critical Heritage,* ed. J. Donald Crowley (London: Routledge and Kegan Paul, 1970), 181 and 216, respectively. Subsequent references to reviews in this volume will be given parenthetically as *HCH.*

19. These reviews are all reprinted in *Hawthorne: The Critical Heritage*

250–52, 253–58, 264–67, and 340–51. If it seems odd that antebellum reviewers saw the *Blithedale Romance* as realistic, despite its title, one need only look at modern academic critics who have done the same. See, e.g., Katherine Kearns, *Nineteenth-Century American Literary Realism: Through the Looking-Glass* (Cambridge: Cambridge UP, 1996), 205–32.

20. *Springfield Republican* June 22, 1876, rpt. in *Nathaniel Hawthorne: The Contemporary Reviews*, ed. John L. Idol Jr., and Buford Jones (Cambridge: Cambridge UP, 1994) 381.

21. Henry James, *Hawthorne* (New York: Harper, 1879) 110, 163, 3, 120.

22. *Springfield Republican* Oct. 2, 1891, rpt. in *Melville: The Critical Heritage*, ed. Watson C. Branch (London: Routledge and Kegan Paul, 1974) 422. Subsequent citations from this volume are given parenthetically as *MCH*.

23. Glazener 127; James, *Literary Criticism*, ed. Leon Edel, 2 vols. (New York: Library of America, 1984) 1: 221.

24. *Atlantic Monthly* Mar. 1877, rpt. in part in *Dickens: The Critical Heritage*, ed. Philip Collins (New York: Barnes and Noble, 1971) 317. Subsequent references to this volume will appear parenthetically as *DCH*.

25. Howells qtd. in Edwin Cady, "'The Wizard Hand': Hawthorne, 1864–1900," *Hawthorne Centenary Essays*, ed. Roy Harvey Pearce (Columbus: Ohio State UP, 1964) 333; James, *Literary Criticism* 1: 130.

26. *North American Review* July 1818, rpt. in *Scott: The Critical Heritage*, ed. John O. Hayden (New York: Barnes & Noble, 1970) 148.

27. Mark Twain, *Life on the Mississippi* (1883; New York: Penguin, 1986) 328.

28. William Dean Howells, *Criticism and Fiction and Other Essays*, ed. Clara Marburg Kirk and Rudolf Kirk (New York: New York UP, 1959) 17, 38; Howells, *Heroines of Fiction* (New York: Harper, 1901) 99, 110.

29. Bell 8. On the nebulousness and inconsistencies plaguing postbellum conceptions of realism, see also Warner Bertoff, *Ferment of Realism 1884–1914* (New York: Free Press, 1965) 3.

30. James, *Literary Criticism* 2: 978.

31. Howells, "Emile Zola," *North American Review* Nov. 1892: 390; *Criticism and Fiction* 163.

32. "Frank Norris' Weekly Letter," *Chicago American* Aug. 3, 1901, rpt. in *Literary Criticism of Frank Norris*, ed. Donald Pizer (Austen: U of Texas P, 1964) 73–75. Exemplifying further the shape shifting that marked postbellum conceptualizations of genres, Norris on another occasion championed Zola as a romancer, while asserting that "Naturalism is a form of romanticism, not an inner circle of realism" ("Zola as a Romantic Writer," *Literary Criticism of Frank Norris* 72).

33. The phrase "vividly realistic" appeared in a review of *Tom Sawyer* in the *San Francisco Evening Bulletin* Jan. 20, 1877, rpt. in *Mark Twain: The Contemporary Reviews,* ed. Louis J. Budd (Cambridge: Cambridge UP, 1999) 165. For other reviews characterizing Twain's novels as realistic, see 157, 162, 166, 267, 277, 288, and throughout. Subsequent citations from this volume appear parenthetically as *MTCR*.

34. Howells, "Editor's Study," *Harper's Monthly* Jan. 1890 and "The New Historical Romance," *North American Review* Dec. 1900, rpt. in *W. D. Howells as Critic,* ed. Edwin H. Cady (London: Routledge and Kegan Paul, 1973) 173, 310.

35. Howells, "Henry James, Jr.," *Century Magazine* Nov. 1882, *W. D. Howells as Critic* 68.

36. James to Howells, Feb. 21, 1884, qtd. by Kirk and Kirk in Howells, *Criticism and Fiction* 96.

37. Jacques Derrida, "The Law of Genre," *Glyph* 7 (1980): 53, 61.

38. Tony Bennett, *Outside Literature* (London: Routledge, 1990) 92, 101–2.

39. John Frow, *Genre* (London: Routledge, 2006), 29, 17–18, and 102.

40. It should be noted that both Glazener and Barbara Hochman have partially anticipated my argument about postbellum realism by pointing out that "reading practices played a formative role in shaping the realist aesthetic" (Hochman, *Getting at the Author: Reimagining Books and Reading in the Age of American Realism* [Amherst: U of Massachusetts P, 2001] 29) and by calling "high realism," in particular, an "institution of reception" (Glazener 14). Bell also makes a related point by questioning the claim that "a generic tradition of realism," marked by "mimetic practices" within texts, existed in the United States in the last three decades of the nineteenth century. The "true story of the transformation of American fiction after the Civil War," argues Bell, "is less a triumphant saga of the rise of realism . . . than a history of this contention" about such a rise (5).

41. For these tenets of postbellum realism, see Hochman 11–12, 26; and Phillip Barrish, *American Realism, Critical Theory, and Intellectual Prestige, 1880–1995* (Cambridge: Cambridge UP, 2001) 17.

42. Bell 6 and 18–37; Glazener 108–46.

43. Dominick LaCapra, *History and Criticism* (Ithaca: Cornell UP, 1985) 130. This critique has also been raised by Martyn P. Thompson, "Reception Theory and the Interpretation of Historical Meaning," *History and Theory* 32 (1993): 257; and David Perkins, *Is Literary History Possible?* (Baltimore: Johns Hopkins UP, 1992) 23–27.

44. For an extended discussion of the "linguistic turn" in historiography and its effects on the philosophy and practice of history, see Elizabeth A. Clark, *History, Theory, Text: Historians and the Linguistic Turn* (Cambridge: Harvard UP,

2004). For a discussion of that turn as it developed in the journal *History and Theory*, see Richard Vann, "Turning Linguistic: History and Theory and *History and Theory*, 1960–1975," *A New Philosophy of History*, ed. Frank Ankersmit and Hans Kellner (Chicago: U of Chicago P, 1995) 40–69.

45. Rabinow and Sullivan, "The Interpretive Turn: The Emergence of an Approach," *Interpretive Social Science: A Reader*, ed. Paul Rabinow and William M. Sullivan (Berkeley and Los Angeles: U of California P, 1979), 1–21; Mary Fulbrook, *Historical Theory* (London: Routledge, 2002) 5; Hayden White, *Tropics of Discourse: Essays in Cultural Criticism* (Baltimore: Johns Hopkins UP, 1978) 55.

46. Michel de Certeau, *The Writing of History*, trans. Tom Conley (New York: Columbia UP, 1988) 30.

47. Keith Windschuttle, *The Killing of History: How Literary Critics and Social Theorists Are Murdering our Past* (New York: Free Press, 1997).

48. On the relation between the current "crisis in history" and these historical antecedents, see Brook Thomas, "The New Historicism and Other Old-Fashioned Topics," *The New Historicism*, ed. H. Aram Veeser (New York: Routledge, 1989) 182–203. For an overview of the movement in twentieth-century history from "scientific objectivity" and logical positivism to postrucutralist/postmodern problematizations, see Fulbrook 15–27; and George Iggers, *Historiography in the Twentieth Century: From Scientific Objectivity to the Postmodern Challenge* (Hanover, NH: Wesleyan UP, 1997).

49. Hans Kellner, introduction, Ankersmit and Kellner, *New Philosophy of History* 10.

50. Nancy Partner, "Historicity in an Age of Reality-Fictions," Ankersmit and Kellner, *New Philosophy of History* 22.

51. Jacques Derrida, *Writing and Difference*, trans. Alan Bass (Chicago: U of Chicago P, 1978) 279.

52. Stanley Fish, "Commentary: The Young and the Restless," Veeser, *New Historicism* 303–16. More recently, Fulbrook has offered a somewhat similar argument. Though not going so far as to claim that theory can have no impact on historical practice, she has argued that the constructed, interpretive nature of historical explanations "does not logically preclude them from *also* being an effective means of communicating with an audience an insight based on extensive research in the sources, on the basis of which certain generalizations and arguments may be made" (154).

53. Fish 308.

54. Raymond Williams, *Long Revolution* (London: Chatto and Windus, 1961) 53.

55. Fulbrook 189.

Fern, Fanny (Sarah Payson Willis), 274
Fielding, Henry, 75
Fish, Stanley: historical inquiry, 316, 317; response and reception theory, 8
Fishermen of Gamp's Island, The (Chesebro'), 257–58, 290
Fiske, John, 31
Flag of Our Union, 42
Foe in the Household, The (Chesebro'): as art, 293–94; publication history, 291–92; realism, 293–94; reception of, 292–93; success, 292–93
Forum, 308
Foucault, Michel, 15
Freeman, Mary Wilkins, 295
Frow, John, 31, 311–12
Fulbrook, Mary, 315, 319

Galaxy Magazine, 259–60, 291
genres, fiction: advocacy, 32, 55, 56–57, 127, 146, 148, 166–69, 212–13; antebellum popularity, 19, 28–30; criminal, 124–30; gothic (Germanic) tales, 96–101, 103, 105, 106–11, 113, 114, 122, 123, 126, 131, 134, 135, 186–87; vs history and philosophy, 41; postbellum realism, 299–311; satire and burlesque, 57–59, 96–99, 101, 103, 106, 110; social criticism, 56–57; travel, 143–44
Germanic (gothic) fiction, 96, 101, 103, 105, 106–11, 113, 114, 122, 123, 126, 131, 134, 135, 186–87
Glazener, Nancy, 301, 306, 313
Glen Cabin (Chesebro'), 258, 290–91
Glover, Caroline, 60
Godey's Lady's Book, 20, 29, 30, 36–37, 39, 44, 48, 50, 52–53, 55–57, 60–62, 64–65, 70, 72–74, 77, 81–83; and Chesebro', 257, 260–62, 271, 280; and Melville, 185; and Poe, 89, 96; and Sedgwick, 203, 206, 207, 222, 238, 240, 242
"Gold Bug, The" (Poe), 88
Goodrich, Diana, 15
Graham's Magazine, 20, 30, 36, 40–41, 43–44, 49–50, 54–56, 60, 66, 68, 71, 76, 82–83, 302, 305; and Chesebro', 257, 263, 264, 272, 280; and Melville, 150, 158, 161, 165, 176, 186, 190; and

Poe, 87, 89, 96, 125, 134; and Sedgwick, 203, 215, 244
Greenblatt, Stephen, ix, 316
Griswold, Rufus Wilmot, 136–37

Habeggar, Alfred, 300
"Hans Pfaall" (Poe), 96, 97, 102, 104–5, 113
Harland, Marian, 77
Harper Brothers (publisher), 18, 104, 157, 169, 181, 184, 189, 198, 203, 239, 248, 250, 257
Harper's New Monthly Magazine, 20, 44–45, 52, 57–58, 60, 64, 69, 72, 77, 304; and Chesebro', 257, 261, 262, 265, 268, 277, 278, 279, 283, 284, 285, 287, 288, 291, 293, 294; and Melville, 175, 177, 178, 180, 181, 191; and Sedgwick, 252
Harper's Weekly, 251
Harte, Bret, 295
Hartford Courant, 178, 288
Haven, Alice, 65
Hawthorne, Nathaniel, 33, 53–55, 60; allegory, 62; compared to Chesebro', 258, 278, 284, 293; Poe as reviewer of, 91–93, 95; reading character, 67–68; realism, 304–5; relationship with Melville, 139, 140, 164, 170, 171–73, 174, 182
Hawthorne, Sophia, 148, 174, 181
"Hawthorne and His Mosses" (Melville), 139, 140, 163–64, 170–73
Heath, John, 115
hermeneutics, historical, 14, 17–18, 35, 137, 299, 314, 318–20; communal practices, 7; implications, 7–8, 9, 18, 200; patterns of interpretation, 7; production and reception, 15; and Sedgwick, 201; theory of, 8–18. *See also* reception, theory of; reception study
Higham, John, 23
Hill, Harrison, 104
history: of the book and reading, 6–7; interpretive turn, 315–16; problematics, 313–16; textuality, 314–15; theory of, 314–15
Hoffman, Daniel, 110, 121

281, 284; and Melville, 138, 140, 141, 146, 151, 152, 160, 168, 177, 185, 188, 190; and Poe, 88, 89–93, 96–101, 103, 111, 114, 116–19, 122, 125–27, 129, 131, 137; and Sedgwick, 204, 209, 211, 212, 214, 220, 225, 227–29, 231, 233–34, 236. *See also* response, informed

reading and interpretation, theories of, 8–15

reading formations, 12–13, 299

reading materials, production, 18–19

realism, 50, 51, 53, 54, 76, 165, 168, 175, 177, 178, 219, 262, 287, 288, 289, 293–94, 296, 298, 301, 312. *See also* verisimilitude

reception, theory of, 6–7, 8, 314; vis-á-vis production, 14–17. *See also* hermeneutics, historical

reception events, 5, 6, 8, 17, 18, 31, 101, 137, 190

reception study: communal practices, 4; history, ix–x, 4–7; implications, xii, 299, 320; issues, 8–9, 314–15; objectives, 7. *See also* hermeneutics, historical

reception theory, 6-7, 8, 314. *See also* hermeneutics, historical: theory of reception vis-à-vis production, 14-17

Redburn (Melville), 157, 170, 192; reception of, 164–66; sales, 166

Redfield and Company, 257, 280, 285

Redwood (Sedgwick), 205, 208, 220, 228, 233, 234, 238, 240, 246, 249, 255; compared to *A New England Tale*, 215; compared to *Clarence*, 229; reception of, 215–19, 254

Renker, Elizabeth, 140

response, informed, 130, 136, 183

response and audience studies, history of, 4–7

return to history, 4, 5

reviewers and critics, guidance, 31–32, 38–40

Reynolds, David, 125

Richmond Compiler, 98, 101, 104, 135

Richmond Enquirer, 144

Richmond Semi-Weekly Examiner, 185

Richmond Watchman and Observer, 161

Richmond Whig, 102

Rogers, Mary, 122

Russell, W. H., 19

Russell, William Clark, 199

Russell's Magazine, 252

Saintine, Y. B., 53

Sand, George (Amantine Aurore Lucile Dupin), 44–46, 221

Saroni's Musical Times, 39, 159, 167

Sartain's, 245, 250, 257, 261–64, 265–66, 268

Saturday Courier, 96, 107

Saturday Evening Post, 106, 107

Saturday Museum, 122

Schwarz, Daniel, 83

Schweickart, Patrocinio, 7

Scott, Walter, 36, 49, 79, 89, 202, 205, 216, 217, 219, 221, 236, 306, 307–8

Scribner's, 18

Sedgwick, Catharine, 8; anonymous publication, 205, 210; audience expectations, 205; becoming a writer, 210; *Boy of Mt. Rhigi*, 245–46; characterization, 212, 218, 224–27, 230–31, 237–39, 241; *Clarence*, 204, 207, 228, 229–32, 233, 238, 241, 243, 246, 249; compared to Scott, 216, 219; correspondence, 208, 213–14, 216, 218, 222, 228, 229, 231, 235, 245, 249; domestic fiction, 215–16, 230, 247, 251–52; historical fiction, 219, 221–23, 235–37; *Home*, 232–34; *Hope Leslie*, 201, 204, 205, 207, 208, 219-28, 229, 233, 238, 240, 243, 245, 247–49, 255; horizon of expectations, 211, 213, 234, 246; Indians, 223–27; juvenile fiction, 242–49, 250, 254–55; *The Linwoods*, 235–40, 242, 243; literary ambition, 207–8; *Live and Let Live*, 240–43; *Love Token for Children*, 243–44; *Married or Single?* 249–52; *Means and Ends*, 244–45; national American novelist, 202, 211, 215–17, 221–22, 254; *A New England Tale*, 201, 204, 205, 210–14, 215, 227, 233, 240, 249, 255; plotting, 218–19, 231–32, 238; *The Poor Rich Man and the Rich Poor Man*, 205, 233, 240–43, 245–46, 248, 250, 253; Puritans,

verisimilitude, 50, 54, 72, 73, 74, 76, 78, 79; and Chesebro', 262, 265–66, 271, 277–78, 280, 283, 287, 293–94, 296, 298; and Melville, 155, 165, 168; and Poe, 89–90, 102, 105, 113; and Sedgwick, 212, 214, 216, 218–19, 225–27, 230, 231. *See also* realism

Victoria, or the World Overcome (Chesebro'), 296; characterization, 281–83; historical fiction, 281; plot, 281–83; publication history, 281; reception of, 281–85

"Von Jung" (Poe), 97

"Von Kempelen and His Discovery" (Poe), 132

Wallace, James D., 31, 304

Walpole, Horace, 98, 100

Warner, Susan, 19, 28, 202, 203, 252, 256, 290, 296

Washington National Era: and Chesebro', 257, 261–62, 263–65, 269, 270, 272, 273, 277-81, 284–85; and Melville, 186–87

Washington National Intelligencer, 144, 154, 175

Washington Union, 176

Weekly Chronotype, 160

Weinauer, Ellen, 171

Weir, Margaret, 22

Wendell, Barrett, 254, 295

Wentz, Sarah, 61

Western Monthly Review, 225, 227, 228

Whalen, Terence, 94

White, Hayden, 315, 316, 320

White, Thomas, 102, 105

White-Jacket (Melville), 157, 164–66, 170, 189; reception of, 167–69

Whitman, Sarah Helen, 133, 137

Widdleton, William, 285

Wiley, 18

Wiley and Putnam, 123, 142, 157

Williams, Raymond, 317

"William Wilson" (Poe), 106, 110, 114, 115, 116, 119, 123

Windscuttle, Keith, 315

working class, access to print, 26–27, 42

Youth's Keepsake, 243

Zboray, Ronald, 28

Zwicker, Steven N., 7